AF767220

Plato's *Philebus*

OKLAHOMA SERIES IN CLASSICAL CULTURE

Plato's *Philebus*

A Commentary

George H. Rudebusch

UNIVERSITY OF OKLAHOMA PRESS : NORMAN

Publication of this book is made possible in part by a grant from the University Press Language Tutorial Fund.

Library of Congress Cataloging-in-Publication Data

Names: Rudebusch, George, 1957– author.
Title: Plato's Philebus : a commentary / George H. Rudebusch.
Description: Norman : University of Oklahoma Press, [2023] | Series: Oklahoma series in classical culture ; volume 63 | Includes bibliographical references and index. | Summary: "Designed especially for philosophers and advanced ancient Greek students, this commentary places the *Philebus* in historical, philosophical, and linguistic context and elucidates the significance and possible interpretations of each passage of this dialogue, in which Plato deals with the question of whether a good life consists of pleasure or knowing"—Provided by publisher.
Identifiers: LCCN 2022039123 | ISBN 978-0-8061-9174-4 (hardcover) ISBN 978-0-8061-9753-1 (paperback)
Subjects: LCSH: Plato. Philebus.
Classification: LCC PA4279.P5 R83 2023 | DDC 321/.07—dc23/eng20230105
LC record available at https://lccn.loc.gov/2022039123

Plato's Philebus*: A Commentary* is Volume 63 in the Oklahoma Series in Classical Culture.

The paper in this book meets the guidelines for permanence and durability of the Committee on Production Guidelines for Book Longevity of the Council on Library Resources, Inc. ∞

The manufacturer's authorized representative in the EU for product safety is Mare Nostrum Group B.V., Mauritskade 21D, 1091 GC Amsterdam, The Netherlands, email: gpsr@mare-nostrum.co.uk

To Hope

CONTENTS

PREFACE

For those who find the Grand Canyon sublime, it is pure pleasure to follow its trails and wander in solitude. There is another, social pleasure in leading others into the canyon, helping them to explore some section of a subcanyon and sometimes to arrive at a view. The experience of research for this commentary has been a similar pleasure, following and looking for paths through one of Plato's masterpieces. And writing the commentary has allowed me the writer's peculiar quasi-social pleasure of leading others down trails and to points of particular beauty.

The previous such commentary for Greek readers was by Bury, who described Plato's *Philebus* as "a gnarled and knotted old oak-tree, abounding in unexpected humps and shoots, which sadly mar its symmetry as compared with the fair cypress-trees and stately pines by whose side it stands in the grove of Academe" (1897, ix). A century of scholarship later, Barker expanded the image of one tree to many, turning the gnarly oak into an "impenetrable jungle." "Intrepid investigators load their back-packs with the very latest in philological and hermeneutic equipment, together with selected remnants of the scholarly gadgetry of earlier generations, and set off to explore it. Many return babbling in unfathomable tongues. Other emerge waving what purport to be maps of this perplexing terrain, set in mind-warping systems of projection and sprinkled with unfamiliar symbols; but few of their maps seem to agree" (1996, 143). At the time Bury wrote, his intended audience had their primary training in classics but had perhaps only secondary and little-used training in philosophy. The intended audience of the present commentary is the opposite: their primary training is in philosophy, while they might have only secondary and little-used training in classics. The goal of this commentary is to assist such philosophers in considering and developing interpretations of all or part of the *Philebus*, a dialogue that, perhaps more than the others, remains full of undiscovered unities and multiplicities.

Toward this goal, the book sets out the details of about twenty arguments. These argument identifications will not be the last word, but they will serve their purpose if they stimulate more careful examination of the arguments than has been the case. In identifying these arguments, the commentary often points out how inference indicators (that is, the Greek words for "therefore" and "because") can be used to establish the structure of the argument, indicators that are often hard to present in translation. This is the place to recommend another too-little-used tool that is available even to those who read in translation: the manner in which the interlocutor's reply signals assent. A word for "obvious" indicates that a successful interpretation will tend to make this premise *obvious*. Words for "probably" or "perhaps" are also signposts for the interpreter to follow, signposts that set bounds on the range of faithful interpretations.

Scholarly progress in understanding the arguments of the *Philebus* and noticing the manner of the interlocutors' replies will not solve all interpretive problems. The *Philebus* is tough on interpreters in other ways: interlaced word order in sentence constructions; abbreviated sentence constructions; and pronouns that are often ambiguous. This feature of more ambiguity than usual is probably the reason why the transmitted manuscripts feature more variation than normal in a Platonic dialogue, which further muddies the waters of ambiguity. In addition, then, to a focus on argument identification, I try to disambiguate the text where I am able to do so. I have not proposed any new emendations to the text, but I resist some common emendations in the notes, and I occasionally advise changes to Burnet's punctuation. (Plato's Greek text was written before the development of lowercase letters and diacritical and punctuation marks.)

I give piecemeal interpretative remarks on the details of particular passages and, more generally, in the introduction, together with alternative interpretations. I show these paths through the dialogue in order to give tools to readers who will bring to bear their own diverse philosophical perspectives and talents, so that they may wander for themselves and make new and better paths through the beautiful landscape of the *Philebus*.

With my students and collaborators Brianna Zgurich and Hayden Niehus, I have coauthored a companion commentary, *Plato's* Philebus*: Greek Text with Basic Grammar* (2020). That companion, modeled on the commentaries of Geoffrey Steadman, focuses on the vocabulary and grammar needed to understand how in each sentence such things as participles, relative clauses, and accusative-plus-infinitive constructions fit together with the finite verbs and their moods, voices, tenses, and aspects.[1] Thanks to that grammar companion, this commentary has been able to expand its consideration of arguments and ambiguities and reduce the number of basic grammatical observations.

One learns different things about the Grand Canyon by studying photographs of it and by actually hiking and viewing it. Likewise, one learns different things about the *Philebus* by reading it in translation and in Greek. This commentary and its companion are designed to encourage philosophical research on the *Philebus* for the broadest possible range of scholars who want to get to know the dialogue in a different way than through English translation.

I thank my editor, Alessandra Jacobi Tamulevich, for expert guidance as I submitted a proposal and wrote this book. Northern Arizona University made this book possible with two Scholarship and Creative Activity Awards, the first supporting a book proposal for the University of Oklahoma Press in July 2014 and the second for continued support as I worked on the project again in July 2015. In addition, the university provided me with a reduced teaching load in fall 2021 and spring 2022 as I finished the project. I gratefully acknowledge this support of my research and also assistance

1. Geoffrey Steadman, "Greek and Latin Texts with Facing Vocabulary and Commentary," accessed June 27, 2022, https://geoffreysteadman.com/.

from the following, who read or advised me on particular passages: Lloyd Gerson, Gale Justin, Kyle Lucas, Mia Osmonbekov, Christopher Rowe, Christopher Turner, David Yount, and especially Sylvain Delcomminette, who graciously shared with me his translation and notes on the *Philebus*, unpublished at the time. I thank, in particular, Fernando Muniz, who has fundamentally shaped my understanding of many of the issues discussed in the introduction, and I thank him again, together with Arthur Lawton, for reading the *Philebus* with me in spring 2003. With special gratitude I acknowledge the assistance of Barbara Jane Hall, Kyle Lucas, Hayden Niehus, and Brianna Zgurich. Over the course of the spring 2016 semester (in Kyle's case) and the three semesters—spring and fall 2016 and spring 2017 (Jane, Hayden, and Brianna)—they read the *Philebus* with me as I wrote the first draft of this commentary, suggesting ideas, catching errors, and making improvements. Finally, I thank Guillermo Camacho, Mike Egan, Magnus Schuh, and Savanah Winiesdorffer, who helped revise a draft of the commentary as they read selections from the *Philebus* in spring 2020. The many errors that remain are my own.

NOTE ON CONVENTIONS

Page and line numbers. The standard page numbers (11–67) and letters (a–e) derive from Stephanus 1578. I follow the line numbers in Burnet 1901.

Burnet. In my names for the manuscripts—B, T, t, W, Ven. 189—I follow Burnet 1901. The bibliography of some editors of the text before the 1900s are lost to me. I mark these in the text in parentheses as follows: (cited in Burnet).

Forms, kinds, and words. Italics name forms (e.g., the form *unbounded*). Initial capitals name kinds (e.g., the kind Unbounded). Quotation marks name linguistic expressions in English (e.g., the adjective "unbounded"), while only context indicates the naming of Greek words. For example, I name a Greek word in the following sentence: The ancient Greek convention is to mention a word or phrase by putting the neuter singular definite article τό before the word or phrase (see, e.g., notes to 33e2 and 58c1). Also, often after a Greek word I use italics to give an English translation (e.g., "Plato's terms πέρας *bound* and ἄπειρον *unbounded*"). Unless otherwise indicated, translations are my own.

Grave and acute accents. In the notes, I distinguish types and tokens of Greek words as follows. A Greek word with a grave accent on the ultima refers to a *token* of that word (that is, a visible particular instance) in the text. A Greek word with an acute accent on the ultima refers to that *type* of word (that is, the one intelligible abstract object that is instantiated in each of the many tokens. For example, the word παρὰ refers to the token παρὰ at 11a1, while παρά refers to the type of that word.

Argument identification. Complex arguments are identified with the conclusion stated first, followed by premises establishing it. When premises themselves are conclusions, the subpremises establishing them are likewise listed below, indented. For example:

C
Because:
P1
Because:
  P1.1
  P1.2
P2

In the example, conclusion C follows from P1 and P2, while P1 in turn follows from P1.1 and P1.2. About twenty arguments are identified in the commentary (see notes to 12c6–7, 12e2, 13a–b, two at 14c–15a, two at 14d8–e4, 18d4–e1, 20e–22c, 22b–c, 24a–e, 26e1–2, 27e–28a, 28a–30a, 29e2, 30a–e, 40b6–7, 43d4–5—additional arguments are identified in Rudebusch 2016).

ABBREVIATIONS

LSJ	Liddell, Scott, Jones, and McKenzie 1940
OED	*Oxford English Dictionary*
S	Smyth 1956
TLG	*Thesaurus Linguae Graecae* Digital Library

INTRODUCTION

1. DRAMATIC SETTING AND DATE

There are no indicators of dramatic setting, although the way that all sides of the conversation take their setting for granted rules out, for example, that the conversation took place where Socrates was deployed with the army or in prison at the end of his life. Nails lists the *Philebus* as being "without dramatic date" (2002, 327), and certainly there is little information that could lead to a dramatic date. Socrates addresses Protarchus as παῖ *child* (e.g., at 15a1), while Protarchus implies Socrates is old (16a5). Socrates remarks on Philebus' style of addressing Protarchus and his friends as παῖδες *boys* (16b4). The "boys" are old enough to be without chaperones and seem to use sexual double entendres with reference to Philebus (11c7–8). Accordingly, Protarchus and friends would be νεανίσκοι—that is, "young men or youths of adult height who show early signs of facial hair" (Nails 2002, 100). Philebus would be older but still able to view them as sexual partners, with Socrates likely to be still older than Philebus. Unlike in the *Phaedrus*, there is no sexual tension between him and his interlocutor. This places the dramatic date certainly after the *Parmenides* (when Socrates was seventeen) and probably after the *Phaedrus*, when Socrates was in his early fifties.

But the following evidence suggests a precise dramatic date for the *Philebus*: the two or three months before Socrates' death. In the *Phaedrus*, Socrates has a reverential attitude toward masters of dialectic, understood to include the method of collection and division. In the *Sophist,* when he meets the Eleatic Stranger, Socrates is ready to be reverential to him. In the *Philebus,* Socrates continues to value the method as a gift from gods, but he pointedly says that the method has escaped him many times, and no longer talks about godlike masters he'd like to meet. Instead, he uses the method himself with seeming mastery and with no reference to a desire to learn from masters. The best explanation of Socrates' change in attitude and self-confidence is the Stranger. This means that the *Philebus* is set in the month or two after Socrates listened to the Stranger (in spring 399) but before Socrates' trial "in the month of Thargelion, roughly May–June" (Nails 2002, 322).

The details of this evidence are as follows. A distinctive method of collection and division is prominently featured in the *Phaedrus*, the *Sophist*, the *Statesman*, and the *Philebus.* In both the *Phaedrus* (266b3) and the *Philebus* (16b6) Socrates pronounces himself an ἐραστής *lover* of collection and division. In the *Phaedrus,* Socrates states he is a lover for a purpose: ἵνα οἷός τε ὦ λέγειν τε καὶ φρονεῖν *in order to be able to speak and know* (266b4–5). He states that if he supposes some other person to be able εἰς ἓν καὶ ἐπὶ πολλὰ πεφυκόθ' ὁρᾶν *to look into one and on many things that naturally come to be* (266b5–6), he pursues "κατόπισθε μετ' ἴχνιον ὥστε θεοῖο" *in [his] footsteps behind [him] as a god* (266b6–7).[1] Socrates is quoting a formula that appears four times in the *Odyssey:* (1) Telemachus following Athena in the guise of a mortal as she leads him away from murderous suitors in pursuit of knowledge of his father (2.406); and (2) him following her again in the guise of a mortal to try to gain that knowledge from Nestor (3.30); (3) Odysseus following Calypso to a feast after she builds a raft for him to carry him away from her island to return to what might fairly be called reality (5.193); and (4) Odysseus, a transient beggar all alone, following Athena in the guise of a mortal leading him to Nausicaa's father, Alcinous, king of the Phaeacians, who will cause Odysseus at last to be set on the soil of his native land. These contexts for Socrates' quotation emphasize his reverential attitude in the *Phaedrus.* The quotation likens Socrates to Odysseus and

1. Ryan (2012, 274–75) explains the changes Socrates makes in adapting the verse to his purpose.

Telemachus at moments when the hero and his son are desperate for wise guidance to save their lives and who are saved in all four cases by following a god. Instead of Athena or Calypso, Socrates tentatively identifies the masters he would follow as διαλεκτικούς *experts at dialectic* (266c1), an expertise that Socrates views as his salvation in reasoning.

Socrates states his pursuit of such experts using a present general conditional, thus as a law governing his own behavior (ἐάν τέ τιν' ἄλλον ἡγήσωμαι δυνατὸν . . . τοῦτον διώκω *if I ever suppose another is able, I pursue him* [266b5–6]). The dramatic date of the *Phaedrus* is between 418 and 416.[2] To judge by the dramatic dates of other dialogues, to this point in Socrates' life the only master dialectician he has ever met was more than thirty years earlier, Parmenides in August 450, when Socrates was seventeen (Nails 2002, 308). Parmenides gave Socrates a master class as part of what the narrator Cephalus called τοὺς λόγους, οὓς ποτε Σωκράτης καὶ Ζήνων καὶ Παρμενίδης διελέχθησαν *the arguments that Socrates, Zeno, and Parmenides once produced in dialogue* or *with dialectic* (*Parmenides* 126c2: Parmenides himself in the course of the discussion referred to τὴν τοῦ διαλέγεσθαι δύναμιν *the power of carrying on a dialogue* or *of dialectic* [135c2]). Parmenides fits Socrates' description in the *Phaedrus* as able εἰς ἓν καὶ ἐπὶ πολλὰ πεφυκόθ' ὁρᾶν *to look into one and upon many things that naturally come to be* (*Phaedrus* 266b5–6). For Parmenides in the lesson (*Parmenides* 137b–166c) gave a masterly exploration of many hypotheses περὶ τοῦ ἑνὸς αὐτοῦ *about the one itself* (137b3). For example, he took up the hypothesis that οὐκ ἂν εἴη πολλὰ τὸ ἕν the one could not be many (137c4–5) and exhaustively refuted it at 142a6–8, showing many things that "naturally come to be" from such a one. Again, he showed that εἰ ἓν ἔστιν *if one is* (142c3), ἀνάγκη δύ' ἀεὶ γιγνόμενον necessarily it is always becoming two (142e7–a1), and that τὸ ἓν ἄρα αὐτὸ . . . πολλά τε καὶ ἄπειρα τὸ πλῆθός ἐστιν *the one itself therefore is many and unbounded with respect to magnitude* (144e3–5). We may imagine that Socrates, as he listened, pursued the dialectical examination κατόπισθε μετ' ἴχνιον ὥστε θεοῖο *in*

2. Nails (2002, 314) notes this date is controversial but nonetheless judges the dialogue to have a "definite dramatic date" (308), giving reasons (314) that perhaps lead to an unstated conclusion that continued controversy is ill-advised.

[Parmenides'] footsteps behind [him] as a god (266b6–7). Given Socrates' past experience with Parmenides, we can explain Socrates' reverential attitude toward masters of dialectic in the *Phaedrus*.

More than fifteen years after the conversation of the *Phaedrus*, Theodorus the geometrician introduces Socrates to τινὰ ξένον *a xenos* (216a2). The word *xenos,* spoken by Theodorus, refers to a friend who is a visitor from another city and who is a guest at the home of Theodorus: a "guest-friend." This is one of the word's meanings and is found in Homer. Spoken by Socrates, who is not hosting him and does not know even his name, the word takes another Homeric meaning: *stranger.* Likewise, *stranger* is the meaning of *xenos* for us readers of the dialogue. Theodorus introduces his guest as τὸ μὲν γένος ἐξ Ἐλέας *on the one hand, with respect to his nation, from Elea* (216a3), ἕτερον δὲ τῶν ἀμφὶ Παρμενίδην καὶ Ζήνωνα ἑταίρων *but* (*who is*) *other than the disciples of the school of Parmenides and Zeno* (216a3–4),[3] μάλα δὲ ἄνδρα φιλόσοφον *yet very much a man of philosophy* (216a4). Remarkably, Socrates straightaway recognizes that the Stranger is a god: Ἆρ' οὖν, ὦ Θεόδωρε, οὐ ξένον ἀλλά τινα θεὸν ἄγων . . . λέληθας; *Then did it escape your notice, Theodorus, that you're not leading a guest-friend but rather some god?* (216a5–6). φαύλους ἡμᾶς ὄντας ἐν τοῖς λόγοις ἐποψόμενός τε καὶ ἐλέγξων, θεὸς ὤν τις ἐλεγκτικός *Since we are paltry*

3. Modern editors emend ἕτερον *other* to ἑταῖρον *companion,* which leads many in turn to delete in addition the ἑταίρων seven words after: ἑταῖρον δὲ τῶν ἀμφὶ Παρμενίδην καὶ Ζήνωνα *a fellow of the school of Parmenides and Zeno.* The changes are made on the grounds that the Stranger shows himself as a member of the school: he is familiar with the teachings of Parmenides and at 241d5 refers to him as a πατρὸς *father.* But these reasons are weak. For the Socrates of the *Theaetetus* is likewise familiar with the teachings of Parmenides and—quoting Homer to call Parmenides αἰδοῖός τέ μοι . . . δεινός τε *revered and dread,* the words used by Helen, who inserts between them the further epithet φίλε ἑκυρὲ *dear father-in-law* to address Priam as he protects her (*Iliad* 3.172)—is even more reverential to Parmenides than the Stranger. The Stranger dares to criticize Parmenides (*Sophist* 244b–245d), but Socrates refuses (*Theaetetus* 183d–184a). Yet no one would use Socrates' reverence for Parmenides to infer that Socrates is a fellow of the school of Parmenides. On the other hand, if Socrates did happen to be Elean, and you were introducing him to your friends, you might well say, "He *is* Elean, *but* he's not a member of the school of Parmenides and Zeno, *yet* he is very much a man of philosophy." Just so, Theodorus introduces the Stranger, coordinating his three statements with μέν . . . δέ . . . δέ *on the one hand . . . but . . . yet . . .* See Cordero 1993, 281–84 and Delcomminette 2014, 535n6 for other considerations regarding this text.

in arguments, [he is] going to going to look us over and refute us, as he is sort of a god of refutation (216b4–6). Socrates at this moment still remembers with admiration the λόγους παγκάλους *utterly beautiful arguments* of Parmenides (217c5). These passages establish that Socrates retains his reverential attitude toward masters of dialectic such as Parmenides up to this point in his life, and contrasts himself as φαύλους . . . ἐν τοῖς λόγοις *paltry in arguments* by way of comparison.

In the *Philebus* Socrates states that οὐ μὴν ἔστι καλλίων ὁδὸς οὐδ' ἂν γένοιτο *there is not and could not come to be a finer way* (16b5) than the method of collection and division—but then he discounts this statement (δέ *but*), saying that the method of collection and division πολλάκις δέ με ἤδη διαφυγοῦσα ἔρημον καὶ ἄπορον κατέστησεν *many times now, after escaping has left me desolate at an impasse* (16b6–7). Socrates continues to revere the method, saying that it is θεῶν μὲν εἰς ἀνθρώπους δόσις *a gift of gods to human beings* (16c5). He continues to revere οἱ μὲν παλαιοί κρείττονες ἡμῶν καὶ ἐγγυτέρω θεῶν οἰκοῦντες *men of old who were mightier than us and who dwelt nearer to the gods* (16c7–8). But he no longer speaks of a desire to learn from present-day masters of dialectic for the purpose of being able to speak and know: the law governing his own behavior (*Phaedrus* 266b5–6, quoted above) no longer seems to hold. He no longer speaks of himself as paltry in arguments and in future to be refuted by a master. This difference in Socrates' attitude between the start of the *Sophist* and the dramatic date of the *Philebus* calls for explanation, and the only explanation can be the Stranger. There is no other master of dialectic Socrates meets or alludes to meeting after his day with the Stranger in the few months remaining of his life who could have caused that change. For purposes of dramatic date, I can leave aside the question *how* the Stranger produced this change. (Did Socrates absorb the Stranger's wisdom as an apprentice watching a master, or did Socrates recoil from errors he observed in the Stranger's technique?) In whatever way the Stranger explains Socrates' change, we must set the *Philebus* after Socrates' meeting with him. There is additional evidence for such a late date in literary allusions in the *Philebus* to the Stranger. For example, there is the odd image in Socrates' locution at 16b6–7 (quoted above) of the ὁδὸς . . . πολλάκις δέ με ἤδη διαφυγοῦσα *the way [of collection and division] escaping [Socrates].* This odd use of the verb διαφεύγω *escape* in connection with collection and division seems to be a backward reference to the eight instances of φεύγω, with and without prefixes, in the Stranger's two dialogues. For example, in the *Statesman*, the Stranger describes his conversation in the *Sophist* this way: διέφυγεν ἡμᾶς ὁ λόγος *the argument escaped us* (284b8–9, with the other instances at *Sophist* 231c5–6, 235b3, 235c5, 236d3, 260d1, and *Statesman* 268e5 and 275d6). Since Socrates spent his last month in prison, a dramatic date for the *Philebus* after the day with the Stranger leaves a window of only two or three months when the conversation could have occurred.[4]

2. PERSONS OF THE DIALOGUE

The dialogue begins as a conversation between Socrates and Philebus in the presence of several young admirers of Philebus, one of whom, Protarchus, takes the position as Socrates' interlocutor. Only these three characters have speaking parts in the dialogue. Although Socrates sometimes refers to his own views using plural pronouns (see note on 11a2), he appears to be alone (as Protarchus implies with his threat at 16a4). The name "Philebus" "is not known in Greece in ancient times except for a fictional instance" (Nails 2002, 238). Protarchus is identified as a son of Callias (at 19b5), but although "Protarchus" and "Callias" are both common names, "there is no known instance of a Protarchus-Callias [father-son] pair" (Nails 2002, 257). This Callias is often interpreted as being the one mentioned in the *Apology*, but Nails argues against that alternative. It is possible that both Protarchus and Philebus are fictional, but our evidence takes us no further than that possibility.

There is much more to say about Socrates. Nails (2002, 263–69) gives an authoritative overview of the historical Socrates' life, military and political career, depiction in comedy, and his trial. The character Socrates in Plato's dialogues is more or less true to that history, with there being vigorous debate about how much more and less (see Graham and Barney 2016 for

4. Debra Nails has pointed out to me in a correspondence that the openings of both the *Theaetetus* and *Symposium* imply a flurry of activity in those few months near the end of Socrates' life.

an introduction to one thread of the debate, the question of the historicity of Chaerephon's visit to the Oracle).

The character Socrates in dialogues such as the *Apology, Charmides, Euthydemus, Euthyphro, Gorgias, Ion, Laches, Lesser Hippias, Lysis, Meno, Protagoras,* and *Republic* 1 is best understood to have as his motive the conversion of others to philosophy by showing in conversation that they are like him in lacking expertise in how to live an excellent human life (Rudebusch and Turner 2014)—let us call these the *missionary* dialogues. Despite professing his own ignorance, the missionary Socrates is typically self-confident in cross-examining others—from deferential youths to men of the highest reputation for wisdom. The method of the missionary Socrates is *dialectical* and *elenctic.* Socrates is *dialectical* here not in using the method of collection and division but rather in using the highest method described in Plato's Divided Line in the *Republic* (509d–511e). That is, Socrates begins from the premises, whatever they are, supplied by his interlocutors and then leads them by trains of questions to the desired conclusion (on this method see Rudebusch 2007, 57–60). Socrates here is *elenctic* in eliciting from his interlocutor an admission either of ignorance (from those who have claimed expertise) or of their overriding need for knowledge.

The Socrates of dialogues such as the *Cratylus, Crito, Phaedo, Phaedrus, Republic* 2–10, *Symposium,* and *Theaetetus* uses the same dialectical method, but his motives for those conversations appear different and various. There is the practical motive to consider the right course of action (*Crito*). There are more academic motives in discussion of topics that, although treated academically, seem nevertheless to bear on practical life choices (like the nature of love in the *Symposium* and *Phaedrus* or the relative advantages of righteous and unrighteous lives in *Republic* 2–10). And there are the purely academic motives in discussions of the relation of language to reality (*Cratylus* and *Phaedrus*). All such practical and more or less academic motives differ from the motive to convert to philosophy that we find in the missionary dialogues. The Socrates of the *Theaetetus* is remarkable in being both *academic* and *elenctic.* That dialogue takes up an academic topic—the nature of knowledge—but it does so with the missionary motive of establishing recognition of human ignorance in Socrates' interlocutor, albeit a more profound ignorance than in the other missionary dialogues (on the more profound ignorance, see Rudebusch 1990).

Ledger's 1989 computer analysis of stylistic features in Plato's texts turned up a "cluster of Platonic dialogues" remarkable for their stylistic similarities: *Critias, Epinomis, Seventh Letter, Laws, Philebus, Statesman, Sophist,* and *Timaeus* (Nails 1995, 110). Of this cluster of near neighbors, the character Socrates is not present in *Epinomis, Seventh Letter,* or *Laws.* He is present but inactive in the *Timaeus-Critias* duology and in the *Sophist-Statesman* duology. Of this cluster, only the *Philebus* features Socrates leading the conversation with his dialectical method, where his motive again seems more academic, although it bears on human life: "a whole theory about the ingredients of the best life and their proper ordering" (Cooper 1997, 398).

Although not linked closely by Ledger's 1989 stylometric study to this cluster, the *Theaetetus* is dramatically linked with the duology *Sophist-Statesman*, the former ending (*Theaetetus* 210d) with an agreement to meet the next morning, and the latter beginning (*Sophist* 216a) with Theodorus referring to the previous day's agreement. It is tempting for readers to assimilate the philosophy of the Socrates who leads the discussion in the *Theaetetus* and *Philebus* with the philosophy of the Eleatic Stranger, who leads the discussion in the *Sophist* and *Statesman.* Cooper (1997, 398), for example, in his introduction to the *Philebus,* says that Socrates there "pursues the discussion much more in the manner of the Stranger of *Sophist* or *Statesman* than in his own manner in either the [missionary] dialogues or the *Republic.*" This assimilation is overstated. The Stranger chooses to speak from a position of authority, the position of one who professes to have an answer, as Theodorus reports: διακηκοέναι γέ φησιν ἱκανῶς καὶ οὐκ ἀμνημονεῖν *[the Stranger] says that he has heard [the answer] well enough and has not forgotten* (217b7–8). Such professions assimilate the Stranger not to Socrates but to his interlocutors, who often profess wisdom (for example, the eponymous characters at *Laches* 190c and 190e, *Euthyphro* 4e–5a and 5c, and *Protagoras* 318e–319a). Socrates makes no such profession in the *Philebus.* On the contrary, he expresses doubt about the provisional answer he defends at the start of the dialogue (Τί δ' ἂν ἄλλη τις κρείττων τούτων φανῇ; *What if some other [answer] superior to these comes to light?* [11d11]), and indeed that first answer proves to be wrong by 22a–c. Rather than speaking from a position of authority, the Socrates of the *Philebus* speaks as one among equals, cross-examining as a way to develop an account in common with his interlocutor. This is the Socrates who seeks to elicit his answer from the position of his interlocutor, who has just failed to do so with Philebus but who succeeds admirably with Protarchus.

There are additional differences between the form of conversation of the Stranger and Socrates.[5] Socrates gives encouragement to the interlocutor to speak his mind boldly: ἵνα μὴ μάτην θαρρήσῃς, ἀφίημι *I dismiss [my objection to your statement] in order that you do not speak boldly in vain,* (*Theaetetus* 189d4). This encouragement has its proper effect on Theaetetus: ὅτι δὲ κελεύεις προθύμως ἀποκρίνασθαι, παρακινδυνεύων λέγω *because you bid me to answer with a spirit, I'm taking a chance and speaking out* (204b2–3). In fact, Socrates praises Theaetetus when he throws up opposition: Ἀνδρικῶς γε . . . μάχῃ *you're fighting like a man* (205a1). In contrast, the Stranger prefers αὐτὸς ἐπὶ σαυτοῦ μακρῷ λόγῳ διεξιέναι *to go through a long speech all by himself* (217c3), unless his interlocutor responds ἀλύπως τε καὶ εὐηνίως *in a way that is easy to handle and does not cause trouble* (217d1). The Stranger's first interlocutor, Theaetetus, comes close to causing trouble early in the conversation, when the Stranger proposes to divide hunting on land into two parts—namely, hunting of the tame and hunting of the wild. Instead of assenting, Theaetetus questions the Stranger's division: εἶτ' ἔστι τις θήρα τῶν ἡμέρων; *is there any hunting of the tame?* (222b6). The Stranger gives no praise to him for throwing up opposition. He crushes Theaetetus: εἴπερ γέ ἐστιν ἄνθρωπος ἥμερον ζῷον *[there is] if at any rate a human being is a tame animal* (b7) and commands, θὲς δὲ ὅπῃ χαίρεις *posit whatever you like!* (b7–8), spelling out three alternatives that seem designed to make Theaetetus feel like a fool for questioning the Stranger: εἴτε μηδὲν τιθεὶς ἥμερον *either you posit that nothing is tame* (b8—but that

5. I thank Fernando Muniz for discussion, observations, and references about this difference in method.

would be stupid), εἴτε ἄλλο μὲν ἥμερόν τι, τὸν δὲ ἄνθρωπον ἄγριον *or that something else is tame, but the human being is wild* (b8–9—even more stupid), εἴτε ἥμερον μὲν λέγεις αὖ τὸν ἄνθρωπον, ἀνθρώπων δὲ μηδεμίαν ἡγῇ θήραν *or that, while you do say that the human being is tame, you suppose that there is not any hunting of human beings* (b9–10—also stupid). The Stranger then makes a second command that puts Theaetetus in an awkward position: τούτων ὁπότερ' ἂν ἡγῇ φίλον εἰρῆσθαί σοι, τοῦτο ἡμῖν διόρισον *whichever of these you suppose is dear to you to answer, make this division for us!* (b10–11). It seems that Theaetetus has been properly tamed by the Stranger's fierce response to his question. For he meekly says: ἀλλ' ἡμᾶς τε ἥμερον, ὦ ξένε, ἡγοῦμαι ζῷον, θήραν τε ἀνθρώπων εἶναι λέγω *o Stranger, but I suppose we are a tame animal, and I say that there is hunting of human beings* (c1–2). Theaetetus throws up no more opposition in the conversation.[6]

In the missionary dialogues, Socrates speaks of the good only insofar as it bears on practical deliberation about how to live the best life, all things considered. He speaks of it there as being *knowledge*, specifically, expertise at human well-being. In other dialogues, Socrates speaks of a good itself, but only indirectly, either as the uppermost limit of a therapy that leads to numerous revisions in the object of one's love (*Symposium* 210a–211d), or with images like the sun, telling us what that good is *like* but claiming to be unable to give an account of what it *is*, despite the requests of his interlocutors (*Republic* 506b–509c). The Socrates of the *Philebus* is more knowledgeable, giving an account of what the good is. In comparison to the many other characters of Socrates in the many other Platonic dialogues, then, this Socrates of the *Philebus* shows himself unrivaled in knowledge on this theoretical point, although such theoretical knowledge falls short of the practical wisdom about which every character of Socrates knows we are ignorant. (On the difference between theoretical knowledge and practical wisdom, see Rudebusch 2018, 231–32.)

6. As an alternative, Cooper attributes the differences in the pursuit of the respective topics to the interlocutors. Compared to the Stranger's interlocutors, Theaetetus and Young Socrates, Protarchus in the *Philebus* is "much more ready to throw up opposition" (1997, 398).

3. DATE OF COMPOSITION

As noticed above, Ledger's 1989 computer analysis of the stylistic features of Plato's texts turned up a "cluster of Platonic dialogues" remarkable for their stylistic similarities: *Critias, Epinomis, Seventh Letter, Laws, Philebus, Statesman, Sophist,* and *Timaeus* (Nails 1995, 110). If this group of stylistically similar dialogues is taken as evidence that these dialogues were written at the same period of Plato's life, then one ought to predict that other dialogues would likewise group themselves about other periods of Plato's life (even if we do not know which periods correspond to which times of Plato's life). That prediction is false: there are no other groupings of comparable similarity. Thus, Ledger's stylistic similarities might better correlate with other features than Plato's time of life. For example, perhaps the close similarity of these dialogues is explained by Plato's use of a scribe who paraphrased in a strongly idiosyncratic way Plato's dictation. And perhaps Plato's use of such a scribe might in turn be explained by health problems on Plato's part, which might in turn be explained by old age—but for each story of this explanatory house of cards one might produce an indefinite number of alternative explanations. From Ledger's computer analysis, then, it seems that "the only fully warranted conclusion . . . is that there is a group of *stylistically similar* dialogues. Whether that similarity derives from order of composition, subject matter, genre, intended audience, or some other variable, remains unknown" (Nails 1995, 114).

Nevertheless, there is a scholarly consensus dating the *Philebus* as written late in Plato's life. (See Nails 1995, 64, for a table showing the consensus. For recent examples, see Irwin 2019, 73–77 and Meinwald 2019, 338n3.) Such a date would make this Socrates of the *Philebus* Plato's last depiction of him, which is one way to explain why this Socrates displays the greatest knowledge of the good.

4. DRAMATIC MIRRORING OF PHILOSOPHIC THEMES

The *Philebus* begins mid-sentence, with a reference back to an earlier discussion, one that probably took place immediately prior to this dialogue. The prior discussion is summarized as a controversy between Philebus' hedonism and Socrates' own intellectualism. Like the beginning, the end of the dialogue breaks off as if mid-sentence (67b11). Among Platonic dialogues, "the *Philebus* is unique in this feature of beginninglessness and endlessness" (Burnyeat 1997, 19). This feature gives the appearance that the author created the dialogue by setting bounds to an indefinitely longer conversation. This stylistic feature, like the interpretations of Philebus' hedonism discussed above, mirrors the philosophical thesis within the dialogue about bounded and unbounded—namely, that the addition of boundaries is an expert's way of producing a good product out of material that, prior to boundaries, is indeterminate. Proclus' word for this mirroring is "ἐνεικονίζεται, the verb from εἰκών, *image*" (Burnyeat 1997, 19).

5. TOPIC AND STRUCTURE

The topic of the dialogue is set by the question, "Is the good pleasure or knowing?"[7] The answer will be "Neither: the good is measure, beauty, and truth"—but knowing will turn out to be immeasurably more similar to the good than pleasure, and the good for human beings includes both knowing and certain measured pleasures. Curiously, Protarchus and Socrates give two different interpretations of Philebus' position. In terms of the divisions developed later in the dialogue, there are three competing theses about pleasure under discussion. The character Philebus has an open-ended ("unbounded") position about pleasure and the good, and Socrates and Protarchus set bounds to his thesis in different ways. Following Delcomminette (2006, 22) I take Philebus' indeterminacy to be a dramatic reflection of philosophical themes of ἄπειρον *unbounded* and πέρας *bound* featured in the dialogue: the philosophical position of Philebus is ἄπειρον, and the dialogue will apply πέρας to it.

1. *Socrates' interpretation of Philebus*: When we divide the kind Good we find pleasure as one subkind (among possible others, see 11b4–6).
2. *Protarchus' interpretation of Philebus:* The kind Good, without any division, is one and the same as the kind Pleasure (see 11d8).

7. As Delcomminette (2006, 23) observes. He is closer to the text than the alternative interpretation of Gosling (1975, 76) and Irwin (1995, 328), who take it to be, "What is pleasure?" Indeed, the topic is not set by any question of the form "What is X?"

In addition, Socrates has his own thesis about the kind Good and the kind Pleasure:

3. *Socrates' thesis about pleasure:* the kind Pleasure can take on goodness and badness as extrinsic characteristics. Accordingly, we can divide that kind into the subkinds Good Pleasure and Bad Pleasure (see 12c7–8).

If we distinguish these three positions on pleasure, we can understand why the dialogue continues after Protarchus' interpretation of Philebus—namely, the identity thesis—is refuted at 20e–22c. The remainder of the dialogue is aimed at refuting Philebus, as interpreted by Socrates, and establishing Socrates' thesis about pleasure in the context of determining what the good life is for human beings.

The *Philebus* is structured so that the experience of reading it is like spending time in a laboratory as follows: (1) entering the lab to find something and then, after (2) moving an obstacle out of the way, (3) reaching a microscope and then (3, 4, and 5) looking through it at three different objects. Having properly examined the objects, (6) one finds what one is looking for. These six stages appear as follows in the *Philebus*: (1) The dialogue begins with a question: what makes a human life happy? Preliminary competing answers are that pleasure is good and that knowing is better than pleasure. (2) The first moves in the competition run into an obstacle: the paradox that one is many and many is one. The discussion gets past the obstacle by supposing the paradox is a phenomenon introduced by the "microscope" itself—namely, human reason in accordance with the "Divine Method." (3) Accepting the Divine Method allows the argument first to make a Fourfold Division of the world into four kinds, Bound, Unbounded, Mix, and Cause, and to place pleasure into the kind Unbounded and knowing into the kind Cause. Using the Divine Method, (4) the argument classifies relevant kinds of pleasure—the place where it comes to be, restoring pleasures and pleasures of anticipation, a variety of false pleasures, and a significant kind of true pleasure—and identifies pleasure as a process of *coming to be* as opposed to states and acts of *being* like, for example, knowing. Then, with the same method, (5) the argument classifies relevant kinds of knowing from more to less accurate.

Thanks to the classifications, (6) we can answer the original question with a ranking as follows. In the mixture that is a human life, the first rank goes to the effect of Measure (namely, being measured and timely, etc.); the second rank goes to the effect of Measure and Beauty (namely being complete, sufficient, etc.); the third goes to the effect of (Measure, Beauty, and) Truth (namely, the power of knowing and being aware); the fourth to the effects of knowing in the soul (namely, the sciences and kinds of expertise); and the fifth to the effects of activities of science and expertise (namely, pleasures that are free of pain).

If this structural outline promises "a well-directed and fruitful discussion, it has to be admitted that this is a very high-flying view. A low-flying bird will have quite a different perspective. What looks from very high up like a well-ordered landscape turns out, from close up, to be full of crags and ravines, bogs, and apparently unfordable rivers" (Frede 1993, xv). The crags, ravines, bogs, and river obstacles are in many cases caused by stylistic ambiguity.

6. STYLISTIC AMBIGUITY

Readers of the *Philebus* often notice ambiguity as a striking literary feature. Socrates' interlocutors, Philebus and Protarchus, certainly do. They ask for clarification much more often than their counterparts in other dialogues. For example, in the first five pages of the dialogue, more than a third of Protarchus' questions (twelve of thirty-two) ask for clarification: Τὸ ποῖον; *To what?* (11d3); Τὰ ποῖα δὴ λέγεις; *What in the world are you saying?* (13d2); Λέγε πῶς; *Tell me how* (13e1); Τὸ ποῖον δή; *Just what sort?* (13e3); Πῶς; *How?* (13e8); Τὸν ποῖον δή; *Just what sort?* (14c3); Λέγε σαφέστερον *Speak more clearly*! (14c6); Σὺ δὲ δὴ ποῖα, ὦ Σώκρατες, ἕτερα λέγεις; *But what other version are you talking about, Socrates?* (14e5); Πῶς; *How?* (15a8); Πόθεν; *From where?* (15d3); Τίς αὕτη; λεγέσθω μόνον. *What method? Just let it be said!* (16b8); Λέγε μόνον *Just say it* (16c4). As a rough comparison, in his first thirty-two speeches, Euthyphro asks Socrates for clarification just four times, all at the start in order to clarify Socrates' appearance for a legal matter (*Euthyphro* 2a–7b). Thrasymachus (at *Republic* 336b–341d) asks for clarification in just two of his first thirty-two speeches: Τίς . . . ὑμᾶς πάλαι φλυαρία ἔχει, ὦ Σώκρατες; *What nonsense possesses you just now, Socrates?* (336b8–c1) and Τί λέγεις σύ; *What are you saying?* (339d4). Likewise, Theaetetus (144e–147e) asks just two questions: Τὸ ποῖον; *What sort [of difference]?* (145e2) and Πῶς τί τοῦτο λέγεις; *What sort of thing are you saying?* (146d5).

The *Philebus* makes extensive use of two types of ambiguity: *pronominal* and *elliptical*. Pronouns can be ambiguous about their antecedent. For example:

(S) Diotima taught Socrates about love. Plato wants her to instruct him.

In speech S, the pronoun "her" is feminine in gender, singular in number, and unambiguously stands for the only feminine singular antecedent noun, "Diotima." But the masculine singular pronoun "him" might stand for either of two masculine singular antecedents, "Socrates" or "Plato." The pronoun more naturally stands for "Plato," since that noun is nearer the pronoun than "Socrates." But "Socrates" is still a possible antecedent, making the pronoun ambiguous. *Ellipses* (or "brachylogies") are abbreviated, incomplete sentence constructions with suppressed elements that "must be supplied from some corresponding word in the context" (S §3017). For example, in S the sentence *Plato wants her to instruct him* is likely to be short for *Plato wants her to instruct him* <u>*about love*</u>. We complete the phrase in S by looking for antecedent sentences with a structure in some way parallel.

Socrates' ambiguity provokes Protarchus' questions and presents puzzles for the interpreter. Plato's use of such ambiguity in writing the dialogue is a literary style that calls for explanation. Each such ambiguity sets a puzzle and invites the reader to use intelligence in considering context in order to interpret the meaning. In terms of the measure theory developed in the *Philebus* (24a–27b), the intelligence of the reader, in finding the pronominal antecedents or completing an ellipsis, for example, *sets a bound* to a text that was in a way *unbounded*. In this way, the ambiguity in the *Philebus* makes the literary form of the dialogue a mirror of one of its philosophical themes—namely, that *the good is caused by an intelligent setting of bounds to something unbounded*. The commentary points out many cases of such ambiguity in small cases (see notes to 11a1, 12c1–2, 12e7, 16c9 [see note to 16d1], 37a7 and a9 [see note to 37a2–b3], 37e1–3, 49d3, and 58b3) and large (see notes to 15b–c, 16b–e, 35a6–9, 46d7–47a1, 63e9–64a3, and 64c–67a).

7. *NOEIN, PHRONEIN, PHRONESIS,* AND *NOUS*

The main thesis of the *Philebus* is that the life of *phronein* and *noein* is preferable to the life of enjoying and feeling pleasure. Accurate translations and interpretations of these terms are needed to understand the main thesis. I begin with *noein*. The most elegant translation of *noein* is the verb "to mind," (as in "Mind your manners!"). Unfortunately, that elegant verb usually has the meaning *to be bothered by* (as in "Do you mind my asking?") or the meaning *to beware* (as in "Mind the gap!"). Less elegant than "to mind" is "to be mindful of," a copula with an adjective and a preposition calling for an object. Mindfulness has become a term of art in popular psychology as a technique of focusing one's mind with full attention on something. Connotations of the effort and concentration associated with this technique might, like *bother* and *wariness*, distort the meaning of *noein*.

Minding or being mindful is a kind of awareness. Specifically, it is awareness of *imperceptible* or *universal* features of objects. This mental awareness is different from sensory awareness, which is awareness of *perceptible* or *particular* features of objects. The choice-of-lives thought experiment (20c–22c) depends on the difference between *feeling* pleasure (using sensory awareness without mental awareness) and having *mental awareness* of the pleasure (an awareness that does not include feeling the pleasure). Six times in the *Philebus* the verb *noein* is followed by an object or clause. These objects and clauses indicate the sorts of imperceptible features that one might be mentally aware of:

1. How a kind can be one and many (23e6).
2. Any bound in the kind Hotter and Colder (24a8).
3. That the amount of each element (earth, air, water, and fire) in us is relatively small, insignificant, impure, and impotent (29b9).
4. The nature of the largest pleasures (45c7).
5. How a small, pure-of-pain pleasure can be more pleasant than a big, mixed-with-pain pleasure (53b10).
6. About righteousness, what it is (62a4).

For the purposes of this commentary, I use "to be mentally aware" to translate *noein*, leaving the adverb "mentally" to be understood when it produces unidiomatic English or is implicit in context. This choice gives a univocal translation to the nine occurrences of *noein* in the *Philebus,* a translation that will, perhaps, make the verb *noein* more readily intelligible than "to mind" or "to be mindful of," as shown in the following list:

(11b7) τὸ φρονεῖν καὶ **τὸ νοεῖν** καὶ μεμνῆσθαι *to know, **to be mentally aware** and remember.*

(21a14) τοῦ φρονεῖν καὶ τοῦ νοεῖν καὶ λογίζεσθαι *of knowing, of **being mentally aware** and reckoning.*

(23e6) νοῆσαι πῇ ποτε ἦν αὐτῶν ἓν καὶ πολλὰ ἑκάτερον ***be aware** how each is one and many!*

(24a8) πέρας εἴ ποτέ τι νοήσαις ἄν *if you might **be aware of** any bound.*

(29b9) ἐν ἑνὶ δὲ λαβὼν περὶ πάντων νόει ταὐτόν *after grasping [my point] in one [case], **be aware of** the same [point] about all [the cases]!*

(33b4) τὸν τοῦ νοεῖν καὶ φρονεῖν βίον *the life of **being mentally aware** and knowing.*

(45c7) νοῆσαι . . . ἥντινα φύσιν ἔχει ***be aware of . . .** what nature it has!*

(53b10) ἀρκεῖ νοεῖν ἡμῖν αὐτόθεν ὡς *it is enough for us, on the spot, to **be aware** how* [a small pleasure can be more pleasant than a big].

(62a4) φρονῶν ἄνθρωπος αὐτῆς περὶ δικαιοσύνης ὅτι ἔστιν, καὶ λόγον ἔχων ἑπόμενον τῷ νοεῖν *a person who knows, about righteousness itself, what it is, and who has an account that follows his **awareness**.*

These translations are better than the usual translations of *noein* for purposes of an accurate understanding of the Greek text. For comparison, table 1 shows representative translations of *noein* in these passages.

All these alternatives are idiomatic in context. But no column of translations makes *noein* univocal. For example, in the case of Frede 1993, *to understand, to study, to conceive,* and *to prove* give *noein* four different meanings. The verb "to be mentally aware" makes *noein* univocal in this dialogue. The virtue of charity should lead us always to use the same meaning for the same word when permitted by context. Such a univocal translation makes the interlocutors precise in their speech; while the five columns of polysemous translations in table 1 make the interlocutors speak in a less mindful, more scattershot way.

Table 1
Representative translations of *noein*

	Frede 1993	Gosling 1975	Frede 1997	Delcomminette 2020	Muniz 2012
11b7	understanding	thought	*Vernunft*	*être intelligent*	inteligência
21a14	intelligence	thought	*Erkennen*	*intelligence*	inteligência
23e6	to study	to see	*verstehen*	*penser*	*conceber*
24a8	conceive	to see	*erkennen*	*penser*	*conceber*
29b9	to take	to take	*nimm*	*applique la pensée*	*concebe*
33b4	reason	thought	*Vernunft*	*intelligence*	*pensamento*
45c7	to comprehend	to see	*herauszufinden*	*penser*	*discernir*
53b10	to prove	to note	*klarzumachen*	*penser*	*conceber*
62a4	comprehension	under-standing	*Wissen*	*pensée*	*reflexão*

There are six other comparative advantages to a univocal translation of *noein* with a verb of being aware over the representative translations in table 1. First, the verb "to be mentally aware," like other verbs of knowing and perceiving, including *noein* in the *Philebus*, is *factive*. For example, if I am aware how each is one and many, and how a small pleasure can be more pleasant than a big, then each *is* one and many, and a small pleasure *can* be more pleasant. If I am aware or have awareness of a bound, point, or nature, then that bound, point, or nature exists. Unlike being aware and awareness, verbs of thinking (such as the French verb *penser* in table 1) and nouns of thought (such as "thought," the French *pensée,* and the Portuguese *pensamento*) are not factive.

Second, "to be aware" coordinates with "to feel pleasure" in the dispute between Socrates and Philebus. In that dispute, one side proposes as good a life that feels pleasure, not a life that merely has the capacity to feel. As an alternative, the other side proposes a life of acts of knowing, not a life that merely has the potential to know. Nouns like "intelligence" and "reason" seem to refer to a mental *power* to act rather than the act. Nouns like "understanding" and "comprehension" are ambiguous. They might refer to the power or to the act. The articular infinitive *noein* unambiguously refers to an act. It is a virtue of the English infinitive "to be (mentally) aware" and the gerund "being (mentally) aware" that they are likewise unambiguous.

Third, using a verb of awareness to translate *noein* allows an English translation to display rather than to hide the relation of *noein* to its prefixed forms. The first column of table 2 lists *noein* and its prefixed forms found in the *Philebus*. The second and third columns list the number of occurrences and the locations in the text. The fourth column lists my proposed translations in terms of awareness. With the exception of *dianoeisthai*, these translations are univocal and give a sense corresponding to the Greek prefixes. The fifth column lists the translations of Frede 1993 as a representative example of polysemous translations that hide the sense of the Greek prefixes, with the exception of *agnoein*.

Fourth, awareness can be had "on the spot"; knowledge cannot. Knowledge requires a training process that enables remembering to come to mind with awareness. At 53b10 Socrates states: ἀρκεῖ νοεῖν ἡμῖν αὐτόθεν *it is enough for us, on the spot, noein.* No verb of understanding or knowing fits this passage, in which *noein* can arise *on the spot.* Therefore, to translate any other instance of *noein* in the *Philebus* with a word of knowing—such as the English word "understanding" or the German words *Vernunft, Erkennen, verstehen,* and *Wissen* in table 1—makes a univocal translation of *noein* impossible. In contrast, a translation of *noein* everywhere with a verb of awareness is possible and fits the "on the spot" remark well.

Fifth, if we accept that in the *Philebus noein* is everywhere a verb of being aware, Socrates' lists of three cognitive activities at 11b7 (τὸ φρονεῖν καὶ τὸ νοεῖν καὶ μεμνῆσθαι) and 21a14 (τοῦ φρονεῖν καὶ τοῦ νοεῖν καὶ λογίζεσθαι) might take on new significance (see notes to 11b7 and 21a14 for discussion of the variant to both readings in manuscript B). At 11b7 the infinitive μεμνῆσθαι is combined with νοεῖν in that both verbs share the same article τὸ. We can make the linguistic combination visible with this translation of 11b7: *to know and to be mentally aware and remember.* Given that the linguistic combination of νοεῖν and μεμνῆσθαι corresponds to an analysis of knowing in terms of being aware and remembering, it is charitable to take Socrates to give the three listed items as an implicit analysis of *phronein*

Table 2
Noein and its prefixed forms in the *Philebus*

noein	9	11b7, 21a14, 23e6, 24a8, 29b9, 33b4, 45c7, 53b10, 62a4	be (mentally) aware	understanding, intelligence, study, conceive, take, reason, comprehend, prove, comprehension
agnoein	5	21b8, 23b2, 48d8, 62a9, 64d7	be (mentally) *un*aware	be in ignorance, not realize, not know, cannot recognize
dianoeisthai	11	21d1, 22c2, 38e6, 43a8, 45c3, 51b2, 52e7, 55d5, 58d2, 62a5, 62d8	be (mentally) aware *through* (a period of time or an event of reasoning); hence *to keep* or *have in mind* or *to think through*	think, regard, entertain a thought, plan, question, see, find out, reflection, possess comprehension, intention
ennoein	5	17d6, 20b7, 32e3, 57a6, 58e4	be (mentally) aware *in* (some matter)	realize, remember, ascribe
epinoein	1	65e6	to *set* (mental) awareness *on* (something)	to conceive of
katanoein	9	18b2, 18b6, 18b9, 26c5, 35d8, 40e9, 48a10, 51e4, 51e6	become (mentally) aware	grasp, discover, get, consider, distinguish, see,
sunnoein	4	26c4, 31e4, 44e2, 48b2	*share* (mental) awareness (*with* another)	strike, understand, see

in terms of *noein* and *memnēsthai*. Here is an illustration of that analysis. I can feel pleasure from hearing the song of a robin and have that perceptual awareness without knowing what the sound is. Likewise, I can be mentally aware that it is some kind of birdsong without knowing what kind. My being mentally aware turns into knowing when I remember the song a robin makes. The illustration identifies a kind of recognitional knowing that is a combination of being aware and remembering. In addition to recognitional knowing, there is predictive knowing. In this kind of knowing, I am aware of the song, and I can reckon what notes the bird will sing next. This combination of awareness and reckoning is reflected in the linguistic combination at 21a14: τοῦ φρονεῖν καὶ τοῦ νοεῖν καὶ λογίζεσθαι *of knowing and of being mentally aware and reckoning.* It is easy to see how recognitional knowing and predictive knowing are equivalent: if I remember the robin's song, I can reckon what notes come next; and, if I can reckon what notes come next, I must be remembering the robin's song. Socrates confirms the implicit analysis of *phronein* as recognitional knowing when he spells out in greater detail the conditions for gaining recognitional knowledge at 17b3–e4. At 17e5 the infinitive *phronein* is used to name this kind of knowing. (Socrates also says the person with this sort of knowing is σοφός *wise* at 17e1.)

Sixth, identifying a single meaning for *noein* as *being aware* permits us to contrast it with *phronein,* which must be a verb of knowing at least at 17e5. In addition to 17e5, two other occurrences of *phronein* also require translation with a verb of knowing. One occurrence is 55c–59c, where Socrates presents a hierarchy of kinds of expert knowing (*epistēmai*), including music, medicine, carpentry, arithmetic, and dialectic. He refers to these at 63b4, asking the pleasures if they are willing "to live with all *phronesis* or apart from *phronein*" (οἰκεῖν μετὰ φρονήσεως πάσης ἢ χωρὶς τοῦ φρονεῖν). *Phronein* must be translated with a verb of knowing in this passage, too. The other occurrence is 62a2, where Socrates speaks of φρονῶν ἄνθρωπος αὐτῆς περὶ δικαιοσύνης ὅτι ἔστιν *a person who knows, about righteousness, what it is.* In this passage, the knowing must be recognitional knowing, not mere awareness. The verb *phronein* occurs six other times (11d9, 12d4 [twice], 33a8, 33b4, and 55a7) in contexts that are neutral between competing translations. Socrates uses the verb *phronein* at 11d9, 33a8, and 55a7 to refer to everything that is akin to *phronein.* He uses *phronein* conjoined with *noein* at 33b4 to refer to everything that is akin to *phronein* and *noein.* These occurrences are neutral between different translations of *phronein.* In the remaining two occurrences, both at 12d4, Socrates uses *phronein* in opposition to τὸν ἀνοηταίνοντα, which might mean either *the man who is mentally unaware* or who is *unknowing.* These occurrences, too, are neutral. Since all eleven occurrences either require a verb of knowing or are neutral, it is possible to provide a univocal translation of all eleven instances in the *Philebus.*

I endorse Frede's 1993 translation of the articular infinitive *to phronein* at 11b7 with the gerund "knowing." For accuracy, I recommend translating the same articular infinitive with the same gerund everywhere. The noun *phronēsis* is equivalent to the articular infinitive knowing at its first occurrence (12a1), where Socrates asks, κρατεῖ δὲ ὁ τῆς ἡδονῆς τὸν τῆς φρονήσεως; *does the life of pleasure conquer the life of phronēsis?* The Greek word and its English translation, "pleasure," unambiguously mean *the act of feeling pleasure.* The English translation of *phronēsis* should likewise mean *the act of knowing.* The gerund "knowing" has this as a primary meaning. The noun "knowledge" does not do as well as "knowing" at suggesting to the reader the act of knowing. "Knowledge" in this context more likely suggests the possession, in memory, of facts or know-how. This meaning is unsuitable as a translation of *phronēsis*, because Socrates' candidate life, coordinate with the Phileban life, is not a life of possession but a life of activity. The translator might consider that the gerund "knowing" is already in use for the articular infinitive. This consideration might be grounds for using a different translation. I propose as a glossary entry "(act of) knowing." This gives a univocal translation for *phronēsis* everywhere in the *Philebus.*

If we recognize that *phronesis* refers to an activity, not a possession, we will for the same reasons translate *nous* with an activity word, not a possession word. For example, at 13e4 Socrates reminds Protarchus of what he "said at the start were good things"—namely, φρόνησίς τε καὶ ἐπιστήμη καὶ νοῦς *knowing, expert knowing, and awareness.* Since these items are competing with the family of pleasure, enjoyment, and so on, we ought to translate *all* of Socrates' goods with activity words like "knowing," not possession words like "knowledge." In particular, it is misleading to translate *nous* here as "mind" or "reason." The nouns "mind" and "reason" refer to things one can possess without activating, which does not fit the context. It is true that the discussion frames the dispute in terms of κτημάτων *possessions* at 19c6. But even in this passage, the possessions Philebus puts forward are ἡδονὴν καὶ τέρψιν καὶ χαρὰν *pleasure, delight,* and *joy* (19c7), which are *states* of perceptual awareness, not *capacities* to be in those states. Correspondingly, Socrates' candidates here need to be translated as states, not capacities: νοῦν, ἐπιστήμην, σύνεσιν, τέχνην *awareness, expert knowing, comprehension, craft understanding* (19d4–5). There is no passage requiring that *nous* be given a different meaning from *awareness*. This permits us to give *nous* that univocal meaning in every occurrence.

The noun *phronesis* at 13e4, 21d9, 28a4, 28d8, and 60d4 (when, typically, it is part of a list mentioning other subkinds of the same general kind) has only its literal meaning, referring to the kind Knowing, although that kind is never collected. There is a larger kind of factive cognition, never collected and never named. Socrates indicates the extent of this larger kind with such words as φρόνησις, ἐπιστήμη, νοῦς, μνήμη πᾶσα, δόξα ἀληθής or ὀρθή, and ἀληθεῖς λογισμούς. *Phronesis* is used as a figure of speech (part-for-whole synecdoche) to refer to this larger kind twenty-one times—typically, when it is opposed to pleasure: at 12a1, 12a3, 14b4, 18e3, 19b4, 20b7, 20e2, 20e4, 21b9, 27c5, 27d2, 59d10, 60b4, 60c8, 60e3, 61c6, 61d1, 63a9, 63b4, 65a8, and 65d5. *Phronesis* occurs in conjunction with *nous* when it figuratively refers to the larger kind seven times: 22a3, 58d7, 59d1, 63c5, 63c7, 65e4, and 66b6. And at 64c8 *nous* figuratively refers to that larger kind. It should be clear in context when I use "knowing" figuratively to refer to the larger kind.[8]

8. *GENOS*, *PHUSIS*, AND *EIDOS*[9]

The noun γένος has the root meaning *offspring*, and hence also the meanings *family* and *race* of living things, and by extension the word in its many occurrences in Plato can refer not only to biological kinds such as the human race,[10] but also political and economic kinds of human beings, as well as biological, chemical, physical, mathematical, metaphysical, and epistemological kinds. Reference to γένη *kinds* is indispensable in the Divine Method (16c–19b): any "one" there divided is a kind, and the "many" that are the result of that

8. I thank the anonymous referee whose penetrating criticisms led me to revise my translations of these words.
9. I thank Fernando Muniz for much helpful discussion about γένος and εἶδος.
10. τὸ ἀνθρώπινον γένος *the human race* (e.g., *Statesman* 262c10–d1, 262e5, and 266c4) is just τὸ τῶν ἀνθρώπων γένος *the kind of human beings* (e.g., *Statesman* 266b1), which is ἡμῶν τὸ γένος *our kind* (e.g., *Timaeus* 72e5).

division are also kinds—that is, subkinds. Any such kind, although in itself one thing, may be divisible into many parts that are subkinds. For example, in figure 1 (in note to 16e–17a) the kind Vocal Sound (or Letter) is divided into thirty-five subkinds. Any one kind is in addition unbounded—that is, it contains indefinitely many objects that come and cease to be members of the kind; these are the temporary, observable particulars, in contrast with the eternal, intelligible kinds.

The twenty-eight instances of γένος in the *Philebus* are all best translated with the same word—"kind." In one instance, the word is used adverbially (in the dative case to limit an adjective): γένει ἕν *one in kind* (12e7). In another it is used as part of a predicate: εἶναι γένους *to be of a kind* (52d1). In sixteen instances the noun is modified with a definite article that is singular or plural (τὸ γένος/τὰ γένη *the kind[s]*) (11b5, 24a9, 25a1, 27a12, 28c9, 30a10, 31a5, a8, a9–10, b4, c2, 32d2, 44e7, 51e1, 53a2–3, 65e2). Once it is modified with an interrogative pronominal adjective, οὗ γένους *of which kind?* (31a1), expecting a demonstrative as answer: *of this kind.* In the final nine cases, the noun γένος is modified by a quantifier word—πολλά *many* (26c9), ὅσα *as many as* (52e6), τι *some* (26e2), τι *any* (63c1), τρίτου *third* (27d7–8), and τετάρτου *fourth* (23d5)—and three interrogative quantifiers, ἐν τίνι γένει *in which kind?* (27e2), expecting a quantifier in answer: *in some kind*, and ὁποίου γένους *of what sort of kind?* (27d5 and 28c4), also expecting a quantifier in answer: *of some sort of kind.* It is the occurrence of such quantifiers that is significant for Socrates' ontology. For such quantification sentences in effect state or entail the statement that kinds exist. A theory stating that kinds exist ought to have them in its ontology.[11]

11. I follow a standard account of ontological commitment:

> In using the predicate "is red" or the adjective "seven," one is not thereby committed to the existence of colors or numbers, though one is committed when one says that there are primary colors from which the others may be generated, or that there are prime numbers between 6 and 12. In general one is committed to the existence of Fs when, and only when, one says that there are Fs. This is the simple idea behind Quine's slogan, "To be is to be the value of a bound variable." The point is not that to exist amounts to nothing more than being the value of a bound variable, but that to *commit* oneself to the existence of something is nothing more than *to say* that there is such a thing. To commit oneself to "things that are F" is to say something the proper regimentation of which [that is, the proper

An occasional alternative translation of γένος is "sort" (thus, for example, Fowler [1925] translates the very first instance at 11b5). The nouns "sort" and "kind" are nearly synonymous in English, but translators, by an oddity of the English language, often need the noun "sort" to translate certain Greek adjectives. About three dozen times Protarchus uses the interrogative pronominal adjective ποῖον (-α); "What sort(s)?" The expected answer to such a question uses demonstrative and relative pronominals—τοιόνδε (or τοιοῦτον) οἷον *[it is] this sort, that* or *[it is] such as . . .* —to correlate with the interrogative (e.g., 29b4–9, although in dialogue they are often implicit). Likewise, the English noun "sort" can translate the Greek indefinite pronominal enclitic adjective τις, as happens about nine times in Socrates' speeches:

(18c1) φθόγγου . . . τινος *a sort of uttered sound*
(44c6) τινι δυσχερείᾳ *a sort of disgust*
(48c6) πονηρία . . . τις *a sort of baseness*
(49d1) λύπη τις ἄδικός . . . καὶ ἡδονή *a sort of unrighteous pain and pleasure*
(50e6) τινος ἀνάγκης *a sort of necessity*
(56c1) τινι προσαγωγίῳ *a sort of "hold against" tool*
(61b4) τις λόγος *a sort of argument*
(62c5) θυρωρὸς . . . τις *a sort of doorkeeper*
(64e1–3) τις . . . συμφορά *a sort of jumble*

In colloquial English, there is a pronunciation of "sort of" that may be treated as an adjective—"sorta"—as in "what sorta thing?—this sorta thing" or "a sorta jumble." The colloquial adjective better corresponds to the grammatical structure of the Greek. English readers interested in understanding Socrates' metaphysics need to know that although the noun "sort" might be used to translate Greek adjectives into standard English, that noun does not carry ontological weight. To avoid compounding this problem, translators should never use the weightless noun "sort" both to translate adjectives and to translate the noun γένος. Then Socrates, at least in translation, will speak of both sorts and kinds, but he will only require kinds in his ontology.

---

translation into predicate logic] is, or entails, a quantificational sentence ∃x Fx the truth of which requires the existence of at least one object *o* that makes Fx true when *o* is assigned as value of "x" (Soames 2009, 426).

Another alternative translation of γένος is "class," a word favored by, among others, Gosling (1975) in his translation of γένος in the Fourfold Division at 22d–30e (at 23d5, 24a9, 25a1, 27a12, 27d5, 27d7–8, 27e2, 28c4, 28c9, and 30a10). Classes, like kinds, have the advantage of being able to divide into many subclasses and also to contain unboundedly many particulars. For English readers interested in understanding Plato's metaphysics, the problem with using "class" as a translation of γένος is that "class" is ambiguous in a way that γένος is not. On the one hand, it might mean a class as used in the mathematical theory of classes. It is true that both such classes and γένη contain members. But mathematical classes are defined "extensionally"—that is, by their membership. According to the Axiom of Extensionality, Class 1 = Class 2 just in case Class 1 and Class 2 possess the same members. Unlike such classes, a single γένος, such as Unbounded or Mix, can possess members that come and go even while it remains the same γένος. The power of a γένος to persist even as its members change makes it like another meaning of "class," as when we speak of social classes. For example, the rich and poor remain with us as classes even as their membership changes. In contrast with mathematical classes, what gives a γένος *kind* its identity is not its membership but rather its distinctive εἶδος *form* (see Muniz and Rudebusch, n.d.)—that is, its φύσις *nature.*

The φύσις of a γένος K is what one looks to in trying to understand what K is. About a third of the instances of the word φύσις in the *Philebus* make this point:

(12c5–6) To understand the kind Pleasure (which is one and many), δεῖ καὶ σκοπεῖν ἥντινα φύσιν ἔχει *it is necessary indeed to examine what nature it has.*

(18a8–9) To understand a given kind taken as a "one," οὐκ ἐπ' ἀπείρου φύσιν δεῖ βλέπειν εὐθὺς ἀλλ' ἐπί τινα ἀριθμόν *with respect to [its] nature it is necessary not to look on unbounded [particular instances of K], but rather upon some number [of subkinds of K].*

(25a3–4) To collect many things and identify the kind Unbounded, χρῆναι . . . μίαν ἐπισημαίνεσθαί τινα φύσιν *one ought to put the sign of some one nature on [them].* Socrates here uses the noun φύσιν exactly as the Stranger uses the noun εἶδος (*Statesman* 258c3–8)—that is, as the internal accusative of this verb of *setting* X (accusative) *as a* σῆμα sign *on* Y (dative).

(28a1–3) To identify what provides some part of the good to the kind Pleasure, ἄλλο τι νῷν σκεπτέον ἢ τὴν τοῦ ἀπείρου φύσιν *we must examine something other than the nature of the [kind] Unbounded.*

(44e7–8) εἰ καὶ τὸ τῆς ἡδονῆς γένος ἰδεῖν ἥντινά ποτ' ἔχει φύσιν βουληθεῖμεν *if we were to wish to see what nature the kind Pleasure has.*

(45c7) νοῆσαι γὰρ δεῖ φαμεν ἥντινα φύσιν ἔχει *for we say it is necessary to be aware of what nature [the kind Pleasure] has.*

The φύσις of a γένος K is what one looks at to understand K because of the distinctive effects that φύσις has on K's members. Another third of the instances of the word in the *Philebus* make this point: [12]

(22b4–6) The φύσις of the kind Choiceworthy (αἱρετόν) makes the life that is its member ἱκανὸς καὶ τέλεος *sufficient and complete.*

(25e7–8) τὴν ὑγιείας φύσιν *the nature of [the kind] Health* comes to be from the right mix of Bound and Unbounded.

12. In the remaining third of passages, it is less clear whether it is a form, a kind, or many things (perhaps in virtue of being associated with a kind), that have a φύσις:

(44d9–e1) εἰ βουληθεῖμεν ὁτουοῦν εἴδους τὴν φύσιν ἰδεῖν, οἷον τὴν τοῦ σκληροῦ *if we were to wish to see the nature of any form whatsoever, for example the nature of the [form]* hard. This might be a passage where εἶδος *form* is used figuratively to refer to γένος *kind*. On the other hand, if literal, it is evidence that forms, like kinds, possess distinctive forms, i.e., natures. For example, the nature of the form *choiceworthy* might include *sufficient* and *complete* (see 22b4–6, quoted above).

(48c4) ἰδὲ τὸ γελοῖον ἥντινα φύσιν ἔχει *see what nature the [form or kind]* laughable *has.*

(26e6–7) ἡ τοῦ ποιοῦντος φύσις οὐδὲν . . . τῆς αἰτίας διαφέρει *the nature of the [form or kind]* making thing *differs in no respect from the cause.*

(44a10) χωρὶς τοῦ μὴ λυπεῖσθαι καὶ τοῦ χαίρειν ἡ φύσις ἑκατέρου *the nature of each [form or kind], of not feeling pain and of enjoying, is separate.*

(50e4–5) Κατὰ φύσιν . . . πορευοίμεθ' ἂν *we might proceed according to the nature [of our (form or kind of) inquiry].*

(60b2–3) τό τε ἀγαθὸν καὶ ἡδὺ διάφορον ἀλλήλων φύσιν ἔχειν *that the [form or kind] good and the [form or kind] pleasant have a nature different from each other.*

(60b10) Τὴν τἀγαθοῦ διαφέρειν φύσιν *that the nature of the [form or kind] good differs.*

(64e5–6) καταπέφευγεν ἡμῖν ἡ τοῦ ἀγαθοῦ δύναμις εἰς τὴν τοῦ καλοῦ φύσιν *the power of the good has for us fled for refuge into the nature of the [form or kind] beautiful.*

(27a5) The φύσις of the kind Making (τὸ ποιοῦν) makes each member of that kind ἡγεῖται *lead*.

(29a9–10) Τὰ περὶ τὴν τῶν σωμάτων φύσιν ἁπάντων τῶν ζῴων . . . καθορῶμέν *we observe the things that have to do with the nature of the [kinds of] bodies of all living things.*

(30b6–7) The kind Cause μεμηχανῆσθαι τὴν τῶν καλλίστων καὶ τιμιωτάτων φύσιν *has devised the nature of the finest and most precious things [namely, wisdom, awareness, and soul]* for the celestial bodies.

(31c2–3) Ἐν τῷ κοινῷ μοι γένει ἅμα φαίνεσθον λύπη τε καὶ ἡδονὴ γίγνεσθαι κατὰ φύσιν *together in the kind Mix pain and pleasure seem to come to be by [their] nature.*

(31d8–9) When the harmony that was destroyed εἰς τὴν αὑτῆς φύσιν ἀπιούσης ἡδονὴν γίγνεσθαι *returns into the nature of its own [kind], pleasure comes to be.*

(32a2) The undergoing of stifling heat is διάκρισις δέ γ' αὖ καὶ διάλυσις ἡ παρὰ φύσιν *the separation and dissolution beyond [a living thing's] nature* (likewise παρὰ φύσιν at 32a6 and 32b1).

(32a3) κατὰ φύσιν δὲ πάλιν ἀπόδοσίς τε καὶ ψῦξις *a return again and a cooling according to [a living thing's] nature* (likewise, κατὰ φύσιν at 32a8 and 42d5).

(32d5–6) ἀγαθὰ μὲν οὐκ ὄντα, ἐνίοτε δὲ καὶ ἔνια δεχόμενα τὴν τῶν ἀγαθῶν . . . φύσιν *not being good things, but sometimes some [of them] accepting the nature of good things.*

(49c4–5) ἡ δ' ἀσθενὴς ἡμῖν τὴν τῶν γελοίων εἴληχε τάξιν τε καὶ φύσιν *the [foolishness] of the weak has been allotted the rank and nature of things laughable for us.*

In the above sentences, the noun γένος is usually implicit. This is typical of what linguists call generic predications. For example, "'Birds fly' is true even though penguins can't, 'Bees sting' is true even though mason bees don't, and 'Dogs bark' is true even if poodles are polite" (Liebesman 2011, 409)—the subjects, respectively, are not any particular birds, bees, and dogs, but the kinds Bird, Bee, and Dog.

The noun εἶδος has the root meaning *that which is seen*, hence *visible shape* and *intelligible form*. As noticed above, the notion of intelligible form is essential to the identity of a γένος *kind* K. While kinds are like cattle herds in having members by virtue of which they can divide, a form is like the brand, one and the same feature shared by the many livestock that come and ago while the herd remains constant (Muniz and Rudebusch, n.d.). For example, the Hashknife brand has defined a herd of cattle in northern Arizona for a century and a half, the herd remaining the same even as it loses members to death or gains new members when calves are branded each spring. Just as cowboys easily distinguish herds from brands, one might predict that Socrates and Protarchus likewise manage to distinguish γένη *kinds* from εἴδη *forms.* Of the fourteen instances of εἶδος in the *Philebus,* ten confirm the prediction: they are easily translated *form* as opposed to *kind* or *particular members* of a kind. In four of those cases the noun εἶδος is limited by a genitive noun. In one of these cases the limiting genitive is plural:

(18c2) τρίτον δὲ εἶδος γραμμάτων *a third form of letters.*

In this case the third form is the single feature—being ἄφωνον *mute*—shared by certain kinds of Greek letters or vocal sounds, namely π, τ, κ, φ, θ, χ, and σ (see figure 1 in note to 16e–17a). In the remaining three such cases the limiting genitive is plural:

(19b2) εἴδη . . . ἡδονῆς *forms of pleasure:* the εἴδη *forms* are what identify the subkinds of pleasure.

(32c4) ἡδονῆς καὶ λύπης ἕτερον εἶδος *another form of pleasure and pain:* namely, the form shared by pleasures χωρὶς τοῦ σώματος αὐτῆς τῆς ψυχῆς *of the soul itself, [pleasures] apart from the body.*

(35d9) βίου γὰρ εἶδός τί *some form of life* that identifies the kind of living that goes on ἐν τῷ πληροῦσθαι καὶ κενοῦσθαι καὶ πᾶσιν ὅσα περὶ σωτηρίαν τέ ἐστι τῶν ζῴων καὶ τὴν φθοράν *in all that has to do with the destruction and preservation of the organism, such as depleting and repleting.*

There remain six other cases that conform to the prediction of a distinction between εἶδος and γένος.

(23c12) Τούτω δὴ τῶν εἰδῶν τὰ δύο τιθώμεθα *among forms, let's posit these two,* namely, the forms *unbounded* and *bound,* which identify the kinds Unbounded and Bound and are shared by the members of those kinds.

(23d2) κατ' εἴδη διιστὰς *separating form by form* or *according to forms.* Just as a cowboy might separate a herd into subherds by finding identifying brands and separating according to those, so Socrates here separates the kind Things That Are Ever Said to Be into the subkinds Unbounded, Bound, and so on by means of the forms *unbounded, bound,* and so on that identify the subkinds.

(44e1) εἴδους τὴν φύσιν . . . οἷον τὴν τοῦ σκληροῦ *the nature of a form, such as the nature of the [form] hard,* the form shared by all kinds of hard things.

(48e8) τὸ τρίτον εἶδος *the third form* (namely, the form *soul* or, if we accept the Badham/Burnet emendation, the form of *the things in the soul*: see note to 48e8–9).

(49e1) ἐν τρισὶν . . . εἴδεσιν γίγνεσθαι *[that the self-ignorance of friends] comes to be in three forms*—namely, the forms *self-ignorance about one's wealth, beauty,* and *wisdom.*

(51e5) ταῦτα εἴδη δύο *these* (the *more divine* form of sights and sounds and the *less divine* form of smells are) two forms (of pure pleasures).

In these cases the noun εἶδος is not limited by a genitive, but it is natural to understand such a limit: these passages refer to the forms, respectively, of the kinds Unbounded and Bound, of the kind Hard, of the kind Soul, of the subkinds Self-Ignorance about Wealth, Beauty, and Wisdom, and of the more and less divine kinds of Pure Pleasure.

So far, so good. But there is a fly in the ointment. There are four remaining instances of εἶδος in the *Philebus* that cannot literally mean *form* in the sense of a single "brand" shared by many members of one "herd." Two cases speak of forms as the objects resulting from division:

(20a6) ἡδονῆς εἴδη σοι καὶ ἐπιστήμης διαιρετέον *one must divide into forms of pleasure and knowing.*

(20c4) τὴν διαίρεσιν εἰδῶν ἡδονῆς *division into the forms of pleasure.*

The Hashknife brand looks like a *T* with a long bar serif as foot (representing the handle of a hash knife), while the arm on top of the stem is arched like the blade of a hash knife. Literally dividing the Hashknife brand would mean something like detaching the blade and handle from the stem of the brand.

But Socrates in these two passages means a division of the kind Pleasure into its subkinds, not a division of the form *pleasure* into its subforms—even if such a division were intelligible (on difficulties with dividing forms into subforms, see Muniz and Rudebusch 2018, 397–98). It is understandable, therefore, why Frede (1993) translates εἴδη in these two passages as "kinds"—and such a translation destroys the εἶδος/γένος distinction drawn above.[13]

The next passage raises a similar problem:

(33c5–6) τό γε ἕτερον εἶδος τῶν ἡδονῶν . . . πᾶν *the other form of pleasures . . . all [of it].*

There is no problem in speaking of εἶδος τῶν ἡδονῶν *a form of pleasures:* one form shared by many kinds of pleasures. The problem is to speak of "all" that form. To speak literally of "all" the Hashknife brand would be to speak of the brand as the whole Hashknife icon containing its parts such as the blade, handle, and stem. This is not Socrates' meaning here. He is speaking of all the other *kind* of pleasures—that is, of the kind as a whole containing its subkinds as parts. Once again, it is understandable why Frede (1993) translates εἶδος in this passage as "kind"; again, such a translation destroys the εἶδος/γένος distinction drawn above.

The fourth passage speaks of an εἶδος as a thing that has come to be:

(32b1) ἔμψυχον γεγονὸς εἶδος *a form having become ensouled.*

The Hashknife brand came to be when a cowboy constructed the first such branding implement inspired by the distinctive shape of a camp cook's hash knife, and the herd came to be shortly after. As Socrates posits them (15a1–2), neither forms nor kinds come to be or cease to be like this brand and herd. They simply and eternally are. Only the unboundedly many particular members of kinds come and cease to be. English translations of this passage tend to be very free, hiding the puzzle from the reader. Hackforth (1945)

13. The translation issue in turn misleads interpreters, most recently, Meinwald (2019): "The same word, *eidos,* lies behind both many key assertions we put in terms of forms (e.g. *Republic* 476a5–6) and many central passages (e.g. *Phaedrus* 265e1–2) translated as concerning species" (2019, 345n23); "it is important to realize that 'genus' and 'species' in connection with Plato . . . can be used whenever one wishes to indicate that one kind (the species) is a subkind of another (the genus)" (2019, 345n25); "genera and species—our old friends, the forms!" (2019, 349).

translates εἶδος as a "state" that is "constituted." Frede (1993) translates εἶδος "combination" and γεγονὸς with the verb "forms" ("the natural combination of limit and unlimitedness that forms a live organism"). Gosling (1975) adds to the text a reference to the particular "things" and then has "them," not the form, come alive ("the form of *things* whose natural combination . . . makes *them* alive").

The fly is removed from the ointment by seeing Socrates' speech in those four passages as figurative, not literal (following Muniz and Rudebusch, n.d.). Socrates, like every user of natural language, occasionally uses figures of speech, including, in particular, metonyms. Metonymy is a classical trope "traditionally defined as the substitution of a figurative expression for a literal or proper one. In metaphor, the substitution is based on resemblance or analogy; in metonymy, it is based on a relation or association other than that of similarity," some relation of *contiguity* rather than of *similarity* (Johnson 2000, 41). As examples of metonymy based on a *participation* relation, Socrates uses θέατρον *a place for seeing* or *theater* to refer to the people who share that space, the spectators (*Symposium* 194b3 and 194a6). Likewise, he uses συμμαχία *alliance* for the people who share in the alliance, the allies (*Republic* 560c9). As an example of the *part/whole* relation (a kind of metonymy called *synecdoche),* Socrates uses κεφαλή *head* to refer to the person as a whole (*Phaedrus* 234d6 and 264a8). The solution to the puzzle of εἶδος is that, although the word literally refers to a form, in a natural, figurative usage it can refer either to a kind (by synecdoche, insofar as a kind as a whole is composed of its members with its defining form) or to members of a kind (by metonymy, in that the members participate in that form).

English speakers sometimes use the word "brand" literally, as in:

(S1) "I don't know whether defendant has ever branded any cattle with this brand or not" (Wheeler v. Kassabaum, 76. Cal. 90, 120).

Such usages are similar to the literal uses of εἶδος that were easily translated as *form* in the first ten εἶδος passages above (18c2 through 51e5), passages in which an εἶδος is as different from a γένος as a brand is from a herd. But English speakers sometimes use the word "brand" as a metonym to refer to a herd, as in:

(S2) "The first contract between me and Mr. Zirker was that Mr. Zirker was to take the cattle as they run—was to take the whole brand" (Wheeler v. Kassabaum, 76. Cal. 90, 120).

In S2 the adjective "whole," like the adjective πᾶν in 33c5–6 (quoted above), indicates that the noun "brand" must be figuratively referring to a herd. Sentence S2's metonymy is similar to 20a6, 20c4, and 33c5–6, in which the noun εἶδος is a metonym for a γένος. Likewise, English speakers sometimes use the word "brand" as a metonym to refer to members of a herd. The *OED* attests this usage of "brand" (I.4.e—remarkably, the *OED* does not list this usage as a "transferred"—that is, figurative—sense):

(S3) "It is seldom they kill their own brands" (Romspert 1881, 186).

Sentence S3's metonymy is similar to the figurative use of εἶδος in 32b1 above to refer to particular members of a kind.

As "brand" is used figuratively to refer to a herd, so in English "form" is used figuratively to refer to a kind. The *OED* entry for "form" (I.4.a) lists the usage I have assigned the word for the translation of εἶδος: "that which makes anything . . . a determinate . . . kind." It also lists what I have called the metonymic or figurative usage of form (I.5.b): "a species, kind, or variety." Like its listing of "brand" as *members of a herd*, it does not call this usage "transferred." (But the *OED* does list as "transferred" the meaning for "brand" [I.6]: "A particular sort or class of goods [such as a herd of livestock], as indicated by the trademarks [or 'brand marks'] on them.") For εἶδος LSJ lists as the same meaning (II.1) "*form, kind*, or *nature,*" and it lists as a third meaning (III.1) "*class, kind*" (citing only Plato, Aristotle, and an Aristotelian genus/species usage in Dioscorides Pedanius). The LSJ entry for εἶδος does not observe the two stages of transferred meaning, first from *visible shape* to *intelligible form* or *nature*, and then from *intelligible form* or *nature*, by metonymy, to items determined by that form or nature: *kinds, species, varieties, and classes.*

According to the hypothesis in the section of the introduction titled Dramatic setting and date, Socrates leads the conversation in the *Philebus* after listening to the Eleatic Stranger demonstrate his method of collecting and dividing kinds in the *Sophist* and the *Statesman*. Socrates' use of collection and division fit this hypothesis. He appears knowledgeable of the Stranger's four-step method, while putting it to his own use. In contrast, the four steps do not appear in the *Phaedrus*. For example, the first kind of mania collected there, the kind Prophecy, relies upon linguistic data for evidence (244b6–d5). The lack of expertise in the *Phaedo* is appropriate: Socrates at the dramatic date of the *Phaedrus* has not yet met the Stranger.

The Stranger gives a paradigm of collecting and dividing to define what the kind Angler is by beginning with the hypothesis that the kind Angler is within the kind Expertise. Dividing that kind in two, he repeats the dichotomous division only of the subkind inhabited by the Angler, until at the end his division produces the kind Angler by itself. The Stranger divides a kind reached at any given level by collecting exhaustive and exclusive subkinds of it. The Stranger does not enumerate the steps needed to collect each subkind, but Rudebusch and Muniz (2018, 401–5) identify in the paradigmatic division four steps: (1) list many items, (2) identify a form, (3) recognize that the listed items share that form, which is to gather them under the heading of that form, and (4) give a name to the kind just collected at step 3.

For example, to collect the kind Productive Expertise, the Stranger first lists γεωργία μὲν καὶ ὅση περὶ τὸ θνητὸν πᾶν σῶμα θεραπεία, τό τε αὖ περὶ τὸ σύνθετον καὶ πλαστόν, ὃ δὴ σκεῦος ὠνομάκαμεν, ἥ τε μιμητική *farming, and whatever is an attendance for any living body, and whatever is an attendance for any composite or molded body—anything we call an* artifact—*and the imitative expertise* (*Sophist* 219a10–b1). Then, second, he identifies the shared form: πᾶν ὅπερ ἂν μὴ πρότερόν τις ὂν ὕστερον εἰς οὐσίαν ἄγῃ, τὸν μὲν ἄγοντα ποιεῖν, τὸ δὲ ἀγόμενον ποιεῖσθαί πού φαμεν *with respect to anything whatsoever, if it does not exist beforehand, but someone afterward brings it into being, we say, I suppose, that the one who brings it into being* makes, *and the thing being brought into being* is made (219b4–6). Third, he collects the listed things under the heading of the shared form: τὰ δέ γε νυνδὴ <ἃ> διήλθομεν ἅπαντα εἶχεν εἰς τοῦτο τὴν αὐτῶν δύναμιν *the things we just now went through held their power, all together, in this [i.e., in making]* (219b8–10). Finally, fourth, he names the newly collected kind: ποιητικὴν τοίνυν αὐτὰ συγκεφαλαιωσάμενοι προσείπωμεν, *after bringing them under a head with [their form], let us call them* Productive Expertise (219b11–12).

When Socrates collects the kind Unbounded in the *Philebus,* he begins, like the Stranger, first by listing items in the kind. Whereas the Stranger listed about five items, Socrates lists only a pair: θερμοτέρου καὶ ψυχροτέρου *hotter and colder* (24a7–8). There are plenty more items he could have listed. Indeed, later he lists ξηρότερον καὶ ὑγρότερον . . . καὶ πλέον καὶ ἔλαττον καὶ θᾶττον καὶ βραδύτερον καὶ μεῖζον καὶ σμικρότερον, *drier and wetter . . . more and less, faster and slower, and larger and smaller* (25c8–10). But Socrates lists only the duo *hotter and colder* before going on to name the form he has in mind: μᾶλλόν τε καὶ ἧττον γιγνόμενα καὶ τὸ σφόδρα καὶ ἠρέμα δεχόμενα καὶ τὸ λίαν καὶ ὅσα τοιαῦτα πάντα *becoming more and less and accepting the intense, the mild, the excessive and all such things* (24e7–25a1). After listing members and naming the form, Socrates names the kind—τὸ τοῦ ἀπείρου γένος *the kind Unbounded* (25a1)—in the context of collecting the listed things under the heading of the shared form into a single kind: εἰς τὸ τοῦ ἀπείρου γένος ὡς εἰς ἓν δεῖ πάντα ταῦτα τιθέναι *it is necessary to put all these things into the kind Unbounded as into a one* (25a1–2). He explains this *putting many into one* κατὰ τὸν ἔμπροσθεν λόγον *by reference to the earlier account* (25a2)—namely, as he recalls it here: ὅσα διέσπασται καὶ διέσχισται συναγαγόντας χρῆναι κατὰ δύναμιν μίαν ἐπισημαίνεσθαί τινα φύσιν, *as far as we are able, we ought to put the sign of some one nature on whatever has been split apart and scattered* (25a1–4). Socrates in the *Philebus* follows this method, in more or less abbreviated ways, to collect the four kinds in the fourfold division and the subkinds of pleasure and knowing.

COMMENTARY

PART I. HAPPINESS

1. The Happiness Question: What makes a human life happy, pleasure or knowing?

11a–12a: Socrates and Protarchus agree to a contest between pleasure and knowing. Socrates hints there might be something better than either pleasure alone or knowing alone. The winner of the contest will be whichever of the two candidates, pleasure or knowing, proves either to be or to be more closely related to that which makes life good.

11a1 **Ὅρα δή** *So, take a good look at . . .* The δή, as often below, seems to mark both a transition (*"so"*) and emphasis (*"good"*). The first words Plato chooses for each dialogue are full of meaning (Burnyeat 1997, following Proclus' commentary on Plato's *Parmenides* 658.33–659.23). Perhaps more than any other dialogue, the reader of the *Philebus* must "take a good look" in reading, in order to determine the meaning of fragmentary, ambiguous, or otherwise indeterminate sentences. This stylistic feature mirrors the main theme of the dialogue—that when facing something unbounded we should use understanding to insert appropriate bounds to create something good.

Πρώταρχε without ὦ in conversation marks either that the object of address has shifted (as if, perhaps, Socrates has turned from Philebus to Protarchus) or that the address is emphatic. In either case, the dialogue begins abruptly, with a reference to an earlier discussion that took place apparently just before the opening words.

11a2 **πρὸς . . . ἀμφισβητεῖν** *to dispute against.* The verb suggests a metaphor of advocates seeking courtroom victory, a metaphor continued throughout the dialogue.

τίνα τῶν [λόγων] *which of the statements.* Editors, including Burnet (1901), tend to emend this τῶν in the manuscripts to τὸν so that the text becomes πρὸς τίνα [λόγον] τὸν παρ' ἡμῖν [μέλλεις] ἀμφισβητεῖν, *which statement on our side are you going to dispute?* But Socrates will give not one but several statements in summarizing his response to Philebus: an anti-pleasure statement (μὴ ταῦτα *not these*, 11b7), and both a comparative (ἀμείνω καὶ λῴω *better and more desirable*, 11b7–9) and superlative (ὠφελιμώτατον *most beneficial*, 11c1–2) pro-knowing statement. Someone who affirms pleasure is good might dispute that knowing is good, or dispute only that knowing is better than pleasure for certain creatures, or dispute only that knowing is best of all. So, it makes good sense for Socrates to direct Protarchus to consider well "which of the (several) statements on our side you are going to dispute."

παρ' ἡμῖν *on our side.* The plural pronoun here and below is unusual for Plato's character Socrates. To judge from Protarchus' threat at 16a4–6, Socrates seems to be the sole advocate of knowing who is present at this discussion. Perhaps Plato intends the reader to infer that there are other advocates of knowing, even if not then present, whose side Socrates has been defending.

11b1 **σοι κατὰ νοῦν** *according to your awareness.* The idiom prefigures one of Socrates' pro-knowing strategies in the course of the dialogue, which is to draw attention to the hedonist's intellectual commitments.

11b4 **ἀγαθὸν εἶναί . . . τὸ χαίρειν** The subject of this indirect discourse is the articular infinitive τὸ χαίρειν, and the complement is the word ἀγαθὸν (S §1150, 1153, 1168). When the complement is an adjective agreeing in gender and number with the subject—as here, where both are neuter singular—the complement regularly functions as a predicate adjective, exactly as in the English translation, *to enjoy is good*. Such a statement leaves open that many other things might be good, such as, for example, knowing.

There is a sophisticated alternative translation. Grammar, idiosyncratic Platonic style, later restatements in the *Philebus* of 11b4–5, and immediate context have convinced many that the sentence instead must (or might) mean *to enjoy is the good*—an identity statement rather than a mere predication. The identity of enjoyment and the good entails that knowing cannot be the good and can only be good insofar as it is pleasant. The motive to construe ἀγαθὸν εἶναι τὸ χαίρειν *to enjoy is good* as τὸ ἀγαθὸν εἶναι τὸ χαίρειν *to enjoy is the good* is the worry that the plain meaning of the sentence entails that Socrates is fallaciously equivocating between the predicate adjective "good" here and the substantive complement "the good" later. Rudebusch (2019) argues against the sophisticated reasons given for this alternative and argues that the worry is unfounded.

11b4–6 **ἀγαθὸν εἶναί . . . ὅσα τοῦ γένους ἐστὶ τούτου σύμφωνα** Socrates attributes four theses to Philebus' hedonist side of the dispute. *For all creatures* (πᾶσι ζῴοις):

H1 ἀγαθὸν εἶναι τὸ χαίρειν, *To enjoy is good (or a good thing).*

H2 (ἀγαθήν [or ἀγαθόν] εἶναι) τὴν ἡδονὴν, *Pleasure is good (or a good thing).*

H3 (ἀγαθήν [or ἀγαθόν] εἶναι τὴν) τέρψιν, *Delight is good (or a good thing).*

H4 (τοσάδε ἀγαθὰ εἶναι) ὅσα τοῦ γένους ἐστὶ τούτου σύμφωνα, *All things that are consonant with this kind are goods (or good things).*

11b7 **μὴ ταῦτα** *not these.* This sentence fragment requires interpretation to complete its meaning. The negation μὴ rather than οὐ indicates that the words stand for a dependent clause stating what τὸ ἀμφισβήτημα *the point of contention* is. This dependent sentence is constructed with the accusative ταῦτα plus an unstated infinitive and complement that we must supply by finding the correct parallel construction. The audience, hearing this sentence said in conversation, at the first moment of hearing these words, will naturally supply the parallel from 11b4: μὴ ταῦτα ἀγαθὸν εἶναι πᾶσι ζῴοις, *But these things are not good for all creatures.*

Such a thesis would simply contradict the four Phileban theses H1–4. But as soon as Socrates completes the sentence begun here, his intended construction will become clear.

τὸ φρονεῖν *to know.* The verb is a near synonym of ἐπίσταμαι *to expertly know.* See introduction: *Noein, Phronein, Phronesis,* and *Nous.*

τὸ νοεῖν *to be mentally aware.* On this meaning, see introduction: *Noein, Phronein, Phronesis,* and *Nous.*

μεμνῆσθαι *[to] remember.* Manuscript B is an exception to the other manuscripts, adding the definite article τὸ μεμνῆσθαι *to remember.* For the possible significance of the nonexceptional text, see introduction: *Noein, Phronein, Phronesis,* and *Nous.*

Remembering is an unforgettable Platonic theme at *Meno* 81b–86c and *Phaedo* 72e–76c, where the activity of memory explains knowledge that we are able to have (such as geometry) that cannot be gained from sense perception.

11b8 **τὰ . . . συγγενῆ** *things of the same kind as.* The word indicates that there is a larger kind of factive cognition, never collected and never named. Nor are its subkinds ever collected. Socrates indicates the extent of this larger kind with terms that include the following: φρόνησις, ἐπιστήμη, νοῦς, μνήμη πᾶσα, δόξα ἀληθής or ὀρθή, and ἀληθεῖς λογισμούς. This larger kind is opposed to the larger kind of pleasure, indicated by the terms τὸ χαίρειν, ἡδονή, and τέρψις. Bury (1897) supposes that συγγενῆ connotes a more intrinsic relation than σύμφωνα, a word that is connected with guesswork at 56a. But Socrates must regard τὸ χαίρειν, ἡδονή, and τέρψις also as συγγενῆ, since he refers to the single *genos* that they belong to at 11b5. The word connected to guesswork, σύμφωνα, is more likely used to indicate that neither the larger kinds nor their respective subkinds have been properly collected at this point. See Introduction: *Noein, Phronein, Phronesis,* and *Nous.*

δόξαν *opining.* In this dialogue, δόξα is opposed to ἐπιστήμη *expert knowing* and τὸ νοῦν ἔχειν, *having mental awareness,* as in the *Republic* (477b–478d, 505d8, 506c6, 508d8).

λογισμούς *reckoning* (my translation follows Vogt 2019, 26). The phrase δόξαν . . . λογισμούς is in apposition to τὰ . . . συγγενῆ. τὸ λογιστικόν is "the rational" part of the soul at *Republic* 440e–441a.

11b9 **ἀμείνω . . . λῴω** are complements of the verb γίγνεσθαι: *prove to be better and more desirable.* The comparatives ἀμείνω and λῴω *better and more desirable* refer to degrees of intrinsic goodness. The kind that contains knowing is not the greatest intrinsic good (which Socrates argues at 64c–67a is the trinity of measure, beauty, and truth), but "at least" (γε, b9) it is better than the kind Pleasure. It will turn out to be "by an immeasurable degree" (μυρίῳ, 67a11) closer than the kind Pleasure to the greatest good.

ὅσαπέρ [ἐστιν] αὐτῶν δυνατὰ μεταλαβεῖν *as many as are able to partake of them*, opposite to Philebus' πᾶσι ζῴοις *for all creatures* and much more restricted, since very few kinds of creatures partake of such knowing. Thus, Socrates' point of contention opposes four intellectualist theses to Philebus' hedonism. *For as many creatures as are able to partake of knowing:*

I1 τὸ φρονεῖν τῆς γε ἡδονῆς ἀμείνω καὶ λῴω γίγνεσθαι *To know turns out to be better and more desirable than—at least—pleasure.*

I2 τὸ νοεῖν τῆς γε ἡδονῆς ἀμείνω καὶ λῴω γίγνεσθαι *To be mentally aware turns out to be better and more desirable than—at least—pleasure.*

I3 [τὸ] μεμνῆσθαι τῆς γε ἡδονῆς ἀμείνω καὶ λῴω γίγνεσθαι *To remember turns out to be better and more desirable than—at least—pleasure.*

I4 τὰ τούτων αὖ συγγενῆ, δόξαν τε ὀρθὴν καὶ ἀληθεῖς λογισμούς, τῆς γε ἡδονῆς ἀμείνω καὶ λῴω γίγνεσθαι *The things of the same kind as the knowing, the being aware and remembering—[such as] correct opining and true reckoning—turn out to be better and more desirable than, at least, pleasure.*

Given these parallel constructions, Socrates' audience can correctly complete the sentence fragment μὴ ταῦτα as follows. *For as many creatures as are able to get a share of knowing, being mentally aware and remembering, and the like:*

I5 μὴ ταῦτα τοῦ γε φρονεῖν καὶ τοῦ νοεῖν καὶ μεμνῆσθαι καὶ τῶν τούτων αὖ συγγενῶν ἀμείνω καὶ λῴω γίγνεσθαι *These things [to enjoy, pleasure, and delight] are emphatically not better and more desirable than knowing, being mentally aware and remembering, and things of the same kind as these.*

11c2 εἶναι *is.* Scholars have had trouble finding a subject for εἶναι. The recent tendency is to translate as Gosling (1975, 1): "they are of the greatest possible benefit." Such translations supply a plural pronoun referring to the plural subject in the previous clause, τὸ φρονεῖν καὶ τὸ νοεῖν καὶ μεμνῆσθαι καὶ τὰ τούτων αὖ συγγενῆ. The problem is that the subject ought to be singular to agree with the singular complement ὠφελιμώτατον. Stallbaum's 1842 reading, discussed by Bury (1897), makes μετασχεῖν the subject as follows: *to have a share is most beneficial of all.* (S §1984 gives examples of anarthrous infinitives used as subject with εἰμί.) On this reading, while to know is *better* than to enjoy, *best* of all is to possess a share of knowing. It is a problem for this alternative that, as Socrates argues elsewhere (*Euthydemus* 280c–d), to possess a good capacity is inferior not superior to activating that good.) I propose (in the spirit of Badham's 1855 solution, discussed in Bury 1897) to read the fragment ὠφελιμώτατον ἁπάντων εἶναι as short for four single sentences, each with a singular neuter subject rather than as short for one sentence with a plural subject as follows. *For all creatures that are and will be capable of having a share:*

O1 τὸ φρονεῖν ὠφελιμώτατον ἁπάντων εἶναι *To know is, of all things, a most beneficial thing.*

O2 τὸ νοεῖν ὠφελιμώτατον ἁπάντων εἶναι *To be mentally aware is, of all things, a most beneficial thing.*

O3 τὸ μεμνῆσθαι ὠφελιμώτατον ἁπάντων εἶναι *To remember is, of all things, a most beneficial thing.*

O4 ἕκαστον τῶν τούτων αὖ συγγενῶν ὠφελιμώτατον ἁπάντων εἶναι *Each of the things of the same kind is, of all things, a most beneficial thing.*

τοῖς οὖσί τε καὶ ἐσομένοις [δυνατοῖς μετασχεῖν] limits πᾶσι to *the ones that are and will be able to have a share* (of knowing). The superlative ὠφελιμώτατον *most beneficial* refers to the utility—the extrinsic goodness—of knowing, while the remainder of the dialogue discusses only intrinsic goodness. Such utility would be a small point to show in the overall scheme of the dialogue. Accordingly, the claim of maximum utility for knowing might be σμικρὸν ἔτι τὸ λοιπόν *the small point still remaining*, to be shown at the conclusion of the dialogue, 67b11.

11c4 **Πάντων μὲν οὖν μάλιστα** *[not "sort of"] but "most of all" [is how we each spoke]!* I see this as a case where the spirit of the μὲν οὖν is affirmative, while the letter is adversative (Denniston 1966, 475). Philebus is replying to Socrates' question, which expects the answer οὕτω πως λέγομεν ἑκάτεροι *we each spoke in this sort of way.* Philebus' answer agrees with the expected answer, as far as it goes, but he shows he regards the approximative πως *in this sort of way* as inadequate by substituting the superlative πάντων μάλιστα *most of all.*

11c8 **ὁ καλὸς ἀπείρηκεν** *the handsome [Philebus] has refused* or *has sunk from exhaustion.* The sexualizing epithet ὁ καλός *the handsome* apparently introduces a double entendre alluding to Philebus' pederasty. The verb in sexual contexts means *has denied us sexual favors* (perhaps because of detumescence—that is, *sinking from exhaustion*).

11c9–10 **τρόπῳ παντὶ** may be another double entendre: the colorless *by every means* or the sexual *by turning every way.*

περανθῆναι *to be brought to an end, fulfilled,* emphasized as the last word in the Greek sentence. This passive form can have the obscene sense *to be penetrated* (Henderson on περαίνεσθαι [1991, 158] and on ἀπεῖπον [1991, 161]). I thank Chris Turner for pointing out the double entendres in c8–10. And there is another level of word play here. The two verbs ἀπείρηκεν and περανθῆναι presage the main metaphysical contrast of the dialogue, between πέρας and ἄπειρον. The etymological meaning of the verb περανθῆναι is *to be brought to a* πέρας *bound.* And the verb ἀπείρηκεν, although not cognate with ἄπειρον *unbounded,* nevertheless suggests that word by its sound.

11d–12b: ***As the starting point of the contest between pleasure and knowing, Socrates gets Protarchus to agree that each side will advocate that their candidate is the one and only good that provides the life of happiness.***

This starting point is the first "turn" of the contest between pleasure and knowing (see note on 11c9). Socrates gets Protarchus to agree that each side in the contest will defend the thesis that their candidate is *the good*—that is, "the one able to provide the life of happiness" (11d5–6). As it happens, at 20b–22c Socrates will refute both these claims—that *the good is pleasure* and that *the good is knowing*—claims that we might call *unmixed hedonism* and *unmixed intellectualism*. Why did Plato contrive the dialogue to prove Socrates wrong? One explanation is that the disproof of Socrates is *implicit criticism* by Plato either of the historical Socrates or of discussions of pleasure in earlier dialogues. For further discussion, see Gosling and Taylor (1982), Rudebusch (1999), and Bravo (2003). Another explanation is *characteristic pedagogy*. Self-deprecation is part of Socrates' character throughout Plato's dialogues. There is a pedagogical advantage in discussion if the teachers point out their own errors. Teachers who do so are more likely to avoid oppositional behavior from students.

The refutations of *unmixed hedonism* (that the good in human life is pleasure) and *unmixed intellectualism* (that it is knowing) do not bear on the opposed positive and comparative claims of Socrates and Philebus (see notes to 11b4–6 and 11b9). In order to refute Philebus' hedonism—that *pleasure is (all of it) good*, and that *it is better than knowing*—Socrates after 22c will turn to a different method. I follow Delcomminette (2006) in distinguishing Socrates' initial *summary*, with its positive, comparative, and superlative claims, from the *first turn* of the investigation, which takes up hedonism and intellectualism as unmixed claims about the nature of the good. This distinction avoids an interpretive dilemma. Either the dialogue is inconsistent in its statements about hedonism or we need to read ἀγαθόν at 11b4 as meaning τἀγαθόν, in which case both Philebus and Protarchus are refuted in the first eleven pages of the dialogue (by 22c), which, as a consequence, requires us to struggle to find literary unity with the remaining forty-five pages of the dialogue.

11d2 **Ἴθι δή, πρὸς τούτοις διομολογησώμεθα καὶ τόδε** *come then, let us in addition to these things also agree to the following.* With this exhortation, Socrates marks the first turn of the investigation.

11d4–6 **ἕξιν** *possession* . . . **διάθεσιν** *ordered condition.* Following Harte (1999, 386), I interpret διάθεσιν as specifying more precisely the ἕξιν: it is a possession that is the result of an act of *placing in order,* from the verb διατίθημι. Bury's alternative interpretation relies on Aristotle, who discusses the difference between the two words at *Categories* 8b27–9a13, distinguishing a ἕξις as more stable and longer-lasting than a διάθεσις. Referring to Aristotle's discussion, Bury (1897) says the two are "combined so that one or the other may cover every possible case of psychic δύναμις," an appropriate way to begin an investigation. Both a feeling of pleasure and an act of awareness seem in this conversation to count as a ἕξις or διάθεσις. See introduction: *Noein, Phronein, Phronesis,* and *Nous.*

τὴν δυναμένην . . . τὸν βίον εὐδαίμονα παρέχειν *the power to provide the truly happy life.* In Socrates' summary of the earlier discussion with Philebus at 11b4–6 he did not attribute the identity thesis *Pleasure is the good* to Philebus nor did he attribute to his side the identity thesis *Knowing is the good.* But here, at this first turn of the investigation, he invites Protarchus to agree to frame the point of contention in terms of competing identity theses. Each side will try to show that their favored candidate is "the" cause of human well-being. (See Rudebusch 2019 for discussion.) The goal of this first turn of the dialogue is to identify "the condition *able to provide* well-being." Thus, the goal is not to identify well-being itself but rather its cause. In terms of the kinds distinguished later, the goal is to identify a member of the kind Cause (αἰτία 27b1) rather than a member of the kind Mix (μεικτὸν 25b5). I interpret this cause to be the most immediate proximal cause, not the entire chain of cause and effect leading to a happy life, and not any of the distal causes. Thus, although both agree that this proximal cause is a condition *of the soul,* this is consistent with there being distal external causes of that psychic condition, such as a well-organized society. Thus, 11d4–6 need not "disqualify" such external causes as playing a causal role in human well-being, nor need it "presuppose" that the good is "located" in the soul, as Delcomminette states (2006, 37). Finally, the goal is to understand the cause of *human* happiness, as opposed to, say, *divine* or *porcine* happiness. Thus, this passage refutes the too-broad interpretation of Damascius' professor (Damascius 1959, §6): "The subject under discussion is [the good] that is present *in all animals*, from the divine down to the lowest." Damascius' professor follows Plotinus' interpretation of the *Philebus* (*Enneads* 6.7 [38].25.11–16). Nor, therefore, is the subject of the *Philebus* the even broader good of *Republic* 509b—not, that is, "the good that pervades *all things generally*" (as Damascius [1959, §6] correctly sees).

11d8–9 **Οὐκοῦν** *isn't it the case that?* expecting assent to an inference. The question this adverb introduces is a sentence fragment. What has just received assent at d4–7 is that each side ἕξιν ψυχῆς καὶ διάθεσιν ἀποφαίνειν τινὰ ἐπιχειρήσει τὴν δυναμένην ἀνθρώποις πᾶσι τὸν βίον εὐδαίμονα παρέχειν *will attempt to show some state or ordered condition of soul to be the one able to provide a truly happy life for all human beings*. This allows us to complete the fragment: ὑμεῖς μὲν [ἀποφαίνειν ἐπιχειρήσετε αὐτὴν εἶναι] τὴν τοῦ χαίρειν, ἡμεῖς δ' [ἀποφαίνειν ἐπιχειρήσομεν αὐτὴν εἶναι] αὖ τὴν τοῦ φρονεῖν *you will try to show it to be the state or condition of enjoying, while we will try to show it to be the state or condition of knowing.*

11d11 **Τί δ' ἂν** *but what if*? This question sets the stage for the superior cause of true happiness revealed in the course of the dialogue. The passage 11d11–12a1 correctly predicts the course of the dialogue: its hypothesis that the cause of true happiness is more like knowing than pleasure is confirmed by the dialogue's end.

11e2 **τοῦ ταῦτα ἔχοντος βεβαίως βίου** *by the life securely possessing these things*. Scholars have had trouble identifying an antecedent of the neuter plural ταῦτα that agrees with it in gender and number. The sense seems to require that ταῦτα refer to the subject of the verbs of appearing in the previous two sentences—namely, ἄλλη τις [ἕξις ψυχῆς καὶ διάθεσις] κρείττων *some other superior [possession or ordered condition of the soul]*. Since this subject is feminine singular, some even propose emending the text from ταῦτα to ταύτην. I suspect that, with this slight anacoluthon, Plato is accurately representing Socrates' oral habits of speech. As Smyth (1956, §3004) says, anacoluthon "is natural to Greek by reason of the mobility and elasticity of that language." I recommend preserving the neuter plural in translation as does Gosling (1975: "the life which secures these characteristics") and perhaps Frede (1993: "a life that firmly possesses that").

11e2–12a1 **ὁ τῆς ἡδονῆς τὸν τῆς φρονήσεως** *the life of pleasure . . . the life of knowing.* In its first appearance here in the dialogue, the noun ἡδονή is used as an abbreviation for τὴν [sc., ἕξιν καὶ διάθεσιν] τοῦ χαίρειν *the state or ordered condition of enjoying* (11d8). And in its first appearance the noun φρόνησις is an abbreviation for τὴν ἕξιν καὶ διάθεσιν τοῦ φρονεῖν *the state or ordered condition of knowing.*

12a8 **γνώσῃ** *will come to know.* When the verb is used absolutely with an intensive pronoun, as here, the idiom may mean "you shall judge for yourself" (*Laches* 187c2) or even "you shall do as you please," as at *Gorgias* 505c9. Philebus is not so much predicting as commanding. Hence, Smyth (1956, §1917) uses this passage to illustrate how the future tense can be used to command, the "jussive future." Protarchus' defensive reply suggests that he hears a tone of disapproval in this jussive future.

12a9–10 **οὐκ ἂν . . . εἴης.** Here I think that the potential optative with a negative states a future propriety as an opinion of the speaker *you should no longer be in charge* (S §1824).

τοὐναντίον. Since τοὐναντίον is accusative rather than genitive, it cannot function as a substantive (*the opposite*) coordinate with ὁμολογίας and must therefore be adverbial: *contrariwise.*

12b1 **ἀλλὰ γὰρ** *But [what you just suggested—that I might be going to try to be in charge—is out of the question] for* (see Denniston 1966, 100–101).

ἀφοσιοῦμαι. The primary meaning is religious—*purify oneself of guilt or pollution*—hence the secondary ethical meaning *discharge oneself from an obligation* or *absolve oneself.* Since αὐτὴν τὴν θεόν *the goddess [Aphrodite] herself* is part of the context, the religious connotation is primary.

12b3–4 **ἡμεῖς . . . συμμάρτυρες ἂν εἶμεν** Here the potential optative is imperative in force, stating a command, exhortation, or request to every observer of Philebus' absolution (S §1830): *let's be witnesses together!* The effect, says Bury (1897), is "of a veiled threat" (*we'll be watching you!*).

ἀλλὰ δὴ progressive rather than adversative, indicating a change of topic: *well now* (Denniston 1966, 241).

12b5 **ὅμως** *nevertheless* introduces πειρώμεθα περαίνειν *let us try to reach a conclusion* and discounts μετὰ Φιλήβου ἑκόντος ἢ ὅπως ἂν ἐθέλῃ *in company with Philebus, whether he is willing or whatever he wants.* The ὅμως is regularly before the clause it introduces. Its being thrown out of place—hyperbaton—here is for emphasis (S §3028).

12b6 **ἢ ὅπως ἂν ἐθέλῃ** is a euphemism (S §3024) or, as Bury (1897) puts it, "Attic urbanity" for ἢ καὶ ἄκοντος *or indeed unwillingly.*

περαίνειν (echoing περανθῆναι of 11c9–10) *to penetrate [X], to go through [X] to the end,* whether pleasure, knowing, or some third thing is the state or condition of soul with the power to provide a truly happy life for all human beings.

2. To resolve the Happiness Question, we need to get agreement to the One-Many Thesis.

12b–d*: The initial zeal to determine the truth turns into a dispute that threatens to scuttle the inquiry. The dispute begins when Socrates makes a verbal division of pleasure—which is* one *thing, even revered as a single goddess—into* many, *even opposite pleasures, such as wise and foolish pleasures.*

12b7–9 **δὴ** emphasizes **αὐτῆς**: *her very self.*

ἀπ[ό] *from* plus genitive seems to require some verb of beginning, such as ἀρκτέον *one must begin.* Bury (1897) solves the problem by pointing out that "Πειρατέον implies commencement" (likewise **ἀπ[ό]** at 12c5–6). The literal English translation is intelligible: *we must try from the goddess.*

τῆς θεοῦ, ἣν ὅδε Ἀφροδίτην μὲν λέγεσθαί φησι, τὸ δ' ἀληθέστατον αὐτῆς ὄνομα Ἡδονὴν εἶναι *the goddess, whom [Philebus] here says is called Aphrodite, while her truest name is Pleasure.* The two accusative-plus-infinitive constructions—ἣν Ἀφροδίτην μὲν λέγεσθαί [sc., ὑπὸ τῶν πολλῶν] *who is called Aphrodite [by the many]* and τὸ δ' ἀληθέστατον αὐτῆς ὄνομα Ἡδονὴν εἶναι *while the truest name of her is Pleasure*—both report what ὅδε φησί *[Philebus] here says*. Frede's 1993 translation correctly puts both claims in Philebus' mouth: "This fellow claims that though she is called Aphrodite her truest name is pleasure." Gosling's 1975 translation, in contrast, puts only the first claim in Philebus' mouth and makes the second Socrates' direct discourse: "Philebus calls her Aphrodite, but the most accurate name for her is pleasure." If Socrates were himself asserting Aphrodite's truest name to be Pleasure, we would find direct discourse—Ἡδονή ἐστιν *is pleasure*—not the accusative plus infinitive of indirect discourse, Ἡδονὴν εἶναι *to be pleasure*.

12b10 **Ὀρθότατα** *(you have spoken) most correctly.* I assume that Protarchus does not have a strong opinion from whom exactly Socrates ought to make the attempt, and so what ὀρθότατα must affirm is that Socrates is "most correctly" reporting the Phileban doctrine about the true name of Aphrodite.

12c1–2 **Τὸ . . . δέος** *fear.* On Socrates' "scrupulosity in manner of address to gods" (Bury 1897) see *Cratylus* 400d–401a and *Phaedrus* 246d.

κατ' ἄνθρωπον *what you'd expect for a human being.* κατά plus accusative of fitness or conformity (LSJ). There is an ambiguity in the conforming, either to an *object* of fear who is a human being, or conforming to a fearing *subject* who is Socrates, a human being. In other words, Socrates might be saying that his fear of naming gods goes beyond any fear he has of mere human beings, or he might be saying that his fear of gods goes beyond the sort of fear that human beings in general would seem capable of—beyond even panic. In either case, Socrates begins the philosophical discussion with reference to excess without bound, prefiguring a metaphysical theme of the dialogue.

12c4 **ποικίλον** complement to the implied feminine subject cannot function as a predicate adjective and must be a substantive. Since it lacks a definite article, it is best to translate it as an indefinite substantive: *a complex* or *manifold thing.* This clause introduces the argument that follows (12c6–d6), with a preliminary statement of the conclusion that pleasure, while one thing, is also manifold or many. This will be generalized from pleasure to include all things. That generalized thesis is a metaphysical theme of the dialogue. Socrates will elicit the one-many conclusion about pleasure from two main premises,—that pleasure is one and that it is many.

12c5 **ἀπ[ό]** *from* plus genitive with the verb of beginning ἀρχομένους.

12c6 **γάρ** *for* introduces the reasoning why it is necessary that we examine what pleasure's nature is—namely, because pleasure is, paradoxically, both one and many.

μὲν introduces the thesis that pleasure is one while coordinate δὲ at c7 introduces the antithesis that pleasure is many.

12c6–7 **[ὡς] ἀκούειν . . . οὕτως ἁπλῶς** *to hear* [the singular noun *pleasure*] *merely so, without qualification.* In this parenthetical clause the demonstrative adverb οὕτως *so* means *merely so* or *without a word more* (LSJ A.IV) and correlates with an implied relative adverb ὡς (LSJ Ab.II.1). The implied contrast to *unqualified* is *qualified by other words,*—for instance, in the noun phrases "wise pleasure" or "foolish pleasure," as in the examples Socrates will give just below at d1–4. Scholars (at least since Bast [1809, 37]) tend to read the parenthetical clause as limiting the truth of the main clause. Thus Frede (1993): "if one just goes by the name it is one single thing." On this reading, Socrates completes his thought by discounting the unity of pleasure: "but in fact it comes in many forms." The problem with such a reading is that it avoids rather than promotes the one-many puzzle Socrates aims to establish here and later in the dialogue. As a way to better fit the context, then, I propose we read the parenthetical clause not as limiting but as a reason for the main clause:

P1 ἀκούομεν ἡδονὴν οὕτως ἁπλῶς *We hear [the word] pleasure merely so: unqualified.*

C1 [ἡ ἡδονή] ἐστιν ἕν τι *[Thus] pleasure is one thing.*

There is another version of such an argument, from the language used to describe an object to the oneness of the object, at *Sophist* 237d6–10 (defended by Rudebusch [1991, 521–23]).

12c7 **ἕν τι** *[pleasure is] one thing.* ἕν τι has no article, which indicates it is not the subject but must be a predicate noun (S §1150). This is the first main premise of the reasoning leading to the paradox.

12c7–8 **δήπου** *I presume* combines the certainty of δή with the doubtfulness of που (Denniston 1966, 267), and expresses the confidence of the speaker in his statement while recognizing at the same time that the listener might not share that confidence.

ἰδὲ γάρ· *for consider:* introduces the examples at 12c8–13a6, illustrating that there are all sorts of pleasure, even sorts that are unlike each other.

12c8–d4 **ἥδεσθαι** *to take pleasure.* Its four occurrences at c8–d3 take accusatives as subjects (τὸν ἀκολασταίνοντα ἄνθρωπον, τὸν σωφρονοῦντα, τὸν ἀνοηταίνοντα καὶ ἀνοήτων δοξῶν καὶ ἐλπίδων μεστόν, τὸν φρονοῦντα). Absolute ἥδεσθαι means *to take pleasure*, while with a dative object (αὐτῷ τῷ σωφρονεῖν, αὐτῷ τῷ φρονεῖν) it means *to take pleasure in.* The intensive pronoun αὐτῷ here means *by itself* or *alone* (S §1209a), while τῷ σωφρονεῖν and τῷ φρονεῖν are articular infinitives: *thinking soundly* and *knowing.* It is not clear how these first examples of pleasure, the pleasure of αὐτῷ τῷ σωφρονεῖν or of αὐτῷ τῷ φρονεῖν fit Socrates' definition of pleasure later in the dialogue as perceived replenishment. The pleasure of being sound-minded reappears in the final mix at 63e4–5.

τὸν . . . ἄνθρωπον *the human being.* The article indicates that the accusative ἄνθρωπον is subject of the infinitive ἥδεσθαι, here and thrice more at d1–4 (S §1150).

12d4–6 **τούτων τῶν ἡδονῶν ἑκατέρας** *each of these two pleasures*—that is, in the contrasting cases of wanton/sound-minded pleasure and mindless/wise pleasure.

πῶς ἄν τις . . . οὐκ ἀνόητος φαίνοιτο ἐνδίκως; *how could it be possible that anyone [who says each is similar] not quite justly look like a fool?* Both the interrogative adverb πῶς *how* and the negative οὐκ *not* (S §1826a) in a question give the potential optative the force of a strong assertion. The final position of the adverb ἐνδίκως *justly* makes it emphatic.

12d–13a: ***Protarchus posits that unlike pleasures (such as unsound and sound pleasures, likewise foolish and intelligent pleasures) are unlike in their causes, but not unlike as pleasures.***

Protarchus explicitly accepts the self-identity of pleasure (τοῦτο αὐτὸ ἑαυτῷ *this the same as itself,* 12e1) and evidently accepts its oneness and being while denying the complexity dividing that one into many different and even opposite units. He provides an alternate explanation of the truth of Socrates' unlikeness thesis, drawing a distinction between a pleasure and its source. Given the distinction, he argues that the premises show only that sources of pleasure are different and opposed, not that pleasures themselves are. In disputing Socrates' division, Protarchus in effect denies the One-Many Thesis as it applies to pleasure.

Socrates appears to accept the possibility of Protarchus' "inspired" (ὦ δαιμόνιε, 12e3) distinction between an instance of pleasure and its source or cause. But Socrates mentions additional phenomena of color and shape that do not seem susceptible to that causal distinction: the colors black and white are unlike and opposite each other, and likewise shapes (for example, concave and convex) may be unlike and opposite each other. Such opposite colors and shapes do not *come from* opposites; they *are* opposites. Thus, Protarchus' causal distinction fails in the case of opposite colors and opposite shapes, and so he cannot, Socrates says, trust the causal distinction to explain away all instances of seemingly opposite pleasures. Protarchus takes Socrates' point and allows the possibility of unlike pleasures ("Ισως *perhaps,* 13a6).

12d7 **εἰσί . . . γὰρ** *yes, they are, because* assents to Socrates' thesis and examples. The εἰσί is short for something like ἡδοναί εἰσί τινα τρόπον ἀνόμοιοι ἀλλήλαις *pleasures are in a way unlike each other,* while the γάρ indicates the reason why Protarchus assents (on assentient γάρ, see LSJ γάρ I.d and Denniston 1966, 86).

12d7–8 **μὲν γὰρ . . . οὐ μὴν** *yes, well [the unlike pleasures are from opposite actions], but [they're] not [themselves opposites].* The two clauses together admit but discount Socrates' observation about the way we speak of unlike pleasures (LSJ μὲν A.II.6, Denniston 1966, 335).

12e1 **μὴ οὐχ** ***[How could]n't [a pleasure] not [be most similar to a pleasure?]*** The μή is problematic. Some, like Burnet (1901), bracket it as ungrammatical. Others, like Bury (1897), find a rule of grammar ("redundant μή") to explain it. Even if not regular grammar, perhaps the redundancy portrays passion in an outburst by Protarchus. All sides agree that Protarchus' double negative (or, if μὴ is removed, his single negative) in a question gives the potential optative ἂν εἴη the force of a strong assertion, echoing Socrates' potential optative at d5 (S §1826a).

12e2 **ἡδονῇ γε ἡδονὴ** is Burnet's 1901 invention. Manuscript T has ἡδονή γε ἡδονῇ *pleasure [most similar] at any rate [to] pleasure*, where the dative is the complement to ὁμοιότατον. Manuscript B has ἡδονήν γε ἡδονὴ, the more difficult reading of the two, both in itself and if Socrates' reply at 12e3 (καὶ γὰρ χρῶμα . . . χρώματι) is parallel. By the rule *lectio difficilior potior (the more difficult reading is preferable)*, then, we should prefer B, but the accusative ἡδονήν calls for explanation.

I propose the following interpretation of the Protarchan argument, given manuscript B.

P1 Each pleasure, whether sound-minded or unrestrained, intelligent or mindless, obviously shares the feature of being a pleasure, and this feature is the same as itself in every instance.

C1 Thus, a pleasure is, of all things, a thing most similar with respect to being a pleasure, at least.

C2 Thus, pleasures themselves are not opposite to each other, but rather each is similar to the others.

In the text we find the argument in reverse order. I have provided the version of C1 corresponding to the text of manuscript B.

C2 οὐ μὴν αὐταί γε ἀλλήλαις ἐναντίαι [ἀλλ' ἑκατέραι ὁμοῖαι ἀλλήλαις] *These at any rate [the pleasures in the cases unsound/sound pleasure and foolish/intelligent pleasure] are not opposite to each other, but each of the two is like each other.*

$C1_B$ [τὸ εἶναι] ἡδονήν γε ἡδονὴ ὁμοιότατόν ἐστι πάντων χρημάτων *Pleasure is of all things most similar with respect to [being a] pleasure.*

P1 τοῦτο [τὸ εἶναι ἡδονήν] αὐτὸ ἑαυτῷ *This [the feature of being a pleasure] is the same as itself.*

The two inferences in this argument are indicated by the γάρ at 12d8 and the circumstantial participle τοῦτο αὐτὸ ἑαυτῷ [ὄν] *this [being] the same as itself* (S §2054a). Apart from the brackets, the English version is a straightforward translation of the Greek. The only substantial addition that the bracketed material makes to the argument is in the English P1—that two pleasures share the feature of being pleasure—a premise that readily might go without saying. My move from the accusative noun ἡδονήν to the articular infinitive τὸ εἶναι ἡδονήν gains support from Socrates' parallel move from χρῶμα to τὸ χρῶμα εἶναι at 12e4. As interpreted, the argument relies on an implicit distinction between an instance of pleasure among all other items that come and go (ἡδονὴ πάντων χρημάτων), on the one hand, and the feature of being pleasure (τὸ εἶναι ἡδονήν) that is shared by all the many instances, on the other. Socrates will soon make this distinction explicit.

12e3 **Καὶ γὰρ** *yes, and.* Here καί is connective and the γάρ assentient.

χρῶμα . . . χρώματι [ὁμοιότατον ἂν εἴη] *color [can be most similar] to color,* parallel to 12e1, if we accept manuscript T.

δαιμόνιε *heaven-sent.* An idiomatic translation of this vocative might be *by your inspired thought.*

12e3–4 **κατά γε αὐτὸ τοῦτο . . . τὸ χρῶμα εἶναι**: *with respect to this alone: being a color.* Κατά of conformity (LSJ B.IV) with accusative αὐτὸ τοῦτο *this very thing* and articular infinitive τὸ χρῶμα εἶναι *the feature of being a color* in apposition. Limitative γε, confining the applicability of οὐδὲν διοίσει to the stated respect alone (*none will differ in this respect at least),* and implying that the applicability is unlikely to extend to other respects (Denniston 1966, 114–15).

οὐδὲν [χρῶμα] διοίσει . . . πᾶν *no [color] will in any way differ* (LSJ πᾶν D.III as adverb with negative).

12e4 **γε μὴν** is adversative *nonetheless* (Denniston 1966, 348), discounting the previous sentence.

12e4–5 **τὸ . . . μέλαν τῷ λευκῷ** moved for emphasis (hyperbaton, S §3028) from its grammatical place after **ὡς** = ὅτι *that.*

12e6 **ὂν τυγχάνει** *is actually.* The verb can be a slightly emphatic ἐστίν.

καὶ δὴ καὶ *and likewise* is connective, indicating that the statement will add another example of the same sort (Denniston 1966, 248).

σχῆμα σχήματι [ὁμοιότατον ἂν εἴη] *shape [can be most similar] to shape,* parallel to 12e3.

12e7 **κατὰ ταὐτόν** *in the same way,* κατά of conformity (LSJ B.IV).

γένει ἐστι πᾶν ἕν *[shape or shapes] is/are all one in kind,* with an ambiguous subject. Gosling (1975) makes the subject plural: "In kind they are all one," which makes sense: different shapes are one in kind. But Frede's (1993) singular subject also makes sense—"shape is all one in kind"—if we think of shape as consisting of many parts, which is how Socrates is thinking of it in this context. The lack of a definite article indicates πᾶν ἕν is a predicate noun (S §1150).

13a1–2 **τὰ δὲ διαφορότητ' ἔχοντα μυρίαν που τυγχάνει** *[some are most opposite,] while others have, I suppose, an immeasurably great difference.* Gosling (1975: "countless differences") and Frede (1993: "others differ in innumerable ways") translate the singular noun phrase διαφορότητ(α) . . . μυρίαν *immeasurable difference* as plural. The final position of the adjective μυρίαν *immeasurable* in the μὲν . . . δὲ construction gives greater emphasis to the immeasurable difference than to the difference of being ἐναντιώτατα *as opposite as can be.*

13a4–5 **φοβοῦμαι . . . μή . . . εὑρήσομεν** *I am afraid—and it looks very likely—that we will find.* The future indicative after μή is rare with verbs of fearing and makes a stronger prediction about the future. Smyth (1956, §2229) translates: "I apprehend that we shall find some pleasures opposite to other pleasures."

13a6 **τοῦθ'** *this* refers to the object of Socrates' fear on behalf of Protarchus' thesis—namely, that certain pleasures, such as sound or intelligent pleasures, will turn out to be opposite to certain other pleasures, such as unsound or foolish pleasures.

ἡμῶν . . . τὸν λόγον *our thesis* might refer to the Protarchan thesis in its stronger first turn at 11d8–9, that pleasure is the good (which rules out knowing as a good), or to the weaker thesis that Protarchus inherited from Philebus, that all pleasures are good (which leaves open that some or all knowing is good). Socrates' restatement at 13a8, λέγεις . . . ἀγαθὰ πάντ' εἶναι τὰ ἡδέα *you say that all pleasures are good*, shows that he thinks that the existence of opposite pleasures will harm even the weaker thesis.

13a–b: ***According to Socrates, to admit that some pleasures are unlike each other raises a problem for the "pleasure is good" thesis.***

According to Socrates, an unlikeness among pleasures would raise an explanatory problem for hedonism. To illustrate the basic idea, consider a *colorist* and a *shapist* thesis:

Colorism: Color makes *living space* good.
Shapism: Shape makes *furniture good.*

An opposition of colors—such as an intelligent versus a foolish color for a living room—raises problems for the *colorist* thesis, because if there can be such an opposition of color to color, why would a colorist think that it is *color* that makes a space good, rather than *intelligent color?* Likewise, if there is an opposition of shapes—such as sound and unsound shapes for a piece of furniture—why would a shapist think that it is *shape* that makes a good piece of furniture, rather than *sound shape?* As soon as such oppositions within color and shape are recognized, colorism and shapism are threatened. The same is the case, Socrates reasons, for the hedonist thesis that *pleasure makes human life good.*

I interpret Socrates' argument at 13a6–b5 as follows:

P1 Protarchus says that all pleasures are good (a8, restated at b2).
P2 If someone were to press the point, Protarchus might admit that these pleasures (namely, the ones that Socrates distinguishes as bad and as good) are unlike each other (b2–3).
P3 If Protarchus were to admit that these pleasures are unlike, he would need to say *what the good is* in those pleasures (the ones that Socrates

distinguishes as bad and as good), and it will have to be the same with respect to all pleasures (b3–5).

C1 Therefore, if Protarchus admitted such pleasures are unlike, then at P1 his word "good" would be inapt (stated at a7–8, indicated as a conclusion by γὰρ at a8).

C2 Therefore, to admit that these pleasures are unlike will harm Protarchus' thesis that pleasure is the good (stated at a6, indicated as a conclusion by "Ὅτι *because* at a7).

Premise P3 appears in the text as a question, a question that is not rhetorical but that indicates the need for an explanation. I supply the *if* clause ("If Protarchus were to admit that these pleasures are unlike") as a continuation from P2, as indicated by the οὖν *then* at b3, which indicates the continuation of a narrative (LSJ II).

Socrates makes two other statements in the text, but he discounts them, marking them as outside the inferential structure of the argument with a preceding μὲν οὖν *now then* at 13a9 and a following ὅμως *nevertheless* at b2. Typically discounted statements are background information, as they seem to be here:

D1 No argument disputes that pleasures are pleasant (a8–9).

D2 Socrates affirms that there are many bad pleasures as well as good (b1).

Some have accused Socrates in this passage of circular reasoning. This is uncharitable. Socrates in this passage is not assuming that there are good and bad pleasures in order to prove that not all pleasures are good. He is explaining why the admission that pleasures are unlike would harm Protarchus' hedonist thesis.

13a7 **"Ὅτι** *because* is inferential answering the preceding τί *why [will the existence of opposite pleasures like sound/unsound or wise/foolish pleasures harm the thesis that pleasure is the good]?*

αὐτὰ *things*—namely, Socrates' examples of sound and unsound, or wise and foolish, pleasures (12c8–d6), to which Protarchus agreed (12d7).

13a7–8 **προσαγορεύεις αὐτὰ ἀνόμοια ὄντα ἑτέρῳ, φήσομεν, ὀνόματι** *you call these things that are unlike [such as a sound pleasure and an unsound pleasure] by another, we shall say, name.* Stallbaum (1820) wrote that these words "have been the subject of many doubts" *(multis obnoxia fuere dubitationibus).* The challenge is not the grammar, nor even the meaning (since it is restated at 13d2), but to understand how this text answers the question τί *why?* There is no apparent harm to Protarchus' position that it calls sound and unsound pleasures, which are unlike, by another name, "good." Gosling (1975), following Jowett (1892) and Bury (1897), takes the participle ὄντα to express opposition (S §2066): "I should object that despite their dissimilarity you are applying another term to them." But this oppositional participle reading does not point to any harm. And so I prefer to translate ἑτέρῳ ὀνόματι as *by an inapt name*—that is, *a name other [than should be]*, as at *Phaedo* 114e3 and *Euthydemus* 280e5. (LSJ ἕτερος A.III.2). A clue that Socrates has this meaning in mind is the placement of the verb φήσομεν after ἕτερος. Protarchus has readily agreed that he labels unlike pleasures by the "other" or "new" name "good." But Protarchus has not agreed that this name is "inapt." Only Socrates' side of the dispute makes that claim. The placement of the verb φήσομεν indicates that it has within its scope only the contentious adverb phrase in which it is embedded: *by an inapt—[as] we shall say—word.* (On Socrates' use of the first-person plural, see note to 11a2.) Socrates, in the rest of his speech (13a8–b5), will explain why calling them all "good" is inapt.

ἀγαθὰ πάντ' εἶναι τὰ ἡδέα *that all pleasant things are good.* The accusative plus infinitive after a verb of speaking reports what is said. ἀγαθὰ has no article, indicating it is the complement, while τὰ indicates πάντ' . . . τὰ ἡδέα is the subject.

13a8–9 **τὸ . . . μὴ . . . ἡδέα εἶναι τὰ ἡδέα** articular infinitive with emphatic μὴ after ἀμφισβητεῖ *[disputes] the fact that pleasures are pleasant.* "After verbs signifying (or suggesting) to hinder and the like, the infinitive admits the article τό" (S §2744a, mentioning this passage as an example). Smyth's examples show that the verb of hindering may appear with zero, one, or as here (μὴ οὐχὶ) two negatives with no change in meaning beyond different degrees of emphasis.

οὐχὶ . . . λόγος οὐδεὶς ἀμφισβητεῖ *no theory, none at all, disputes.*

13a9 **μὲν οὖν** *now then* with "brusque" tone (Denniston 1966, 167) assents to Protarchus' statement τοῦτο αὐτὸ ἑαυτῷ *this is the same as itself* (12e1), restating it in other words (Denniston 1966, 477).

13b1 **κακὰ δ' ὄντα αὐτῶν τὰ πολλὰ καὶ ἀγαθὰ δέ [ἐστιν]** *while most of them are bad, there [are] also good ones.* I read the participial phrase κακὰ δ' ὄντα αὐτῶν τὰ πολλὰ as concessive ("while") to the main clause. But the conjunction ὅμως also permits this entire clause to be participial, with a second implicit ὄντα instead of ἐστίν.

καὶ . . . δέ *but also* is "a natural enough combination, the former particle denoting that something is added, the latter that what is added is distinct from what precedes" (Denniston 1966, 200).

ὡς ἡμεῖς φαμέν *as we say.* Socrates' side of the argument must affirm that there are at least some good and bad pleasures to establish that some pleasures are unlike and even opposite to others.

13b3 **εἴ** *if* plus optative, with present indicative in the apodosis, refers here to present general time (S §§2359–60). The apodosis is expressed in the participle ὁμολογῶν (= ὁμολογεῖς, S §2350) The mood of the expressed participle is indicative, since there is no particle ἄν (S §1846b): *agreeing that they are unlike [= you agree that they are unlike], were anyone to compel you by the force of reason.*

προσαναγκάζοι The prefix προσ- denotes *in addition: if anyone were to compel-you-in-addition [to the statement that all pleasant things are good].*

13b4 **ἐν ταῖς κακαῖς ὁμοίως καὶ ἐν ἀγαθαῖς ἐνὸν** *being present in the same way in both the bad and good [pleasures]* participial phrase modifying the accusative ταὐτὸν *the same thing.* As an alternative, Bury (1897) suggests this phrase is accusative absolute.

13b3–5 **τί . . . ταὐτὸν . . . πάσας ἡδονὰς ἀγαθὸν εἶναι προσαγορεύεις;** *what thing, the same with respect to all pleasures, do you call being good?* I think it is unnecessary to propose, as some have, that the text is corrupt. The two accusatives that agree in gender and number are τί . . . ταὐτὸν *what same thing?* and ἀγαθὸν *good.* Thus, they are most naturally taken as the double complement to προσαγορεύεις: *what same thing do you call good?* (As an alternative, LSJ [προσαγορεύω A.4] makes πάσας ἡδονὰς one object of the verb when they quote this passage, which raises unsolved problems in translating.) In Greek, as in English, a word denoting sameness often calls for specification: *in what respect* the same thing? It is natural, then, to take the third accusative, πάσας ἡδονὰς *all pleasures,* as an accusative of respect restricting ταὐτὸν *the same thing* (S §1600): *what thing, the same with respect to all pleasures, do you call being good?* Socrates, with this question, asks what feature makes both good and bad pleasures *good.* This is a familiar Socratic request, such as at 34e4: Πρὸς τί ποτε ἄρα ταὐτὸν βλέψαντες οὕτω πολὺ διαφέροντα ταῦθ' ἑνὶ προσαγορεύομεν ὀνόματι; *We call these very much different things by a single name, having looked toward what selfsame thing?* Another similar example is *Laches* 192a8–9: τί λέγεις τοῦτο ὃ ἐν πᾶσιν ὀνομάζεις ταχυτῆτα εἶναι; "What do you say this is that you refer to as *swiftness* in all [these cases]?"

13b–c: ***Protarchus, on the basis of a καθ' ὅσον*** **insofar as** ***distinction, denies that pleasures can be unlike. The near breakdown of the conversation is a dramatic example of the problems that the One-Many Thesis raises for truth-seeking investigations.***

Protarchus denies that any pleasure is opposite or unlike any other "insofar as they are pleasures" (13c5). Protarchus' position is that two things, like a foolish pleasure and a wise pleasure, can be opposites, and hence most unlike, but not insofar as they are pleasures. Insofar as they are each pleasures, they must be alike, just as, insofar as black and white are each colors, they are alike, and insofar as concave and convex are each shapes, they are alike, and, in general, for any form *F*, insofar as two things take that form *F*, they are alike. Socrates, in reply, proposes the following parallel argument to show that Protarchus' reasoning leads to absurdity. Let *F* be the form *unlike.* Then take any two things that are most *unlike.* According to Protarchus' reasoning, insofar as the two are most *unlike*, they must be "the most *like* of all" (13d4–5)—which is absurd. I suppose that Protarchus might try to escape from Socrates' *reductio ad absurdum* by distinguishing qualitative forms such as *pleasure, color,* and *shape* from relational forms such as *unlike.* Of course, such a distinction would seem to grant that *forms*—even insofar as they are *forms*—can be unlike, which in turn might be in tension with Protarchus' general denial of such opposition. My point is that, although Protarchus does not object, Socrates' reply is open to objection. But I do not see grounds to call Socrates' parallel argument a "trap" or "fallacy" (Frede 1993, xviii, 4). My interpretation of Socrates' argument follows Gosling (1975, 78). In addition, Gosling proposes a second possible interpretation: Black and white are both colors; thus, they "must both closely resemble each other" (Gosling 1975, 78). But it is not clear why Protarchus, with his *insofar as* distinction, would find this conclusion absurd.

13b6 **γάρ** is explanatory, introducing Protarchus' motive for asking Πῶς λέγεις *what do you mean* (Denniston 1966, 60) *[I ask,] because do you suppose that anyone will agree . . . ?*

13b7 **ἡδονὴν εἶναι τἀγαθόν** *the good is pleasure* is a restatement of the identity thesis that Protarchus agreed to defend as the first turn of the topic. See note introducing 11d–12b.

13c1–2 **τὰς μὲν . . . τινας . . . ἡδονάς, τὰς δέ τινας ἑτέρας . . .** *while some pleasures . . . , others . . .* "Added to a noun with the article, [τινας] denotes the indefiniteness of the pleasures referred to" (S §1267). The two articles τὰς indicate that ἡδονάς and ἑτέρας are the subjects of their coordinate accusative-plus-infinitive constructions.

13c3 **Ἀλλ' οὖν . . . γε** *but surely . . . at least.* In answers "introduces a protest" (Denniston 1966, 442).

13c8 **τὰ παραδείγματα** that is, the examples color and shape (12e3–7).

13d–14b: ***Socrates and Protarchus agree that there can be many and unlike kinds of both pleasure and knowing.***

That such ones as pleasure and knowing can also be many are instances of the One-Many Thesis. Socrates, having asserted that pleasure is both one and many, begins to generalize the One-Many Thesis: knowing, too, shares the perplexing feature of being both one and many. The recognition that even the paradigms of unity, the ungenerated and imperishable ones such as the good, are also many, marks a turning in Plato's metaphysics. In dialogues such as the *Phaedo, Republic*, and *Symposium*, these sorts of objects are only one, not one and many, whereas in the *Philebus, Theaetetus, Sophist, Statesman,* and *Parmenides*, these sorts of objects are both one and many (as Rickless [2007] argues). This fundamental change in Plato's metaphysics would be a reason for Plato to emphasize the principle in this dialogue.

13d6 **νεώτεροι τοῦ δέοντος** *younger than what is needed*, hence too inexperienced to do what is needed (LSJ νεώτερος A). See note introducing 16c–19b for a discussion of Socrates' pejorative adjective νέος *young.*

ἐκπεσὼν *after falling out.* According to Bury (1897), this is a "metaphor from a ship stranded in a storm: the rhythm suggests a tragic citation." Taking the ultima of ἡμῖν as an anceps, Socrates might have chanted the rhythm of the words μῖν ἐκπεσὼν οἰχήσεται (x ¯ ˘ ¯ / x ¯ ˘ ¯) as iambic trimeter. Bury continues: "The marine metaphor is carried on from εἰς τὸν αὐτὸν φερόμεθα λόγον [*carried back to the same argument*] above [13c6], and continued in ἀνακρουώμεθα *back her out* [as at] Herodotus *Histories* 8.84.2." Gosling (1975, 78) says,

> Certainly *ekpiptein* can be used of shipwreck, but is also a common verb for orators or stage-performances being hissed off. With *logos* as a subject, one might most naturally take the latter sense. There is no doubt, however, that *anakrouesthai* is a familiar nautical term for backing water. One could, therefore, with Hackforth 1945 [following Bury 1897], preserve the metaphor throughout, or take the hissing as the most natural sense, and take the "back up" metaphor to be so weak as not to be discordant. In this case the immediate move to a wrestling metaphor would be fairly easy, as both arguments and law-cases were often spoken of in terms of combat.

13d7–8 **τάχ' ἀνιόντες . . . ἴσως ἂν** *perhaps coming back . . . perhaps.* Both manuscripts B and T have ἀνιόντες, which Stallbaum (1820 and 1842) accepts without comment. Burnet (1901), following Bury (1897), prefers ἂν ἰόντες, found in manuscript Ven. 189, also without comment. Both variants—τάχ' ἀνιόντες *perhaps, coming back* and τάχ' ἂν ἰόντες, *perhaps, coming*—are intelligible. The ἂν ἰόντες reading repeats ἄν in a permitted though unnecessary way. Such an ἄν is placed early in the sentence before the participle "in order to direct attention to the character of the construction" (S §1765). Yet, while ἴσως is frequently joined with ἄν or τάχ' ἄν (using *TLG*, in Plato I found ἴσως τάχ' ἂν twice, ἴσως . . . τάχ' ἂν twice, τάχ' ἂν ἴσως seven times, τάχ' ἂν . . . ἴσως five times, and ἴσως ἄν eight times), I could find no instances of ἴσως ἄν joined with τάχ' ἂν anywhere else in Plato or indeed in any Greek text. Style also gives a reason to prefer ἀνιόντες to ἰόντες. The prefix ἀν- echoes the prefix in ἀνακρουώμεθα, and gives an apt metaphor of this stage of the dialogue, an image of wrestlers who have broken apart, just as Protarchus and Socrates have broken apart in the conversation, and then come *back* using similar holds on each other. See note to 13e2 on how the holds might be similar.

εἰς τὰς ὁμοίας [**λαβάς**] *into similar holds* is a metaphor from wrestling. The same metaphor is at *Phaedrus* 236b9–c1 (εἰς τὰς ὁμοίας λαβάς) and *Republic* 544b5 (πάλιν . . . ὥσπερ παλαιστής, τὴν αὐτὴν λαβὴν πάρεχε *just like a wrestler, let me again have the same hold*). Bury (1897) compares the quick change from marine to fighting metaphors with Shakespeare's "take arms against a sea of troubles."

13d8 **συγχωρήσαιμεν** *we might reach agreement with (each other).* It is possible to classify this potential optative as the apodosis of a future less vivid conditional, by letting the participle ἀνιόντες stand for the protasis εἰ ἀνίοιμεν *if we were to come back* (S §2344).

13e1 **Λέγε πῶς;** This is the punctuation of Stallbaum (1842), Badham (1855 and 1878), Bury (1897), Burnet (1901), and Diès (1949). With the question mark at the end of the sentence, we must understand the interrogative πῶς to introduce a direct question: *tell [me]: how?* Such a reading requires these two words to represent two independent clauses. Thus, Stallbaum (1820) adds the comma to his text: Λέγε, πῶς; I recommend instead the punctuation of Stephanus (1578), which has a period at the end of the sentence, not a question mark: Λέγε πῶς. This punctuation permits the πῶς to introduce an indirect question after the imperative Λέγε. The English translation can mark the imperative mood with an exclamation mark: *tell how!*

13e2 **Ἐμὲ θὲς ὑπὸ σοῦ . . . ἐρωτώμενον** *Put* me *under* you *as I am being questioned!* Socrates' first four words recall the wrestling metaphor. Protarchus has been under Socrates, who has been trying to pin him to an admission that some pleasures are unlike and opposite each other. This command makes clear how the two wrestlers will resume their session by coming back together into similar holds: Protarchus, to be in control, would hold Socrates in the same way that Socrates just held him—that is, as asking—while Socrates will now be in the same position Protarchus was—that is, as answering. My translation attaches the prepositional phrase ὑπὸ σοῦ to the verb of placing θὲς and also understands it with the passive participle ἐρωτώμενον. As an alternative, LSJ (τίθημι B.I) attaches the prepositional phrase only to the passive participle ἐρωτώμενον, which they make an attributive substantive: *make me the one who is answering questions.*

13e5–6 **ὅτι ποτ' ἐστὶν ἀγαθόν** *what is good?* or *what is a good thing?* is the reading in manuscript B, while T has ὅτι ποτ' ἐστὶν τἀγαθόν, "what is the good?" Socrates' answer is a list of cognitive states. The question that best correlates with a list is *What is good?* not *What is the good?* Socrates himself often asks questions of the form *What is the F?*—or, equivalently, *What is F-ness?* If his interlocutors answer that form of question with a list of *F* things or a list of things that are *F*, he typically chides them for giving a list rather than a definition (for example at *Euthyphro* 6c–d, *Meno* 72a–b, and *Theaetetus* 146d). We may assume that Socrates is careful to correlate questions and answers of this form. Thus, his answer suggests that the text of B is correct.

Socrates here reminds his audience that he had made a positive claim that the listed cognitive powers are ἀγαθά *good things*. This passage is sometimes interpreted as a (somewhat inaccurate) restatement of

11b7–9, where he made a comparative claim that cognitive acts are *better and more desirable* than pleasures. The words at e5, κατ' ἀρχὰς *at first,* might refer to the first words of this dialogue, but there is an alternative. According to LSJ, the circumstantial participle διερωτώμενος means *being cross-questioned* or *being continually questioned.* (I am not able to defend Frede's [1993] translation, "when I tried to answer the question.") Socrates was not being asked a train of questions at 11b7–9. Thus, Socrates might here be referring, and referring accurately rather than inaccurately, to a prior, off-stage part of his conversation with Philebus.

14a4 **οἴχοιτο** *would vanish, would be ruined.* The subject is ὁ λόγος *the discussion.* According to the *Lexicon* of Photius (M 279.1), μῦθος ἐσώθη *the story was saved* is a formula said after a story with a happy ending, comparable to our formula *and they lived happily ever after.* Evidently μῦθος ἀπώλετο *the story was destroyed* was the opposite formula for stories with sad endings: *and they came to a bad end.* Likewise *Republic* 621b8–c1 (μῦθος ἐσώθη καὶ οὐκ ἀπώλετο *the story was saved and not destroyed*), *Theaetetus* 164d9 (μῦθος ἀπώλετο), and *Laws* 645b1–2 (ὁ μῦθος . . . σεσωμένος ἂν εἴη *the story would have been saved*).

σῳζοίμεθα ἐπί *we would be rescuing ourselves on.* The verb suggests that the story ends with a reef that wrecks the ship/dialogue, while saving the sailors/speakers who rescue themselves on it.

14a5 **ἀλογίας** *lack of reason, irrationality.* In Socrates' imagined case, the ἀλογία that would save him from losing the competition, while at the same time destroying the dialogue, would be the insistence that no kind of knowing can be opposite or unlike any other. In Protarchus' case, it would be the same insistence about pleasure.

14a6 **Ἀλλ' οὐ μὴν** *but surely not* is a strong adversative indicating a protest with a complete rejection of what precedes (Denniston 1966, 147 and 335–36).

14a7 **τό . . . ἴσον** = ἰσότης (as at 25a7) *the equality of [the discussion].* What the hedonist Protarchus approves here is the very proportion and measure that Socrates will make part of the nature of the good by the end of the dialogue.

γε μήν *moreover* is progressive (Denniston 1966, 349), linking two reasons for Protarchus' approval, saving the dialogue and equal treatment.

14b1–2 **Τὴν . . . διαφορότητα . . . τοῦ ἀγαθοῦ τοῦ τ' ἐμοῦ καὶ τοῦ σοῦ** *my good's fact of difference and your good's fact of difference.* There is no need to bracket the τοῦ ἀγαθοῦ as Burnet (1901) does (following Bury 1897). The genitive case denotes the possession of difference by Socrates' good and by Protarchus' good. In other words, both knowing (Socrates' good) and pleasure (Protarchus' good) possess types that are unlike. In contrast, a similar genitive usage denotes comparison not possession at *Republic* 587e5–588a1 (τῆς διαφορότητος τοῖν ἀνδροῖν, τοῦ τε δικαίου καὶ τοῦ ἀδίκου *the difference between the two men, the righteous and the unrighteous*). The difference between these two usages is that τοῦ ἀγαθοῦ is singular while τοῖν ἀνδροῖν is dual.

14b3 **τολμῶμεν** *let us dare!* responds to φοβηθείς at 14a2. With accompanying participles μὴ ἀποκρυπτόμενοι and κατατιθέντες δὲ, it means *let us dare not to hide away but to place* (LSJ A.II.2).

μηνύσωσι *they reveal, disclose.* The subject of the two courtroom verbs ἐλεγχόμενοι *being cross-examined* and μηνύσωσι is not clear. Stallbaum (1842) proposes αἱ διαφορότητες, but this requires emending the masculine ἐλεγχόμενοι to the feminine ἐλεγχόμεναι. Bury (1897) proposes οἱ λόγοι, but this requires deleting the words τοῦ ἀγαθοῦ and understanding λόγου with ἐμοῦ and σοῦ. I propose without emendation to make the subject ὁ ἀγαθός ὁ τ' ἐμοῦ καὶ ὁ σοῦ *my good and yours.* The courtroom metaphor is to examine these two claimants in order to make them reveal the truth, in order that the examiners may find out if either has a valid claim.

14b5 **γὰρ οὐ δήπου . . . γε** *for, I presume, [we are] not at any rate [loving victory].* This common Platonic combination of particles (Denniston 1966, 268) here supports the exhortation to admit the fact of difference within the kinds Pleasure and Knowing in the previous sentence by an appeal to the unacceptability of the alternative, to care merely for victory in debate. On δήπου see note to 12c7–8.

14c–15a: ***With respect to the One-Many Thesis (that one is many and many is one), Socrates distinguishes a*** vulgar ***version about objects that come and cease to be in space and time from an*** aristocratic ***version about nonspatial, nontemporal ones ("forms"). It is easy to raise problems for either the aristocratic or the vulgar thesis. There are three problems for the aristocratic thesis that raise significant controversy among those who believe in forms.***

Protarchus will relate the following argument from opposites for a One-Many Thesis, asking if this is the sort of One-Many Thesis that Socrates has in mind.

A Argument that one Protarchus is many:

P1 [Protarchus is one.]

P1.1 Because Protarchus is one by nature. 14d1

P2 [Protarchus is many.]

Because:

P2.1 [There is a tall Protarchus, short Protarchus, heavy Protarchus, light Protarchus, and endless other Protarchuses.]

P2.1.1 Because Protarchus is tall and short, heavy and light, and endless other things. 14d2–3

P2.2 There are even opposite Protarchuses. 14d1–2

P2.2.1 [Because there are a tall Protarchus and a short Protarchus, a heavy Protarchus and a light Protarchus, and endless other pairs of opposite Protarchuses.]

P2.2.1.1 Because Protarchus is tall and short, heavy and light, and endless other [pairs of opposite] things. 14d2–3

B Run backward (πάλιν, 14d1), the same argument shows that the many Protarchuses are the same one.

P1 [Protarchus is many.]

Because:

P1.1 [There are a tall Protarchus, short Protarchus, heavy Protarchus, light Protarchus, and endless other Protarchuses.]

P1.1.1 Because Protarchus is tall and short, heavy and light, and endless other things. 14d2–3

P1.2 There are even opposite Protarchuses. 14d1–2: καὶ ἐναντίους

P1.2.1 [Because there are a tall Protarchus and a short Protarchus, a heavy Protarchus and a light Protarchus, and endless other pairs of opposite Protarchuses.]

P1.2.1.1 Because Protarchus is tall and short, heavy and light, and endless other [pairs of opposite] things. 14d2–3

P2 [Protarchus is one.]

P2.1 Because Protarchus is one by nature. 14d1

There have been two main alternative interpretations of the argument for 14c11–d1.

Alternative 1. The Cynic-logic interpretation. Some interpreters think that the argument requires, in Friedländer's words (1969, 317–18), "the [false] principle in Cynic logic . . . according to which each thing should be designated only 'by its own name' and not by any other predicate." This false principle evidently underlies Striker's representation of the argument (1970, 13):

(1) You are one.
(2) You are both big and small (*sowohl groß als auch klein*).
(3) Whatever is big cannot be small.

Therefore, you are equally one (from premise 1) and many (from premises 2 and 3).

According to this interpretation, the false Cynic principle would be needed to establish premise 3.

Alternative 2. The confused-copula interpretation. Some interpreters think that the argument requires, in Löhr's words (1990, 30), "that the 'is' of predication [*die Prädikationskopula*] be confused with the 'is' of identity." "In such a case one could accept that something is identical with some other object, perhaps in the sense in which we say that the Prime Minister of Great Britain *is* (identical with) Mrs. Thatcher" (Löhr 1990, 28). According to this sort of interpretation, the argument would run as follows: "If Protarchus *is* big (i.e., is the Big), then it follows that he cannot at the same time be small (= be the Small), for in that case the Big would have to be identical with the Small" (Löhr 1990, 30). Hence, big Protarchus is different from small Protarchus; hence they are two, hence Protarchus is one and many.

As it seems to me, there is no need to attribute a false premise or logical flaw to the argument. The inference from there being a tall Protarchus, a short Protarchus, and so on (14d2–3), to there being many Protarchuses is sound as it stands.

One way to see that P2.1 establishes that there are many Protarchuses is in terms of *persistence conditions*—that is, different periods of existence for different Protarchuses. Consider, for example, the Protarchus who is tall *in relation to his older sister* but also short *in relation to his younger brother.* Certainly Protarchus was not always taller than his older sister; he became so at some time—say, at the age of ten. And he was not always shorter than his younger brother; he became so at some time—say, at the age of fifteen. Suppose that Protarchus' present age is eighteen years. Then we have different persistence conditions for *Protarchus* (who has persisted for eighteen years), *taller-than-older-sister Protarchus* (a Protarchus who has persisted for eight years), and *shorter-than-younger-brother Protarchus* (a Protarchus who has persisted for three years). Since they have persisted for different times, these are distinct Protarchuses. I use persistence conditions to show the validity of the inference from tall and short Protarchus to multiple Protarchuses. But my claim, that Protarchus' argument is sound, is not a claim that Protarchus argued by reference to persistence conditions. Indeed, it seems to me that persistence conditions imperfectly represent the argument. For example, the distinction between taller-than-older-sister Protarchus and shorter-than-younger-brother Protarchus would exist even if, by some odd chance, these two Protarchuses happened to persist for exactly the same period of time. The difference between tall and short Protarchus is the cause, not the effect, of the difference between (or, in the odd case, the identity of) the persistence conditions of these two Protarchuses.

14c1 **Τοῦτον . . . τὸν λόγον** *this statement* must refer to the statement of unlikeness (see note to 14b1–2) that they have just agreed to put on center stage, since Socrates is exhorting them to proceed, by additional agreement, to establish it even more securely. Protarchus in his reply will ask Socrates for further specification of τοῦτον.

14c8 **ἓν . . . τὰ πολλὰ εἶναι καὶ τὸ ἓν πολλὰ** *that many are one and one many.* This is one way of putting into words the fact of unlikeness to which Socrates and Polemarchus agreed, when each conceded that their good (knowing or pleasure) could possess unlikeness, requiring it to be many. Protarchus in effect made these theses into a point of dispute, when he denied that one pleasure could be opposed to another insofar as they were both pleasures.

14c11 **Ἀρ . . . οὖν** *then.* The οὖν indicates the kind of inference where the question is prompted by the preceding statement (Denniston 1966, 426).

14d1 **τοὺς ἐμὲ** *me's.* Protarchus cannot make his point with ἡμᾶς *us,* the regular plural of ἐμὲ *me.* While English most obviously forms a parallel plural from "me" by adding an apostrophe and the letter *s* (to native speakers, "mes" and "me-s" seem not to be so obvious in meaning as "me's"). Protarchus pluralizes ἐμὲ by adding the plural definite article.

14d8–e4 Socrates gives an argument from parts as another proof that a becomer can be one and many.

P All the parts and pieces of a given object *are* that object, just as that object *is* all its parts and pieces.

C Thus, the one object is many, and its many parts are simply one.

The casual and abbreviated presentation of the argument indicates that Socrates assumes that Protarchus has heard it before. Socrates tells Protarchus that it is agreed ὡς ἔπος εἰπεῖν ὑπὸ πάντων *by everyone, so to speak,* that to argue in such ways about becomers is παιδαριώδη καὶ ῥᾴδια καὶ σφόδρα τοῖς λόγοις ἐμπόδια *juvenile, frivolous, and very much impeding their reasoning* (14d5–7). Since Socrates in this section seeks Protarchus' *agreement* to the One-Many Thesis, it is not that thesis—that is, conclusions like C above—that he condemns. Rather, I take it, Socrates is condemning those who take the One-Many Thesis to be a reductio ad absurdum, condemning those who elicit the One-Many Thesis from you so that ἐλέγχῃ καταγελῶν *they refute you by mocking you* (14e2–3).

At *Parmenides* 129c5–d2 Socrates gives an example of a division by μέρη *parts*: ἕτερα μὲν τὰ [μέρη] ἐπὶ δεξιά μού ἐστιν, ἕτερα δὲ τὰ ἐπ' ἀριστερά, καὶ ἕτερα μὲν τὰ πρόσθεν, ἕτερα δὲ τὰ ὄπισθεν, καὶ ἄνω καὶ κάτω ὡσαύτως *my left and right [parts] are different, and my front and back parts, and likewise my top and bottom parts.* These parts, left and right, front and back, up and down, are both ἕτερα *different* and ἐναντία *opposite.* It is easy to extrapolate an example of a division of μέλη: my right and left μηροί *upper legs* are different (indeed opposite), as are my right and left κνῆμαι *lower legs,* βραχίονες *upper arms,* and πήχεις *lower arms.* The hypothetical refuter need not claim every μέλος *member* or every μέρος *part* has an opposite, but the difference and hence duality of opposites is perhaps easier to establish with a stubborn interlocutor. As with the argument that Protarchus is one and many, the conclusion here (τό τε ἓν ὡς πολλά ἐστι καὶ ἄπειρα, καὶ τὰ πολλὰ ὡς ἓν μόνον *that the one is many things, even unbounded things, and the many are one only)* follows from the premises that Socrates is a composite and that a composite is all its parts together. Socrates objects not to this one-many conclusion, but to the juvenile assumption that the conclusions are τέρατα *monstrosities.*

Socrates does not indicate how the refuter might secure agreement that πάντα ταῦτα τὸ ἓν ἐκεῖνο εἶναι *all these are that one.* There is no denying the refuter's first premise, the division in speech of, say, Socrates into different parts and limbs—it is certainly true that Socrates is a whole composed of parts, an organism composed of members. But it seems possible to deny the refuter's inference that "all these parts *are* that one [whole]" (e1–2). At this step the refuter *identifies* the composite with its elements. The denier might propose that the elements *make up* the composite without *being* the composite. The denier, then, posits that the composite is not the elements but rather is something else or something more, arising from the elements, having itself its own shape and being something different from the elements. As part of a discussion of wholes and parts in the *Theaetetus,* Socrates considers this sort of alternative: χρῆν γὰρ ἴσως τὴν συλλαβὴν τίθεσθαι μὴ τὰ στοιχεῖα ἀλλ' ἐξ ἐκείνων ἕν τι γεγονὸς εἶδος *for perhaps it is necessary to posit that the composite/syllable is not the elements/letters, but that out of these a sort of one has come to be, a form* (203e2–5). Harte (2002, 28n54) reports that philosophers today are likely to propose that Gottlob Frege has solved the problem of wholes and parts, by denying that numbers are properties of things:

"While looking at one and the same external phenomenon, I can say with equal truth both 'It is a copse' and 'It is five trees,' or both 'Here are four companies' and 'Here are 500 men'" (*Foundations of Arithmetic*, §46). In order to avoid admitting that one and the same thing can be both one and five, Frege asserts that each such statement of number is, contrary to its overt grammatical form, in fact about a concept not an empirical object. As Frege thereby avoids admitting that the same thing is singular and plural in number, we might likewise avoid admitting that the same thing is both a whole and all its parts. For, while looking at one and the same phenomenon, I can say with equal truth both "It is one whole" and "It is many parts together," or both "Here are four companies" and "Here is the army." And we might avoid admitting that one and the same external phenomenon is both one whole and many parts by asserting that what is whole, contrary to the overt grammatical form, is not the external phenomenon but a posited abstract object (setting aside for this solution the differences between a Fregean concept and Platonic form). See Harte (2002, 28–29) for an alternative discussion of Frege's applicability to the Platonic problem. It seems to me that at *Theaetetus* 203e2–5, Socrates, as a means of avoiding the same problem of identifying an external phenomenon as both one whole and as many parts, anticipates this Fregean alternative. Like Frege, Socrates posits an abstract object to bear the property of being the composite or whole.

On this Fregean alternative, the composite or whole will be different from "the all"—that is, the parts all together (Οὐκοῦν διαφέροι ἂν τὸ ὅλον τοῦ παντός, ὡς ὁ νῦν λόγος; —Ναί, *then wouldn't the whole differ from the all, according to the present argument?—Yes*, 204b5–7). Socrates rejects this distinction with the following reasoning.

P1 The all is *this* all: whenever nothing is missing (τὸ πᾶν δὲ οὐχ ὅταν μηδὲν ἀπῇ, αὐτὸ τοῦτο πᾶν ἐστιν; —Ἀνάγκη, 205a1–3).

P2 Whenever something is absent from a thing, it is neither whole nor all (οὗ δ' ἂν ἀποστατῇ, οὔτε ὅλον οὔτε πᾶν, 205a5).

P3 A thing comes to be at once the same (thing, namely, whole and all together) from the same (condition, namely, not missing anything) ἅμα γενόμενον ἐκ τοῦ αὐτοῦ τὸ αὐτό, 205a6).

C1 A whole will be the same thing as all—namely, that from which nothing is absent in any way . . . A whole and all differ in no way (Ὅλον δὲ οὐ ταὐτὸν τοῦτο ἔσται, οὗ ἂν μηδαμῇ μηδὲν ἀποστατῇ; . . . —οὐδὲν διαφέρειν πᾶν τε καὶ ὅλον 205a4–5, 7).[1]

As a lemma, Socrates has already established that:

L1 (For anything of which there are parts) all (of that thing) is the parts all together (Τὰ δέ γε πάντα μέρη τὸ πᾶν εἶναι, 204e5).

From C1 and L1 it follows that:

C2 For anything of which there are parts, the whole (of that thing)—that is, all (of that thing) will be the parts all together (οὗ ἂν μέρη ᾖ, τὸ ὅλον τε καὶ πᾶν τὰ πάντα μέρη ἔσται, 205a8–9).

Harte (2002, 29) finds Socrates' "identification of a whole with its parts" to be "problematic." But she seems to interpret Socrates to be identifying the whole with all its parts taken any which way—that is, with what she calls a "collection," which term, though grammatically singular, she uses to refer to "many things, plurally quantified" (2002, 27). Moreover, she takes Socrates to defend "the thesis that composition is identity, the thesis underlying both Lewis's [1991] and Baxter's [1988] (more or less successful) claims to the innocence of composition" (2002, 43). And Harte understands that underlying thesis as follows: "Suppose one asks: when is it the case that many things compose one thing, a whole? . . . Lewis answers: whenever there are many things" (Harte 2002, 17). It would be a logical error to take Socrates ever to give this answer. In the *Theaetetus* he makes only the converse claim that οὗ ἂν ᾖ μέρη, τὸ ὅλον ἀνάγκη τὰ πάντα μέρη εἶναι *for anything*

1. Aristotle's discussion of composites and elements at *Metaphysics* 1041b11–33 does not dispute conclusion C1. While Aristotle argues that the composite is more than the elements, he defines "element" there as what is ἐνυπάρχον ὡς ὕλην *present in as matter* (1041b32). He maintains that "the syllable is some particular thing; not merely the letters, vowel and consonant, but something else besides" (ἔστιν ἄρα τι ἡ συλλαβή, οὐ μόνον τὰ στοιχεῖα τὸ φωνῆεν καὶ ἄφωνον ἀλλὰ καὶ ἕτερόν τι, 1041b16–17). "This 'something else' is something that is not an element, but is a cause" (δόξειε δ' ἂν εἶναι τὶ τοῦτο καὶ οὐ στοιχεῖον, καὶ αἴτιόν γε, 1041b25–26)—namely, the formal cause. The μηδαμῇ in Socrates' formulation οὗ ἂν μηδαμῇ μηδὲν ἀποστατῇ shows that the items under discussion are not restricted to things that are present in the whole only *as matter*.

of which there are parts, the whole [of that thing] is necessarily the parts all together (205a8–9).

Moreover, Greek makes a distinction between τὰ πάντα μέρη *the parts all together*, and πάντα τὰ μέρη *all the parts [any which way]* (S §1174). It seems to be a grammatical mistake to take Socrates to identify the whole with the parts present or absent, composed or decomposed, for he never tries to identify the whole with πάντα τὰ μέρη.

14d4 **τὰ δεδημευμένα** *the vulgar* or *commonplace things/versions* (LSJ A.II). A second possible meaning noticed by Harte (2002, 180) is *the published [things]* (LSJ A.III). It is true that similar arguments about one and many have been published by Plato at *Republic* 523c–525a and perhaps *Phaedo* 101, but *Parmenides* 129c and *Sophist* 251a–c have already published versions that Socrates here does not consider to be δεδημευμένα, so the meaning *published/nonpublished* distinction does not seem to fit the distinction Socrates draws here in the text.

14d7–8 **παιδαριώδη καὶ ῥᾴδια καὶ σφόδρα τοῖς λόγοις ἐμπόδια ὑπολαμβανόντων γίγνεσθαι** *understanding (the vulgar arguments) to be juvenile, frivolous, and very much impeding their reasoning,* a circumstantial participle added to the substantive πάντων *everyone* and denoting a reason (S §2054a) for everyone's agreement not to touch the vulgar versions of the One-Many Thesis. In the list παιδαριώδη *juvenile* καὶ ῥᾴδια *easy/trivial/frivolous* καὶ σφόδρα τοῖς λόγοις ἐμπόδια *very much impeding their reasoning,* the first and last items help to disambiguate ῥᾴδια. If Protarchus' version of the One-Many Thesis is easy to understand or trivial, it cannot be much of a hindrance to reasoning, and so ῥᾴδια more probably means *easy to make*. Such a meaning fits well with the fact that rookies can manufacture such versions of the thesis, versions that nevertheless are not easy to understand but on the contrary lead to ἀπορία *impasse* (15d8–16a3). In the *Theaetetus* Socrates describes philosophical conversation as free to choose and change its topic and as having leisure to talk at any length, in contrast to legal advocates in court who must slavishly stick to one topic and watch the clock (172d–e). And Socrates demonstrates extraordinary patience in the *Euthydemus* with juvenile and frivolous arguments, to the point of scandalizing his friend Crito (305a–b). It is a puzzle why those two Socrateses seem to stand in sharp contrast to the Socrates here, who is impatient with newcomers and time wasters. The first two Socrates apparently find plenty of value in that reasoning (see Rudebusch and Turner 2014 for an explanation). Socrates here, in contrast, seems to value the conversation only for the goal of settling the pleasure/knowing controversy. Such a goal would fit the metaphor used to frame the topic of discussion for the *Philebus*, the metaphor of advocates seeking courtroom victory (11a1–12b2). See Annas and Rowe (2003) for possible explanations as to why Plato's character Socrates would change between dialogues in this and other ways.

14e1 **ἑκάστου** *of a given person*. This person is, implicitly, the one from whom agreement is extracted (διομολογησάμενος, e2) and the one who is refuted and jeered at (ἐλέγχῃ καταγελῶν, e2–3) and the one who is compelled to say monstrous things (τέρατα διηνάγκασται φάναι, e3).

μέλη *members* is a butcher's word referring to parts of a body produced by "cutting at the joints" (διατέμνειν κατ᾽ ἄρθρα, *Phaedrus* 265e1, likewise *Statesman* 287c3–5); hence it suggests more possible parts than *limbs* but fewer possible parts than *pieces*.

διελὼν τῷ λόγῳ *after dividing by means of speech*. An interpretation of what it is in this proposition to *divide by means of speech* the body ought to guide the interpretation of 15d4.

15a6 **ἑνάδων** feminine genitive plural noun ἑνάς, *henads*—that is, *ones*. This rare word or perhaps neologism first appears in extant Greek here, although it is later found in *testimonia* of Pythagoras, Zeno, and Xenocrates. It is the only occurrence in Plato. Another neologism perhaps occurs at 30e1: γενούστης.

15a6–7 **ἡ πολλὴ σπουδή** *the great zeal* for the positing of eternal ones such as human being, ox, the beautiful, the good, is contrasted with an ensuing ἀμφισβήτησις *controversy*. These two sentiments can contrast when speaking, for example, of a referendum in a democracy. For example, the great zeal by the Athenians to put to death "the whole adult male population of Mitylene" (reported at Thucydides, *History* 3.35.1) later turned into a controversy when the issue was reconsidered and the population was almost evenly divided over the death sentence (3.47.3). In the same way, as I interpret the text, *before* division of aristocratic ones into manies, there was much enthusiastic support for positing the ones, while *after* division—presumably because many of the enthusiasts now found the marvelous One-Many Thesis to be incredible—the general zeal among the circle of philosophers turned into controversy.

15a7 **μετὰ** plus genitive *in conjunction with* (LSJ A.II). The aristocratic division of the eternal henad human being is parallel to the vulgar division of the ephemeral man Protarchus. As we might divide Protarchus into tall Protarchus, short Protarchus, and so on, we might likewise divide the henad human being into many human beings such as wise human being and foolish human being, sound-minded human being and unsound-minded human being, and so on. There are examples of just such divisions earlier in the dialogue. Socrates, although he had not yet introduced the words ἑνάς *henad* and διαίρεσις *division*, proposed that one might divide the henad human being into wise human being and foolish human being, sound-minded human being and unsound-minded human being at 12d1–4. In the very same passage, he also divided pleasure into wise pleasure and foolish pleasure, sound-minded pleasure and unsound-minded pleasure. And, with the division, the earlier shared zeal for inquiry did turn into a dispute, when Protarchus denied that unsound-minded pleasure and sound-minded pleasure, foolish pleasure and wise pleasure are pleasures unlike or opposite each other.

15b–c: ***Socrates states paradoxes that come with accepting an aristocratic One-Many Thesis. Nevertheless, he stresses the importance of agreeing to the One-Many Thesis for their inquiry and any inquiry.***

Commentators have struggled to interpret the text of 15b. The root of the problem is 15b2–4, the Second Controversy. Grammatically, the Second Controversy is easy to translate: "how *these*—each one always being the same and subject neither to coming-to-be nor ceasing-to-be—nevertheless most stably are *this one*" (15b2–4). The difficulty has been to make the "nevertheless" intelligible: why does Socrates discount the clause that each "one" is always the "same [one]" by saying that *nevertheless* they "most stably are one"? Badham first stated the problem of intelligibility for modern commentators: the question posed at 15b2–4 asks how it is "conceivable that that which is one and imperishable should be nevertheless unchangeably one:—than which nothing could be more absurd" (1878, 10). More than a century later, the problem remained: "What problem is Plato supposed to see in the fact that each of these monads, which are always the same and never admit coming-to-be nor ceasing-to-be, *nevertheless* are each most certainly *one?* Why should the eternally unchanging unities not 'most steadfastly' [*auf sicherste Weise*] forever be ones? This question appears empty" (Frede 1997, 121).

The numerous alternative interpretations may be divided into three: Emendation, Clairvoyance, and Grammatical Revision.

1. *Emendation.* Frede (1997, 122) and Dancy (1984, 162–63) review different changes to the text that have been suggested. Emendation is a last resort, since there are no reported difficulties in the manuscripts for this passage.
2. *Clairvoyance.* Following Dancy (1984), I identify three subalternatives of nonemending readings, adding Dancy's as a fourth type. All four share the same defect in requiring that Protarchus have the power of a clairvoyant to be able to answer as he does.)

Subalternative 2.1. "How can each of these [monads such as human being, Ox, etc.] be *one,* and also *be* or exist?"

Subalternative 2.2. "How can it be that these monads [such as human being, Ox, etc.], each being individually self-identical and eternal, are yet one single [more generic] unity?"

Subalternative 2.3. "How can each of these units be *one* when it is to be distinguished from the One?"

Subalternative 2.4. "When Socrates says that one of the problems is how each unit can be one, although it is not something that comes-to-be or passes-away, he is merely reminding Protarchus that there is nothing controversial about how something that comes-to-be and passes-away can be one."

Frede states the problem shared by these subkinds. "It is legitimate to bring references to discussions in other dialogues into play as complements, but only in the presence of a clearly drawn allusion, not by freely reading things into the text [*ein freies Hineinlesen*], which in all honesty requires the skills of a clairvoyant. We are unwilling to accept that Plato in this passage is putting forward a list of questions on the existence and status of the forms that is so poorly formulated that the questions are . . . taken by themselves, completely unintelligible" (1997, 123).

3. *Grammatical Revision.* The text of 15b naturally seems to consist of three correlative clauses, marked by the sequence Πρῶτον μὲν . . . εἶτα . . . μετὰ δὲ τοῦτ' *first . . . again . . . after this*. But it is grammatically possible instead to take 15b as consisting of only two correlative clauses, putting the words "after this" within the scope of the second clause. The unintelligibility of 15b2–4 is then avoided by hyperbaton—that is, by attaching the word ὅμως *nevertheless* (15b4) to the following clause, instead of taking it with the one it is in. The result of this merger and hyperbaton is then an intelligible point of controversy: how can the unchanging one be that one and *nevertheless after this* be among the unbounded things that come to be? The problem with grammatical revision is that the required case of hyperbaton is unparalleled: "hyperbaton with a preceding ὅμως requires at least a connecting particle, as ὅμως μήν or ὅμως καί" (Frede 1997, 122n17). Hence, this proposal forces us to revise our understanding of Greek grammar.

Muniz and Rudebusch 2004 propose a more satisfactory interpretation. The key to their reading of the Second Controversy begins with a new reading of the First Controversy as follows. After Socrates' claim at 15a4–7 that the intense interest in henads turns, with their division, into controversy, Protarchus asks, Πῶς; *how?* (15a8), meaning, no doubt, "How, with division, does the zeal become controversy?' In reply to Protarchus' "How?" Socrates says: Πρῶτον μὲν εἴ τινας δεῖ τοιαύτας εἶναι μονάδας ὑπολαμβάνειν ἀληθῶς οὔσας *first, if one ought to suppose that there are any such monads truly existing* (15b1–2). Prior to Muniz and Rudebusch

2004, interpreters took the word μονάδας *monads* to refer to the ἑνάδες *henads* ἕνα ἄνθρωπον . . . καὶ βοῦν ἕνα καὶ τὸ καλὸν ἓν καὶ τὸ ἀγαθὸν ἕν *one man and one ox and the one beautiful and the one good* (15a4–6). But it is better to take the antecedent of τοιαύτας μονάδας *such monads* (15b1) to be the nominalized prepositional phrase [τὰ] μετὰ διαιρέσεως *[the things] after division*, in other words, τὰ διαιρετά *the results of the division*, not τὰ διαιρετέα *the things to be divided.* (Another case in which the antecedent of a demonstrative is a nominalized phrase occurs at 15d4–6, where the antecedent of τοῦτο is the nominalized infinitive phrase [τὸ] ταὐτὸν ἓν καὶ πολλὰ ὑπὸ λόγων γιγνόμενα περιτρέχειν πάντῃ *the fact that the same one runs around everywhere, becoming as a result of speech many things.*)

It is better for the following reasons. First, in parallel passages, Socrates has already expressed this sort of distinction between one henad divided into monads, using the terms ἕν τι *a one* and μορφὰς παντοίας *shapes of all sorts* at 12c7, and using the terms γένει *in kind* and μέρη *parts* at 12e7. Second, there would have been no reason for Plato to have coined a new word (or used a rare word), ἑνάς *henad,* if he intended to use it interchangeably with the established word μονάς *monad.* Third, as Frede notes (1997, 119n12), the word ἑνάς connotes the *unity* of a one, while the word μονάς connotes a one's *separation* (*Alleinigkeit*) from other ones—hence, as I take the meaning, *the result of a division.* By the way, such a translation accords with the explanation of these two terms in Damascius (1959, 44.1–3): "He calls the apexes *monads* and *henads.* In relation to the multitudes which depend upon them and originate from them, they are called *henads,* while in relation to the ontologically higher realities [πρὸς δὲ τὰ ὑπερούσια] they are called *monads.*" Fourth, this interpretation connects the First Controversy with antecedent passages in the *Philebus.* Controversy arose between Socrates and Protarchus over the existence not of the *henad* pleasure but of the *monads* such as foolish pleasure and wise pleasure, with Protarchus denying the very existence of such monads at 12d7–8 and 13b6–c2. According to those two speeches—to put it in terms of henads and monads—there do not exist, in addition to the *henad* pleasure, also individual and distinct *monads* such as wise pleasure and foolish pleasure. In contrast, if the words ἑνάς and μονάς are interchangeable, there is no connection between this First Controversy and the actual issues under discussion in the rest of the *Philebus*, for the existence of the *henads* pleasure, knowing, and so on is never disputed by Protarchus or Philebus.

The fifth and biggest advantage of this interpretation is that it makes possible, for the first time, a problem-free interpretation of 15b2–4. We all agree that the grammatical antecedent of the pronoun ταύτας *these* is τοιαύτας μονάδας *such monads*. As now interpreted, the phrase τοιαύτας μονάδας refers to monads like foolish and wise human being, foolish and wise pleasure, and so on. The contrasting singular expression μίαν ταύτην *this one* naturally refers, therefore, to *this one henad*—for example, human being or pleasure. With these antecedents understood, nothing else is needed to give an intelligible translation of 15b2–3 as follows:

> Controversy arises about how *these* (*monads*; for example, Foolish and Wise human being)—each one always being the same and subject neither to coming-to-be nor ceasing-to-be (for example, the monad Foolish human being is always Foolish human being and never becomes Wise human being nor ceases to be Foolish human being)—nevertheless most stably are *this one* (*henad*; for example, human being).

Whereas the First Controversy precisely expresses Protarchus' skepticism about the very existence of such unlike and separated monads as foolish pleasure and wise pleasure, by contrast the Second Controversy expresses precisely what is amazing concerning one and many, should we grant the existence of such monads in addition to the henad. The apposite remark set between hyphens in the translation above, that the monads are always the same and subject neither to coming-to-be nor ceasing-to-be, makes clear that the Second Controversy has to do with the aristocratic version of the One-Many Thesis rather than the vulgar version. This apposite remark makes clear, moreover, why Socrates thinks that the amazement provided by division of such eternal henads as man, ox, the beautiful, or the good is worthy of the aristocrat, unlike the division of a temporary henad such as the human beings Protarchus and Socrates. For it is no wonder if an unstable *becomer* like Protarchus is and is not (as recognized, for example, at *Republic* 478d)—there is, after all, no possible knowledge, properly speaking, of any such objects of perception (*Republic* 478a–b, 510a–b). But how, indeed, can a monad, *eternally selfsame and unchanging*—hence a proper object of knowledge—nonetheless be a henad and be it in that very same unchanging, "most stable" way? As is often noticed, this question is related to the problem, expressed in similar terms, of *Parmenides* 129c–d. But there is no need to look to other dialogues to find this problem: it is present in the prior context of the *Philebus*.

Socrates never explicitly says what these aristocratic ones and manies are, but γένη *kinds* have this metaphysical power. See introduction: *Genos, Phusis*, and *Eidos*.

15b4–7 **ταὐτὸν καὶ ἓν ἅμα ἐν ἑνί τε καὶ πολλοῖς γίγνεσθαι** *that one and the same [monad], at the same time, comes to be in a single thing and in many things*, an accusative plus infinitive plus complement construction indirectly reporting the statement that would appear most impossible of all. I follow those interpreters (e.g., Migliori 1993, 83) who see the parallel with the problems raised at *Parmenides* 131a–c. Either foolish human being itself, for example, is "dispersed"—cut up and divided—among the many particular foolish human beings and hence itself many (absurd!) or foolish human being itself remains whole and undivided so that all of it is present in each of the distinct and separate many foolish human beings, with the absurd consequence that it will become as a whole separated from itself.

15c7–9 **Φίληβον . . . μὴ κινεῖν εὖ κείμενον** *not to stir up Philebus, who is resting nicely*. Corresponding to the English proverb *Let sleeping dogs lie*, the Greek proverb is μὴ κινεῖν κακὸν εὖ κείμενον *not to stir up trouble that is resting nicely*.

PART II: METAPHYSICS

1. A hypothesis to use to get agreement to the One-Many Thesis: Speech causes the one-many puzzles.

15d–16a: ***Socrates hypothesizes that the One-Many Thesis is a product of speech and disparages inept reasoners.***

Socrates describes how inept reasoners controvert any statement by manipulating it to lead to the marvel that one is many and many one, which inept reasoners take to be incredible. Protarchus and the rest of Philebus' circle understand the problem of such inept reasoners, as 16a6 shows. Indeed, Protarchus had experience with the vulgar version of this problem, as he reported at 14c11–d3. Thus, I interpret the statement, "Protarchus is tall," as a vulgar example to illustrate 15e2–3: Protarchus and tall Protarchus are different things, but the youthful controverter can knead the dough of this sentence into a one (see note to 14c11–d1: Protarchus is tall Protarchus) and then unroll it into a many (Protarchus and tall Protarchus are two). Socrates gives examples of aristocratic henads, such as human being, at 15a4–7. And in arguing for the thesis that pleasure, while one thing, is also complex (12c7–8), Socrates has already suggested aristocratic statements analogous to the vulgar statement about Protarchus, such as that pleasure is wise pleasure and foolish pleasure. The youthful controverter can obviously and easily also knead such statements about the eternal two, wise pleasure and foolish pleasure, into a one, pleasure, and then unroll it into many. My interpretation follows Hackforth (1945). Gosling (1975, 148) states the advantages of this kind of interpretation:

> This interpretation has the advantage that it would justify the assertion of [15]d4–5 that *everything* that is said . . . gives an example of many and one becoming the same. For on this view any sentence is of some general form [subject and predicate, or topic and comment], and therefore can be accused either of saying of one thing (e.g., man) that it is two or more (e.g., man and good), or of saying that two things (man and good) are but one. It is a paradox that might well delight the young, and certainly would put an end to philosophical discussion. Furthermore, it is possible to see it as in some sense a good starting-point for tackling the problem of 15b . . . For that problem is essentially: how *can* the one be many?

Gosling raises four "main difficulties for this interpretation" (1975, 148). These difficulties were apt for Gosling's target, the interpretation of Hackforth (1945). But replies are at hand on behalf of my version of that interpretation. The first difficulty is that, according to this interpretation, "Plato expects his reader to read the *Philebus* with the *Sophist* open before him, and to know that this is where to look for clues" (1975, 148). I reply that my interpretation need make no reference to the *Sophist.* I refer only to Protarchus' expressed familiarity with the problem, his earlier apt, if vulgar, example, and an obvious nonvulgar example suggested by Socrates' own previous discussion. The second difficulty is that the Divine Method of 16b–c below should bear on the problem of all speech being easily controverted by immature reasoning (1975, 149). My reading of the Divine Method expressly connects it with this problem. "A third difficulty is that the interpretation supposes that the identification of one and many is a consequence of a *false* theory, . . . whereas the text suggests that it is [not a false theory but] an important fact that can be abused" (1975, 149). In reply, as I showed above in the note to 14c–15a, the identification of one and many does not depend on a false theory (namely, a theory that confuses predication with identification). "The fourth difficulty is that . . . this interpretation . . . seems to have no bearing on the main problem about pleasure" (1975, 149). On my reading, however, the Divine Method does bear on the main problem about pleasure (see heading 8 under Commentary in the table of contents) and is also used in the Fourfold Division (under heading 6) and the division of knowledge (heading 9).

15d4–6 **Φαμέν που ταὐτὸν ἓν καὶ πολλὰ ὑπὸ λόγων γιγνόμενα περιτρέχειν πάντῃ καθ' ἕκαστον τῶν λεγομένων ἀεί** *We say, I suppose, that one and many, becoming the same thing due to statements, run around every which way in each of the things ever said, past or present.* This passage is introduced by the deliberative subjunctive τις . . . ἄρξηται; *how might one make a beginning?* (15d1) and the hedging που *I suppose,* (15d4). Accordingly, I take this proposition to be a hypothesis proposed in order to resolve the aristocratic controversies, which have to do with a one and many that "neither come to be nor cease to be" (15a1–2). As I have translated 15d4–6, the words ἓν καὶ πολλὰ *one and many* are the grammatical subject both of the participle γιγνόμενα *becoming* and the verb περιτρέχειν *run around.* My translation follows, for example, Schleiermacher (1809), Apelt (1922), Diès (1949), Hackforth (1945), Stallbaum (1842), Friedländer (1969), Waterfield (1982), and Migliori (1993). Although this translation is the obvious one, it has been thought that it requires Plato to confuse the "is" of identity with the "is" of predication, or for subtle reasons to have the author attribute the error to the character Socrates. But this charity is misplaced. The puzzle of one and many becoming the same thing need not be the result of philosophical confusion (see note to 14c–15a).

There are three alternative translations of this proposition.

Alternative 1. The grammatical subject is ταὐτὸν ἓν καὶ πολλὰ, *the same one and many [problem].* Paley (1873) (likewise, Badham [1855], Bury [1897], Taylor, and Delcomminette [2020]) translates accordingly: "This same 'One and Many' [i.e., *the doctrine* of the identity of One and Many], called into being by discussions, goes the round of every subject of conversation, whether new or old."

Alternative 2. The grammatical subject is ταὐτὸν *the same thing.* Frede (1993) (likewise, Benardete [1993]) translates accordingly: "It is through discourse that the same thing flits around, becoming one and many in all sorts of ways, in whatever it may be that is said at any time, both long ago and now." This translation may be equivalent to the one I give—one and many become the same. But it has been used as the basis for de Almeida's alternative interpretation of the *Philebus*. De Almeida (2002, 211) interprets the *Philebus* to "define human being as a task [*como tarefa*], namely, the task of enjoying the eternal present moment, realizing at each instant humanity and affirming the beauty of coming-to-be." He finds support for his interpretation in his translation of 15d4–6: "We say that the Same, as one and as many, becomes the same by thought [*é identifacado pelo pensamento*] and that it circulates, now and always, through everything which we say."

Alternative 3. The grammatical subject is ἓν καὶ πολλὰ *one and many*, but there is no predicate. Desjardins (2004) interprets the *Philebus* to describe a dialectical resolution to the conflict between "nature (in the objectivist sense) and "convention (in the relativist sense)" according to which these "mutually opposed elements are brought together as a plurality of parts in such a way as to constitute the unity of a single whole," a compound that is "neither simply one nor simply many, but both one and many" (2004, 49). They are brought together in the same way incommensurables in one dimension are brought together in two-dimensional geometry (2004, 122–27). Her interpretation is based on an alternate interpretation of 15d4–6, which she translates as follows: "It is we who, through reason, bring into being both the many and the one of reality" (2004, 48).

Assessment of alternatives. Löhr states the problem with Alternative 1, and the problem is the same for Alternative 2: "Although the possibility of [grammatical] attraction of [the grammatical number] of *gignomena* [a plural form] to *polla* [plural] cannot be ruled out, still it is to be expected that Plato, for the sake of the clarity of the sentence structure [*um der Klarheit des Satzbaus*], would have written *gignomenon* [the singular form in proper agreement with *tauton*]" (1990, 96). Alternative 3 seems to be a mistranslation. The Greek *gignomena* ("becoming") has a complement that this alternative ignores, *tauton* ("the same thing"). Hence, *gignomena* cannot have the existential meaning, "coming into existence," that this alternative assumes; it must serve as a linking verb with complement, meaning "becoming the same thing." One might defend the alternative interpretation of Desjardins on the grounds that, even if we revise her translation, we still ought to admit that humans in speech cause becoming—if not becoming an existent, then at any rate becoming same or different. However, such an interpretation of 15d4–6 puts it in contradiction with 15a1–6, which asserts that the one and many under discussion are not capable of being brought into being (μήτε γένεσιν μήτε ὄλεθρον προσδεχομένην *accepting neither genesis nor destruction*, 15b3–4). Desjardins gives no explanation for this contradictory consequence of her interpretation of the passage.

15d6 **οὔτε μὴ παύσηταί ποτε** *will surely never cease.* "The subjunctive . . . with οὐ μή may have the force of an emphatic denial" (Goodwin 1890, §295).

15d7–8 **τῶν λόγων αὐτῶν . . . πάθος ἐν ἡμῖν** *an effect in us of speech itself,* genitive of source (S §1410). I take the intensive pronoun αὐτῶν *itself* to indicate that the process (namely, of one and many coming to be the same) and the circulation (namely, of one running to many and many running to one) are nominal or linguistic phenomena. A nonlinguistic representation—imagine a statue or painting of Protarchus—does not have the appearance of impossible contradiction. In contrast, any verbal description of Protarchus, in the hands of an inept reasoner, can be made to appear an impossible contradiction. I take ἐν ἡμῖν *in us* to indicate the location of the effect: we have this experience (as at *Statesman* 277d7 [τὸ περὶ τῆς ἐπιστήμης πάθος ἐν ἡμῖν *our experience in regard to expert knowing*]; *Laws* 644e1 [πάθη ἐν ἡμῖν, *experiences of ours*]). The description of the process and circulation as *an effect or experience in us*, like the intensive αὐτῶν *itself*, rules out the opposing, unstated, contrast, that the process and circulation are *facts of nature*.

An alternative translation would take τῶν λόγων to be a possessive genitive (S §1297—as at 17d: τοῦ σώματος . . . πάθη *experiences of the body*): language itself has the *pathos*, condition or disease—a disease whose symptoms are the process and circulation reported by 15d4–6. On this reading, the ἐν ἡμῖν indicates the location of the speech itself: the speech takes place among us.

15d8 **ἀθάνατόν τι καὶ ἀγήρων** *something undying and ageless*. The two adjectives are found together in a traditional epithet of the gods (Homer, *Iliad* 2.447, 8.539, 12.323, 17.444; *Odyssey* 5.136, 5.218, 7.94, 7.257, 23.336).

15d9 **ἡσθεὶς ὥς** *after delighting as if* . . . In the *Republic* (539a–c), Socrates proposes to censor the practice of dialectic among the young, in order to prevent the young from abusing the power of dialectic (see Frede 1993, 8). But "late learners" can also abuse dialectic (*Sophist* 252a–c). See end of note to 16d1 for more discussion of Socrates' pejorative term, *young*.

15e2–3 **τοτὲ μὲν ἐπὶ θάτερα κυκλῶν καὶ συμφύρων εἰς ἕν, τοτὲ δὲ πάλιν ἀνειλίττων καὶ διαμερίζων** *sometimes rolling and kneading things that are different into one, then again at other times unrolling and dividing into parts*. Protarchus and the rest of Philebus' circle understand the problem of such inept reasoners. See note to 15d–16a.

16a–b: ***Protarchus warns that Socrates' present young audience may find his remarks insulting. Yet the audience recognizes that such immature controverting is a problem.***

16a6–b1 **γὰρ . . . εἴ τις τρόπος ἔστι καὶ μηχανὴ τὴν μὲν τοιαύτην ταραχὴν ἡμῖν ἔξω τοῦ λόγου εὐμενῶς πως ἀπελθεῖν, ὁδὸν δέ τινα καλλίω**

ταύτης ἐπὶ τὸν λόγον ἀνευρεῖν *For if there is some way and contrivance, with respect to such turmoil, for us agreeably to go somehow away outside of the [one-many] thesis and find out some finer path upon the [one-many] thesis.* Evidently, Protarchus and his side seek a device that will lead "away" from the trouble, "outside" and "on" the controversial thesis. Although Socrates has no trouble understanding, readers have found the grammar difficult. I have taken γὰρ *for,* though out of place by hyperbaton, to introduce this present indicative [ἔστι *is*] protasis (subordinate to a future indicative [συνακολουθήσομεν *we shall follow along*] apodosis, S §2360b). I take the pronoun ἡμῖν *for us* plus infinitives of purpose (S §2008) ἀπελθεῖν *to go away* and ἀνευρεῖν *to find out* as complements to τις τρόπος . . . καὶ μηχανὴ *some way and contrivance.* And I take τὴν . . . τοιαύτην ταραχὴν *with respect to such turmoil* as accusative of respect (S §1601b).

An alternative is to take μηχανὴ *contrivance* to introduce an accusative (ταραχὴν *turmoil*) plus infinitive (ἀπελθεῖν *to go away*) construction, "as if Ταραχή were a goddess to be propitiated, in possession of the λόγος, a fort to be captured" (Bury 1897, following Stallbaum 1842). Such an accusative-plus-infinitive construction with μηχανὴ is ad hoc for the μὲν clause, and raises a problem for the δέ clause: what is the accusative subject of ἀνευρεῖν? Stallbaum (1842) makes ὁδὸν the subject of ἀνευρεῖν, as if the active voice were passive (*viae . . . inveniendae* "a road to be discovered"). Bury (1897) instead quotes with seeming approval Badham (1878), who solves the problem by excising the entire δέ clause.

2. After accepting the hypothesis that speech causes the one-many puzzles, we can use the Divine Method.

16c–19b*: Socrates states five propositions that constitute the Divine Method. He illustrates, with the examples of letters, music, and dance, how every investigation should search for the one and the many by discovering all the intermediates.*

Some commentators complain about the trivial content of the Divine Method. As an account of scientific method it is at such a high level of generality as to be of no practical guidance. The complaint seems to miss the point of the

Divine Method. Socrates is not aiming to guide practicing scientists with his account, but only to describe scientific practice in such a way as to secure agreement to the One-Many Thesis. Socrates' description makes explicit the conditions under which scientific research is possible. Using this description to secure agreement to the One-Many Thesis in the face of the controverting of speech by immature reasoning is comparable, then, with Kant's transcendental deductions, which aim to secure agreement to the nature of knowledge in the face of skeptical controverting. It would miss Kant's point to object that his characterization of science there is of no practical guidance.

I interpret all of 16c9–e2 as a statement of the Divine Method. On my reading, the statement of the Divine Method consists of a main verb δεῖν *one ought* (16c10), governing the five infinitives boldfaced in steps 1–5 below. The use of the infinitive δεῖν is a standard indicator of reported discourse, and the infinitive form of the main verbs of all five steps indicates they belong together subordinated to δεῖν. The return of a finite main verb (παρέδοσαν *transmitted)* at 16e3, confirms that the reported, indirect discourse ends with the last words of the previous sentence χαίρειν ἐᾶν *to bid farewell* (e2).

The standard punctuation of this passage (found in Burnet 1901) puts a period after ἐχόντων (16c10). The period requires us to take the ὡς at 16c9 as a conjunction introducing indirect discourse. (The only exception I have found is Stallbaum 1820, which has a raised dot.) Such a construction, though perhaps not unprecedented (Stallbaum's [1842, 31] examples are unconvincing, but Bury [1897, 17] gives two defensible examples: *Laws* 624a7–b3 and *Republic* 437a6–7), is at least odd. With this punctuation, translators tend to follow the analysis of Bury (1897, 17n12), who treats the genitive absolute ὡς . . . ὄντων . . . ἐχόντων as if it were a "more regular" accusative-plus-infinitive construction—that is, as if 16c8–10 were equivalent to the following, which omits the ὡς and converts the genitive absolutes to accusative *τὰ λεγομένα* plus infinitives *εἶναι* and *ἔχειν*:

> ταύτην φήμην παρέδοσαν, ἐξ ἑνὸς μὲν καὶ πολλῶν *εἶναι τὰ* ἀεὶ *λεγομένα* εἶναι, πέρας δὲ καὶ ἀπειρίαν ἐν αὐτοῖς σύμφυτον *ἔχειν they transmitted this report, that the things that are always said to be are out of a one and many, and that they have in themselves by nature bound and unboundedness.*

In addition, the period produces another oddity in the clause that follows it. With the standard punctuation, the following sentence consists only of a subordinate clause: δεῖν οὖν ἡμᾶς . . . *therefore to be necessary for us* . . . Accordingly, interpreters supply an unstated subject and finite verb of telling or commanding. It is open to interpreters to supply as the subject of this main clause ταύτην φήμην *the report* (16c8), as Benardete (1993) does: "The ancients . . . passed it on as a report, 'Whatever are the things that are said to be, they are out of one and many, and they have in themselves an innate limit and unlimitedness.' It intimates, then, that we must . . ." But the punctuation makes the subject of the second sentence ambiguous. The subject might also be οἱ μὲν παλαιοί *the human beings of old* (c7) or perhaps the gods (θεῶν, c5). This ambiguity permits one to interpret the ten lines following δεῖν οὖν ἡμᾶς (to the end of e2) *either* as a continuing statement of the Divine Method *or* as inferences drawn from the Divine Method. Many translations try to capture this ambiguity. For example, Hackforth (1945): "The men of old . . . passed on this gift in the form of a saying: all things (so it ran) that are ever said to be consist of a one and a many, and have in their nature a conjunction of Limit and Unlimitedness. This then being the ordering of things we ought, *they said* . . ." Hackforth inserts the words "they said," leaving ambiguous who said them, the gods as part of the Method, as an aside in giving the Method, or the human beings of old interpreting the Method for us. The expedient of Diès (1949) (likewise, Fowler [1925], Gosling [1975], Waterfield [1982], Frede [1993], and Migliori [1993]) is to leave out any main clause and translate the infinitive δεῖν *to be necessary* as if it were the finite main verb δεῖ *[it] is necessary*: "The ancients transmitted to us this tradition, that all that one may say to exist is made of one and many and contains in itself, associated in origin *[originellement associées]*, limit and the infinite. Therefore, *it is necessary* for us . . ." No interpreter dissents and many interpreters—from Burnet (1901) to Delcomminette (2006)—explicitly follow Bury's (1897) punctuation.

As an alternative, I propose to replace the period between the ἐχόντων and δεῖν with a comma. The effect of this is more natural grammar that unambiguously makes steps 1–5 below the content of the Method. On my reading, the main clause of the statement of the Method (indirectly reported) is δεῖν *that it is necessary* (16c10–d1). The main clause is prefaced by a genitive absolute construction—namely, ὡς ἐξ ἑνὸς μὲν καὶ πολλῶν ὄντων τῶν ἀεὶ λεγομένων εἶναι πέρας δὲ καὶ ἀπειρίαν ἐν αὑτοῖς σύμφυτον ἐχόντων *on the grounds that the things that are always said to be are from a one and many and have in them by nature a bound and an unbounded* (16c9–10)—stating a supporting reason for the main clause. Smyth (1956, §§2070, 2122) gives examples where the Greek conjunction ὡς, introducing a genitive absolute clause, signifies that the speaker takes that clause to be true, so that the conjunction ὡς may be translated *on the grounds that.* Accordingly, I take it that this genitive absolute clause is strictly speaking not part of the Method, but an assumption made by the gods giving it.

The Method itself, then, is a set of instructions constituted by five sentences that are grammatically subordinate to the δεῖν. The δεῖν is an infinitive, which is a standard indicator of indirect discourse (S §2616), which itself indicates that it, and hence the five sentences subordinate to it—ζητεῖν *to search,* σκοπεῖν *to look,* [sc., σκοπεῖν *to look*], προςφέρειν *to apply,* and the infinitive idiom χαίρειν ἐᾶν *to dismiss from mind*—together report the contents of the φήμην *report* (16c8) transmitted to us by human beings of old, a step-by-step prescription for how to discover and learn:

1. ἀεὶ μίαν ἰδέαν περὶ παντὸς ἑκάστοτε θεμένους **ζητεῖν**—εὑρήσειν γὰρ ἐνοῦσαν *having posited that there is in each case always one form for everything,* ***to search*** *for it—for [it is needful that we] shall find it present in them* (16d1–2).
2. ἐὰν οὖν μεταλάβωμεν, μετὰ μίαν δύο, εἴ πως εἰσί, **σκοπεῖν**, εἰ δὲ μή, τρεῖς ἤ τινα ἄλλον ἀριθμόν whenever we comprehend, after one **to look** for somehow there are [two], and if not, for three or some other number (16d3–4).
3. καὶ τῶν ἓν ἐκείνων ἕκαστον πάλιν ὡσαύτως [sc., **σκοπεῖν**], μέχριπερ ἂν τὸ κατ' ἀρχὰς ἓν μὴ ὅτι ἓν καὶ πολλὰ καὶ ἄπειρά ἐστι μόνον ἴδῃ τις, ἀλλὰ καὶ ὁπόσα *[**to look**] into every one of those further ones in the same way, until a person sees, with respect to the starting one, not only that it is one, many, and unbounded, but also how many it is* (16d4–7).

4. τὴν δὲ τοῦ ἀπείρου ἰδέαν πρὸς τὸ πλῆθος μὴ **προσφέρειν** πρὶν ἄν τις τὸν ἀριθμὸν αὐτοῦ πάντα κατίδῃ τὸν μεταξὺ τοῦ ἀπείρου τε καὶ τοῦ ἑνός *not to* ***bring*** *the form of the unbounded* ***into contact with*** *the plurality until one discerns, in the plurality, every number between the unbounded and the one* (16d7–e1).
5. τότε δ' ἤδη τὸ ἓν ἕκαστον τῶν πάντων εἰς τὸ ἄπειρον μεθέντα **χαίρειν ἐᾶν** *just then—after letting each and every one go into the unbounded—****to dismiss them from mind*** (16e1–2).

After these five steps, the repetition of the finite verb παρέδοσαν *handed down* (at 16c8 and e3), confirms that we have reached the end of the indirect discourse that reported the content of the tradition.

16c8 **παρέδοσαν** *handed [X] over, transmitted [X].* I follow the standard interpretation in identifying the "very brilliant fire" with τέχνη *craft*. I agree with Huffman (1999, 11–17), followed by Delcomminette (2006, 64) that Prometheus is a mythical reference with no implications for historical philosophical predecessors. The alternative, more common, interpretation of this proposition is to identify this Prometheus with Pythagoras (see, for example, Gosling [1975, 165]). Delcomminette (2006, 64) points out the problem with such an alternative: it "would entail that no discoveries were made in any of the crafts [*dans le domaine des arts*], according to Plato, prior to the age of Pythagoras."

16c9 **ὡς** introduces a genitive absolute construction and marks the clause as held true by the speaker: *on the grounds that* (LSJ ὡς B.IV.1).

16d1 **ἡμᾶς** *we [newer, inferior human beings].* It solves interpretive puzzles to notice that it is *newer, inferior* human beings who practice the Divine Method. These subjects are the *recipients* of the legacy of the Divine Method. The implied contrast is with οἱ μὲν παλαιοί, κρείττονες ἡμῶν καὶ ἐγγυτέρω θεῶν οἰκοῦντες *the human beings of old who were superior to us and who used to dwell nearer to the gods* (16c7–8), the human beings who transmitted the report. We younger recipients by contrast are inferior to them and dwell further from the gods.

Any reading that does not recognize the implied contrast is vulnerable to a simple argument by Dancy (2005) that proves the incoherence of

16d9–10 with the Fourfold Division at 23c–e. Dancy's argument begins by noticing the ambiguity about τῶν ἀεὶ λεγομένων εἶναι at 16c9. Two meanings are possible, either *the things that are said to exist always* or *the things that are always said to be.* Because of the ambiguity it is not clear if 16c9 refers *exclusively* to the forms, or to the forms *among all the other things* that are "always said to be." The ambiguity makes no difference for Dancy's argument. In either case, the following premise is true:

(D1) In 16c9 τῶν ἀεὶ λεγομένων εἶναι means the forms (and maybe other things).

It obviously follows from 16c9 and D1 that:

(D2) The forms have in them bound and unbounded.

But, in making the Fourfold Division, Socrates makes clear that:

(D3) The kind Mix is the kind whose members contain bound and unbounded (23c12–d1).

It follows from D2 and D3 that:

(D4) The kind Mix contains the forms.

And, according to 26d7–9 below:

(D5) All members of the kind Mix are things that come to be (and perish).

It obviously follows from D4 and D5 that:

(D6) The forms come to be.

The conclusion D6 is absurd. Therefore, the Divine Method is inconsistent with the Fourfold Division.

Dancy's argument makes only three assumptions—D1, D3, and D5—to derive a contradiction. Assumption D3, that *only* Mix contains bound and unbounded, is impossible to deny. Likewise, assumption D5, that the members of the kind Mix come to be, is impossible to deny. If D1 is true—that is, if 16c9 is talking about the forms (and maybe other things)—then Dancy is right and the *Philebus* contains a contradiction at its heart. One way to save the *Philebus* from this contradiction is to say that the phrase, "have in them bound and unbounded," means something different in the two passages, and perhaps such duplicity is implicit in the readings of commentators prior to Dancy who did not emphasize the contradiction.

I propose an alternative that I introduce by reviewing the circumstances in which the gods sent down their gift. According to 16c6, the Divine Method was ἐρρίφη διά τινος Προμηθέως *sent down by some Prometheus* to our ancestors. According to 16c7–8, these human beings of old κρείττονες ἡμῶν καὶ ἐγγυτέρω θεῶν οἰκοῦντες *were superior to us and lived nearer to the gods*. An escape from Dancy's contradiction lies in the answer I propose to the questions: What does it mean to live ἐγγυτέρω θεῶν *nearer to the gods*? And in what way are οἱ παλαιοί *the human beings of old* superior to more recent human beings? I answer these questions by noticing the earlier distinction in the *Philebus* between vulgar and aristocratic versions of the One-Many Thesis (14d4–15a6). Socrates says that the δεδημευμένα *vulgar* (14d4) version of the One-Many Thesis belongs to a παιδαριώδη *childish* (14d7), hence younger, age. Socrates says that in such cases τὸ ἓν μὴ τῶν γιγνομένων τε καὶ ἀπολλυμένων *the one belongs to the realm of things that come to be and cease to be* (15a1–2). In contrast, he says, the nonvulgar (μήπω . . . δεδήμευται, 14e5–6), that is, aristocratic cases of the One-Many Thesis have to do with such things as ἕνα ἄνθρωπον . . . καὶ βοῦν ἕνα καὶ τὸ καλὸν ἓν καὶ τὸ ἀγαθὸν ἓν *one man, one ox, the one beautiful, or the one good* (15a4–6) that neither come to be nor cease to be. Socrates refers to ἡ πολλὴ σπουδὴ *the great zeal* (15a6–7) concerning such objects, for which Plato's *Republic* and *Symposium* give us a sense. For example, in the *Republic* (475a–480e) Socrates makes a distinction between "philosophers" and "lovers of sights and sounds." If you ask lovers of sights and sounds, "What is beauty?" the answer you will get is a perceptible object: "This city," or "this beach," or "that sunset." Philosophers, when asked what beauty is, will refer, by contrast, to the form *beauty*. One theme of the *Republic* is that philosophers are the true aristocrats. Although rare, they have a superior, more divine nature compared to the common or vulgar lovers of sights and sounds.

On the basis of this context, I give the following answer to the questions, what does it mean to live "nearer to the gods?" and in what way are "the ancients" superior to those living today?

(A1) People who recognize the existence of the forms and speak of them live nearer to the gods and are superior to those who do not recognize the existence of the forms and do not speak of them.

The answer A1 solves the problem raised by Dancy. Socrates said that the ancients, who were superior to us and lived nearer the gods, transmitted the Divine Method to inferiors who were living farther from the gods (16c8). If A1 is true, what made the ancients a race of aristocrats and marked them as living nearer to the gods was the fact that they recognized the existence of the forms. These ancients, however, wanted to give this tradition to a younger, more childish, age—that is, by A1, to people who are inferior insofar as they do not recognize the existence of the forms and never speak of the forms. It is, I admit, conceivable that the ancients were poor teachers who did not know how to transmit traditions to the younger generations, but charity requires us to assume, on the contrary, that they were competent teachers who knew what they were doing. Hence, I assume that the ancients knew how to make their tradition comprehensible to the younger, inferior generations. Accordingly, the ancients, when they transmitted the tradition, spoke as any good teachers do, *in terms that the inferior younger generations can understand*. But the younger generations, for the most part, are incapable of recognizing the existence of the forms. Therefore, the only things of which the younger generations speak are the things that come to be and perish. These things, that come to be and perish, are τὰ ἀεὶ λεγομένα εἶναι *the things always said to be* by the younger.

The inferiors did not need to become philosophers in order to use the Divine Method. The Divine Method, as Socrates tells us, is to be used for "research and learning and teaching one another" (16e3–4). Every discovery in any craft was made thanks to this gift (16c2–3). Engineers and doctors, shoemakers and aulos players, without needing to become philosophers, use this gift whenever they inquire, learn, or teach about their craft. Socrates' illustrations of the method in the case of music, dance, and letters (17a–d, 18b–d) show how the Divine Method works. In each of these cases, the Method finds the number and quality of what

Plato calls kinds. Then, as now, musicians, dancers, and grammarians must be able to recognize the objects of their expertises among sensory particulars and be able to classify them correctly. But it is possible to practice the five steps of the Divine Method (see note to 16b–e), as the ancients taught their successors to do, by looking at instances of the forms and making appropriate classifications among them, even for those who do not recognize the ontological commitment to the forms required by their practice.

In sum, when the ancients transmitted the Divine Method to a younger age, they spoke in terms that inferior youth can understand. Accordingly, the words τῶν ἀεὶ λεγομένων εἶναι *the things always said to be* at 16c9 refer to what the *inferiors* are always talking about, namely, the things that come to be and perish. And on this reading premise D1 of Dancy's argument, which requires that 16c9 refers to the forms, is false. That argument assumes the ancients were speaking to others as equals able to recognize the existence of the forms and cannot explain why Socrates takes pains, in introducing the Divine Method, to say that *superiors* deliberately handed it down to *inferiors*. And if D1 is false, the contradiction that Dancy found between the Divine Method and the Fourfold Division disappears.

Socrates and Protarchus disagree about pleasure. Socrates thinks that wise pleasure is opposite to foolish pleasure. Protarchus denies it is possible for pleasure to be divided from itself in this way (12d8). But there is no dispute between Socrates and Protarchus that pleasure *is one* (12c6–7), and no dispute that color and shape *are each one* (12e4). This recognition by Protarchus and Socrates distinguishes them as aristocratic philosophers, not vulgar lovers of sights and sounds. In terms of the *Republic*, ὁ φιλοθεάμων καὶ οὐδαμῇ ἀνεχόμενος ἄν τις ἓν τὸ καλὸν φῇ εἶναι καὶ δίκαιον καὶ τἆλλα οὕτω *the lover of the visible cannot bear to have anyone say that the beautiful or the just or anything is one in any way* (479a3–5). We should not be surprised, then, to find Socrates speaking to Protarchus about such things as man, ox, the beautiful, or the good, that neither come to be nor cease to be (15a4–6). Socrates and Protarchus are not the inferiors who, like ordinary craftworkers, are competent to use the Divine Method in developing and classifying knowledge but have disdain for the talk of philosophers. In general, we can avoid contradiction by paying attention not only to the theoretical claims that are made but also to who makes the claims and to whom.

16d1 **διακεκοσμημένων** *having been arranged.* For similar methods of division, see *Phaedrus* 265a–266b, *Sophist* 218b–231c and 264b–268d, *Statesman* 258b–268d; see also Muniz and Rudebusch (2018) for a discussion of what is being divided.

16d6 **τις** *any [inquirer, student, or teacher].* The indefinite pronoun refers to someone engaged in any of the activities σκοπεῖν καὶ μανθάνειν καὶ διδάσκειν *doing research, learning, or teaching* (16e3–4)—that is, researchers, students, and teachers.

16e–17a: ***Socrates emphasizes the importance of complete enumeration of ones and manies and distinguishes dialectic from eristic discussion and illustrates how vocal sound is one, many, and unbounded.***

According to Gosling (1975), it is difficult to harmonize Plato's description of the Divine Method with the illustrations of it that he provides, because the method apparently can only be used to analyze genus/species relations, yet the illustrations involve relations that are not of this type. Hampton (1990) solves Gosling's problem by interpreting the method to include more than genus/species relations. Such broadening is also required on my interpretation. Every species is a subkind of its genus, but not every subkind is a species of a genus. For example, although Wise Human Being and Foolish Human Being are subkinds of the kind Human Being, that kind is not a genus of which those two subkinds are species. See note to 15b–c.

The Divine Method consists of five steps (see note to 16b–e):

1. ἀεὶ μίαν ἰδέαν περὶ παντὸς ἑκάστοτε θεμένους **ζητεῖν**—εὑρήσειν γὰρ ἐνοῦσαν *having posited that there is in each case always one form for everything,* ***to search*** *for it—for [it is needful that we] shall find it present in them* (16d1–2).
2. ἐὰν οὖν μεταλάβωμεν, μετὰ μίαν δύο, εἴ πως εἰσί, **σκοπεῖν**, εἰ δὲ μή, τρεῖς ἤ τινα ἄλλον ἀριθμόν whenever we comprehend, after one

to look for two, if somehow there are [two], and if not, for three or some other number (16d3–4).

3. καὶ τῶν ἓν ἐκείνων ἕκαστον πάλιν ὡσαύτως [sc., **σκοπεῖν**], μέχριπερ ἂν τὸ κατ' ἀρχὰς ἓν μὴ ὅτι ἓν καὶ πολλὰ καὶ ἄπειρά ἐστι μόνον ἴδῃ τις, ἀλλὰ καὶ ὁπόσα *[**to look**] into every one of those further ones in the same way, until a person sees, with respect to the starting one, not only that it is one, many, and unbounded, but also how many it is* (16d4–7).
4. τὴν δὲ τοῦ ἀπείρου ἰδέαν πρὸς τὸ πλῆθος μὴ **προσφέρειν** πρὶν ἄν τις τὸν ἀριθμὸν αὐτοῦ πάντα κατίδῃ τὸν μεταξὺ τοῦ ἀπείρου τε καὶ τοῦ ἑνός *not to **bring** the form of the unbounded **into contact with** the plurality until one discerns, in the plurality, every number between the unbounded and the one* (16d7–e1).
5. τότε δ' ἤδη τὸ ἓν ἕκαστον τῶν πάντων εἰς τὸ ἄπειρον μεθέντα **χαίρειν ἐᾶν** *just then—after letting each and every one go into the unbounded—**to dismiss them from mind*** (16e1–2).

Socrates uses vocal sound as an example.

> When someone, whether a god or a god-inspired man—there is an Egyptian story that his name was Theuth—observed that sound was unbounded, he was the first to notice that the vowel sounds in the unbounded were not one but many, and again that there were other elements which were not vowels but make a sort of sound [from the vocal cords], and they, too, have a number; and he distinguished a third kind of letter that we now call mutes. Then he divided the unsounded—the mutes—until he distinguished each individual one, and he treated the vowels and the intermediates in the same way, until he knew the number of them and gave to each and all the name "letter." (18b7–c6)

As an illustration, figure 1 shows one way Theuth might have completed his division of the Greek alphabet.

Each box in the figure represents a kind. Each kind is identified by its form and is divisible in virtue of its members (see Muniz and Rudebusch 2018). To understand the kind/form distinction, a helpful analogy is a rancher's herd of cattle, which is defined by a brand and is divisible in terms of its

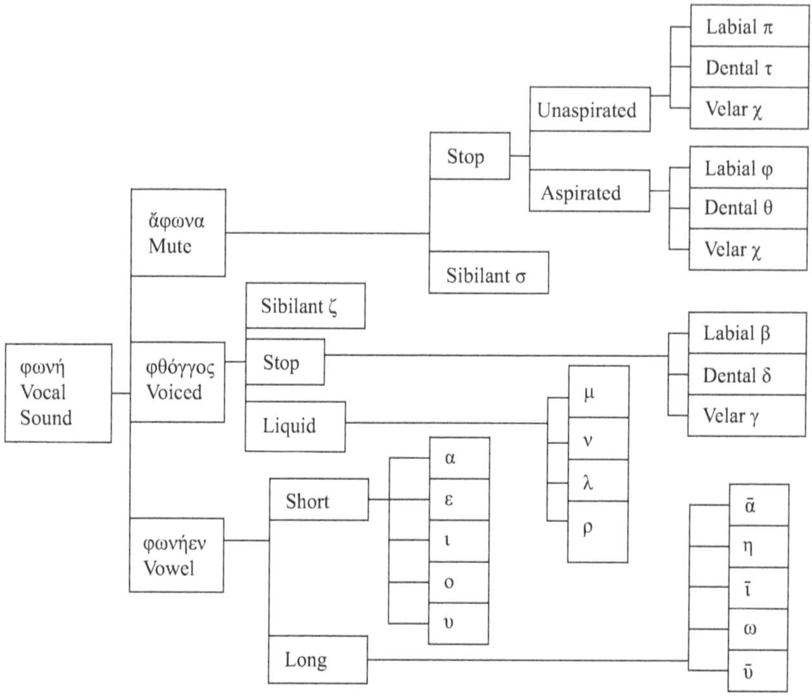

Figure 1. Division of Greek letters. Author's construction showing how Theuth might have divided vocal sound.

members, the individual steers. For example, the kind represented at bottom center, Long, is like a herd defined by its brand, in this case the kind/herd is defined by its form/brand *vocal sound that is a long vowel,* a one shared by each of the kind's five members, represented by the boxes to its right: ᾱ, η, ῑ, ω, and ῡ.

The box on the far left, Vocal Sound, represents the One relative to step 1 of Theuth's inquiry, a kind defined by the form *vocal sound.* According to 18b8–c3, step 2 of Theuth's inquiry found exactly three forms, φωνήεν *vowel,* φθόγγος *voiced,* and ἄφωνα *mute.* As an alternative, Menn (1998, 292) interprets φθόγγος to be the kind including "liquids and nasals and sibilants," and he translates ἄφωνα as "stop"; LSJ, however, notices that at *Theaetetus* 203b3 the definition of the letter sigma is that it is τῶν ἀφώνων. Since sigma is a mute but not a stop, Menn's interpretation of ἄφωνα is inconsistent with that definition. LSJ (φθόγγος II.1) cites *Philebus* 18c1 and gives the meaning of φθόγγου there as "semi-vowel," supporting Menn's interpretation of φθόγγος. LSJ evidently is echoing "the Roman grammarians, who applied the term ("semi-vowel") to the spirants and liquids, including nasals" (*OED*, "semi-vowel"). Such a meaning for φθόγγος would double-list sigma as both φθόγγος (since it is spirant) and ἄφωνα (since it is mute). And such a meaning for φθόγγος would also have Theuth omit from his classification the voiced stops beta, gamma, and delta. It is better, therefore, to translate φθόγγου τινος at 18c1 as "a sort of sound." And which sort of sound is made more precise at 18c5: it is the sort containing τὰ μέσα *the intermediates.* To make the best sense of the text, I propose that τὰ μέσα, intermediate between vowels and mute vocal sounds, are voiced vocal sounds. As figure 1 shows, such an interpretation of Theuth's initial tripartite division could give a proper classification of Greek vocal sound, leaving out only the double consonants *xi* and *psi*, which is as it should be, since each of those written letters represents not one but two vocal sounds.

Socrates does not go through the iterations of step 3 with his example. Figure 1 presents one way to do so. All thirty-six kinds—from Vocal Sound, Mute, Voiced, and Vowel down to the Labials, Dentals, and Velars—represent the Many of Theuth's inquiry. Although many, this division-tree of thirty-six kinds is not unbounded. The Divine Method's step 4 gives us permission τὴν τοῦ ἀπείρου ἰδέαν πρὸς τὸ πλῆθος προςφέρειν *to bring the form of the unbounded into contact with the plurality* of the kinds and subkinds of vocal sound only after figure 1 is established as a complete representation of every kind of vocal sound relative to the research, learning, or teaching at hand. This event of προςφέρειν *bringing into contact* calls for interpretation. Certainly this προςφέρειν requires as its cause someone with expert knowledge of the thirty-six forms associated with the kinds. Those forms will set bounds in various ways on the unbounded mouth noises that the expert can make, such as shorter or longer duration of the noise, more or less aspiration and use of larynx, higher or lower or forward or backward position of tongue, and more or less open position of jaw and lips. I interpret the προςφέρειν as what later is described as μειγνὺς *mixing* (Protarchus introduces the verb with this participle at 25e3), which produces members of the kind Mix.

Socrates defines the third kind, Mix, as ἐν . . . ἐγγιγνόμενα *born among* the things that are more and less (26a2, see also 25e7 and 26a6)—given ἡ ὀρθὴ κοινωνία *the right combination* (25e7) of the kinds Bound and Unbounded. Socrates later will give examples of mixing that produce health and music (25e7–26a4), and it is possible to use vocal sound as another example as follows. Speech comes to be in the realm of mouth noises. As such, the noises are indefinite in length, shorter and longer: "aoi," "aaaooouuuiii." They are indefinitely rougher and smoother: "aaahhhhchchch." They are made by indefinite variations of tongue and lip: "blrrmndzzpt." There is a sense in which, when we learn to speak, we learn the right combination of bounds to these noises. Greek vowels have limited quality—for example, the sound of omicron as opposed to iota—and limited quantity, long vowels being twice as long as short vowels—for example, omega and omicron. Greek consonants are limited to definite labial, dental, and velar forms, with or without definite forms of aspiration and of sound, of nasality, of liquidity, and of stops. The knowledge of vocal sound (in this area of research, learning, or teaching) is the knowledge of the right combinations, so as to give birth, so to speak, among the many discordant noises in the world, to articulate letters, giving birth by putting number into and putting other bounds upon noise. Expert phonetic speech pronounces letters, letters that come in and out of being.

17a1–2 **πολλὰ θᾶττον καὶ βραδύτερον ποιοῦσι τοῦ δέοντος** *they make a many faster or slower than one ought.* Paley (1873), quoted in Bury (1897) suggests how one might do a too-hasty division of pleasure. "Pleasure! oh, of course, pleasures are quite countless and endless." On the other hand, "an example of someone who moves too slowly would be Philebus, who insists at the beginning of the dialogue that pleasure is one, and is reluctant to see that the many pleasures might have very different natures, especially when considered from the point of view of having some of these incorporated into a pattern for successful living" (Moravcsik 1979, 93).

17b–d: ***Socrates illustrates how musical sound is one, many, and unbounded.***

17b7–8 **ἀλλ' ὅτι πόσα τ' ἐστὶ καὶ ὁποῖα** *but because [we know] how many and what sorts [the sound units] are.* The unstated subject of ἐστὶ is neuter plural, not feminine plural, in agreement with the complements πόσα and ὁποῖα. Accordingly, the subject cannot be the feminine plural φωναί *sounds* but ought to be a neuter plural such as τὰ κατ' ἐκείνην τὴν τέχνην *the things conforming to that skill* (see this noun phrase as a neuter singular at 17c1)—namely, units of sound (in Greek, perhaps, φωνήματα, although according to *TLG* this word does not occur in Plato). Protarchus' superlative assent at b10, Ἀληθέστατα, shows he has no trouble understanding that this cause explains why each of us is able to speak and understand speech.

17b11–12 **Καὶ μὴν καὶ τὸ μουσικὸν ὃ τυγχάνει ποιοῦν, τοῦτ' ἔστι ταὐτόν.** *And indeed this, which actually is the thing making [each of us] musical, is the same thing [as that which makes each of us grammatical]*—namely, τὸ πόσα τ' ἐστὶ καὶ ὁποῖα εἰδέναι *to know how many and of what sorts [the sound units] are.* On my analysis the τὸ belongs with ποιοῦν and Socrates in his speech says it out of place in order to echo τὸ γραμματικὸν . . . ποιοῦν at 17b8–9. (As an alternative, Paley [1873] thought the τὸ out of place was owing to a scribe's mistake.)

17b13 **Πῶς;** *how [is the cause of musical skill the same as the cause of grammatical skill]?* Socrates' answer, which I interpret to include 17b1–d2, will explain that in both cases the cause is knowing the quantity and quality of the objects in division-trees belonging to each skill, objects that in both cases are sounds, that is, "sound units."

17c1–2 **Φωνὴ μέν που καὶ τὸ κατ' ἐκείνην τὴν τέχνην ἐστὶ μία ἐν αὐτῇ.** This is the text in manuscripts T and W, which include the words καὶ τὸ. As Delcomminette (2020) says, "It is hard to see [*on voit mal*] how they could have been inserted in error." Given this text, I propose to understand the substantive τὸ κατ' ἐκείνην τὴν τέχνην *the thing conforming to that skill* coordinate with Φωνὴ and introduced by the epexegetic καὶ. Such an explication makes sense, since Φωνὴ has been used for vocal sound and is now clarified to mean sound in a more general sense—namely, the sound units as studied in different ways by both skill at vocal sound and at music. The change in gender from the feminine Φωνὴ *sound* to the neuter τὸ *the [sound unit]* recalls the neuter subject of ἐστὶ at 17b7–8 and is continued in the next speech by the neuter adjectives βαρὺ and ὀξύ. A literal translation would be as follows: *Sound—that is, the [sound unit] conforming to that skill [musical skill] is, I suppose, one in it [i.e., musical skill].*

An alternative analysis of T takes τὸ κατ' ἐκείνην τὴν τέχνην to be an accusative of respect with the meaning of the idiom τὸ κατά given in LSJ κατά B.IV.2 (τὸ κατ' ὑμέας *as far as concerns you*,τὸ κατ' ἐμέ *as far as I am concerned*). According to this alternative, the καὶ is an adverb modifying ἐστὶ. Thus Fowler (1925): "Sound is one in the art of music also, so far as that art is concerned." This appears to be the manuscript and the analysis behind the translation of Frede (1993): "Sound is also the unit in this art, just as it was in writing."

Finally, there are two possible readings of ἐκείνην τὴν τέχνην *that skill.* Both Fowler and I take it "with reference to what has gone immediately before" (LSJ ἐκεῖνος I.1)—namely τοῦτο ὃ τυγχάνει μουσικὸν τὸ ποιοῦν *this thing actually making [each of us] musical* at 17b11. Frede, alternatively, takes ἐκείνην τὴν τέχνην to be *skill at writing* (better: *vocal sound)*—that is, *the more remote* of the two skills, in opposition to *the nearer* skill at music. But sense does not require this alternative, and it faces a problem. According to LSJ, the remote as opposed to nearer reading of ἐκεῖνος *that* requires an instance of οὗτος *this.* But there is no instance of οὗτος in this sentence, only the nondemonstrative pronoun αὐτῇ *it.*

In contrast, manuscript B and other manuscripts omit the words καὶ τὸ: *sound is a one in it [musical skill] in accordance with that skill [at vocal sound].* Frede (1997) endorses this alternative, giving this free translation: Der Ton, der zu dieser Kunst gehort, erweist sich bei ihr als Einheit *the sound, which belongs to this art, shows itself in it as unity.*

Gosling (1975) chooses a text that retains the καὶ but omits the τὸ and also omits the ἐν αὐτῇ *in it* (not *in itself,* as Gosling [1975, 86] translates in his discussion): Φωνὴ μέν που καὶ ~~τὸ~~ κατ' ἐκείνην τὴν τέχνην ἐστὶ μία ~~ἐν~~

αὐτῇ *sound I suppose according to that skill is also a one.* His translation gives κατά the meaning *in* (LSJ B.I.2): "You will grant that vocal sound in the skill of letters also is one."

17c4–5 **ὁμότονον** *same-in-tone,* as in Nicomachus (1895, 11.5.7).

17c11–e3 **ἐπειδὰν λάβῃς τὰ διαστήματα ὁπόσα ἐστὶ . . . , καὶ ὁποῖα, καὶ τοὺς ὅρους τῶν διαστημάτων, καὶ τὰ . . . συστήματα . . . ἔν τε ταῖς κινήσεσιν αὖ τοῦ σώματος ἕτερα . . . ἐνόντα . . . —ὅταν γὰρ αὐτά τε λάβῃς οὕτω, τότε ἐγένου σοφός, ὅταν τε ἄλλο τῶν ἓν ὁτιοῦν . . . ἕλῃς, οὕτως ἔμφρων περὶ τοῦτο γέγονας** *whenever you grasp how many intervals there are . . . and what sorts [of intervals there are], and the boundaries of the intervals, and the scales . . . and moreover other things that are in the movements of bodies . . . —yes, whenever you grasp them in this way, then you become wise, and whenever you take hold of any other of the ones whatsoever, in this way you have become wise concerning this thing.* The ἐπειδὰν *whenever* condition requires that one grasp the number of musical intervals, and their qualities and boundaries, and also the musical scales, and associated dance rhythms, too, in order to become wise. Socrates summarizes and generalizes from the ἐπειδὰν condition with a pair of ὅταν conditionals introduced with a confirmatory γάρ, "yes, whenever you grasp them [i.e., intervals, scales, and dance rhythms]" before he states the τότε *then* clause with a gnomic aorist: *then you become wise [in that field].*

The τε . . . αὖ *and moreover* at 17d4 coordinates the noun phrase ἔν ταῖς κινήσεσιν τοῦ σώματος ἕτερα ἐνόντα *other things that are in the movements of bodies* with the previous four noun phrases (ὁπόσα, ὁποῖα, ὅρους, and συστήματα) coordinated by three instances of καί (LSJ τε A.I.4 "a single τε [*and*] joins a . . . clause or sentence to what precedes"). The two instances of τε at 17e1 coordinate their two ὅταν conditional statements. Scholars have found "some cause for suspicion both in οὕτως and γέγονας after the aorist" (Bury 1897) in the last conditional at 17e1–3. As Badham (1878) says, "the tenses are strangely chosen, ὅταν λάβῃς, ἐγένου—ὅταν ἕλῃς, γέγονας." Adam (1900) proposes a plausible emendation of ἕλῃς to ἔχῃς (LSJ ἔχω A.I.9 "*possess mentally, understand*"), noting the advantage: "as ἔχω with this meaning is the perfect of λαμβάνω,

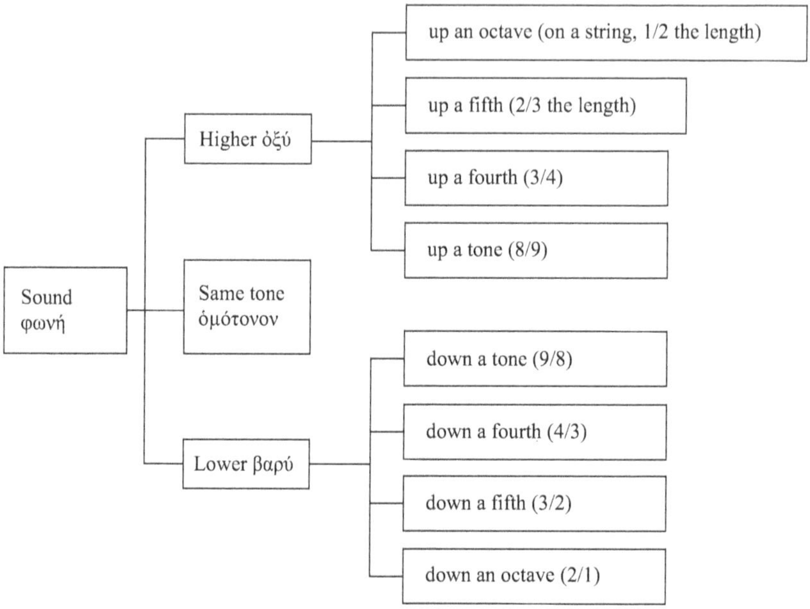

Figure 2. Division of Greek musical intervals. Author's construction showing the division Socrates might mean.

the tenses fall into their proper sequence: ὅταν λάβῃς, ἐγένου—ὅταν ἔχῃς, γέγονας" *whenever you grasp, you become—whenever you possess, you have become.*

As Delcomminette says (2006, 130), "the type of musical theory to which Socrates refers here is not entirely clear." In figure 2 I have not speculated on how to complete the division beyond the clue given by *Republic* 400a5–6—namely, that harmony of intervals is a four-part division. Accordingly, I have divided the *intervals of highness and lowness* into four each: up (and down) by an octave, a fifth, a fourth, and a tone. I ignore the traditional modes: Dorian, Ionian, and so on.

17d: ***Socrates sketches how dance movement is one, many, and unbounded.***

17d4–6 **ἕτερα τοιαῦτα . . . πάθη γιγνόμενα, ἃ δὴ δι' ἀριθμῶν μετρηθέντα δεῖν αὖ φασι ῥυθμοὺς καὶ μέτρα ἐπονομάζειν** *[whenever you grasp] other things such as [i.e., similar to music] that come to be effects [of music],* *which [effects], after they have been put into measures by numbers, they say we ought to name rhythms and measures.* The kind Dance is divided not by sound, but rhythm, where the unbounded includes the fast and the slow. The Greeks seem to have classified dance steps relative to the time the foot is lifted up (ἄνω χρόνος) and the time it is stepping down (κάτω χρόνος). At *Republic* 400a4–5 Glaucon says, τρί' ἄττα ἐστὶν εἴδη ἐξ ὧν αἱ βάσεις πλέκονται *there are some three forms from which the dance steps are woven.* These forms were the three kinds of rhythms defined by the ratios of the length of time for the up stepping to the down stepping. These ratios are 1:1, found in dactyls (a long up followed by two short downs:—˘˘); 1:2, found in iambs (˘—); and 2:3, found in paeons (—˘˘˘). See Moutsopoulos (1959, §§48–50) and West (1992, 129–53 and 242–45), summarized in Delcomminette (2006, 141–42).

17d–e: ***Socrates generalizes from the examples: a successful demonstration must produce a complete division of the subject at hand, identifying all the intermediates between one and many.***

17e3 **τὸ δ' ἄπειρόν σε ἑκάστων καὶ ἐν ἑκάστοις πλῆθος ἄπειρον ἑκάστοτε ποιεῖ τοῦ φρονεῖν καὶ οὐκ ἐλλόγιμον οὐδ' ἐνάριθμον** *the unbounded multitude of each and in each on each occasion makes you unacquainted with being intelligent and not to be taken into account or counted,* a play on the two meanings of ἄπειρόν, with further play on the adjectives of prestige, ἐλλόγιμον and ἐνάριθμον, with etymologies derived from counting and number.

18a–d: ***Socrates generalizes from the examples: a successful research program must produce a complete division of the subject at hand, identifying all the intermediates between one and many. He discusses grammar as a research and teaching discipline.***

18a8–b2 **οὐκ ἐπ' ἀπείρου φύσιν δεῖ βλέπειν εὐθὺς ἀλλ' ἐπί τινα ἀριθμόν, οὕτω καὶ . . . μὴ ἐπὶ τὸ ἓν εὐθύς, ἀλλ' [ἐπ'] ἀριθμὸν αὖ τινα πλῆθος ἕκαστον ἔχοντά τι κατανοεῖν** *one ought not look immediately at a nature of an unbounded but at some number, and in this way . . . not [look] immediately at the one, but at some number, each [number] having some* *quantity to understand*. This translation does not bracket ἐπ' at b1 but preserves the text of the manuscripts by letting βλέπειν *look* govern all four ἐπί *at* phrases. Following Diès (1949) and Delcomminette (2020) it takes κατανοεῖν to limit the meaning of the substantive πλῆθος (S §2001, 2004). The alternative of Burnet (1901) (followed by Gosling [1975] and Frede [1993]) is to bracket ἐπ' and to make ἀριθμὸν *number* the direct object of κατανοεῖν *understand*.

18b8 **λέγων – ὅς** Following Delcomminette (2020) and *pace* Burnet (1901), I end the interjection here, "on pain [*sous peine*] of making Theuth, the Egyptian god, the inventor of the *Greek* alphabet."

18c2 **εἶδος** *form* here and below, not "kind" or "class." See introduction: *Genos*, *Phusis*, and *Eidos*.

18d–20a: *The method of collection and division is necessary for Socrates and Protarchus to investigate how knowing or pleasure is the good for human beings.*

18d4–e1 *The Divine Method is relevant to the inquiry between knowing and pleasure*. The premises for this conclusion are as follows:

P1 The inquiry was, "Which is preferable in a human life, wisdom or pleasure?" (18e3–4).

P2 The Divine Method requires the inquirers (namely, Socrates and Protarchus) to explain:

- a How is it that knowing is one and many (18e9)—that is, whether there are forms of knowing (19b2–3).
- b How is it that pleasure is one and many (18e9)—that is, whether there are forms of pleasure (19b2–3).
- c What number (of forms) pleasure possesses before that (number) become unbounded (19a1–2).
- d What number (of forms) knowing possesses before that (number) becomes unbounded (19a1–2).
- e How is it that pleasure is not immediately unbounded (18e9–a1); that is, what are the qualities of each of the forms of pleasure (19b3).

f How is it that knowing is not immediately unbounded (18e9–a1); that is, what are the qualities of each of the forms of knowing (19b4).

The Divine Method requires answers to questions a–f because:

P2.1 The inquirers (namely, Socrates and Protarchus) agree that knowing is one and pleasure is one (18e6).

P2.2 The Divine Method shows that the inquirers are competent only if, for each *one, similarity,* and *identity* (in their account), they are able to answer the questions a–f (19b5–8).

19b5 **ὦ παῖ Καλλίου** *son of Callias.* Although this Callias is often identified as Callias III, Nails (2002, 257) reasons that such an identification is "unwise." Callias III had two sons (mentioned by Socrates in Plato's *Apology* 20a). One is Hipponicus III; the other is unnamed but born in or after 412, making him too young to have had a conversation with Socrates, who died in 399. Both "Protarchus" and "Callias" were common names at the time.

19b6–8 **κατὰ παντὸς ἑνὸς καὶ ὁμοίου καὶ ταὐτοῦ . . . καὶ τοῦ ἐναντίου** in regard to each *thing that is one, that is like, that is the same,* and *that is opposite* (i.e., *many, unlike, different).* This is a restatement of the requirement at 19b3 (itself a restatement of 17b7–8), that relevant skill about *X* requires one to know what kinds and subkinds of *X* there are, including their number and qualities.

δυνάμενοι *being able.* This plural participle is circumstantial to the singular γένοιτο, despite the difference in number. It expresses the condition εἰ μὴ δυναίμεθα τοῦτο . . . δρᾶν *if we were not able to do this,* a future less vivid protasis (S §2344, 2067).

19c2–3 **καλὸν μὲν τὸ σύμπαντα γιγνώσκειν τῷ σώφρονι, δεύτερος δ' εἶναι πλοῦς δοκεῖ μὴ λανθάνειν αὐτὸν αὑτόν** *to know all things [is] fine for the man of sound mind, but a "second sailing" [for the sound-minded man who is inexpert] seems to be not to escape noticing himself [i.e., his ignorance].* Brianna Zgurich suggests Hesiod's ranking may be in the back of Protarchus' mind:

οὗτος μὲν πανάριστος ὃς αὐτὸς πάντα νοήσῃ,
ἐσθλὸς δ' αὖ κἀκεῖνος ὃς εὖ εἰπόντι πίθηται.
ὃς δέ κε μήτ' αὐτὸς νοέῃ μήτ' ἄλλου ἀκούων
ἐν θυμῷ βάλληται, ὃ δ' αὖτ' ἀχρήιος ἀνήρ.

That man is altogether best who considers all things himself,
and he, again, is good who listens to a good adviser;
but whoever neither thinks for himself nor keeps in mind what another tells him,
he is an unprofitable man. (*Works and Days* 293–97, trans. Hugh G. Evelyn-White)

The figure of speech δεύτερος . . . πλοῦς *second sailing* means *a second-best course of action* or *the next best way.* The figure is from those who use oars when the wind fails (LSJ πλόος). Burnyeat (2004, 85) argues the proverb here is "bound to evoke" its use at *Phaedo* 99c9–d1, since in both cases the speaker is "mindful of his own ignorance," and "recoiling from a vastly ambitious explanatory enterprise beyond their power." Socrates seems to repeat the figure of speech at *Philebus* 59c4 δεύτερος [sc., πλοῦς], and the Eleatic Stranger uses it at *Statesman* 300c2.

19c3–4 **τί δή μοι τοῦτο εἴρηται τὰ νῦν;** *Just why has this been stated by me, with respect to the present events?* "With passive verbs (usually in the perfect and pluperfect) . . . the person in whose interest an action is done, is put in the dative. The notion of agency does not belong to the dative, but it is a natural inference that the person interested is the agent" (S §1488).

19d5–6 **<ἃ> κτᾶσθαι δεῖν** The ἃ is found in manuscript Ven. 189 but not B or T. The addition of ἃ creates a relative clause: *which things [you say] it is necessary to possess.* Without ἃ, the infinitive construction κτᾶσθαι δεῖν lacks a conjunction coordinating it with the previous clause (asyndeton, S §3016): *[reason . . . is a good,] is necessary [for us] to possess.*

19e1–2 **πρὶν ἂν . . . πέρας . . . γένηταί τι** *until a sufficient determination had been made* (πρὶν with aorist subjunctive after negation = ἕως, "to express an action preceding the action of the antecedent clause, the verb in which [ἀφήσομεν] is future," LSJ πρὶν II.2.a).

καθάπερ οἱ παῖδες *like children* "may be an allusion to Socrates' ὦ παῖδες in 16b" (Bury 1897).

19e4 **τῶν ὀρθῶς δοθέντων ἀφαίρεσις οὐκ ἔστι** "*one can't take back what is given by the rules* [*dans les règles*]" Delcomminette 2020.

20a5–6 **ἡδονῆς εἴδη σοι καὶ ἐπιστήμης διαιρετέον** *one must divide forms of pleasure and expert knowing.* Kinds can be divided into subkinds, but forms cannot be divided into subforms. Socrates is using εἴδη *forms* figuratively to refer to kinds. See introduction: *Genos, Phusis,* and *Eidos.*

3. The identity of the good is complex; it cannot be identified simply with either pleasure or knowing.

20b–c: ***Socrates' two thought experiments.***

20b3 **πρὸς δὲ αὖ τοῖς** is the variant in manuscript B. This reading makes sense only if τοῖς has the older, poetic meaning τούτοις, hence the meaning *in addition to these things.* This variant requires us, implausibly, to postulate a then-familiar but now-lost catchphrase. That catchphrase would be comparable to a contemporary English speaker using "thou" for "you," to evoke the solemnity of Socrates' recall of (another ancient) divine gift. The second variant πρὸς δὲ αὐτοῖς is in two manuscripts. To make sense of this we might take αὐτοῖς to intensify ἡμῖν, hence the meaning *in reference to us ourselves,* which is farfetched. The third variant is in manuscript T: πρὸς δὲ τούτοις *in addition to these things,* so that Socrates would be saying that "he has not only lost fear but also gained new light—two conditions for proceeding with the argument" (Bury 1897). This third variant is so plain that it falls under the suspicion of being a scribe's fix of a corrupt manuscript

20b4 **τίς . . . θεῶν** *some one of the gods.* Socrates introduces his two thought experiments as divine revelation, giving great emphasis to his confidence in them and their refutation of the first turn of the inquiry (see note to 11d–12b), which framed the question in exclusive terms: "What condition of the soul—pleasure or knowing—is the good?"

20b6–7 **ὄναρ ἢ καὶ ἐγρηγορώς** *in a dream or quite awake.* Socrates reports here the experience of not being sure if it was a visitation of a god (perhaps

Aphrodite herself?) who awoke him or if the god conveyed the experience in a dream. Burnyeat (2004, 85) sees in these words a reference to the distinction Socrates draws at *Republic* 476b–d between those in a dream state (as I interpret it [see note to 16d1], these are the lovers of sights and sounds who think all there is to beauty is beautiful perceptible objects, i.e., nominalists) and those who are quite awake (the philosophers who recognize the existence of the intelligible form *beauty* apart from perceptible objects). "Only philosophers are awake . . . because they alone are aware of the difference between Forms and their sensible participants" (Burnyeat 2004, 85). It is a problem for Burnyeat that he does not discuss two other instances of the opposite states in the formula ὄναρ οὔθ' ὕπαρ *in a dream or awake* (*Philebus* 36e5 and 65e5).

20b9 **καίτοι** *and yet*. The use of this particle likely indicates that Socrates is "pulling [the inquiry] up abruptly" (Denniston 1966, 557), in abandoning, at least here in the first turn, the claim that the answer requires the skill of one able to discriminate the number and quality of pleasures and expertises.

20c4 **Τῶν δέ γε εἰς τὴν διαίρεσιν εἰδῶν** *of the forms in division*. Kinds are divided into subkinds with reference to their distinctive forms. Those forms are the "forms in division."

οὐδὲν ἔτι *[In order to see that neither the kind Pleasure nor the kind Knowing is the same as the kind Good, they will] no longer [need to divide Pleasure into subkinds—that is, use the Divine Method]*. Socrates does not seem ever to take back this claim that he no longer needs a division of forms of pleasure. This raises the difficult question why he made so much of the method a few pages earlier. The square brackets I have added to this proposition follow Delcomminette (2006, 164). An alternative interpretation (Striker 1970, 9; Gosling 1975, 177, 211–12; Waterfield 1982, 37) in effect looks at this proposition as follows: "The inquirers will no longer have additional need of the division of the kinds of pleasure [throughout the remainder of the dialogue]." This alternative must explain away the Fourfold Division (22d–30e) and the division of the kinds Pleasure (31a–55b) and Expert Knowing (55d–59d).

20c5–6 **δείξει** *it will be evident*. The active voice of this verb, when intransitive, can have a middle meaning (Bury 1897).

20d7–8 **Τόδε . . . περὶ αὐτοῦ ἀναγκαιότατον . . . εἶναι λέγειν** *[it is] most necessary to say that this thing [i.e., the sufficient] is a feature of ["is about"] it [namely, the good],* an accusative-plus-infinitive construction after λέγειν, which is infinitive after ἀναγκαιότατον. Smyth's (1956, §3008g) alternative analysis is that this sentence is the sort of anacoluthon where the "verb that should have been principal" has been attracted into a relative clause, so that εἶναι properly should be ἐστὶ. His translation is: "this indeed is, as I think, most necessary to state about it."

20d8 **ἐφίεται [αὐτοῦ]** *aims at [it]. TLG* finds the middle voice of ἐφίημι twenty times in Plato; in every instance but this it had a genitive object, which I supply from the previous line.

20d9 **ἑλεῖν [αὐτὸ] καὶ [αὐτὸ] περὶ αὑτὸ κτήσασθαι** *to get [it] and to secure [it] about oneself.* The prepositional phrase περὶ plus accusative after a verb of possession is often used with persons who are about one as "attendants, connexions, associates, or colleagues" (LSJ περί C.I.2).

20d10 **τῶν ἄλλων οὐδὲν φροντίζει πλὴν τῶν ἀποτελουμένων ἅμα ἀγαθοῖς** *[anything aware of the good] is not concerned with other things except those things that are produced together with goods.* Bury (1897) found this a curious remark, leading him to "doubt the correctness of the text." But it is reasonable for things hunting and aiming at the good only to be concerned with nongoods when those things come as a package with good things. Socrates' example at *Gorgias* 468b1–4 is that one only walks because one supposes that walking will occur together with something better than what happens with nonwalking, while standing still only supposing it to occur together with something better than what happens with walking.

20e–22c: ***A thought experiment shows that even pleasure maximizers desire to include thought and knowing in their lives.***

The conclusion that *even pleasure maximizers desire to include thought and knowing in their lives* follows immediately from the single premise that *the life possessing only pleasure (and lacking thought and knowing) does not possess the good.* That premise in turn is the conclusion of the following argument:

P1 The good must be complete, sufficient, and choiceworthy (22b4–5 and 20d1–10).

P2 The life possessing only pleasure is neither sufficient nor [complete nor] choiceworthy for any human being or any animal (22b1–2).

P2.1 Because the life possessing only pleasure is choiceworthy to no one (21e4).

P2.1.1 Because [a thought experiment, with Protarchus as arbitrary subject] shows that he would not choose the life possessing only pleasure (21e3–4).

In that thought experiment:

P2.1.1.a The lives of pleasure and of thought are separated, such that there is no thought in the life of pleasure (20e4–5).

P2.1.1.a.1 Because if pleasure is the good it must have no need of anything else to be added to it, and if it has such a need, it ceases to be possible for it to be our true good (20e5–21a2).

P2.1.1.b Protarchus would (if possible) choose to live his whole life in the enjoyment of the greatest pleasures (21a8–9).

P2.1.1.c But, living [a life of pleasure separated from knowing], Protarchus would not always enjoy the greatest pleasures throughout his life (21b3–4).

Because:

P2.1.1.1 Because Protarchus' life of the most possible pleasures would need knowing, awareness, remembering, expert knowing, and true opining (in order to enjoy the greatest pleasures throughout his life) (21a14–b1, 21b6–8).

Because:

P2.1.1.1.1 Protarchus would not recognize whether he was or was not enjoying himself (21b7–8).

P2.1.1.1.1.1 Because he would be void of all knowing (and awareness) (21b8–9).

P2.1.1.1.2 Protarchus would not remember that he had been enjoying himself; of the pleasure he encountered at one moment not a trace of memory would be left at the next (21c2–4).

P2.1.1.1.2.1 Because he would not possess memory (21c1).

P2.1.1.1.3 Protarchus would not believe that he was enjoying himself when he was (21c4–5).

P2.1.1.1.3.1 Because he would not possess true thought (21c4).

P2.1.1.1.4 Protarchus would not reckon that he was able to enjoy himself later on (21c5–6).

P2.1.1.1.4.1 Because he would lack the power of reckoning (21c5).

P2.2 [Without knowing and the like] Protarchus would live the life not of a human being but of some sort of sea lung or one of those creatures of the ocean whose bodies are encased in shells (21c6–8).

The argument for this proposition works as follows. A hedonist, considering the prospect of nonstop pleasure all his life, has two options: (1) merely sensing the pleasure his whole life; (2) Sensing, knowing, being aware of, remembering, expertly knowing, and truly opining about his pleasure his whole life. If the hedonist, like Protarchus and Philebus, wants the *most* pleasure, then he will choose the second option, since it provides additional pleasures (the pleasures requiring knowing and the like).

The inference from P2.1.1 to P2.1. is valid. It is an instance of what in predicate logic is called *universal instantiation*: to show some predicate holds true universally of every subject, one shows it holds true of an arbitrary subject—in this argument, Protarchus. This interpretation of the argument agrees with Damascius (1959), for whom the argument proves its conclusion by deduction (as opposed to division). An alternative, less charitable interpretation (Hampton 1990) is to take the argument not as establishing a universal truth but merely as ad hominem against Protarchus.

The thought experiment works as follows. We assume (1) that the arbitrary subject's life contains pleasure but no remembering (or knowing and the like). There is no hidden contradiction in such an assumption, which is approximated by human beings suffering memory loss (or other mental disabilities). Moreover, we assume (2) that the subject's preference is to live enjoying the greatest pleasures throughout his life. But, we point out, (3) there will be *more* pleasure if the subject not only *feels* or *perceives* pleasure but remembers it, because (it goes without saying) remembering a pleasure is or causes a pleasure. The argument does not need to make a claim as to whether memory can *be* or merely *causes* pleasure. Take away memory and the subject's capacity to take pleasure from life is diminished. In the same way, for each distinct rational faculty, the loss of that rational faculty deprives the subject of the class of pleasures that are or are the effect of that faculty. In addition to memory, it is possible to distinguish also mental awareness and knowing from sense perception (see introduction: *Noein, Phronein, Phronesis,* and *Nous*).

After the thought experiment, at 22d4, Socrates says, ἂν αἴτιόν τις ὑπολάβοι πότερον αὐτῶν εἶναι *one might suppose that either [pleasure or knowing] is the cause [of the mixed life being good].* He does not take the thought experiments to show that knowing or pleasure is the *cause* of the goodness of such a mixed life. It is an error to interpret the argument to aim to show that the exercise of rational faculties is such a cause, an "intrinsic" good, as Cooper (2003) and Irwin (1995) do. Such an interpretation not only makes Socrates' statement at 22d4 mysterious, it leads to contradiction in the text, as Cooper (2003) and Irwin (1995) notice: their interpretation, that pleasure is an intrinsic good, conflicts with the conclusion at 54d6–7 that pleasure belongs to the kind Becoming and thus cannot be intrinsically good.

Along the same lines, a standard objection to the argument is that hedonists might, for all the argument shows, still hold that nothing but pleasure is good in itself, maintaining that knowing and the like are valuable only as a means to get more pleasure. The reply, as in the preceding paragraph, is that the guiding question (see 11a–12a) is not "What is intrinsically good?" but "What condition of the soul is able to provide the life of well-being for all human beings?"—hence extrinsic as well as intrinsic goods are part of the answer. Gosling (1975) notices this limit to this argument: the victory for the mixed life has not yet established that there are any other ingredients than pleasure that possess intrinsic value: thought may be merely of extrinsic value, organizing or otherwise enabling more pleasures than are available to a creature capable merely of sensation. The dialogue goes on to establish that thought is of greater intrinsic value than pleasure by showing that thought is more akin to the good at 64c–67a.

The conclusion of the argument is that the capacity for feeling pleasure and nothing else in a soul is not able to provide happiness, even on the hedonist's own terms (that a happy life has the most pleasure possible). *Pace* Gosling (1975), the argument does not assume that pleasure must *be* activities of thinking as opposed to the *effects* of such activities. *On either assumption*, the conclusion follows that without thought overall pleasure is diminished.

21a4 **βασανίζοντες** *putting [these things] to the test [in you].* The word suggests a formal cross-examination.

21a8 **Δέξαι' ἄν;** *would you find it acceptable?* Formally to question someone about what they would accept might suggest the language used in business negotiation to settle an important contract. This expression might also have been used in a courtroom examination of a witness who required that a question be worded in a particular way in order to give assent.

Πρώταρχε without vocative here does not, I think, indicate that "the object of address is shifted" (Bury 1897, 1) and does not express "astonishment, joy, contempt, a threat, or a warning" (S §1284) but continues the mock formal tone that was introduced by the participle βασανίζοντες (a4) and continued with the elaborate preface to the question (a6–7).

21a8–9 **σὺ ζῆν τὸν βίον ἅπαντα ἡδόμενος ἡδονὰς τὰς μεγίστας;—Τί δ' οὔ;** *[Protarchus would if possible choose] to live his whole life in the enjoyment of the greatest pleasures.* This premise establishes that Protarchus is a hedonic maximizer: more is better. (If the arbitrary subject of the thought experiment happens not to be a hedonic maximizer, the conclusion P2 will also follow.)

21a14 **Ὅρα δή** *so, take a good look at*, repeating 11a1.

τοῦ φρονεῖν καὶ τοῦ νοεῖν καὶ λογίζεσθαι *to know and to be mentally aware and reckon.* According to Diès (1949), manuscript B is an exception among manuscripts in leaving off the second τοῦ, reading τοῦ φρονεῖν καὶ νοεῖν καὶ λογίζεσθαι *to know, be mentally aware, and to reckon.* (Burnet [1901] attributes the exception to manuscript T instead of B.) For the possible significance of the non-exceptional manuscripts, see introduction: *Noein, Phronein, Phronesis,* and *Nous.*

21a14–b1 **Ὅρα δή, τοῦ φρονεῖν καὶ τοῦ νοεῖν καὶ λογίζεσθαι τὰ δέοντα καὶ** [sc., **πάντων**] **ὅσα τούτων ἀδελφά, μῶν μὴ δέοι' ἄν τι;** *wouldn't you stand in need in any way of knowing, of being mentally aware, of reckoning what is needful, and of whatever things are brothers to these?* The verb δέοι(ο) must take a genitive complement, so that the neuter accusative τι must be adverbial. As translated, the accusative τὰ δέοντα is the object of λογίζεσθαι (following Fowler [1925], with Gosling [1975] and Delcomminette [2020]).

Badham (1878), Diès (1949), and Frede worry that "a 'calculation of needed things' [*Bedarfsberechnung*] would already give away that a life of pleasure must contain something like that" (Frede 1997, 25). Frede accepts "the conjecture of Klitsch et al." that τὰ δέοντα is a corruption that has slipped a line too high. This conjecture would move τὰ δέοντα after πάντα at 21b2 (πάντα γὰρ ἔχοιμ' ἄν *I'd have all things* would become πάντα τὰ δέοντα γὰρ ἔχοιμ' ἄν *I'd have all the things I need).*

According to the standard punctuation, which Burnet (1901) follows, the imperative Ὅρα is intransitive. As a third option, I propose removing the comma after Ὅρα and replacing the comma after ἀδελφά with a raised dot: Ὅρα δή τοῦ φρονεῖν καὶ τοῦ νοεῖν καὶ λογίζεσθαι τὰ δέοντα καὶ [sc., πάντων] ὅσα τούτων ἀδελφά· μῶν μὴ δέοι' ἄν τι; With the comma gone, the verb Ὅρα takes τὰ δέοντα as its object, and τὰ δέοντα takes the genitive articular infinitives as its object: *take a good look at the things that stand in need of knowing, of being mentally aware and reckoning, and of whatever things are brothers to these [i.e., to knowing, being mentally aware, and reckoning]. Surely, it's not the case that you wouldn't stand in any need?* Other occurrences of the neuter plural participle τὰ δέοντα with a genitive complement in Plato are at *Laws* 820e2–3 (ὄντα τῶν δεόντων μαθημάτων *being a part of things that stand in need of instruction)* and *Statesman* 273e8–9 (τὰ μὲν . . . ὀλίγου δέοντα ἠφανίσθαι *things standing in need of little to disappear*—that is, things that are close to disappearing*)*. Protarchus shows by his answer at 21b2 (Καὶ τί; πάντα γὰρ ἔχοιμ' ἄν που τὸ χαίρειν ἔχων *Why? Having pleasure, I'd have everything)* that he cannot imagine needing anything that requires knowing and so forth. Socrates then points out items that the hedonic maximizer would need, items that do require knowing and so forth. These items include knowing and not being ignorant that one is feeling pleasure (21b7–8), remembering that one has felt pleasure (21c2) and that one's present pleasure is continuing from the past (21c3–4), seeming to oneself to feel pleasure (21c4), and being able to reckon that and how one will feel pleasure in the future (21c5–6). Protarchus prefers a life of the most and greatest pleasures. A life that merely perceives pleasure has fewer pleasures than a life in which one's experience of pleasure is also understood, remembered from the past, thought while perceiving, and reckoned as what will be in the future. If my punctuation of the passage is accepted, we can avoid emendation.

I take it that the four Greek nouns—νοῦν *awareness*, μνήμην *remembering*, ἐπιστήμην *expert knowing*, and δόξαν ἀληθῆ *true opining*—refer to four kinds of mental awareness, none of which is αἴσθησις *perception*. One might feel pleasure without possessing these kinds of awareness (see introduction: *Noein, Phronein, Phronesis,* and *Nous*). As I interpret the argument (following Hackforth [1945]), it assumes there is a distinction between *perception* of pleasure and four kinds of *mental awareness* of pleasure. Ficino's alternative interpretation (2000, 32) does not seem to distinguish perception from mental awareness: "No pleasure is present in a soul that does not think." Delcomminette (2006, 122) follows Ficino in taking the argument to lead to a self-contradiction: "a life of pleasure [without thought] is a self-contradiction."

21b1 **μῶν μὴ δέοι' ἄν τι** Burnet (1901) accepts the emendation of Klitsch instead of the μηδὲ ὁρᾶν *and not to see* of manuscripts B and T. The **μῶν** = μὴ οὖν expects a negative answer, while "with a negative, the potential optative might have the force of a strong assertion" (S §1826a), while τι adverbially "joined with Verbs [means] *somewhat, in any degree, at all*" (LSJ τις A.II.11.c): *surely it's not the case that you wouldn't stand in any need?*

21b6–7 **Νοῦν δέ γε καὶ μνήμην καὶ ἐπιστήμην καὶ δόξαν . . . ἀληθῆ** *awareness, remembering, expert knowing, and true opining.* Bury (1897) anticipates an objection: "We might expect that μνήμην should be here omitted, as this clause deals only with knowledge of the *present*, whereas in the next clause that of the *past* is first mentioned." And he provides a reply: The clause "πρῶτον . . . φρονήσεως explains νοῦν only, while μνήμην, δόξαν ἀληθῆ and ἐπιστήμην are explained in the next clause." In other words, Socrates begins the passage by mentioning four possessions—awareness, remembering, expert knowing, and true opining—and then explains the consequences of the loss of each, beginning with νοῦς *awareness,* and then in his following speech taking up μνήμην *remembering,* δόξαν ἀληθῆ *true opining,* and ἐπιστήμην *expert knowing,* the last of which enables us to predict and control the future through λογισμός *reckoning.*

21b7–8 **κεκτημένος . . . ἀνάγκη . . . σε** *[you, not] possessing . . . , [it is] necessary that you.* Anacoluthon of nominative in suspense (S §3008e). The nominative circumstantial participle ought to accompany the action of the main verb, which should have a masculine singular subject. Thus, readers expect σὺ ἀγνοήσεις *you will be ignorant* instead of σε ἀγνοεῖν *that you be ignorant* after ἀνάγκη *[it is] necessary.*

21c1 **Καὶ μὴν** introducing "something new or deserving special attention" (LSJ μὴν A.II.2) *and besides.* I interpret Καὶ μὴν ὡσαύτως (21c1) to introduce the elaboration of *how* lack of knowing causes ignorance of one's own pleasures. Hence, above I interpret propositions P2.1.1.1.1–4 (21b7–8, 21c2–4, 21c4–5, and 21c5–6) as premises supporting P2.1.1.1 (21a14–b1, 21b6–8).

21c7 **πλεύμονος** *sea lung.* Aristotle in the *Parts of Animals* describes the sea lung (a kind of jelly fish) as a creature on the very boundary between the kinds of life forms that do and do not possess sensation. As he sees it, "nature passes from lifeless objects to animals in such unbroken sequence, interposing between them beings which live and yet are not animals, that scarcely any difference seems to exist between two neighbouring groups owing to their close proximity" (681a12–15). On the one hand he says that sea lungs "have no sensation [αἴσθησιν], and their life is simply that of a plant separated from the ground" (681a19–20). But he wavers: "inasmuch as they have a certain flesh-like substance, they must be supposed to possess some degree of sensibility [αἴσθησιν]" (681a27–28; translations by Ogle in Barnes 1984).

21c8 **μετ' ὀστρεΐνων** *among things living in hard shells*, not μετ' ὀστράκων *between hard shells*. The ὄστρεον is the *shellfish*; the ὄστρακον is the *hard shell*; and the ὀστρέϊνον is a *thing living in a hard shell*. Plato, anticipating Aristotle, ranks sea life as the lowest form of animal life in his account of the transmigration of souls in the *Timaeus*. "The fourth kind of animal, the kind that lives in water, came from those men who were without question the most stupid and ignorant of all . . . Instead of letting them breathe rare and pure air, they shoved them into water to breathe its murky depths. This is the origin of fish, of all shellfish, and of every water-inhabiting animal" (92a7–b7; translation by Donald Zeyl in Cooper 1997).

22a5–6 **οὐχ ὁ μέν, ὁ δ' οὔ** *[it's] not [the case that] one man [will choose it] while another [won't]*—that is, it's not the case that opinions will differ about this choice. For the idiom, Bury (1897) cites Aeschylus, *Persians* 802, Herodotus, *Histories* 1.138, 2.37, Plato, *Laws* 923b, and *Republic* 475b.

22b–c: ***A thought experiment shows that knowing by itself is not choiceworthy for anyone.***

Socrates reaches the conclusion that *his candidate, knowing, is not the good* (22c3–5) from a single premise: *the life possessing knowing without pleasure does not possess the good* (22b3–4). I identify the subpremises for this single premise as follows:

P1 The good must be complete, sufficient, and choiceworthy (22b4–5 and 20d1–10).

P2 The life possessing only knowing is neither sufficient nor complete nor choiceworthy for any human being or any animal (22b1–2).

P2.1 Because the life possessing only knowing is choiceworthy to no human being or animal (21e4).

P2.1.1 Because [a thought experiment, with Protarchus as arbitrary subject] shows that he would not choose the life possessing only knowing (21e3–4).

In that thought experiment:

P2.1.1.a The lives of pleasure and of knowing are separated, such that there is no pleasure in the life of thought (20e4–5).

P2.1.1.a.1 Because if knowing is the good it must have no need of anything else to be added to it, and if it has such a need, it ceases to be possible for it to be our true good (20e5–21a2).

P2.1.1.b The arbitrary subject would (if possible) live possessing knowing, awareness, expert knowing, and every memory of everything (21d9–10).

P2.1.1.c (But, living a life of thought separated from pleasure, the arbitrary subject would not live possessing knowing, awareness, expert knowing, and every memory of everything.)

P2.1.1.c.1 Because he has no share of pleasure great or small, nor of pain, and is altogether insensible to all such things (21e1–2).

22b4 (and 20d1–10) ἦν γὰρ ἄν ἱκανὸς καὶ τέλεος καὶ . . . αἱρετός *the good must be sufficient, complete, and choiceworthy.* Cooper (2003) gives an alternative translation of τέλεον. Instead of "complete," he translates τέλεον as *final* in the technical sense of Aristotle's *Nicomachean Ethics* I.5: *that for the sake of which all else is done*. It is doubtful that introducing a technical sense improves the argument (as Delcomminette [2006, 109–10n289] shows). As Delcomminette (2006, 111) states: "Each criterion [being complete, sufficient, and choiceworthy] is necessary and sufficient for the other two." I take Bury (1897, 211–14, in his Appendix G) to outline the connection between the three criteria as the following: "complete" refers to the object's nature; "sufficient" refers to facts about its relation to the needs of another; "choiceworthy" refers to its value to another. In effect, the argument finds a way to test the criterion of completeness by connecting it to a testable criterion, desirability for an arbitrary individual. Since "choiceworthy" or choiceworthiness is necessary to the other criteria, it is sufficient to show that choiceworthiness is lacking.

22b3–8 **πᾶσι φυτοῖς καὶ ζῴοις** *for all plant and animals.* Why are plants mentioned here? Plato in the *Timaeus* says that the kind Plants is "totally devoid of thought, reckoning, or mental awareness, though it does share in sensation, pleasant and painful, and desires. For throughout its existence it is completely passive, and its formation has not entrusted it with a natural ability to discern and reflect . . . Hence, it is alive [but] lacks self-motion" (77b5–c5; translation by Zeyl in Cooper 1997).

22c1–2 **τήν γε Φιλήβου θεὸν οὐ δεῖ διανοεῖσθαι ταὐτὸν καὶ τἀγαθόν** *We must keep in mind that Philebus' goddess [namely, Aphrodite = Pleasure] and the good are not the same.* Socrates says that in this argument they will "not yet [οὐδὲν ἔτι] need the division-induced forms of pleasure" (20c4–5). As Delcomminette (2006, 164) explains, this is because Socrates, from the beginning of the dialogue, had two theses opposed to his own proposition (that knowing, being mentally aware, remembering, and the like are at least better and more choiceworthy than pleasure, for all who are capable of them; and that to take part in these is of all things most beneficial for all able to do so [11b7–c2]): the generic proposition that pleasure is *a* good, and the identity thesis that pleasure is *the* good. The argument that refutes the identity thesis (with its conclusion stated here at 22c1–2) does not need to divide pleasure into its different and opposing forms. The later discussion (31a–55b), showing that pleasure is not generically a good, will need such a division.

22c: ***Socrates limits his conclusion about knowing to non-divine lives.***

22c4 **ἕξει που ταὐτὰ ἐγκλήματα** *[knowing] will have the same charges [against it].* The argument for 22c4 is best interpreted as parallel to that for 22c1–2 (see notes to 20e–22c and 22b–c for my identification of the two arguments). The text of 21d9–10 (Εἴ τις δέξαιτ' ἂν αὖ ζῆν ἡμῶν φρόνησιν μὲν καὶ νοῦν καὶ ἐπιστήμην καὶ μνήμην πᾶσαν πάντων κεκτημένος *whether any one of us would choose to live possessing knowing, awareness, expert knowing, and every memory of everything*) is parallel to 21a8–9 (Δέξαι' ἄν, Πρώταρχε, σὺ ζῆν τὸν βίον ἅπαντα ἡδόμενος ἡδονὰς τὰς μεγίστας; *would* you, *Protarchus, choose to live your whole life enjoying the greatest pleasures?*). The text of 21e1–2 (ἡδονῆς δὲ μετέχων μήτε μέγα μήτε σμικρόν, μηδ' αὖ λύπης, ἀλλὰ τὸ παράπαν ἀπαθὴς πάντων τῶν τοιούτων *having neither a large nor small share of pleasure, nor of pain, but entirely without experience of all such things*) is likewise parallel to 21a14–b1 (Ὅρα δή τοῦ φρονεῖν καὶ τοῦ νοεῖν καὶ λογίζεσθαι τὰ δέοντα καὶ ὅσα τούτων ἀδελφά· μῶν μὴ δέοι' ἄν τι; *take a good look at the things that stand in need of knowing, of being mentally aware and reckoning, and of whatever things are brothers to these. Surely, it's not the case that you wouldn't stand in any need?).* Finally, 21e3–4 (Οὐδέτερος ὁ βίος, ὦ Σώκρατες, ἔμοιγε τούτων αἱρετός, οὐδ' ἄλλῳ μή ποτε, ὡς ἐγᾦμαι, φανῇ *neither life of the two of these, Socrates, is choiceworthy to me at any rate, nor does it ever appear [choiceworthy] to another, so I think*) treats the conclusions identically. Accordingly, in my identification of the argument that knowing *is not the good,* I supply premise P2.1.1.c parallel to premise P2.1.1.c in the argument that *pleasure is not the good.* The arbitrary subject, valuing all knowing, wants as much as possible in his life. On his terms, then, he needs pleasure, since a life deprived of all knowing and the like of every pleasure (and perhaps pain) will be a greatly diminished life. It seems to me that alternate interpretations, if they do not explain why *on his terms* this knowing maximizer will need pleasure, are inferior. An additional benefit of my interpretation is that it explains why the argument that knowing *is not the good* applies to Socrates' mind but not to divine knowing. Since it is unbecoming for the divine to feel any pleasure (see 33b10–11), it is no diminishment to the divine knowing, as opposed to human knowing, to delete all thought of pleasure. Parallel to the argument that *pleasure is not the good*, in the argument that *knowing is not the good* pleasure is not recognized as intrinsically good, but rather as needed to complete the life of the subject who values nothing but thought.

22c5–6 **τόν γε ἀληθινὸν ἅμα καὶ θεῖον** *the true and divine [awareness].* Socrates leaves undiscussed the nature of divine awareness here because it is "not immediately under discussion—not a claimant for the place of τἀγαθόν—but is 'on a different footing' [ἄλλως πως ἔχειν]" (Bury 1897). Plato gives no clue in this dialogue why divine knowing is choiceworthy for the gods. But (1) his account of pleasure in the *Philebus* as nothing but processes of repletion or anticipation (see 31a–55b) excludes the kind of pleasure that Aristotle attributes in the highest degree to God—namely, pleasure as unimpeded activity according to one's nature. See Rudebusch (2006) for a discussion of Aristotle's account in comparison to Platonic repletion theories. Not only is there a gap in Plato's account, but (2) Plato in earlier writings appeared to recognize such activity pleasures as well as repleting pleasures, in particular in the *Apology* and the *Protagoras* (see Rudebusch 1999 for an account of such "modal" pleasures in Plato). Since (1) there is a gap in Plato's account of pleasure and (2) Plato appears in other dialogues to be aware of this gap, I speculate that Socrates' hedge at 22c5–6 is a reminder of the possibility of alternative definitions of pleasure.

22c7–d1 **οὐκ . . . πω** *not yet*, which "seems to imply that such a claim will be urged later on" (Bury 1897), presumably for the divine type of awareness—but this claim is not urged in the *Philebus* and may perhaps be one of the "small things" still left to discuss at the dialogue's end. One way Socrates might urge this claim would be to argue that the exercise of awareness is not a pleasure in the sense of refilling but a pleasure in the sense of a "modal pleasure" (Rudebusch 1999, 124–26) or "act of power" (Rudebusch 2009b, 409–12). An alternative interpretation (Badham 1878, followed by Waterfield 1982) is to cut the word πω *yet* from the manuscript.

τῶν . . . δευτερείων . . . πέρι neuter genitive plural δευτερεῖα [sc., ἆθλα] *concerning second prize.* This marks the beginning of the second turn of the investigation. "The κοινός or μικτὸς βίος [*common or mixed life*] gains the νικητήρια [victory], without further dispute" (Bury 1897).

4. The Fourfold Division: Since the identity of the good is complex, the answer to the Happiness Question requires that we make use of four metaphysical kinds—Bound, Unbounded, Mix, and Cause.

22d–23b: *The issue between Socrates and Protarchus is now whether knowing or pleasure is the cause of and more closely resembles the goodness of the mixed life.*

The two thought experiments (20b–c) show that pleasure and thought are both needed for life to be choiceworthy, but they leave open for the hedonist to argue that thought is only of extrinsic value in the mixed life (pleasure being the only intrinsic value or "cause" of that life's goodness), and they leave open for the intellectualist to argue that pleasure is only of extrinsic value (thought being the only intrinsic value). While Socrates has refuted the Protarchan thesis that pleasure is identical to the good, a more sophisticated form of argument (ἄλλης μηχανῆς *other machinery*, 23b7) is needed to refute the Phileban thesis that pleasure is generically good (see note to 11d–12b). Socrates needs to employ the Divine Method and make the relevant divisions of pleasure and expert knowing. But first, with the Fourfold Division, Socrates will provide background information to give perspective on the nature of pleasure, knowing, and what causes a "mixed" life of the two to be good.

22e2 **μετόν** (sc., εἶναι) accusative plus implicit infinitive after λέγοιτο, where the accusative is the present neuter singular participle of the impersonal verb μέτεστιν, which takes a dative of possessor *X* plus genitive *Y* *that there is something being a claim by X to Y* (Badham 1878, followed by Bury 1897). The alternative analysis of Stallbaum (1842) claims this is a rare case of a participle instead of an infinitive after a verb of speaking to report indirect discourse, but the few examples given by Matthiae (1827, 1091–92) are unpersuasive: Euripides, *Iphigenia at Aulis* 425–26 (πέπυσται γὰρ στρατός—ταχεῖα γὰρ διῆιξε φήμη—αἶδα σὴν ἀφιγμένην *the army has learned that your daughter has arrived—for rumor travels quickly)* and 1503 (θανοῦσα δ' οὐκ ἀναίνομαι *although dying, I did not say no)*; Sophocles, *Antigone* 995 ("Εχω πεπονθὼς μαρτυρεῖν ὀνήσιμα *having felt [them], I am able to attest [your] benefits)*; and Aeschylus, *Agamemnon* 583 (νικώμενος λόγοισιν οὐκ ἀναίνομαι *being overcome by speeches, I do not say no*).

22e3 **τῷ ἐμῷ νῷ** *to my awareness* echoes Philebus' words to Socrates, ὁ σὸς νοῦς *your awareness* (22c3).

22e4 **Ἀλλὰ μήν** *yet truly*, to allege something not disputed (LSJ μήν A.II.3).

22e6 **κεῖται** *has fallen*, said of wrestlers (LSJ A.6).

23a1 **νοῦν . . . ἐμφρόνως.** Awareness "showed its sense . . . by declining to enter the field, . . . since it would have fared no better than Pleasure" (Bury 1897).

23a4 **πρὸς τῶν αὐτῆς ἐραστῶν** *in the eyes of her lovers.* "Here ἡδονή is regarded not as θεός but rather as a mistress, beloved for her κάλλος" (Bury 1897).

23b5 **συχνοῦ μὲν λόγου τοῦ λοιποῦ** *What a long remaining argument!* Genitive of cause after exclamation Βαβαῖ (S §1407).

23b6 **ῥᾳδίου** is Burnet's (1901) and most editors' emendation to the manuscripts' ῥᾳδίον. If we accept the change, the genitive ῥᾳδίου coordinates with the genitive of cause in the previous line: *[what a long remaining argument and not an] easy [argument].* If we retain the manuscripts, we may take δὲ to introduce an independent clause, supply ἐστί, and let ῥᾳδίον be a nominative neuter predicate adjective: *[and it is not an] easy [thing].*

καὶ γὰρ δὴ The καὶ emphasizes the γὰρ *for indeed.* The δὴ either adds more emphasis to γὰρ *for yes indeed* or emphasizes φαίνεται *for indeed it does appear.*

23b7–8 **δεῖν ἄλλης μηχανῆς ἐπὶ τὰ δευτερεῖα ὑπὲρ νοῦ πορευόμενον οἷον βέλη ἔχειν ἕτερα τῶν ἔμπροσθεν λόγων** *to be necessary, marching to the capture of second prize on behalf of awareness, to have as it were missiles of another device, different from the earlier arguments.* This is Karl Lehrs's reading (as cited in Bury 1897). An alternative reading is Stallbaum (1842), followed by Burnet (1901), who inserted a comma after μηχανῆς, making ἐπὶ τὰ . . . ἔμπροσθεν λόγων stand in apposition: *that there is need of another device, [namely, that it is necessary,] marching to the capture of second prize on behalf of awareness, to have as it were different missiles from the earlier arguments.* As Bury (1897) notices, it is "harsh" to expect δεῖν to take both a genitive noun and an infinitive. Lehrs's reading is cryptic to decode to the same sort of degree that so much of Socrates' speaking style has been.

I take the "missiles" (βέλη) to be the kinds Unbounded, Bound, and Mix. I take the "other device" (ἄλλης μηχανῆς) to be the measure theory intuited by the character Socrates and the author Plato (see Rudebusch 2021), and I take the missiles that are "perhaps the same" (ἴσως . . . ταὐτά) to be the method of division that Socrates uses in the fourfold division (see Muniz and Rudebusch 2018), which is perhaps an instance of the "gift of the gods" (Θεῶν . . . δόσις, 16c5) already used at 16c–19b, just as Socrates says.

23b9 **ἔστι δὲ ἴσως ἔνια καὶ ταὐτά** *but perhaps some [missiles] also are the same.* In trying to capture the city of second prize, it is not clear which of the "earlier" arguments or devices will be reused.

23b9–10 **οὐκοῦν χρή;—Πῶς γὰρ οὔ;** *don't we have to?—How could we do otherwise?* Socrates appears to be asking Protarchus to confirm that they may need new weapons. How can he expect Protarchus to be able to answer? I would have expected Protarchus to answer, as he so often does, with a request for clarification: "What sort of missiles?" But instead Protarchus assents as if Socrates' question were obvious: "How could we do otherwise?" (This strange exchange led Badham [1878] to propose emending the text to give the question **οὐκοῦν χρή;** to Protarchus and the answering question **Πῶς γὰρ οὔ;** to Socrates.) If I were staging this dialogue, rather than emend it, I would direct the actor playing Protarchus to roll his eyes and speak in a sarcastic tone in his reply.

23c–e: ***Socrates distinguishes the metaphysical kinds Unbounded, Bound, Mix, and Cause.***

My hypothesis is that the method, kinds, and forms used by Socrates in this division are the same sorts of things used by the Eleatic Stranger in Plato's *Sophist* and *Statesman,* as if the Socrates of the *Philebus*—unlike the Socrates of the *Phaedrus*—has by this dramatic date observed the Stranger's method of division. See introduction: Dramatic Setting and Date. On this hypothesis, Socrates' nontechnical vocabulary distinguishes between kinds and forms. Ordinary language users have no trouble distinguishing between a *herd* of livestock, on the one hand, and the *brand* marking each member of the herd, on the other. Just as a herd contains many head of livestock, all sharing the same brand, so also for Socrates in the *Philebus* a *kind* contains many members, all sharing the same *form.* See introduction: *Genos, Phusis,* and *Eidos.* Socrates proposes to divide "all the things there are now in the universe" (πάντα τὰ νῦν ὄντα ἐν τῷ παντὶ, 23c4) by collecting four kinds of those things. Socrates, like the Stranger, collects each kind in four steps: first, stating an open-ended list of items; second, identifying the power shared by those items; third, bringing those items together under a heading according to that power; and fourth, naming the kind. Like the Stranger, Socrates sometimes abbreviates an episode of collection. If his interlocutor apprehends the third step alone, Socrates can produce an understanding of the given division without explicitly going through either or both of the first two steps. See Muniz and Rudebusch 2018 and Muniz and Rudebusch n.d. for this interpretation of the Stranger's method.

Benitez (1989, 63–65) proposes reading the Fourfold Division as a parody of the Divine Method, but his objections to taking seriously the Fourfold Division fail, as Delcomminette (2006, 132–33) has shown. I consider here the two most important objections to a serious reading.

Objection 1: Socrates' Fourfold Division is incomplete. Socrates does not enumerate all the subkinds of Bound and Unbounded, nor does he divide these kinds into their ultimate, indivisible subkinds. The reply is that *no* division aims at a complete enumeration. Notice, for example, in the division of letters of ancient Greek (see fig. 1 in note to 16e–17a), that only the mute stops—π, τ, and κ—have aspirated forms: φ, θ, χ. This is incomplete as an enumeration of sounds that come out of the mouth. Ancient Sanskrit, for example, uses aspirated and unaspirated forms of the voiced stops. That is, in addition to *b*, *d*, and *g*, Sanskrit also distinguishes *bh*, *dh*, and *gh*. This incompleteness as an enumeration of vocal sound is not a flaw in the division of ancient Greek, because *for the purposes of studying and teaching ancient Greek,* there is no need to distinguish the aspirated voiced stops. Division differs from enumeration, therefore, in that it only goes as far as needed in order to master the skill under investigation. Whether we divide the kinds Vocal Sound or Bound, it is unnecessary as well as impossible to give a complete enumeration. The point is to divide according to the goal at hand: Socrates does precisely this in the case of both Vocal Sound and the Fourfold Division.

Objection 2: Socrates' Fourfold Division treats the unbounded as if it is a form. This seems impossible to interpreters such as Grube (1935, 303) and Gosling (1999, 43–45). The reply is that there *is* a Form *unbounded,* just as, in the *Sophist* (254d) there is a Form *motion* as well as *rest.* To be unbounded, after all, is a feature shared by many different things and an object of scientific study. Hence, by the Platonic argument from science, it is a form.

23c4 **Πάντα . . . διχῇ διαλάβωμεν** *let us divide all into two.* There seems to be an allusion to the Stranger's penchant for dichotomous division in this remark, an echo of πάντα δίχα διαλαβεῖν (*Statesman* 261b4), with the correction from bisection to trisection to quadrisection perhaps a bit of mockery of the Stranger's penchant. The earlier illustrative divisions were of the kinds Vocal Sound and Musical Sound. Notice that each of these kinds is one. By contrast, the present division is not of one kind but of many things: "all things that now exist in the world" (23c4). Most naturally, "now" includes temporal beings. As Benitez (1989, 68) notes, the words "in the world" (ἐν τῷ παντὶ) in each of its later occurrences (29b10, c2, d2, d6, 30c3) refers to the physical world. This is the world that nominalists recognize, the world to which the Divine Method is meant to apply, the world that, as was revealed by that method, is *of* two elements, bound and unbounded (23c9–10).

23c9–10 **Τὸν θεὸν ἐλέγομέν που τὸ μὲν ἄπειρον δεῖξαι τῶν ὄντων, τὸ δὲ πέρας** *we said* [at 16c5–10] *that God pointed out the unbounded and the bound of beings.*

23c12 **Τούτων δὴ τῶν εἰδῶν τὰ δύο τιθώμεθα** *let us posit the two [unbounded and bound] of these [three] forms.* Stallbaum (1842) changes neuter genitive plural Τούτων of manuscripts to neuter accusative dual Τούτω: *let us posit these [to be] two of the forms.*

23d2 **κατ' εἴδη διιστὰς** *separating by forms.* An alternative translation is *separating into forms.* Kinds can be separated, *by reference to* their defining forms, into subkinds, but forms cannot be separated *into* subforms. On this alternative, Socrates would be using εἴδη figuratively to refer to kinds. See introduction: *Genos*, *Phusis*, and *Eidos*.

23d9–11 Following Ritter (1923, 174) and Hackforth (1945, 44), Delcomminette (2006, 254) proposes why Socrates considers this fifth cause: because mixes like health or seasonable warmth, which are good, often do disintegrate into bad things like illness or unseasonable cold. And Delcomminette in the same place proposes why Socrates, having considered this fifth cause, rejects for present purposes a need for such a cause: because "bad things like illness and winter cold are not by means of a positive cause, but rather by nothing more than the *absence*" of a positive cause.

23e1 **βίον** is in all the manuscripts, but no one understands how it can make sense. The context requires that the "fifth" be not a manner of living but a form or kind.

23e3 **τῶν τεττάρων τὰ τρία διελόμενοι** *after dividing three [kinds, as parts] away from the four [as a whole].* The middle voice is indirect reflexive [*for our purposes*—that is, *our inquiry*]. Active or middle, the verb διαιρέω with an accusative plural object *X* and a genitive of separation *Y* means *divide X from* or *of Y* as in "dividing pieces of a pie"—the division is within *Y*, not *X*, a division that separates the parts *X* away from the whole *Y*. In just this way the verb διαιρέω takes a plural accusative object and genitive of separation at 14e1 with the same meaning. LSJ II.1 list the idiomatic translation *divide Y into X*. Thus Delcomminette (2020): "taking apart three from the four (*prenons-en à part trois des quatre*)." Instead of a verb of *taking apart* or *dividing*, Fowler (1925), Gosling (1975), and Frede (1993) use verbs of *taking* or *taking up* (and Hackforth [1945] uses a verb of *confining attention to*), which are unattested meanings and which hide from the reader the riddling nature of Socrates' speech.

24a–e: ***Socrates illustrates the unbounded with the relations hotter and colder.***

Socrates gives two arguments for the conclusion that *the hotter and its opposite are unbounded together* (stated at 24b8 and d6–7).

Argument A establishes the conclusion as follows:

P1 The more and the less reside in these kinds (i.e., in the hotter and colder, 24a9; restated as: the more and less are always in the hotter and colder, 24b4–5).

P2 Whenever the more and less reside in a kind, they do not permit the attainment of any end (24b1).

P2.1. Because if an end is reached, the more and less have ended (their residence in the kind, 24b2).

P3 If the hotter and colder are without end, they must be entirely unbounded (24b8).

Argument B establishes the conclusion as follows:

P1 [The intensely and mildly reside in the hotter and colder.]

P2 The intensely and the mildly have the same power as the more and less (24c1–3); wherever the intensely and mildly reside, they do not allow each thing [there where they reside] to have a fixed quantity; on the contrary, always making in each subject matter (i.e., hotter and colder, wetter and drier, etc.) something more intense than something milder and the opposite (i.e., something milder than something more intense), the intensely and the mildly make the intensively more and the intensively less and remove every trace of fixed quantity (24c3–6).

P2.1 Because if the intensely and the mildly do not remove every trace of quantity, but allow it and the proportionate in the domain of the more and less and the intensely and the mildly, these four shall be gone from the domain in which they resided (24c6–d2).

P2.1.1 Because, after accepting the fixed quantity, the hotter and the colder would no longer exist (24d2–3).

Because:

P2.1.1.1 The hotter always goes ahead and does not stop, and the colder does likewise (24d4–5).

P2.1.1.2 But a fixed quantity stops and ceases to go on (24d5).

24a7–8 **θερμοτέρου καὶ ψυχροτέρου πέρι . . . πέρας . . . τι** *any bound about a hotter/more hotly and colder/more coldly.* Socrates collects the kind Unbounded in a roundabout way, beginning by getting Protarchus to agree that we cannot conceive any bound "of a hotter/more hotly and colder/more coldly." Used here without a definite article, the Greek neuter singular comparatives θερμοτέρου and ψυχροτέρου might be the adjectives "hotter" and "colder" or the adverbs "more hotly" and "more coldly." It is consistent with this text to take these comparatives to refer to relations of more and less on a domain (if the comparatives are adjectives) of hot and cold things or (if they are adverbs) heating and cooling actions. For example, regions of the earth make up a domain of hot and cold *things*, where, for instance, Australia is hotter than Antarctica, and Antarctica is colder than Australia. The regions of the earth also make up a domain of hot and cold *actions*. For instance, the sun *shines more hotly* in Australia than it does in Antarctica and *more coldly* in Antarctica than in Australia.

Although Socrates does not say so, it is consistent with the text to take the relations *hotter/more hotly* and *colder/more coldly* on a given domain as antisymmetric, transitive, and inverse relations on that domain. The elicited agreement that there is no conceivable bound to these relations indicates that the relations are unbounded (as defined by Rudebusch [2021, 57]) on that domain. There is the same adjective/adverb ambiguity in the case of the words Socrates uses to list other members of the kind Unbounded. In the rest of this commentary, I have, for the sake of brevity, used only the English adjective "hotter" instead of "hotter/more hotly" and likewise with the other such relations, trusting that the reader will bear in mind the ambiguity in the Greek.

24a9 **ἐν αὐτοῖς . . . τοῖς γένεσιν** *in them, the kinds* (appositive) or perhaps *in the kinds themselves*. The reference to these two kinds tells us how to interpret the previous note in a more accurate way. The previous note states that the singular comparatives θερμοτέρου and ψυχροτέρου refer to many relations of *hotter* and *colder*. It is more accurate to take each singular comparative to refer to one object, not many. That one object is the kind Hotter, which contains many relations on many domains (or the kind Colder, which contains the inverse relations on the same domains). The adverbs μᾶλλόν *more* and ἧττον *less* modify adjectives or verbs, not nouns. We might take these adverbs to refer to two features of relations on domains of either things or actions. Thus, "the more and less dwell in the kinds Hotter and Colder" by virtue of being a feature of the members of these kinds. I take these features *more* and *less* to be the powers of *being ever more* and *ever less*—that is, being *unbounded*.

οἰκοῦν<τε> Manuscripts B and T have οἰκοῦν. By adding τε, Burnet (1901), following other editors, produces **οἰκοῦντε** (the present active neuter nominative dual participle of οἰκέω *inhabit, occupy, dwell*) in agreement with the dual finite verbs sharing the same subject, ἐνοικῆτον and ἐπιτρεψαίτην.

24b1 **ἕωσπερ ἂν ἐνοικῆτον, τέλος οὐκ ἂν ἐπιτρεψαίτην γίγνεσθαι** *so long as [the more and less] are dwelling in [a relation of hotter or colder], [the more and less] could not permit an end to come to be [in that relation].* As I interpret: if the more and less are features of merely antisymmetric and transitive inverse relations, then those relations are unbounded.

24b4 **ἔν τε τῷ θερμοτέρῳ καὶ ψυχροτέρῳ** *in the hotter and colder.* Again, the Greek neuter singular comparatives might be adjectives or adverbs (see note to 24a7–8). This clause contains an exception to the rule that "τέ usually follows the word with which the . . . sentence-part to be connected is most concerned" (S §2983). The exception is that "τέ may stand after a word . . . which, though common to two members of a clause, is placed either at the beginning (especially after a preposition) or in the second member" (S §2983c).

24b4–5 **Ἀεὶ . . . ἔν τε τῷ θερμοτέρῳ καὶ ψυχροτέρῳ τὸ μᾶλλόν τε καὶ ἧττον ἔνι** *the more and less are always in the hotter and colder.* As I interpret, the relations *more* and *less* (which as forms and powers are always present in the kinds Hotter and Colder, forms that cause those kinds of relations to be as expressed at 24b7–8, where the causality is indicated by the inferential τοίνυν *therefore* at 24b7). I take the relations *hotter* and *colder* to be *two* merely antisymmetric and transitive inverse relations on a given domain. The alternative interpretation, defended, for example, by Benitez (1989), is that the hotter and colder is but *one* member of the kind Unbounded: "the-hotter-and-colder," to give it its own name. As Delcomminette (2006, 219) points out, this alternative has trouble explaining why the hotter and colder are referred to using the plural forms αὐτοῖς . . . τοῖς γένεσιν at 24a9.

24b7–8 **Ἀεὶ τοίνυν ὁ λόγος ἡμῖν σημαίνει τούτω μὴ τέλος ἔχειν** *therefore the argument indicates that these two do always have no end*—that is, these two kinds of relations are always unbounded, as defined by Rudebusch (2021, 57). I take the word "always" to indicate that the more and less are *necessarily* features of these two kinds of relations.

24c1 **ἀνέμνησας ὅτι καὶ τὸ σφόδρα τοῦτο** *you have reminded me that also this word "intensely."* These words separate argument A and argument B as identified in the note to 24a–e. The inference indicator "according to this reasoning" (κατὰ δὴ τοῦτον τὸν λόγον, 24d6) shows that Socrates is giving arguments for 24d6–7 (ἄπειρον γίγνοιτ' ἂν τὸ θερμότερον καὶ τοὐναντίον ἅμα *the hotter and its opposite are unbounded together*), which is a restatement of 24b8 (παντάπασιν ἀπείρω γίγνεσθον *[the two hotter and colder] are entirely unbounded*).

24c1–3 **τὸ σφόδρα τοῦτο . . . καὶ τό γε ἠρέμα τὴν αὐτὴν δύναμιν ἔχετον τῷ μᾶλλόν τε καὶ ἧττον** *the intensely and the mildly have the same power as the more and less.* I take this statement, premise 2 of argument B, to be parallel to premise 2 of argument A (as identified in the note to 24a–e). I take this statement to show that there are forms *intensely* and *mildly,* like the forms *more* and *less,* sharing the power to cause relations to be unbounded. Socrates' reason for positing the same power for these forms is ὅπου γὰρ ἂν ἐνῆτον, οὐκ ἐᾶτον εἶναι ποσὸν ἕκαστον *because wherever [the forms intensely and mildly] are present, they do not allow each item [there] to be a quantity* (24c3). He explains what it means to *forbid quantity*: ἀεὶ σφοδρότερον ἡσυχαιτέρου καὶ τοὐναντίον ἑκάσταις πράξεσιν ἐμποιοῦντε τὸ πλέον καὶ τὸ ἔλαττον ἀπεργάζεσθον, τὸ δὲ ποσὸν ἀφανίζετον *by always creating in every matter [something] more excessive than [something] more mild and the opposite [i.e., by always creating something more mild than something more excessive], the intensely and mildly produce the greater [thing] and the lesser [thing], and [in this sense] destroy quantity* (24c4–6). On my reading (Rudebusch 2021), this destruction of "quantity" is an effect of removing upper and lower bounds on a given scale. For a scale to possess quantity, then, might be for it to have *some finite number of intervals* between its lower and upper bound. As shown in Rudebusch (2021, 56–57), such a scale must at least be ordinal.

24c6–d2 **μὴ ἀφανίσαντε τὸ ποσόν, ἀλλ' ἐάσαντε αὐτό τε καὶ τὸ μέτριον ἐν τῇ τοῦ μᾶλλον καὶ ἧττον καὶ σφόδρα καὶ ἠρέμα ἕδρᾳ ἐγγενέσθαι, αὐτὰ ἔρρει ταῦτα ἐκ τῆς αὑτῶν χώρας ἐν ᾗ ἐνῆν** *by not suppressing quantity, but instead by allowing it and measure to come to be in the abode of the more and less and intensely and mildly, these things themselves flow* *out of their space, [the space] in which they were present.* This passage tells us more about the "quantity" suppressed by the power of the more and less and intensely and mildly, telling us that quantity and measure seem to come and go together. Rudebusch (2021, 55–57) reviews three different scales of increasing order above the partial scale: ordinal and interval, which do not possess measure, and ratio, which does. It is not clear how to distinguish the three scales in Greek mathematics, since their binary operation of arithmetic did not possess the identity element 0. In any case, Socrates does not distinguish the three. His contrast seems only to be an informal distinction between merely partial scales, on the one hand, and ratio scales as the more ordered scale, on the other. For Socrates' purposes, if a scale possesses quantity, it also possesses measure and is a bounded ratio scale, while if it lacks quantity and measure, it is a merely partial unbounded scale.

24d2–3 **οὐ γὰρ ἔτι θερμότερον οὐδὲ ψυχρότερον εἴτην ἂν λαβόντε τὸ ποσόν** *for a hotter or colder could no longer exist after getting quantity.* Used here without a definite article, the Greek neuter singular comparatives might be adjectives or adverbs (see note to 24a7–8). The inferential γάρ *for* indicates that this statement is presented in support of the general claim of the incompatibility of quantity with more and less and intensely and mildly. The support seems to take the form of an illustrative example of that general incompatibility in the case of hotter and colder. This speech is clearly true, if we take θερμότερον καὶ ψυχρότερον *a hotter and colder* to be a merely partial scale consisting of the relations *hotter* and *colder* on a given domain, and if we take "quantity" to be the features that change a merely partial scale into a ratio scale, with the greater order that such features give to the relations *hotter* and *colder.* As reviewed in Rudebusch (2021, 55–57), every ratio scale is a partial scale, but no ratio scale can be a *merely* partial scale.

24d4–5 **προχωρεῖ γὰρ καὶ οὐ μένει τό τε θερμότερον ἀεὶ καὶ τὸ ψυχρότερον ὡσαύτως, τὸ δὲ ποσὸν ἔστη καὶ προϊὸν ἐπαύσατο** *for the hotter is always going on and not staying put, and the colder likewise, but quantity comes to a stop and ceases to go on.* This passage supports the claim (with inferential γάρ) of the incompatibility of hotter and colder with quantity. I take this speech, an elaboration of 24b7–8, to be an intuitive way of saying that it is the nature of the hotter and colder to be a scale containing the merely antisymmetric, transitive, inverse relations *hotter* and *colder* on a domain D such that, for any x in D, there is a y such that y is hotter than x and there is a z such that z is colder than x. See note to 24a7–8. Plato's account here of the unbounded as always going on and not stopping, like Aristotle's definition of the ἄπειρον as that "of which there is always something outside" (*Physics* 4.6 207a1), is a recognizable ancestor of the modern definition of an ordered infinite set: "for all y, there is an x such that $y < x$."

24d6–7 **κατὰ δὴ τοῦτον τὸν λόγον ἄπειρον γίγνοιτ' ἂν τὸ θερμότερον καὶ τοὐναντίον ἅμα** *indeed, according to this statement [that the hotter and colder always go on], the hotter and the colder [in a given domain] would prove to be unbounded at the same time.* I translate γίγνοιτο as "prove to be" rather than "come to be." The hotter and colder cannot *come to be* unbounded, since you cannot come to be something you always are (24d2–3). But they can *prove to be*—that is, come to be understood as—unbounded. I interpret the phrase κατὰ δὴ τοῦτον τὸν λόγον *indeed* [emphatic δὴ] *according to this statement* to be inferential, indicating an inference from *jointly always going on* to *being unbounded at the same time.* When Socrates speaks of the hotter and colder as always going on and therefore always unbounded, I take him to speak only of what I have called the unbounded merely antisymmetric, transitive, inverse relations *hotter* and *colder.* Certainly, the relations *hotter* and *colder* can exist either in an unbounded partial scale or in a bounded ratio scale.

24d9–e2 **τὸ δὲ εἰς αὖθίς τε καὶ αὖθις ἴσως λεχθέντα τόν τε ἐρωτῶντα καὶ τὸν ἐρωτώμενον ἱκανῶς ἂν συμφωνοῦντας ἀποφήναιεν.** There are two puzzles about this sentence. What is the function of the article τὸ (which Badham [1855] proposed to rewrite as τάχα *perhaps*), and what is the plural subject of ἀποφήναιεν? Stallbaum (1842): "hardly anyone has given a reason [*vix quisquam probaverit*] for the plural number." Bury (1897): "a curious sentence." I propose that the article τὸ makes a substantive of the compound prepositional phrase: **τὸ . . . εἰς αὖθίς τε καὶ αὖθις** *the repetitions [of what Socrates is saying].* Such a substantive, although singular in grammatical form, is plural in sense (a "collective singular," S §996) and may take a plural verb (S §950) both as participle λεχθέντα and finite verb ἀποφήναιεν: *perhaps the repetitions [of what Socrates is saying], after being stated, will show that the questioner and the answerer are in sufficient concord.*

24e4–5 **ἄθρει τῆς τοῦ ἀπείρου φύσεως εἰ τοῦτο δεξόμεθα σημεῖον, ἵνα μὴ πάντ' ἐπεξιόντες μηκύνωμεν** *in order that we do not speak too long going through all [the list], see if we will accept this sign of the nature of the unbounded.* To this point, Socrates has only listed one pair of members of the kind Unbounded he is collecting: the relations *hotter* and *colder* on a given domain. But this passage states his wish to abbreviate the project of collecting the kind. It will suit Socrates later, however, to list other items in the kind Unbounded, as part of his collection of the third kind, Mix: ξηρότερον καὶ ὑγρότερον . . . καὶ πλέον καὶ ἔλαττον καὶ θᾶττον καὶ βραδύτερον καὶ μεῖζον καὶ σμικρότερον *drier and wetter and superior and inferior and faster and slower and larger and smaller* (25c8–10). I take each of these pairs, like "hotter and colder," to be merely antisymmetric and transitive inverse relations on a given domain.

24e7–25a2 **Ὁπόσ' ἂν ἡμῖν φαίνηται μᾶλλόν τε καὶ ἧττον γιγνόμενα καὶ τὸ σφόδρα καὶ ἠρέμα δεχόμενα καὶ τὸ λίαν καὶ ὅσα τοιαῦτα πάντα, εἰς τὸ τοῦ ἀπείρου γένος ὡς εἰς ἓν δεῖ πάντα ταῦτα τιθέναι** *All these things—as many things as show themselves becoming more and less and accepting the intensely and mildly and the excessively and all such things—it is necessary to place into the kind of the unbounded as into a one.* This passage presents the second, third, and fourth steps of collecting the kind Unbounded (on these steps, see note to 23c–e). The second step, identifying the power shared by every member of the kind, is at the words μᾶλλόν τε καὶ ἧττον γιγνόμενα καὶ τὸ σφόδρα καὶ ἠρέμα δεχόμενα καὶ τὸ λίαν καὶ ὅσα τοιαῦτα πάντα *becoming more and less and accepting the intensely and mildly and the excessively and all such things.* The third step—εἰς τὸ . . . γένος ὡς εἰς ἓν δεῖ πάντα ταῦτα τιθέναι *it is necessary to place all these things [that share the same power] into the kind . . . as into a one*—is bringing the items in the kind together εἰς ἓν *into a one* according to the power identified in the second step. The fourth and last step is naming the kind: τὸ τοῦ ἀπείρου γένος *the kind of the unbounded.*

25a–26d ***Socrates identifies equal, double, and number as providing bound to a scale and describes mix as the result of adding bounds to an unbounded domain.***

25a6–b2 **τὰ μὴ δεχόμενα ταῦτα, τούτων δὲ τὰ ἐναντία πάντα δεχόμενα, πρῶτον μὲν τὸ ἴσον καὶ ἰσότητα, μετὰ δὲ τὸ ἴσον τὸ διπλάσιον καὶ πᾶν ὅτιπερ ἂν πρὸς ἀριθμὸν ἀριθμὸς ἢ μέτρον ᾖ πρὸς μέτρον, ταῦτα σύμπαντα εἰς τὸ πέρας ἀπολογιζόμενοι καλῶς ἂν δοκοῖμεν δρᾶν τοῦτο** *With respect to the things that do not accept [the intensely and the mildly and the excessively,* see 24e8*], but do accept all the things opposite to these—in the first place the equal and equality, and after the equal the double and anything that is a number to a number or a measure to a measure—if we were to render an account of all these together in regard to the [kind] Bound, we would seem to accomplish this [task of first collecting as many things as are scattered and dispersed and then putting on them the sign of some one nature,* see 25a2–4*] in a manner worthy of praise.* It is ambiguous when Socrates makes this statement whether the list τὸ ἴσον . . . τὸ διπλάσιον . . . *the equal . . . the double, and so on* in this passage is appositive to τὰ μὴ δεχόμενα ταῦτα *the things that do not accept [the intensely, mildly, and excessively]*—that is, the things that accept *the equal and equality, and after the equal the double and anything that is a number to a number or a measure to a measure* or whether it is appositive to τούτων δὲ τὰ ἐναντία πάντα *the things opposite to [the intensely, etc.]*

In collecting the kind Unbounded, Socrates identifies the members of that kind as the hotter and colder and (later) the drier and wetter, superior and inferior, faster and slower, and larger and smaller, which I have interpreted as unbounded merely antisymmetric, transitive, inverse relations on given domains—that is, unbounded partial scales.

My hypothesis is that the list is appositive to 25a6: *the things that do not accept [the intensely, mildly, and excessively*]. In other words, the equal and double are examples of things that do not accept excessivity, so that Socrates is collecting the equal, double, and so on into the kind Bound. On this hypothesis, while the kind Unbounded contains partial scales as members—namely, unbounded, merely antisymmetric and transitive inverse relations like *hotter* and *colder* on various domains—the kind Bound contains as members the equality relation and ratio relations like *double, triple,* and so forth—that is, the relations themselves rather than those on a given domain. Socrates lists some of these relations as a first step in collecting this second kind at 25a7–8. As an indication of the second step, Socrates also outlines how one might identify the power shared by every member of the kind: *accepting all the things opposite to* intensely *and* mildly *and* excessively (25a6). But he does not render an account of what these opposites are there (I take it that these things are the measured, proportionate, and beautiful). Instead, Socrates speaks conditionally, using the participle of a verb of rendering an account to mark the condition of a future less vivid conditional (ἀπολογιζόμενοι = εἰ ἀπολογιζοίμεθα, Smyth §2344): *if we were to render an account . . . we would seem to accomplish this.*[2] And he indicates what the fourth step would be in naming the kind "Bound." It is only a potential and not yet an actual collection, as Socrates confirms: "we did not do the collection" (οὐ συνηγάγομεν, 25d7). Socrates' speeches at 25d2–e2 (see note there) add support to my hypothesis about the appositive at 25a6.

25b2 **ἂν δοκοῖμεν δρᾶν τοῦτο** *we might seem to accomplish this [collection of the kind Bound].* Socrates uses the potential optative of a verb of seeming because he is potentially but not yet actually collecting the kind Bound (see previous note). Socrates confirms that this collection

2. LSJ I.2 gives a different, ad hoc meaning for ἀπολογίζομαι in this passage: "ἀ. εἴς τι *refer to* a head or class, Pl.*Phlb.* 25b," but they provide no support why ἀπολογίζομαι, a verb of rendering an account or calculating, when modified by εἰς + accusative becomes a verb of referring into. The verb ἀπολογίζομαι does not change meaning in this way in its single other collocation (according to *TLG*) with the preposition εἰς (Xenophon, *Economics* 9.8: δίχα δὲ καὶ τὰ εἰς ἐνιαυτὸν ἀπολελογισμένα κατέθεμεν *we set apart the things calculated [to last] for a year*). In Xenophon's passage the prepositional phrase εἰς ἐνιαυτὸν is an idiom with the meaning *for a year* (LSJ II.2). Unlike verbs of collecting or referring, the verb ἀπολογίζομαι does not move its direct object, not even as an object of thought, and so the preposition εἰς following it naturally expresses relation, *in regard to,* rather than motion *into.*

is merely potential, not actual, at 25d7: οὐ συνηγάγομεν *we did not do the collection.*

25b5 **Εἶεν· τὸ δὲ τρίτον** *well then; [what form does] the third [kind have]?* This speech marks a transition from the second to the third kind, although the second in fact remains uncollected.

25c5–6 **Θερμότερον . . . καὶ ψυχρότερον** *hotter and colder.* Used here without a definite article, the Greek neuter singular comparatives might be adjectives or adverbs (see note to 24a7–8).

25c8–10 **ξηρότερον καὶ ὑγρότερον . . . καὶ βραδύτερον καὶ μεῖζον καὶ σμικρότερον** *dryer and wetter . . . and slower and larger and smaller.* See previous note.

25c10 **ἐν τῷ πρόσθεν** *in the time before,* referring to 24e7–25a5, when Socrates collected many things sharing a single feature into the kind Unbounded.

There is a problem, going back at least to Jackson (1882), with Socrates' statements at 25e–26b that the members of Mix are good, while sickness, wintry weather, and stifling summer heat belong not to Mix but to Unbounded (likewise 64d9–e7). As Delcomminette (2006, 247) well states it: "It is hard to see why, for example, a 'bad' fever of 41°C would be less perfectly determined than a 'good' temperature of 37°C. In the same manner, might one not say that even an excessively cold frost corresponds to a temperature as determinate as what corresponds to more favorable weather conditions?" On my reading (Rudebusch 2021), it is incorrect to describe individual temperatures as elements of Mix: only scales $\langle G, <_k \rangle$ are elements. And the text supports a distinction between the scales $\langle S, <_k \rangle$ inhabited by quantity (the quantity that "stops and ceases to go on," 24d5) and those scales $\langle G, <_k \rangle$ born from the right partnering of the kinds Bound and Unbounded (25e7–8). Every case of "putting in measures and symmetries" is a case of "inserting number" (25e1–2), but the text never says that every case of inserting number will produce measure and symmetry. Certainly the centigrade scale of temperatures bounded by 30 and 45 is as much "inhabited by quantity" as the scale bounded by 36 and 38—but only the latter bounds make it possible for health to come to be for a human body; only the latter scale meets my interpretation of a *mix* as a ratio scale with bounds appropriate for some good or other, as indicated by the examples listed at 25e7–26b7.

25d2–e2 Socrates' speeches at 25d2–e2 (see note there) add support to my hypothesis about the appositive at 25a6. The "genre" (γένναν, 25d3) Bound is the kind that possesses as members "the equal and double and whatever puts a stop to things being at odds with each other and, putting in proportionate and harmonious things, produces a number" (τοῦ ἴσου καὶ διπλασίου, καὶ ὁπόση παύει πρὸς ἄλληλα τἀναντία διαφόρως ἔχοντα, σύμμετρα δὲ καὶ σύμφωνα ἐνθεῖσα ἀριθμὸν ἀπεργάζεται, 25d11–e2). An equality relation and proportion on a domain constitute a ratio scale. The kind Bound, then, as I take it, contains equality relations and proportions that are not themselves on any domain, but that, when are added to a given domain, produce ratio scales.[3]

25d2 **τὸ μετὰ ταῦτα** adverbial *next* or the direct object of συμμείγνυ, *mix* or *breed the next thing ["the thing after these"]—the kind Bound—in with it.*

25d3 **γέννανv** *genre* is rare in prose (LSJ), a poetic synonym for γένος *kind* (used most recently above at 25a1). Socrates seems to be asking Protarchus to mix or breed the kind, the "genre," Bound with the nature of the unbounded. Protarchus is wise to ask for clarification. Socrates' clarification, which follows, is that he is speaking of that which *needed* to be collected into a single kind but has not yet been collected, the kind Bound. This has puzzled commentators who believe Socrates has already collected that kind at 25a6–b3 (but see note to 25b2).

25d5–9 **τὴν τοῦ περατοειδοῦς** [sc., γένναν] *the [genre] of the bound-form* [i.e., the kind Bound]. Socrates coins the compound word.

25d8 **<εἰ>** Burnet (1901) would insert this before τούτων ἀμφοτέρων. We can avoid the addition, if we put a raised dot after δράσει and accept asyndeton in the final clause: "But perhaps it will accomplish the same

3. Thomas (2006, 223), although not offering it as an interpretation of the kind Bound, makes the suggestive remark that "right ratios . . . are determined relative to the domain in which they operate."

thing; in collecting *both* [Unbounded and Bound], that one [Mix] will also become visible."

25d8 **τούτων ἀμφοτέρων συναγομένων** *both together being collected,* genitive absolute. "Both together" refers to the mix. As I interpret this, Socrates is saying that by collecting the kind Mix, κἀκείνη = καὶ ἐκείνη (γέννα) *also that* (still uncollected kind Bound) will become apparent.

25d11 **Τὴν** [γένναν] answers Ποίαν, and καὶ ὁπόση answers πῶς [γέννα] *[I mean] the [genre] . . . and as much [of the genre] as.* This "genre" is the kind Bound—that is, the kind of proportion and arithmetical quantities.

26a2–4 **'Εν δὲ ὀξεῖ καὶ βαρεῖ καὶ ταχεῖ καὶ βραδεῖ, ἀπείροις οὖσιν, ἆρ' οὐ ταὐτὰ ἐγγιγνόμενα ταῦτα ἅμα πέρας τε ἀπηργάσατο καὶ μουσικὴν σύμπασαν τελεώτατα συνεστήσατο;** *these same things [i.e., the equal, double, etc.], being bred into sharp and flat and fast and slow, which are unbounded, produce a bound and compose most perfectly music as a whole.* I follow Frede (1993), leaving out the raised dot after ταῦτα and keeping ἐγγιγνόμενα. Burnet (1901) unnecessarily brackets ἐγγιγνόμενα and inserts a raised dot after ταῦτα.

26b8 **ἡ θεός** Aphrodite is mother of Harmony (Hesiod, *Theogony* 975) and mistress of the seasons (*Homeric Hymn* 6 line 5).

ὦ καλὲ Φίληβε ***handsome Philebus.*** Vocative adjectives such as καλὲ *fine* sometimes translate well as asides in English: *Philebus—by all that is fine!—.*

αὕτη . . . ἡ θεός *this goddess.* Frede (1993) and others change αὕτη to αὐτή, *the goddess herself.*

26b9–10 **νόμον καὶ τάξιν πέρας** ***ἔχοντ'*** **ἔθετο** is manuscript T. Since ἔθετο as a verb of making can take two accusatives (LSJ τίθημι B.I.3), we can translate: [*the goddess*] *made law and order [to be] things that have limit*—that is, when she created law and order, she created them as things that have limit.

νόμον καὶ τάξιν πέρας ***ἐχόντων*** **ἔθετο** is manuscript B. Since ἔθετο can take one accusative (LSJ τίθημι A.VI), we can translate: [*the goddess*] *established a law and order* [*among things*] *having a limit.*

26d4–5 **τό γε πέρας οὔτε πολλὰ εἶχεν, οὔτ' ἐδυσκολαίνομεν ὡς οὐκ ἦν ἓν φύσει.** As I read it, the two clauses (τό γε πέρας . . . πολλὰ εἶχεν *Bound contained many [subkinds* (sc,. γένη from 26d1)*]* and οὐκ ἦν ἓν φύσει *[Bound] was not one by nature*) are both subordinate to ἐδυσκολαίνομεν ὡς: *we complained neither that Bound had many [subkinds] nor that it was not one in nature.* That both εἶχεν and ἦν are imperfect permits both to be subordinate. It may help make Socrates' meaning clear to restate using direct discourse: "We didn't complain as follows: 'Eww, it has many subkinds! Eww, it's not one in nature!' [And so we shouldn't make the same complaint now.]" The alternative does not subordinate both clauses to ἐδυσκολαίνομεν ὡς. See, most recently, Delcomminette (2020): "Without correction, the text would mean: 'As to Limit, it does not have many kinds, and we weren't irritated on the pretext (*irrités sous prétexte*) that it would not be one by nature'—which is both contradictory and excluded by the context."

26d7–9 **τρίτον φάθι με λέγειν, ἓν τοῦτο τιθέντα τὸ τούτων ἔκγονον ἅπαν, γένεσιν εἰς οὐσίαν ἐκ τῶν μετὰ τοῦ πέρατος ἀπειργασμένων μέτρων** *deem me to say the whole progeny of these [Bound and Unbounded] is third, [me] positing this to be one [kind—namely, the kind Mix], a birth into being out of the measures that have been productive/produced by aid of Bound.* On this translation, τρίτον . . . τὸ τούτων ἔκγονον ἅπαν [sc., εἶναι] *that the whole progeny of these is third,* is an accusative plus infinitive construction after λέγειν *to say,* while ἓν τοῦτο [sc., εἶναι] *that this is one* is after τιθέντα *positing.* An equivalent translation makes τρίτον an accusative of respect and puts a single accusative after the verb of speaking: λέγειν . . . τὸ τούτων ἔκγονον ἅπαν *to refer to the whole progeny of these* (e.g., Fowler 1925: "as to the third . . . I mean every offspring of these two"; likewise, Delcomminette 2020). The deponent perfect participle ἀπειργασμένων *[measures] that have been productive/produced* might be active or passive (see, e.g., Fowler 1925; Gosling 1975; Delcomminette 2020) in meaning. In either case, it seems sensible to translate μετὰ plus genitive as *by aid of* (LSJ A.II), so that the measures are either productive (of the birth) with the aid of Bound or the measures are themselves produced by aid of Bound. Bury (1897) tentatively proposes the variant in

W, ἀπειργασμένην, agreeing with οὐσίαν *a being produced out of the measures of Bound* (followed by Diès 1949, and Frede 1993 and 1997). Finally, as Badham noted, γένεσιν εἰς οὐσίαν *birth into being* is a pleonasm: every birth produces a being. Delcomminette (2006, 243) explains the curious phrase as preparing for the difference to be drawn between coming-to-be and being, a difference that will be discussed at 53d3–54c12 and even at 32b3 (τὴν δ' εἰς τὴν αὐτῶν οὐσίαν ὁδόν *the way to their being*).

26e–27b: ***Socrates argues that Cause is a fourth distinct metaphysical kind because of its craftworking intelligence.***

26e1–2 **πρὸς τρισὶ τέταρτόν τι . . . εἶναι γένος** *there is a kind, a fourth besides the three (Unbounded, Bound, and Mix).* I identify the argument for this proposition as following from two main premises: Cause exists, and Cause is distinct from the other three kinds.

P1 [The kind Cause exists.]

P1.1 [Because] it is necessary that everything that comes to be comes to be through some cause (26e2–4).

P1.1.1 Because, Protarchus rhetorically asks, how could anything come to be without a cause (26e5)?

P2 The kind Cause, craftworking all these (i.e., mastering Unbounded and Bound to make Mix), is fourth, other than Unbounded, Bound, and Mix (27b1–2).

P2.1 The maker and the cause are rightly called one (26e7–8).

P2.1.1 Because there is no difference between the nature of what makes and the cause, except in name (26e6–7).

P2.2 It is the same with what is made and what comes into being (i.e., they are rightly called one, 27a1–2).

P2.2.1 Because they also do not differ except in name (27a2).

P2.3 [Cause and Mix] are different (27a8).

P2.3.1 Because What makes (i.e., Cause) is always leading in the order of nature, while the thing made (i.e., Mix) follows (27a5–6).

P2.4 The cause and what is slaving for cause (going) into a process of coming to be (i.e., Unbounded and, likewise, Bound) are not the same (27a8–9).

P2.5 The things coming to be and the things out of which they come to be amount to the three kinds (Mix, Unbounded, and Bound, 27a11–12).

27a8 **Ἄλλο ἄρα καὶ οὐ ταὐτὸν αἰτία τ' ἐστὶ καὶ τὸ δουλεῦον εἰς γένεσιν αἰτίᾳ.** The diacritical marks provided for ἄρα and the punctuation were accepted by all, including Burnet (1901), until Delcomminette (2005, 614):

> (The ἄρα) makes the whole sentence a conclusion drawn from 27a5–7, and the only way of understanding it is to take it as merely tautological, which implies that we should take τὸ δουλεῦον as a synonym of τὸ ποιούμενον. This interpretation could seem to be confirmed by the use of the verb ἡγεῖται at 27a5, which could already bring a touch of domination justifying the subsequent use of such a strong term as τὸ δουλεῦον. But this is hardly convincing: first, because it is really difficult to see how "what is made"—that is, the product itself—could be said to "serve" the cause *εἰς γένεσιν*, which can only refer to its own production, precisely because, as Socrates has just stated, the product always comes "after" the cause—and also, necessarily, "after" it has been produced; and secondly because, in this case, one could really not understand what allows Socrates to state at 27b1–2 that he has distinguished the fourth genus *from the first three*, and should rather agree with G. Striker (1970, 69–70) and E. Benitez (1989, 84) that he has only distinguished it from the third, τὸ μεικτόν, and not from τὸ ἄπειρον and τὸ πέρας.

Ἄλλο ἆρα καὶ οὐ ταὐτὸν αἰτία τ' ἐστὶ καὶ τὸ δουλεῦον εἰς γένεσιν αἰτίᾳ; This is an alternative proposed by Delcomminette (2005, 615–16), changing ἄρα to ἆρα and replacing the period with a question mark, and thereby turning the sentence into a question. This question, in effect, asks Protarchus to assent to the equivalent of premise P2.4. Delcomminette's identification of this new premise saves the argument from the two problems facing the standard reading, pointed out in the quotation above from Delcomminette (2005, 614).

Ἄλλο ἄρα. καὶ οὐ ταὐτὸν αἰτία τ' ἐστὶ καὶ τὸ δουλεῦον εἰς γένεσιν αἰτίᾳ. This is the other alternative proposed by Delcomminette (2005, 616), which he attributes to a suggestion by David Sedley. The period after ἄρα permit the first two words, Ἄλλο ἄρα, to draw the conclusion

P2.3 in my identification of the argument, while the rest of the passage states premise P2.4.

27b1 **τὸ πάντα ταῦτα δημιουργοῦν** *the thing crafting all these.* Drozdek (2000, 140) interprets these words to mean that Cause *makes* all three other kinds. This conflicts with the order in which Cause was introduced—not as soon as Bound and Unbounded were introduced but only after Mix was introduced, because all becoming needs a cause. Better to understand the Greek δημιουργοῦν, like the English verb "to craft," as able to take as direct object either *the thing worked up* (e.g., the bracelet) or *the things worked on* (e.g., silver and turquoise). In this sense of "craft," Cause crafts the thing worked up (Mix) and the things worked on (Bound and Unbounded).

27c–d ***Socrates reviews to show that the answer to the Happiness Question is something in the third kind, Mix.***

27c8–10 **ταῦτα . . . διειλόμεθα** *we divided into these [four kinds].* The direct object of the verb διαιρέω, in the active or middle voice, can be the object divided (LSJ I.1) or the objects produced by division (LSJ III.1). Here ταῦτα *these* refers to the four kinds produced by the division of πάντα τὰ νῦν ὄντα ἐν τῷ παντὶ *all things that now exist in the world* (23c4).

27d8–9 **οὐ γὰρ δυοῖν τινοῖν ἐστι μικτὸς ἐκεῖνος ἀλλὰ συμπάντων τῶν ἀπείρων ὑπὸ τοῦ πέρατος δεδεμένων** *for that [life of pleasure and knowing] is not a mix of a two [i.e., of pleasure* as one *and knowing* as *one] but [is a mix] of all the unbounded [things] that are tied down by Bound [in that life].* This is the text of B. As an alternative, manuscript T adds a definite article before δυοῖν: οὐ γὰρ ὁ δυοῖν τινοῖν ἐστι μικτὸς ἐκεῖνος *for the [life] of a two [i.e., of pleasure as one and knowing as one] is not that mixed life.* This text changes the grammatical subject of the clause, but the meaning comes to the same thing as in B. Another alternative is Christian Gottfried Schütz (cited in Bury 1897), who emends μεικτὸς ἐκεῖνος, *that mixed [life]* to μεικτὸν ἐκεῖνο *that mixed [kind].* Bury (1897) argues on behalf of Schütz: "It would be absurd to say that the mixed *life* is compounded of all limited ἄπειρα." We might avoid the absurdity by taking the participle δεδεμένων, which modifies the substantive συμπάντων τῶν ἀπείρων, to limit the substantive in the obvious way, to say: "that life is mixed of all the unbounded things that are tied down by Bound" *in that life.*

27e–28a: ***Socrates assigns unmixed pleasure to the kind Unbounded.***

Socrates' assignment follows from a single premise, that *the duo pleasure and pain do not have a bound but accept the more and less* (27e5–6). This premise in turn follows from two premises, expressed as present, contrary-to-fact conditionals.

P1 Pleasure could not be all good if it were not by nature unbounded in plenty and increase (27e7–9).

P2 Pain could not be wholly bad if it were not by nature unbounded in plenty and increase (28a1).

27e7–9 *Pleasure could not be all good if it were not by nature unbounded in plenty and increase.* I interpret ἄπειρον as unbounded: If a set of objects is *unbounded*, it is ordered by a duo of relations (like hotter and colder) such that there is no bound to how hot or how cold: the set keeps going on and never stops. Some alternative interpretations make the ἄπειρον indeterminate in some sense. Indeterminacy interpretations face a problem in this passage, because it is inconceivable that Philebus would see indeterminacy as the necessary condition of pleasure's goodness.

27e8–28a1 **πᾶν ἀγαθὸν . . . πᾶν κακόν** *all good . . . all bad.* Delcomminette (2020) follows Bekker (1817), who emends to πανάγαθον *absolutely good* and πάγκακον *absolutely bad.* I do not see a convincing reason to change the text in this way.

5. Note: Knowing should be assigned to the kind Cause.

28a–30a: ***While conventional arguments that the universe is designed and guided by knowledge might be challenged, Socrates gives a grand cosmological argument to show that divine knowing and the knowing of particular human beings belongs to the fourth kind Cause.***

After assigning Philebus' candidate to Unbounded, one of the four kinds, Socrates here assigns his original candidate to Cause, another of the four. I identify the argument for the proposition that *knowing should be assigned to the kind Cause* (28a4–6, restated at 28c3–4, 30d10–e2, and 31a7–8) as follows.

As alternatives, Carpenter (2003, 100) "outlines" the argument, while Rheins (2016, 17–19) represents it in twenty-one premises. Introducing the argument, Socrates says that the authoritative saying of the wise—that is, premise P2 below (restated in the subordinate clause of 28a6–8)—makes it "easy" (28c6) to establish the proposition. In P1, "Manages" translates ἐπιτροπεύειν (28d6). "Arranges and steers" translates συντάττουσαν διακυβερνᾶν (28d9).

That 30d10–e2 (one statement of the conclusion) is a conclusion is indicated by the participial phrase πεπορικὼς ἀπόκρισιν *having provided an answer,* which modifies the implied subject ("this argument" οὗτος ὁ λόγος) to the verb ἐστί *is* at 30e1: "[This argument belongs to the human beings of old, the argument] having provided an answer to my inquiry [i.e., the inquiry stated at 28a4–5: "Into which of the four kinds might we place, without impiety, knowing and expert knowing and awareness?"]. Arguments "provide answers" by drawing conclusions.

P1 [Whatever manages—that is, arranges and steers—the universe should be assigned to the kind Cause.]

P2 Awareness and an amazing knowing arrange and steer this whole universe (28d7–8, 28e3, 30c2–7, 30d8).

Because of the following three arguments:

A Socrates' "easy" argument from authority (inference indicated by Ἀλλὰ μὴν ῥᾴδιον . . . γὰρ *but it is easy [to see the truth of the conclusion], because . . . ,* 28c6).

A.P.1 The wise say with one voice that awareness is king of our heaven and earth (28c6–8).

A.P.2 The wise are perhaps speaking well (second premise indicated by [γῆς.] καὶ [ἴσως] *and,* 28c8).

B Protarchus' three independent, conventional arguments:

B.P.1 The alternative (that the forces of Randomness and Chance run the universe [28d6–7]) does not appear to be pious to say (inference indicated by γὰρ *because,* 28e1–2).

B.P.2 The only account that can do justice to the wonderful spectacle presented by the cosmic order of sun, moon, and stars and the revolution of the whole heaven, is that awareness orders (διακοσμεῖν) it all (second argument indicated by δὲ *and,* 28e2–5).

B.P.3 Protarchus could never give any other account. (That is, the conclusion 28c6–8 is incorrigible. This third argument is indicated by καὶ *and,* 28e5.)

C Socrates' "lengthy" argument:

C.P.1 A kingly soul and kingly awareness are inbred, through the power of Cause, into the nature of Zeus (30d1–4).

Because (inference indicated by Οὐκοῦν *surely then,* 30d1):

C.P.1.1 [Let "Zeus" refer to whatever rules the universe, allowing the possibility that Zeus is "the force of Unreason or Chance" (28d6–7).]

C.P.1.2 The body at our level has a soul (30a3–4).

C.P.1.3 If the body of the universe were not ensouled, the body at our level [would have its soul] after taking it from nowhere (i.e., it would not have a soul) (30a5–8).[4]

Because (implicit inference):[5]

C.P.1.3.1 The bodies at our level as a whole are sustained and take and hold, from the body of the universe, all the things they have (29e5–7).

Because (inference indicated by οὖν *then,* 29e5):

C.P.1.3.1.1 Each element—fire, water, air, and earth—in living things at this level is small and weak and inferior and is sustained and born from and grows out of the same element in the universe, where that element is amazing in magnitude and beauty and in every power that has to do with being that element (29d1–3, 29b6–8).

4. There is no question that the pair of premises C.P.1.2 and C.P.1.3 are coordinate: the question eliciting C.P.1.3 is a sentence fragment needing completion by reference to C.P.1.2: "[The body that is with us has a soul] after taking it from where?" (Πόθεν . . . λαβόν, 30a5). The two premises follow the form of two premises of a modus tollens inference, although Socrates does not elicit their conclusion, that the body of the universe is ensouled.

5. There is no inference indicator in the text marking this entailment. But there are other markers: the verbs of having (ἔχω) and taking (λαμβάνω) in C.P.1.3 recall the very same verbs of having and taking in C.P.1.3.1, and the concessive participle ("even though having the same possessions but still more beautiful in every way") that is attached to the protasis of C.P.1.3 ("If the body of the universe were not ensouled") recalls the argument establishing C.P.1.3.1.

Because (the inference is implicit, but Socrates introduces the following five premises—C.P.1.3.1.1.1–5—by saying Ἴθι δή, τὸν ἐπιόντα . . . λόγον ἄθρει *come then, look at the following argument*, 29a6–7):

C.P.1.3.1.1.1 We observe that fire, water, air, and earth, in synthesis, are present in the nature of the bodies of all living things (29a9–11).

C.P.1.3.1.1.2 The same holds true for every element as for the element fire (29b8–10).

C.P.1.3.1.1.3 The element fire at our level is something small and weak and inferior (29c1–2).

C.P.1.3.1.1.4 The element fire in the universe is amazing in magnitude and beauty and in every power that has to do with being fire (29c2–3).

C.P.1.3.1.1.5 The fire at our level—of you and me and other living things—is sustained and is born from and grows out of the fire of the universe (29c5–9).

C.P.1.3.1.2 There is a body of what we call the cosmos (29e1–2).

Because (inference indicated by δὴ *then* at 29e1, by the introduction of C.P.1.3.1.2.1 with the words τὸ μετὰ τοῦτο ἑξῆς ἕπου *follow along with respect to the next thing in order after this*, 29d6–7, and by the statement of C.P.1.3.1.2 as a causal circumstantial participle):

C.P.1.3.1.2.1 Fire, air, water, and earth laying together in a unity we (rightly) call body (29d7–8).

C.P.1.3.1.2.2 The cosmos is a unity put together out of fire, air, water, and earth (29e2–3).

C.P.1.4 Wisdom and awareness could never come to be without a soul (30c9–10—the coordination of this premise with C.P.1.5 is indicated by the μὴν at c9 [progressive μήν, Denniston (1966, 337, III.1.i "marking the transition from major to minor premise").[6]

6. Although the pair C.P.1.2 and C.P.1.3 are clearly coordinate, and the pair C.P.1.4 and C.P.1.5 are clearly coordinate, the text does not explicitly link these two pairs of premises with each other. Nonetheless, there are three reasons to see a link

C.P.1.5 In addition to a great deal of unbounded in the universe and a sufficient amount of bound in it, there is a cause, not paltry, ordering and arranging years and seasons and months, (a cause that is) most justly called *wisdom and awareness* (30c2–8).

Because (inference indicated by Οὐκοῦν *surely then,* 30c2):

C.P.1.5.1 It absolutely would not stand to reason that the kind Cause would not have devised for the great parts of the astronomical whole the nature of the finest and most valuable things (30a9–c1).[7]

Because (inference from C.P.1.5.1.1 indicated by its statement as genitive absolute to μεμηχανῆσθαι *would have devised,* and inference from C.P.1.5.1.2 indicated by the structure of the sentence a9–b7—namely, Οὐ . . . δοκοῦμέν . . . μὲν . . . δ' οὐκ ἄρα . . . *we do not think on the one hand that* [C.P.1.5.1.2] *and then on the other hand not [think] that* [C.P.1.5.1]):

C.P.1.5.1.1 The great parts of the whole astronomical body are surpassingly fair and pure (30b4–6).

C.P.1.5.1.2 The kind Cause is called every sort of wisdom (30b4).

---

between these two pairs: (1) The two pairs are separated by lines 30a9–c1. Those lines are nothing but an argument subordinate to both pairs, that is, they are a lemma supporting both P.1.3 and P.1.5. The lemma is that "the kind Cause has devised for the great parts of the astronomical whole the nature of the finest and most valuable things" (30a9–c1). The explicit inference from this lemma to C.P.1.3 is indicated by γάρ *because* (30a9). The explicit inference from the lemma to C.P.1.5 is indicated by Οὐκοῦν *surely then* (30c2). And so this ten-line lemma explains the lack of an explicit linking word in natural language. (2) No conclusion is drawn after the statement of C.P.1.2 and C.P.1.3. The audience must wait for the conclusion to be stated later. (3) The first eligible conclusion to be stated is C.P.1, explicitly indicated after the statement of the pair C.P.1.5 and C.P.1.4 by Οὐκοῦν *surely then* (30d1).

7. I interpret the principle established at 30a9–b7 (that anything at our level happens better at the macrolevel) to be used twice in the argument (as premise C.P.1.5.1 and as premise C.P.1.3.1.1), as indicated by the two inference indicators, γάρ *because* at 30a9 and Οὐκοῦν *surely then* at 30c2. This interpretation, in addition to being faithful to the inference indicators, also strengthens the argument by using the principle twice: first to support that the universe has an ensouled body and then to support that the universe is ordered and arranged by wisdom and awareness. The principle established at 30a9–b7 is established by two further premises, but I present them only once (as C.P.1.3.1.1.1 [at 30b4–6] and C.P.1.3.1.1.2 [at 30b4]), with their support in turn.

Because (inference indicated by statement of premises C.P.1.5.1.2.1–4 as participles circumstantial to ἐπικαλεῖσθαι *is called)*:

C.P.1.5.1.2.1 The kind Cause provides a soul in the (bodies) at our level (30b1–2).

C.P.1.5.1.2.2 The kind Cause builds into (souls at our level) trainer's skill (to rule bodies, 30b2).

C.P.1.5.1.2.3 The kind Cause builds into (souls at our level) medical skill (to rule bodies, 30b2–3).

Because (inference from C.P.1.5.1.2.3.1 indicated by its statement as genitive absolute to C.P.1.5.1.2.3):

C.P.1.5.1.2.3.1 A body can stumble (into injury or disease, 30b2).

C.P.1.5.1.2.4. The kind Cause puts together other things in other areas, healing everything (30b3).

The strategy for proving P2 is to argue for the first of the following two alternatives: either awareness and knowing run the universe by arranging and steering it, or unreason and chance run it (28d5–9). *Arguments from design* infer from the orderly aspects of the universe that there is "a deliberative and directive mind behind those phenomena" (Ratzsch 2005). Both Protarchus' briefly stated argument (that only the hypothesis of awareness can adequately explain the phenomenon of cosmic order, B.P.2 = 28e2–5) and Socrates' argument C (that only the hypothesis of awareness can explain the phenomenon of a visible cosmos that is like a human body in having a soul that runs it) are arguments from design.

Modern arguments from design typically reason "as if they thought the world the *workmanship* of God" (Hume [1779] 1998, 40). In contrast, Socrates' argument C reasons that the visible cosmos is the *body* of a divine soul. Hume's character Philo appears to refer to Socrates' argument C and compares it favorably to the workmanship argument: "It must be confessed, that as the universe resembles more a human body than it does the works of human art and contrivance; if our limited analogy could ever, with any propriety, be extended to the whole of nature, the inference seems juster in favour of the ancient than the modern theory" (Hume [1779] 1998, 40).

Although the visible cosmos is a body, Socrates relies on the "workmanship" model when he infers that a wise Cause must have "devised for the great parts of the astronomical whole a nature that is the fairest and most valuable" (C.P.1.5.1 = 30a9–c1), which leads him to conclude that the soul of the universe, "ordering and arranging years and seasons and months" must itself possess "awareness and wisdom" (C.P.1.5 = 30c2–8). Thus, Socrates' argument C establishes the following ultimate causal order. Some primordial member of the craftworking kind Cause, prior to the space and time of the universe, craftworks Bound and Unbounded into the particular mix that comes to be as the universe with its fairest and most valuable nature. That original craftworker does not leave the rule of that universe to chance, but creates a soul (which we call "Zeus") and endows it with awareness to rule the universe as any soul moves its body. This ruling soul causes such things as the order of years, seasons, and months.

The universe's soul Zeus, while a personal member, a "genus-man" (γενούστης) of the fourth kind or 'genus' Cause, is not itself identical with its own cause, some primordial member of the kind Cause. Likewise, the *Timaeus* makes a causal distinction between the transcendent god at 28c and the created world and its soul at 30b. Although the argument in the *Philebus* has no need to draw a further inference, we can: that the primordial member of the kind Cause, since it is craftworking, wise, and cognitive, must itself possess a soul. There is similar reasoning in other later dialogues of Plato. For example, arguing dialectically against those who believe that only the forms are real, the Eleatic Stranger infers that what is "perfectly real" must have awareness and hence soul and hence live and move (*Sophist* 248e6–249a2).

An alternate interpretation (by, e.g., Hackforth 1945, Menn 1995, and Migliori 1993) is that Zeus in some sense is prior to his created existence as ruler of our universe. Such an alternative is at odds with the *Timaeus* and appears obscure in itself. See Rheins (2016) for discussion.

Socrates introduces his argument C when he bids Protarchus to consider "the argument that is relevant to (ἐπιόντα) this topic" (29a6) and ends it at 30d6–8. The argument relies on some false but easily updated scientific assumptions. For example, proposition C.P.1.3.1.2.1 (= 29d7–8) falsely asserts that material bodies in general are composed of the four elements earth, air, fire, and water. Likewise, proposition C.P.1.3.1.2.2 (=29e2–3) falsely asserts that the cosmos is composed of earth, air, fire, and water. Such false propositions make the argument as a whole unsound. It is easy to revise false propositions such as these with up-to-date scientific propositions about the atomic elements of the universe. And so the falsity of such premises is not a serious flaw in Socrates' argument C.

There is another scientific assumption that is false and not easily updated. To show that the body of the universe has a soul, Socrates needs to establish that "the body of the universe has [at its macrolevel] the same things as [bodies at this level] yet even finer in every way" (C.P.1.5.1.1=30b4–6). Then, with the additional premise that bodies at this level—the organic life forms on the surface of the earth—must have souls that are the source and ruler of their motions, it would follow that the astronomical body of the universe has an even finer soul, the source and ruler of its celestial motions. But the premise C.P.1.5.1.1 (=30b4–6) is false. Newton's law of universal gravitation explains the wondrous celestial motions with no need of heavenly elements being "finer" than terrestrial elements. Since Newtonian gravity is sufficient to explain *both* the wondrous order of celestial motion *and* a terrestrial rockfall, celestial motion no more shows that the cosmos is a living body than the motion of a falling rock shows that the earth is a living body. And this premise (C.P.1.5.1.1=30b4–6) is not easily updated or avoided in revising Socrates' argument C. Yet without it (C.P.1.5.1.1=30b4–6), the exciting consequence—that a cosmic soul possesses "wisdom and awareness" (C.P.1.5=30c2–8)—does not follow.

Thus, there is a false and not easily updated premise in Socrates' argument C, making that argument unsound. Nonetheless, as it seems to me, a reader of the *Philebus* who was unaware of a theory of universal gravitation would have found the argument highly plausible. Indeed, writing almost a century after Newton's discovery in 1687 of a theory of universal gravitation, Hume expected his readers to find more plausibility in the conclusion that the visible cosmos is the animate body of a divine soul than that it is the product of "workmanship," on the basis of its greater resemblance to the human body than to any "works of human art and contrivance" (Hume [1779] 1998, 40).

Since C.P.1.5.1.1 (=30b4–6) is the only destructively false premise I find in the argument, and as I find no uncontroversially invalid inferences, I explain the argument's unsoundness on the grounds that the scientific understanding of Plato's day turned out to be false. Alternate interpretations as to *why* the argument is unsound are that the argument is intentional sophistry (Gosling 1975, 206–8) or a game with a purpose other than sound inference to its conclusion (Delcomminette 2006, 263, 266–67). It is a problem for such interpretations that the argument would have been plausibly sound prior to Newton's theory of universal gravitation.

Although the conclusion of this argument is that knowing is part of the kind Cause, an alternative interpretation is that knowing is part of the kind Bound (e.g., Damascius 1959 §127, p. 61 and §134, p. 65; Ficino 2000, 385; Ferber 1912, 159–60; and Robin 1950, 574–75). The reasoning is that, if the mixed life (of pleasure and knowing) is part of the kind Mix (which is a mix of Bound and Unbounded), then either knowing belongs to the kind Bound, or the dialogue equivocates on "mix." This reasoning mistakes the way in which pleasure is bound: not by the kinds of knowing present in the mixed life (including the inexact building and musical skills, 62b–c) but by *number* to produce measure and symmetry. For example, as shown below, pure pleasure is limited by a ratio of one to one with the amount of depletion that can be unperceived. There is no equivocation on "mix," because there is no suggestion at 20b–22c that the good mixed life contains only pleasure and knowing as sole constituents of the mixed life in the way that Bound and Unbounded are sole constituents of Mix. Indeed, 22d1–2 explicitly leaves open the possibility that other ingredients are present in the mix besides pleasure and knowing, a possibility realized in the final account of the mixed life at 64c–67a, where measure, beauty, and truth are the dominant ingredients. As the deliberations in 60a–64b show, both pleasure and knowing are capable of being more or less present in the mixed life. Relative to that mixed life—that is, as effects in the mix of the craftworking agent craftworking—both are unbounded in contrast to the bound provided by measure, beauty, and truth.

28a3–4 **τούτων δή σοι τῶν ἀπεράντων γεγονὸς ἔστω** *let [pleasure] be, for you, among these unlimited things [i.e., the members of the kind*

Unbounded], the reading of B and T. One alternative is Burnet's (1901) revision: τούτω δή σοι τῶν ἀπεράντων γε γένους ἔστων *let these two [i.e., pleasure and pain] for you be of* the kind *of the unlimited things.* Another alternative is Frede, who adopts a correction made in manuscript Ven. 189: τοῦτο δή σοι τῶν ἀπεράντων γεγονὸς ἔστω, *let* this *[i.e., the pleasant] be for you among the unlimited things.* Frede first (1993) translates this as follows: "But take note that pleasure is thereby assigned to the boundless." Later (1997, 35), however, she translates it thus: "let it for you belong [*mag es für dich . . . gehören*] to the boundless."

28d6–9 **ἐπιτροπεύειν** *be in charge . . .* **διακυβερνᾶν** *steer through.* The first verb is consistent with randomness being in charge, while the second verb requires rational agency.

28e7 **δῆτά** *then.* Used in questions, this word in most cases marks an inference or consequence of what was previously said.

29a6 **νῦν ἡμῖν** *for us now* contrasts with τοῖς πρόσθεν *for those earlier* at 28d7–8, e7.

29a10 **καὶ γῆν** *land ho!* ("land indeed!")–perhaps a sailor's cry on sighting land. Socrates is noticing a pun in his list of the four elements: "fire, water, air, and 'land ho!' [i.e., earth]—as storm-tossed sailors say." In her speech of welcome to Agamemnon, Clytemnestra, using a metaphor for his appearance home, says that he is καὶ γῆν φανεῖσαν ναυτίλοις παρ' ἐλπίδα *land appearing to sailors [who had been] past hope* (Aeschylus, *Agamemnon* 899–900).

29b1 **Καὶ μάλα** *[we] very much [observe those things] indeed!* is the natural way to interpret this, until Protarchus establishes his thesis (with the inferential γὰρ) by referring to the company's aporia. Then the meaning seems to be *very much [storm tossed] indeed!*

29b3 **τῶν παρ' ἡμῖν** *the things by us*—that is, the things at our (microcosmic) level such as fire, water, air, and earth. Eventually, soul will be added to the list of things that are put together in bodies.

29b9 **πάντων** *all things . . .* **τῷ παντί** "the all" = *the universe* (in almost all occurrences in *Philebus*). There are different meanings between the plural without the definite article and the singular with the definite article.

29c3 **πάσῃ δυνάμει τῇ περὶ τὸ πῦρ οὔσῃ** *In all the power that is [realized] about fire.* There are different meanings for δύναμις. When modified by a participle *X*-ing it means the *activated* power *X*-ing (two instances in *Philebus*; see also 32a1). When limited by an infinitive (one instance in *Philebus*, at 58d3–4), it is the *inactive* power to *X*. When limited by a genitive (ten instances in *Philebus*—e.g., 28d7), it is the *inactive* power of *X*-ness.

29c5 **ἄρχεται** *[the fire present to us] is subject [to the fire of the universe].* As an alternative, Burnet (1901) (following Jackson) emends ἄρχεται to αὔξεται *[the fire present to us] grows [by the fire of the universe].*

29c5–9 *The fire at our level—of you and me and other living things—is sustained and is born from and is subject to the fire of the universe.* In my interpretation there are no premises supporting this proposition (C.P.1.3.1.1.5). I take it that Socrates, if pressed for a reason, would have appealed to common observations such as the following: the fire of the sun warms the earth and its inhabitants; we do not warm the sun.

Migliori (1993, 173) provides an alternative interpretation according to which there is an argument in the text for 29c5–9, an argument that can be made just as well for the other elements besides fire, as follows: "The matter appears obvious for several reasons: [first] from the principle nothing comes from nothing and [second] because reflection upon the processes which constitute reality [*processi costitutivi della realtà*] shows that the direction of the process is always from more pure to less pure, from pure elements to mixed products."

Delcomminette (2006, 265) interprets the argument to rest on two different undefended speculative metaphysical principles: "a rule of bi-univocal [*biunivoque*] correspondence, according to which all that is present in us is also present in the universe," and "a rule of hierarchy, according to which that which is present in us is infinitely inferior to that which corresponds to it in the universe, upon which it depends and by which it is sustained." These principles are "applied" at four levels: the elementary level of fire, water, air and earth; the level of "their organization into a body, the level of the soul, and the level of "intelligence and the three other kinds" (2006, 265). Like Migliori's interpretation, Delcomminette's interpretation attributes undefended metaphysical principles to the argument and is at odds with the inference indicators in the text.

According to Gosling (1975), this premise cannot merely be the true point that the microcosmic bodies take in any increase of a given element from the environment, which is too weak for the notion of nourishing. His implication is that any stronger version of the premise is false. But, as I have interpreted it, the argument need not make more than the obvious claim that the warmth in our bodies derives from such things as the sun.

According to Hampton (1990), Plato is suggesting here that the macrocosmic fire is ontologically prior to the microcosmic bits of fire. But we need not interpret the argument to presuppose this nonobvious philosophical notion of ontological priority.

29c7 **ὑπ' ἐκείνου** [πυρός] is an antithesis to the preceding ὑπὸ τοῦ παρ' ἡμῖν πυρός and calls for a verb in the passive voice such as ἄρχεται *is subject to* or αὔξεται *is increased by*, but Socrates by the end of the sentence uses the active form ἴσχει *holds fast*.

29e2 **[διὰ] τὸν αὐτὸν γὰρ τρόπον** *on account of the same manner*. Badham raised the problem: if we cannot explain the causal διὰ found in the manuscripts with τρόπον, we ought to edit out the διὰ. Bury (1897) and Burnet (1901) cannot explain, and they do edit out the διὰ. Translators tend to follow them: for example, Frede (1993): "It will turn out to be a body in the same sense, since it is composed of the same elements" (see also Delcomminette 2020). The following reconstruction of the argument avoids changing the text and gives a meaning to the causal διὰ with τρόπον, granting Badham's point that "the cause of its being a body is given in σύνθετον . . . αὐτῶν [composed of the same elements]."

P1 If earth, air, fire, and water lie together in a unity; we legitimately call them a body.

P2 Earth, air, fire, and water lie together in the unity we call the cosmos.

Thus, διὰ τὸν αὐτὸν τρόπον *on account of the same manner [of inference as from antecedent to consequent in P1]:*

C1 The cosmos would be a body.

Later logicians established one sense of τρόπος as "mode of inference," according to LSJ τρόπος VI.

30a–e: ***Socrates concludes the cosmological argument that Knowing belongs to the kind Cause***

For ease of reference I restate here the main steps of Socrates' argument C that *knowing should be assigned to the kind Cause* (see note to 28a–30a for all premises of this lengthy argument).

P1 [Whatever manages—that is, arranges and steers—the universe should be assigned to the kind Cause.]

P2 Awareness and an amazing knowing arrange and steer this whole universe (28d7–8, 28e3, 30c2–7, 30d8).

Because:

C.P.1 A kingly soul and kingly awareness are inbred, through the power of Cause, into the nature of *Zeus* (i.e., *that which runs* or *he who rules* this universe, 30d1–4).

Because:

C.P.1.1 [Let "Zeus" refer to whatever rules the universe, allowing the possibility that Zeus is "the force of Unreason or Chance" (28d6–7).]

C.P.1.2 The body at our level has a soul (30a3–4).

C.P.1.3 If the body of the universe were not ensouled, the body at our level [would have its soul] after taking it from nowhere (i.e., it would not have a soul) (30a5–8).

C.P.1.4 Wisdom and awareness could never come to be without a soul (30c9–10).

C.P.1.5 In addition to a great deal of unbounded in the universe and a sufficient amount of bound in it, there is a cause, not paltry, ordering and arranging years and seasons and months, [a cause that is] most justly called *wisdom and awareness* (30c2–7).

Because:

C.P.1.5.1 It absolutely would not stand to reason that the kind Cause would not have devised for the great parts of the astronomical whole the nature of the finest and most valuable things (30a9–c1).

Because:

C.P.1.5.1.1 The great parts of the whole astronomical body are surpassingly fair and pure (30b4–6).

C.P.1.5.1.2 The kind Cause is called every sort of wisdom (30b4).

Because:

C.P.1.5.1.2.1 The kind Cause provides a soul in the [bodies] at our level (30b1–2).

C.P.1.5.1.2.2 The kind Cause builds into [souls at our level] trainer's skill (to rule bodies, 30b2).

C.P.1.5.1.2.3 The kind Cause builds into [souls at our level] medical skill (to rule bodies, 30b2–3).

Because:

C.P.1.5.1.2.3.1 A body can stumble (into injury or disease, 30b2).

C.P.1.5.1.2.4. The kind Cause puts together other things in other areas, healing everything (30b3).

30a5–6 **Πόθεν . . . λαβόν, εἴπερ μὴ τό γε τοῦ παντὸς σῶμα ἔμψυχον ὂν ἐτύγχανε, ταὐτά γε ἔχον τούτῳ καὶ ἔτι πάντῃ καλλίονα;** *If the body of the universe were not actually ensouled—a body having the same possessions as this [body with us] but still more beautiful in every way—the body at our level [would have its soul] after taking it from where?* Protarchus affirms in answer οὐδαμόθεν ἄλλοθεν *from nowhere else,* giving Socrates premise C.P.1.3 (the body at our level takes its soul from nowhere if the body of the universe is not actually ensouled). This premise is conditional: neither Socrates asking the question nor Protarchus giving his answer affirms here that the universe has a soul.

Lorenz (2019, 94) translates as follows: "But from where . . . does it obtain soul, unless the body of the universe turns out to be ensouled, given that it has the same attributes as our kind of body, but still more beautiful in every way?" Lorenz's "unless" clause inaccurately translates a Greek contrary-to-fact condition, contrary to fact because the tense of the verb ἐτύγχανε is imperfect (LSJ εἴπερ II). Many translators suppose that an English "unless" clause may translate a Greek *neutral* (as opposed to *counterfactual*) "if . . . not" condition. This is inaccurate. An "unless" clause ought only to translate a neutral "except if" condition (πλὴν εἰ, as at Plato, *Apology* 18d1). See Geis (1973) and von Fintel (1992).

Mason (2014, 146) interprets these lines to say, "we get our souls from the world-soul (just as our bodies are derived from the world body)." In addition to being far from the text, such a reading makes the argument assume at this point what it needs to prove.

Carpenter (2003, 100) interprets the reasoning as follows: if the cosmic body were not ensouled, then "our soul, and the very fact that we are living *organisms*, would be no more than merely accidental and contingent—that is, there would be no explanation at all for the organisation which makes a body." The importation of "contingency" is unnecessary and does not strengthen the argument.

30a9–b7 **Οὐ γάρ που δοκοῦμέν γε, ὦ Πρώταρχε, τὰ τέτταρα ἐκεῖνα, πέρας καὶ ἄπειρον καὶ κοινὸν καὶ τὸ τῆς αἰτίας γένος ἐν ἅπασι τέταρτον ἐνόν, τοῦτο ἐν μὲν τοῖς παρ' ἡμῖν ψυχήν τε παρέχον καὶ σωμασκίαν ἐμποιοῦν καὶ πταίσαντος σώματος ἰατρικὴν καὶ ἐν ἄλλοις ἄλλα συντιθὲν καὶ ἀκούμενον πᾶσαν καὶ παντοίαν σοφίαν ἐπικαλεῖσθαι, τῶν δ' αὐτῶν τούτων ὄντων ἐν ὅλῳ τε οὐρανῷ καὶ κατὰ μεγάλα μέρη, καὶ προσέτι καλῶν καὶ εἰλικρινῶν, ἐν τούτοις δ' οὐκ ἄρα μεμηχανῆσθαι τὴν τῶν καλλίστων καὶ τιμιωτάτων φύσιν** (=C.P.1.5.1). Scholars have struggled with the grammar of this sentence. Table 3 below gives my analysis (in the style of Bailly 2003). I follow Bury (1897): "Though the sentence begins with mention of all four γένη, the true subject of the whole is the fourth only, τὸ τῆς αἰτίας γένος, which in the first clause is resumed by τοῦτο as accusative (agreeing with the participles παρέχον, ἐμποιοῦν, συντιθέν, ἀκούμενον) before the infinitive ἐπικαλεῖσθαι, and in the second clause (after the genitive absolute) as accusative subject to μεμηχανῆσθαι."[8]

8. I am grateful to Mason (2014, 148n6) for defending Bury's identification of "the true subject," correcting my identification of the subject of this passage in Rudebusch (2016).

Table 3
Analysis of 30a9–b7

1	οὐ γάρ που δοκοῦμέν γε, ὦ Πρώταρχε *for I suppose, Protarchus, that we do not think*	Main clause. Verb of thinking δοκοῦμέν followed by indirect discourse in two clauses (clauses marked by μέν at row 5 and δέ at row 10), an accusative (τοῦτο at row 4) plus infinitive (ἐπικαλεῖσθαι at row 8 and μεμηχανῆσθαι at row 10) construction.
2	τὰ τέτταρα ἐκεῖνα *with respect to those four*	Accusative of respect limiting δοκοῦμέν.
3	πέρας καὶ ἄπειρον καὶ κοινὸν καὶ τὸ τῆς αἰτίας γένος ἐν ἅπασι τέταρτον ἐνόν *Bound, Unbounded, Shared, and the kind Cause, a fourth that is present in all things*	Appositive to τὰ τέτταρα ἐκεῖνα, naming "those four."
4	τοῦτο *that this*	Demonstrative pronoun in apposition to its antecedent, τὸ τῆς αἰτίας γένος. It is the accusative subject of the indirect μέν and δέ clauses after δοκοῦμέν begun but suspended for the conjunction in row 5.
5	ἐν μὲν τοῖς [σώμασι] παρ' ἡμῖν ψυχήν τε παρέχον καὶ σωμασκίαν ἐμποιοῦν καὶ *providing a soul in the [bodies] at our level and building in physical trainer's skill*	Conjunction of participial phrases (expressing actions performed by the subject, τοῦτο, which actions cause the action of the main verb, ἐπικαλεῖσθαι, of the μέν phrase begun but suspended for the construction in row 6.

(continued)

6	πταίσαντος σώματος *when a body stumbles*	Genitive absolute construction expressing circumstances (a body stumbling), causing the action of the third conjunct, ἐμποιοῦν ἰατρικὴν.
7	ἰατρικὴν καὶ ἐν ἄλλοις ἄλλα συντιθὲν καὶ ἀκούμενον πᾶσαν *and medical skill and in other cases putting other things with [soul] and giving remedies for everything*	Conjunction of participial phrases at row 5 resumed and completed.
8	καὶ παντοίαν σοφίαν ἐπικαλεῖσθαι *is called every sort of wisdom*	The μέν clause begun at row 4 is here resumed and completed. The main verb of this μέν clause is the infinitive ἐπικαλεῖσθαι. The subject is τοῦτο.
9	τῶν δ' αὐτῶν τούτων ὄντων ἐν ὅλῳ τε οὐρανῷ καὶ κατὰ μεγάλα μέρη, καὶ προσέτι καλῶν καὶ εἰλικρινῶν *since these same things [as are found at our level, that is, bodies composed of fire, water, air, and earth lying together in a unity] are in the whole sky in big parts, [which are] surpassingly fair and pure*	Genitive absolute construction expressing circumstances causing the action of the main verb μεμηχανῆσθαι of the δέ clause of the indirect discourse. Restated with a finite verb, the participial phrase reads τὰ δ' αὐτὰ ταῦτά ἐστιν ἐν ὅλῳ τε οὐρανῷ καὶ κατὰ μεγάλα μέρη, καὶ προσέτι καλὰ καὶ εἰλικρινά.
10	ἐν τούτοις δ' οὐκ ἄρα μεμηχανῆσθαι τὴν τῶν καλλίστων καὶ τιμιωτάτων φύσιν *but that [this, i.e., the kind Cause] has not devised the finest and most precious nature in those [heavenly body parts].*	This δέ clause coordinates with the μέν clause above, with same subject τοῦτο.

30a9–10 **τὰ τέτταρα ἐκεῖνα** *with respect to those four.* This noun phrase at first appears to be the subject of the indirect discourse after δοκοῦμέν. Rather than an accusative of respect, Stallbaum's (1842) alternative reading is that the sentence is an anacoluthon: τὰ τέτταρα ἐκεῖνα is the subject of the indirect discourse at first, and Socrates switches mid-sentence to a different subject.

30b1 **ἐν ἅπασι τέταρτον ἐνόν** *[Bound, Unbounded, Mix, and the kind Cause,] a fourth that is present in all things.* We have it already from 23c4–5 that the first three kinds are present *in all things.* An alternative interpretation of ἐν ἅπασι τέταρτον ἐνόν is that it claims that Cause is present *in the kinds Bound and Unbounded as well as Mix* (Delcomminette 2006, 268). This alternative seems at odds with the plain sense of the text, as well as with 27a8–12 and 27b1–2.

30b1–2 **ἐν μὲν τοῖς [σώμασι] παρ' ἡμῖν ψυχήν τε παρέχον** *[the kind Cause] providing a soul in the [bodies] at our level.* As Liebesman (2011, 411) observes, "kinds can inherit properties from their members in much the same way that ordinary objects inherit properties from their parts." The Kind Cause provides souls to bodies in the same sense that it craftworks Unbounded and Bound to give birth to Mix at 27b1–2—namely, in having members that are such causes. In arguing for C.P.1 = 30d1–4 (that the body of this universe has a soul and mental awareness), it would be circular reasoning to assume the existence of that macrosoul. As I interpret the argument, there is no such fallacy. The argument assumes at C.P.1.5.1.2.1 -4 = 30b1–3 only the existence of the kind Cause, already established at 27b1–2. There is similar reasoning about kinds in other dialogues of Plato. For example, the kind Motion cannot be at rest and so it must be moving (*Sophist* 255a). In the same dialogue, arguing dialectically against those who believe that only the forms are real, the Eleatic Stranger infers that what is "perfectly real" must have awareness and hence soul and hence live and move (248e6–249a2). Certainly such statements are absurd if Plato has a set theoretical account of kinds and subkinds. And we should infer that his account of kinds and subkinds does not identify them with sets (on the nature of kinds, see Muniz and Rudebusch 2018 and n.d.).

An alternative interpretation is that a mind in some sense, rather than the kind Cause, would have to be the subject of the participle παρέχον *providing.* Thus, Striker (1970) deletes ψυχήν τε παρέχον *providing soul* from the text on the grounds that the whole point of the argument here is to show that there is such a thing as a divine or world mind and soul, and such a soul is not established until 30c–d. Frede (1997) proposes a different emendation. As she reasons, since it seems wrong to say that awareness *gives* (παρέχον) the soul to the body, but rather orders it and maintains it, it would be preferable to emend the text to read something like κατέχον *possess* or *master.* Another interpretation of this passage is Gosling (1975, 99), according to whom the kind Cause is a category. As a consequence, he cannot understand "supplies" (παρέχον) in a causal way. As he reads this passage, therefore, "the kind Cause supplies souls to bodies" means simply that *souls are in the category Cause.* Likewise, to say "the kind Cause builds skill into souls" (30b2–3) would seem to mean simply that *skill and knowing are in the category Cause.* Since it is the burden of Socrates' argument precisely to *prove* that knowing is in the "category"—that is, the kind Cause—this interpretation seems to make the argument circular.

More recently, Rheins (2016, 19 and 36) has argued that the subject is neither the kind Cause nor an intellect but the cosmos itself on the grounds that "this subject (which is *a* cause), cannot be intellect in 30b1–7, and it is extremely unlikely to be the fourth kind itself, rather than a particular member of it." In reasoning this way, Rheins seems not to notice that, as Liebesman (2011, 411) observes, "kinds can inherit properties from their members in much the same way that ordinary objects inherit properties from their parts." We can say, for example, that the honeybee pollinates plants or that the human race developed atomic energy in the twentieth century. The meaning of γένος *kind* permits τοῦτο *this (kind Cause)* to be present everywhere (in virtue of its members being present everywhere) and to devise the nature of the cosmos (in virtue of one of its members devising the cosmos).

30b2–3 **σωμασκίαν ἐμποιοῦν καὶ πταίσαντος σώματος ἰατρικὴν** *given that a body stumbles [into weakness or disease, the kind Cause] builds into* *[souls at our level] physical trainer's skill and medical skill.* The genitive absolute πταίσαντος σώματος *given that a body stumbles* provides an explanation why the kind Cause builds these things into us.

30b4 **τῶν δ' αὐτῶν τούτων** *these same things [as are found at our level—that is, bodies composed of fire, water, air, and earth lying together in a unity].* The demonstrative pronoun's most immediate and natural antecedent is τοῖς [σώμασι] at 30b1. Bury's alternative antecedent is *these same [four kinds—Bound, Unbounded, Mix, and Cause].* Such an alternative seems to weaken the subargument for C.P.1.5.1 (30a9–c1).

30b6 **μεμηχανῆσθαι τὴν . . . φύσιν** *[the kind Cause] devises the nature.* The verb here is middle in meaning and transitive. The kind Cause devised the nature of the cosmos in the same sense that the human race devised nuclear weapons—namely, in virtue of one or some of its members devising it (as Liebesman [2011, 411] observes, this sense is to be expected in generic predication).

As an alternative, Mason (2014, 148) argues that the meaning of μεμηχανῆσθαι here is passive and that the subject of this verb is τὴν φύσιν "the . . . nature has been built." Mason gives two arguments against a middle, transitive reading, from the meaning of μεμηχανῆσθαι and from the grammar of μεμηχανῆσθαι. In the argument from the meaning of μεμηχανῆσθαι, Mason observes that the kind Cause is described at 30b1 as ἐν ἅπασι ἐνόν *present in all things* and rightly points out that it takes a particular soul to have devised (μεμηχανῆσθαι) the nature of the cosmos. But it does not follow from this observation and point that the meaning is passive rather than active. As Liebesman (2011, 411) observes, "kinds can inherit properties from their members in much the same way that ordinary objects inherit properties from their parts." The meaning of γένος *kind* permits τοῦτο *this [kind Cause]* to be present everywhere (in virtue of its members being present everywhere) and to devise the nature of the cosmos (in virtue of one of its members devising the cosmos). In the argument from the grammar of μεμηχανῆσθαι, Mason reasons that the verb μεμηχανῆσθαι must have a passive meaning, "since a middle sense is out of the question here (Plato would of course never say that soul 'has built itself' into the cosmos)" (Mason 2014, 147). Mason seems not to notice that the middle sense may have, in addition to the direct reflexive sense (which "represents the subject as acting directly *on himself*" [S §1717], for example, "to build *oneself*"), also an indirect reflexive sense (which represents the subject as acting *for himself, with reference to himself,* or *with something belonging to himself*" [S §1719], for example, when the kind Cause devises *with things belonging to itself* some nature). LSJ (μηχανάομαι II.B.1) attests an indirect reflexive sense for the perfect middle of the deponent μηχανάομαι in Plato at *Gorgias* 459d5–6 (πειθὼ . . . μεμηχανημένος *having devised a persuasion for himself)* and at *Laws* 904b6–7 (μεμηχάνηται . . . τὸ ποῖόν τι *has devised the sort of thing with something belonging to himself).* Other such instances in Plato are *Laws* 649a3 (φάρμακον οὔτε αὐτοὶ μεμηχανήμεθα *neither have* we *devised a drug for ourselves)* and *Timaeus* 47a6 (μεμηχάνηνται . . . ἀριθμόν *devised number with reference to themselves).*

τούτοις The most immediate and natural antecedent of the demonstrative pronoun τούτοις is μέρη parts.

30b7 **τῶν καλλίστων καὶ τιμιωτάτων** *[the nature] of the finest and most valuable things.* The plural is used because the argument requires that "the finest and most valuable" refers to three things: soul, awareness, and wisdom. As an alternative interpretation, Hackforth (1945, 56) states that the plural indicates that "Plato wavers between a single world-soul . . . and a plurality."

30c4–5 **ἄπειρόν τε ἐν τῷ παντὶ πολύ, καὶ πέρας ἱκανόν, καί τις . . . αἰτία οὐ φαύλη** *a great deal of unbounded in the universe and a sufficient amount of bound [in it], and a cause, not paltry.* The substantives ἄπειρόν *unbounded,* πέρας *bound,* and αἰτία *cause* are modified, respectively, by ἐν τῷ παντὶ πολύ *a great deal of [unbounded] in the universe,* ἱκανόν *a sufficient amount of [bound in the universe],* and τις . . . οὐ φαύλη *a [cause], not paltry.* These modifiers show that in this premise the words ἄπειρόν *unbounded,* πέρας *bound,* and αἰτία *cause* do not refer to the kinds Unbounded, Bound, and Cause, but to particular members of those kinds, members that exist at the cosmic level. In particular, the word αἰτία *cause* refers to the wisdom and awareness that order events at the cosmic level. This is the first time that *that* wisdom and awareness, as opposed to the kinds Wisdom and Awareness, are mentioned in the course of the argument.

30c6–7 **σοφία καὶ νοῦς λεγομένη δικαιότατ᾽ ἄν** (=ἣ σοφία καὶ νοῦς λέγοιτο δικαιότατ᾽ ἄν) *that might most rightly be called wisdom and awareness.* "The present . . . participle with ἄν represents . . . the present optative with ἄν" (S §1846).

30d1 **ἐν μὲν τῇ τοῦ Διὸς . . . φύσει** *in the nature of Zeus.* Lorenz (2019, 99), following Mason (2014, 146), identifies the Zeus in this passage "with the living, intelligent, and embodied being that is the universe" (99). He gives no explicit argument for his interpretation, although he mentions a consideration that could count in its favor: "the expressions 'a kingly soul' and 'a kingly intelligence' are no doubt meant to refer to the world soul and its intelligence" (Lorenz 2019, 99). The consideration may be true, but it would make a weak argument. Just as Socrates identifies himself with his soul, not his soul *and* body (e.g., at *Phaedo* 115c2–d6), it is safe to assume that Socrates likewise identifies Zeus with the soul governing the body of the universe, not with that soul *and* that body. Socrates' account of personal identity, therefore, gives us one argument that Zeus is the agent ruling the universe, not the agent ruling *and* the body ruled.

There are two more arguments. The second is that Socrates presents conclusion C.P.1 as the answer to the question raised at 28d5–9, which asked "whether the force of unreason and chance manages things altogether and the so-called 'whole', or, as those before us used to say, awareness [νοῦς], that is, a sort of amazing knowing [φρόνησις], arranging [it], steers [it] along?" The question, then, is not "What is the nature of the universe?" but "Who or what rules the universe?" And *Zeus*, with his revealed nature, is the answer to this question. Thus, Zeus is the *ruler* of the universe, not *the universe.*

The third argument is that, although Socrates introduces Zeus' name for the first time in the *Philebus* here in his conclusion at 30d1, he has already referred to the traditional deity in asking the question. He did this when he cited the view of traditional wisdom that "νοῦς is king of heaven and earth for us" (28c7–8). In that wisdom tradition, the "king of heaven and earth" can only refer to Zeus (see, e.g., Homer, *Iliad* 15.192–93), a Zeus who is traditionally associated with νοῦς (e.g., in Hesiod, Zeus has "great νοῦς" [*Theogony* 37]; "it is not possible [even for Prometheus] to deceive the νοῦς of Zeus" [*Theogony* 613]; and "it is not possible in any way to escape the νοῦς of Zeus" [*Works and Days* 105], a "Zeus who knows everlasting arts [ἄφθιτα μήδεα εἰδώς]" [*Theogony* 545]). Protarchus shows he accepts these sorts of elements of traditional wisdom when he answers Socrates' question as to whether unreason or awareness is the ruler. For Protarchus' answer is "it does not appear to be reverent" to say that unreason might rule the universe (28e2). Finally, Protarchus (at 34e5, 36a4) and Socrates (at 60a4) both invoke Zeus by name using traditional expletives. There is no evidence, therefore, to suppose that Socrates and Protarchus have come to a nontraditional pantheistic view of Zeus as the ensouled universe in this dialogue; there is much evidence against such a view; and such pantheism would not give Socrates a better argument.

It is better, then, to interpret Zeus to be *whatever rules the universe, be it chance or awareness.* It is conceivable for Greeks to think of Zeus in this sort of open-ended way. For example, Hecuba describes that deity with the following formula: "Zeus, whether necessity of nature or νοῦς of mortals" (Euripides, *Trojan Women* 886).

30d1–4 **ἐν μὲν τῇ τοῦ Διὸς ἐρεῖς φύσει βασιλικὴν μὲν ψυχήν, βασιλικὸν δὲ νοῦν ἐγγίγνεσθαι διὰ τὴν τῆς αἰτίας δύναμιν** *A kingly soul and kingly awareness are inbred, through the power of Cause, into the nature of Zeus.* See note to 28a–30a for my identification of the argument for this conclusion (C.P.1). As I interpret it, the conclusion answers the question asked at 28d5–9: Is it awareness or chance that rules the universe? Seen as an answer to that question, this conclusion does not posit the existence of a new entity Zeus but establishes, rather, the kingly animation and wise awareness of whatever it is (call it "Zeus") that rules the universe.

30d3 **καθ' ὅτι φίλον ἑκάστοις λέγεσθαι** *according to whatever [is] pleasing for each to be called.* This reverence toward the naming of gods recalls 12c3–4: καὶ νῦν τὴν μὲν Ἀφροδίτην, ὅπῃ ἐκείνῃ φίλον, ταύτῃ προσαγορεύω *and now I address Aphrodite in whatever way is dear to her.*

30e–31a: ***The cosmological argument shows that Knowing belongs to the kind Cause***

30e1 **γενούστης** I follow T and the consensus of the ancient commentators (Porphyry, Proclus, Olympiodorus, Hesychius, and Suidas) in accepting γενούστης at 30e1 as an apparent neologism. Hesychius glosses it as ὁ γεννητικός *someone genetically related,* Suidas as γεννήτης ἢ συγγενὴς ἢ ἔγγονος *either parent or sibling or offspring,* Olympiodorus as συγγενής *kindred.* I coin a word, "genus-man," to make the Greekless reader aware of the neologism. (Another apparent neologism occurs at 15a6; see note there.) Examples of how the suffix –της works:

ἔρος *love*	ἐραστὴς *lover*
ὄρος *mountain*	ὀρέστης *mountaineer*
κόλἄσις *chastisement*	κολαστής *chastiser*

I agree with Stallbaum (1820) that Plato coined it as part of the "well-made jest" (*faceto lusu)* referred to in Socrates' next speech (30e6), the jest being this riddle: "This flawless argument belongs to the human beings of old, who have provided an answer to my inquiry [the inquiry begun at 28a], that awareness is a 'genus-man' of the Cause of all things, stated of the Four, of which it was, for us, one. Now you have our answer" (30d10–e3). In other words, the question was: Which of the four kinds contains Awareness? The answer is: Of the four kinds, one, the kind Cause, contains Awareness as a subkind or "genus-man."

The alternative in manuscript B is to read two words, γένους τῆς, instead of the single word γενούστης. This produces awkward grammar instead of a neologism. The feminine definite article τῆς would take the feminine noun ἀπόκρισιν *answer* as antecedent, meaning: "This flawless argument belongs to the human beings of old, who have provided an answer to my inquiry [the inquiry begun at 28a], that awareness is a kind of the Cause of all things, stated of the [answer] of the Four, of which it was, for us, one. Now you have our answer." The proposition affirmed by this text is not significantly different.

Other alternatives resorted to by modern editors are to cut troublesome words from the text to eliminate the riddling speech. Thus, Burnet

(1901) follows Badham (1878), who brackets τῶν τεττάρων ὧν ἦν ἡμῖν ἓν τοῦτο as "a marginal note on which all correction is thrown away." If we interpret 30d10–e2 as riddling, there is no need for such an emendation. The elaborate and riddling composition do not seem out of place in the *Philebus.* Plato alludes to a children's riddle at *Republic* 479c that was apparently similar in style to his speech here.

30e2 **ὧν** *of which.* Although manuscripts B and T both omit ὧν at 30e2 (although it is added in the margin to T), I retain this relative pronoun in my translation, following the majority of the manuscripts (see Bury 1897, 58 for discussion). The alternative, to make ἦν ἡμῖν ἓν τοῦτο *[of which] this [i.e., Cause] was one for us* an independent clause, is more awkward and less lucid, but does not significantly change the meaning.

PART III. CLASSIFICATIONS OF PLEASURE AND KNOWING

1. Having agreed to the One-Many Thesis, we can use the Divine Method and the kinds produced by the Fourfold Division to classify the forms of pleasure in order to answer the Happiness Question.

31a–c*: The kind Pleasure comes to be in the kind Mix. The classification will be in terms of* location *and* circumstance.

The text at 31a–c does not claim that the kind Pleasure is a member of the kind Mix (it is a member of the kind Unbounded, 31a8–10). This text makes a claim about the location where pleasures come to be: in organisms that are members of the kind Mix.

31a1 **Νῦν** *at present.* An alternative is Diès (1949) and Delcomminette (2020), both of whom follow Bekker's (1817) emendment to νοῦς *awareness,* making it the explicit subject of the verbs ἐστὶ and κέκτηται.

31a2 **τὰ νῦν** *the things now* is an accusative of respect, so that the subject is understood to be νοῦς *awareness*, echoing 30d10–e1. An alternative reading makes τὰ νῦν the nominative subject of ἐστὶ *are* and κέκτηται *possess.*

31a3 **δεδήλωται** *it has been shown* that Awareness belongs to the kind Cause and has the power to order, arrange, and rule the cosmos by producing mixes of Unbounded and Bound.

31a7–8 **νοῦς μὲν αἰτίας ἦν συγγενὴς καὶ τούτου σχεδὸν τοῦ γένους** *Awareness is kindred of Cause and basically of this kind.* In other words, Awareness is a subkind of the kind Cause. It is rare to have the genitive αἰτίας instead of dative as complement to συγγενὴς.

31a10 **ἐν αὑτῷ ἀφ' ἑαυτοῦ** *in itself from itself.* The ἀφ' ἑαυτοῦ leaves open that the kind Unbounded—specifically, its subkind Pleasure—might have bounds in itself *from another.*

31b9 **αὐτῶν** *them.* Plural not dual form is small evidence that Socrates has switched from referring to each of the two kinds, pleasure and pain, to each of the pleasures.

31c2 **'Εν τῷ κοινῷ . . . γένει** *in the shared kind.* Although pleasure and pain are of the kind Unbounded, they arise in the kind Mix.

31c6 **"Εσται ταῦτ' εἰς δύναμιν.** The εἰς δύναμιν might be an idiom—*these things will be [recalled] to the best of my ability*—but it might also describe Socrates' process—*these things will be [recalled, each] in [its distinctive] power.* Protarchus perhaps recognizes the word play with his reply Καλῶς εἶπες *you said [that] in a pretty way.*

ὦ θαυμάσιε *my wonderful [man].* Socrates uses this adjective twice in addressing Protarchus, and Protarchus uses it once in responding to Socrates. It is a common vocative in Plato, used thirty-eight times. A synonym is θαυμαστός, which is Socrates' favored adjective for describing the paradox of one and many.

31c11 **ἁρμονίαν** *harmony.* Socrates put ὑγίεια *health* by name into the kind Mix at 25e7–8. Bury (1897) asks, "But when had harmony been so classed?" It was undeniably so classed at 26a2–4, even if not by name.

31d: *How the kind Pleasure is one:* in *organisms,* from *the circumstances of disintegration and restoration. Organisms (i.e., ensouled bodies) are a mix of bound and unbounded. While the right proportions of that mix disintegrate, there is pain. While the right proportions are being restored, there is the pleasure of restoring.*

Hackforth (1945, 83) interprets the thesis to say that only *filling,* not *restoration* in general, is pleasant, and he sees 42c9–d8 as not merely a restatement but as a change in thesis, as fillings there come to be recognized as possibly painful. Delcomminette (2006, 413) more charitably interprets the present passage (31d4–32d5) as already a general scheme in terms of disintegration and restoration rather than filling and emptying. Certainly, filling and emptying can both be processes leading toward or away from harmony in an organism's nature.

31e–32b*: Bodily pleasures. The easiest kind of pain as disintegrating and pleasure as being restored is in the body.*

31d1 **Κάλλιστ' εἶπες** *you said [that] in the prettiest way.* Socrates makes superlative Protarchus' preceding term of praise and applies it to Protarchus, I suppose, for his accurate recall of the conversation (see note to 31c6).

31d10 **ῥηθῆναι** *be stated,* agreeing with the passive verbal adjective λεκτέον at d9.

δι' ὀλίγων περὶ μεγίστων *in a few [words] about the longest [topics].* Not "weightiest" (Frede 1993)—Socrates does not think pleasure is the most important thing. Socrates here completes his account of pain as a one and pleasure as a one, acknowledging at the same time the unboundedly many particular instances of disintegration and restoration within organisms. Following the Divine Method, he will turn next to identifying different kinds of pleasure.

31e3 **τὰ δημόσιά που καὶ περιφανῆ** *[it is easiest to understand] the common and obvious things.* Pain and pleasure as disintegration and restoration are easiest to understand in the body. Socrates begins here to collect the first subkind of pain and pleasure, which he completes at 32b6–7. It is harder to see the disintegration and restoration in the other subkinds,

31e10 **φθορὰ . . . καὶ λύσις** *a destruction and a disintegration.* Burnet (1901) and others bracket καὶ λύσις on the grounds that λύσις and φθορὰ are synonyms. But they are not. A disintegration is a specific kind of destruction. Some things, like pains, are destroyed by order not disintegration.

32a1 **ἡ . . . πληροῦσα δύναμις ἡδονή** *the power, when filling . . . [is] a pleasure.* When δύναμις is modified by an attributive participle (as here and also at 29c3, δυνάμει τῇ . . . οὔσῃ, *the power being [active]*), it refers to the activated power, in contrast to when it is modified by the genitive substantive—for example, ἡ τῆς πληρώσεως δύναμις *the power of filling*—which refers to the power whether or not activated. Likewise, when δύναμις takes a complementary infinitive, it refers to the mere power, not necessarily in action, as at 58d3–4 (τις . . . δύναμις ἐρᾶν *a certain power to love*). Only the active and not the inactive power is a pleasure.

32a6 **ῥίγους ἡ . . . τῆς ὑγρότητος πῆξις** *from freezing cold the solidifying of the fluids.* The noun πῆξις is modified by two genitives: ῥίγους a genitive of source (S §1410) and ὑγρότητος an objective genitive.

32a7 **ἀπιόντων** *when [the harmony] comes back.* As Bury (1897) says, the prefix here (and in the one other occurrence of this verb) means *back* not *away*. The prefix has this same function in ἀπόδοσις at 32a3.

32a7–8 **διακρινομένων** *when [the things] go back and separate.* I follow Stallbaum (1842), who takes this to be an ellipsis for a genitive absolute. For the subject of the verbs, he supplies τῶν ὑγρῶν, *the fluids,* from ὑγρότητος at a6–7.

32a9 **ἂν φῇ** *[the argument] which states,* subjunctive plus accusative (τὴν . . . φθορὰν) plus infinitive (εἶναι). The subjunctive plus ἂν expresses generality in present time (S §2545c). Listening to Socrates speak, one would at first suppose that the accusative τὸ . . . εἶδος *the form* is the accusative subject of the indirect discourse, but by the time he finishes the sentence one would realize it must be φθορὰν *destruction,* so that εἶδος is an accusative of respect.

32a9–b1 **τὸ . . . ἔμψυχον γεγονὸς εἶδος** *the form that has come to be ensouled.* Neither forms nor kinds come to be. Socrates is using the word εἶδος figuratively to refer to the members of the kind Living Thing. See introduction: *Genos, Phusis,* and *Eidos.*

ἐκ τῆς ἀπείρου καὶ πέρατος *(ensouled) out of the (association) of Unbounded and Bound.* The feminine definite article has no obvious antecedent, but one might supply a word like κοινωνία (as at 25e7) or μεῖξις (27b9). Stallbaum's (1842) alternative, followed by Bury (1897) is to emend the τῆς to τοῦ *[out of] the [kind Unbounded].*

32b3 **τὴν δ' εἰς τὴν αὑτῶν οὐσίαν ὁδόν** the first τὴν goes with ὁδόν *way* the second with οὐσίαν *state of being.* τὴν αὑτῶν οὐσία *its own state of being* will possess ἁρμονία τῆς φύσεως (*harmony of its nature,* 31d4–5) or κατὰ φύσιν (*according to nature,* 32a8) relative to the specific ἔμψυχον εἶδος *life form.*

32b5 **τύπον γέ τινα ἔχειν** (Socrates' *logos* at 32a9 seems) *to give, at least, some idea.* Getting "some idea" or "a first sketch" (*une première esquisse,* Delcomminette 2006, 303) of *X* is contrasted with getting *X* σαφῶς *clearly* at 61a4. Socrates will later make this initial account more precise: the processes of destruction and reintegration *must be perceived by the soul.*

32b6–7 **Τοῦτο . . . ἓν εἶδος . . . λύπης τε καὶ ἡδονῆς** *this [to be] one form of pain and pleasure,* namely, ὅταν τὸ ἐκ τῆς ἀπείρου καὶ πέρατος κατὰ φύσιν ἔμψυχον γεγονὸς εἶδος φθείρηται, τὴν μὲν φθορὰν λύπην εἶναι, τὴν δ' εἰς τὴν αὑτῶν οὐσίαν ὁδόν, ταύτην δὲ αὖ πάλιν τὴν ἀναχώρησιν πάντων ἡδονήν *whenever the life form [that, out of Unbounded and Bound, has come to be according to (its own) nature] is destroyed, the destruction is a pain, and the road back to its proper state of being, this return, is a pleasure for all [creatures].* This is the first form of pleasure and pain, involving both body and soul. The second form (ἕτερον εἶδος, 32c3–4) will be in the soul alone.

32b7 **ἐν τούτοις τοῖς πάθεσιν ἑκατέροις** *in each of these experiences [events of suffering and enjoying]*—namely, the events of starving and eating (31e6–8), thirsting and rehydrating (31e10–32a2), overheating and cooling down (32a2–3), getting too cold and warming up (32a6–8).

32b8 **Κείσθω** *let it be posited,* answering the deliberative τιθώμεθα at b6.

32c–35d: ***Pleasures of anticipation. Socrates defines memory, recollection, and perception and argues that pleasures of soul depend on memory. He argues that desire cannot be a matter of the body. The soul in addition to feeling pain of desire can at the same time feel the pleasure of hope for replenishment.***

Socrates argues that τό γε ἕτερον εἶδος τῶν ἡδονῶν, ὃ τῆς ψυχῆς αὐτῆς ἔφαμεν εἶναι, διὰ μνήμης πᾶν ἐστι γεγονός *the entire second form of pleasure, the one belonging to the soul itself, arises from remembering [as well as from expectation].* In answer to Protarchus' Πῶς; *how?* Socrates gives an explanation. I identify the premises of this explanation as follows:

P1 Of the various effects on the body, some are extinguished within the body before they reach the soul, leaving it unaffected (32d2–4).

P2 Of the various effects on the body, others go through both body and soul and provoke a kind of disturbance that is peculiar to each but also common to both of them (32d2–6).

P3 *Definition of perception*: *Perception* is that shared movement when the soul and body share in being moved in a single shared effect (34a3–5).

P4 *Definition of escaping notice:* Let us say that the bodily effects that do not go through the soul *escape the notice* of the soul, while those that do go through the soul *do not escape the notice* of the soul (33d8–10).

P5 *Definition of nonperception:* Whenever the soul is unaffected by the disturbances of the body, instead of saying that the state of escaping the notice of the soul is *forgetting*, call it *nonperception* (33e10–a1).

P6 The state of escaping notice, as defined here, is in no way the process of forgetting (33e2–3).

Because (inference from P6.1 indicated by γὰρ *because* at 33e2, while δ' *and* and δὴ *now* at 33e4 coordinate P6.1 with P6.2 and P6.3):

P6.1 (Definition) *Forgetting* is the departure of memory (33e3).

P6.2 In the case in question here, no memory has yet occurred (33e4).

P6.3 It would be absurd to say that there could be any losing of something that neither is nor has come to be (33e4–5).

P7 *Definition of memory:* Memory is the preservation of a perception (34a10–11).

P8 Recollecting differs from memory (34b2).

Because (inference indicated by Socrates' answering Protarchus' Τὸ ποῖον; *[differs] with respect to what?)*:

P8.1 *Definition of recollection*: recollection occurs in two cases:

a. When the soul takes up again, as far as possible, within herself, without the body, that (movement) which she had once undergone together with the body (34b6–8).

b. When, after the loss of memory of either a perception or something learned, the soul plows up again this memory for itself (34b10–c1).

P9 All these cases of recollection (namely, either [*a*] the soul taking up again without the body that motion it had undergone with the body, or [*b*] when that motion has been lost, the soul plowing it up again) are also memories (34c1–2).

P10 Every impulse and desire and source of action of the whole animal belongs to the soul (by means of memory) (35d2–3).

Because (inference indicated by ἄρα *therefore,* 35d1):

P10.1 [In every case of impulse and desire] the soul [of an animal that is in any respect empty relative to something fuller] does contact filling [relative to something emptier] (35b11–c1).

Because (inference indicated by ἄρα *therefore,* 35b11):

P10.1.1 There is no source from where one, beginning empty, could be in contact with filling, neither through perception of this (emptiness) that one is at present undergoing, nor prior memory that one ever underwent it (35a6–9).

P10.1.2 In some way some part of the one who thirsts is connected with filling (35b6–8).

Because (inference indicated by ἄρα *therefore,* 35b6):

P10.1.2.1 The one desiring desires something (35b1).

P10.1.2.2 An animal that is empty desires the opposite of what it undergoes (35a3–4). (I take this premise to be restated twice: at 35b3, "What it desires is not what it undergoes"; and at 35c12–13, "The impulse leads toward something opposite to the things being undergone.")

Because (inference indicated by ἄρα *therefore,* 35a3):

P10.1.2.2.1 Whenever something thirsts, it is empty. 34e9–11 (I take this premise to be restated at 35b3–4, "It thirsts, and this is being empty.")

P10.1.2.2.2 Thirst is a desire for filling with drink. 34e13–35a1 (I take this premise to be restated twice: at 35a4, "Being empty, it loves to be filled," and at 35b4, "The [empty animal] desires filling.")

P10.1.3 It is impossible that the body [could be in contact with filling at the time it is desiring] (35b9).

P10.1.3.1 Because (γάρ) it is empty (35b9).

My interpretation of the argument supporting 33c5–6 is supported by 34c4–8: the reason why he has said "all these things" is "in order that we might somehow grasp as completely and clearly as possible the pleasure of soul apart from body, and at the same time desire, for through these [statements] both pleasure of soul apart from body and desire are likely to be revealed."

Plato distinguishes different items in his analysis, such as desire and pain. I follow Aristotle in my interpretation. Aristotle criticizes Plato's pleasure-as-repleting theory in the *Nicomachean Ethics* (1153a13–15, see Rudebusch 2009b). But he "takes it for granted" (ὑποκείσθω) in his *Rhetoric* that "pleasure is a kind of movement, [a movement that is] both an ongoing restoration of the normal nature and perceived" by the soul (1369b33–35). In his *Rhetoric,* Aristotle follows the distinctions drawn in the *Philebus* when, for instance, he defines *orexis* (anger): "Let anger be a desire for revenge, [a desire] accompanied by pain caused by perceived disrespect" (1378a30–31). Aristotle does not identify *orexis* as a pain but *accompanied by* pain, just as in Plato's analysis. It follows at once from this distinction that although the pain *parching* is bodily, the desire *thirst* is as psychological as anger:

Anger = desire for revenge, always *accompanied by* pain caused by perceived disrespect, and usually accompanied either by the anticipatory pleasure of hope that there will be revenge or the anticipatory pain of fear that there will not.

Thirst = desire for drink, *accompanied by* pain caused by perceived parching, and usually accompanied either by the anticipatory pleasure or pain of hope or fear that there will or will not be quenching.

Thirst as much as anger will affect one's judgment, in particular judgments about the choice of risky actions for the object desired. The history of backcountry hiking in the Grand Canyon, for example, shows that the thirsty as well as the angry often choose foolhardy actions, because of judgment impaired by desire. Thus, thirst is something that "affects judgment and is attended by pleasure and pain"—which is precisely Aristotle's definition of πάθη *feeling* in the *Rhetoric* (1378a20–21).

A thought experiment illustrates the distinctions drawn in the *Philebus*. Imagine me at some time in the past *parching*. The parching is a process in which the body is drying out. Next imagine me, still in the past, *quenching*, a bodily process of rehydration. Now imagine me at present, again undergoing the bodily process of parching and in a psychic state of awareness of the parching. The state of awareness of the depleting is a necessary condition for the bodily depleting itself to be a pain. But it is not itself a depleting and thus not itself a pain. Socrates in the *Philebus* begins by defining pleasure and pain as processes of depletion and repletion (31d–e) but refines the definitions later so that pleasure and pain are *perceived* depletions and repletions only (43b7–c6). Add another psychic state, a memory of a quenching that refreshed me in the past. The memory of past quenching itself is neither a depleting nor a repleting and hence neither a pleasure nor a pain. Only now can you add another psychic state to my condition: *thirst*—that is, the *desire for drink*. Thirst, understood as desire for drink, is a kind of psychic "contact" (ἐφάπτεσθαι, 35b11) of the soul with an object. In particular, thirst (which is intentional) is not the same as parching (which is not intentional). The pain is bodily and is a process of depleting; the desire is not a process of depleting and is not physical but psychic. Socrates distinguishes the mere pain of a perceived bodily depleting process from the intentional psychological state of desire at 34e9–35d3. While the body all by itself can "empty" (κενοῦται, 35b9), "the one desiring desires *something*" (35b1), and "it is impossible that the body" have this form of contact with such an object of desire (35b9). Indeed, neither the present perception of one's bodily emptiness nor the memory of past events of parching could establish such contact (35a6–9). Nothing but memory of past repletion could make possible the soul-contact with the object of desire that occurs in events of desire (35c1–2). To make it easier to think of the object of my desire, put into my field of vision a glass of water, add a bodily process involving light rays reflecting from the water stimulating my eyes, and add, as a result of that process, a psychic state of perception of that water. Add another psychic event, an expectation that my parching pain will continue into the future: call it *fear*. If we postulate that fear depletes one's psychic equanimity as parching depletes bodily homeostasis, then we can understand why Plato calls fear a pain. Although fear of continuing bodily depletion is a pain, it is a psychic pain, not a bodily pain, and it is distinct from the bodily thirst. Imagine one more psychic event, an expectation of future quenching of my present thirst: call this *hope*. I take it that this expectation might restore psychic equanimity, which explains why Plato calls hope a pleasure. The psychic pleasure hope is obviously distinct from the bodily pleasure of quenching. Socrates and Protarchus agree that fear and hope are each a "form of pleasure and pain" (ἡδονῆς καὶ λύπης . . . εἶδος, 32c3–6).

According to this analysis, the desire thirst has the following features. It is:

> *For* perceived drink—that is, a sort of contact by the soul with object of desire.
> *Made possible by* memory.
> *Always with* the pain of parching, but not itself this pain.
> *Sometimes with* the pain of fear, but not itself this pain.
> *Sometimes with* the pleasure of hope, but not itself this pleasure.

In Plato's analysis, all the following are distinct: bodily pain (say, parching), perception of thirst, memory of restoration ending that pain (i.e., quenching), fear (i.e., pain of anticipating continued parching), perception of drink, and hope (i.e., pleasure of anticipating quenching).

32c1 **τὸ μὲν [sc., προσδόκημα] πρὸ τῶν ἡδέων ἐλπιζόμενον** *that the one [sort of anticipating], being felt before the pleasures, [is pleasant and confident]*: "as one may hope a hope, so might a hope be hoped" (Bury 1897). An alternative is to take **ἐλπιζόμενον** as middle instead of passive and to read it as appositive: *the anticipating, [where] one (sort of) anticipating is an expecting for one's own purposes.*

32c3–5 **Ἔστι γὰρ οὖν τοῦθ' ἡδονῆς καὶ λύπης ἕτερον εἶδος, τὸ χωρὶς τοῦ σώματος αὐτῆς τῆς ψυχῆς διὰ προσδοκίας γιγνόμενον** *this is another form of pleasure and pain, the form that arises from anticipation, through the soul itself apart from the body.* The contrast between the two types is not between pleasures in *body* and soul, but between pleasures *in organisms* (ἐν τοῖς ζῴοις, 31d4–5) *through restoration* and *in soul itself through expectation* (αὐτῆς τῆς ψυχῆς διὰ προσδοκίας, 32c4). An alternative interpretation (Delcomminette 2006, 304) is that the distinction is between pleasures that happen at the same time as the restoration (whether in body or soul) and pleasures that happen at a temporal distance (*à distance*) from the restoration. Delcomminette raises difficulties for the body/soul contrast but not for the organism/soul contrast.

It is possible to understand an event of *expectation* as enjoyable just in case it is experienced as filling a psychic lack. As *hunger* is a bodily lack, so *the prospect of not eating in the future* is a psychic lack, a lack that might be felt as insecurity. The expectation of eating, if pleasant, would fill some such psychic lack.

32c6–8 **ἐν γὰρ τούτοις . . . εἰλικρινέσιν τε ἑκατέροις γιγνομένοις . . . καὶ ἀμείκτοις λύπης τε καὶ ἡδονῆς** *for in these [cases of anticipatory pleasure and of pain], each of the two [i.e., cases of anticipatory pleasure and cases of anticipatory pain] arises both pure and without mixture of pain and pleasure.* I interpret τούτοις *these* to refer to only anticipatory pleasures and pains and to interpret "pure" to mean *not a mix of pain and pleasure.*

An alternative interpretation (Delcomminette 2006, 308) is that "pure" means *not a mixture of pleasure and knowing.* Delcomminette (2006, 307) recognizes that the reading I choose seems compelled by the text (*il semble qu'il faille comprendre*). But he raises two objections to this interpretation. (1) The words "pure" and "mixed" have not at this point of the discussion been introduced yet in precisely this sense. (2) Anticipatory pleasures are mixed with pain: "there is no sense in anticipating a restoration except when one lacks harmony" (2006, 308). The reply to the first objection is that the text supplies the sense of "pure" immediately, with the coordinate clause ἀμείκτοις λύπης τε καὶ ἡδονῆς *without a mixture of pain and pleasure.* To reply to the second objection, I agree that anticipatory pleasures are replenishments of psychic lacks, just as pleasure in general is a replenishment of lack—but those lacks need not be perceived, and when unperceived the pleasure is unmixed with pain.

The turn to anticipatory pleasures marks the second turn of dialogue. The first turn of the question showed that it is false that pleasure is the same as the good and false that only pleasure is good (see note to 11d2). The false pleasures of anticipation will show that it is false that all pleasures are good.

κατά γε τὴν ἐμὴν δόξαν *according to my opinion* modifies **ἐμφανὲς ἔσεσθαι τὸ περὶ τὴν ἡδονήν** *the [question] about pleasure will be distinct* while word order suggests that **ὡς δοκεῖ** *as it seems* modifies **εἰλικρινέσιν τε ἑκατέροις γιγνομένοις καὶ ἀμείκτοις λύπης τε καὶ ἡδονῆς** *each of the two arises both pure and without mixture of pain and pleasure.* The three expressions of personal opinion have bothered some commentators. I have followed Hackforth (1945) in interpreting them. Hackforth translates the first two as "I think, if I may put my own view" and takes the third to repeat, after the parenthetical remark, that this is a mere statement of Socrates' view (as opposed to a claim dialectically elicited from the interlocutor).

32d2 **ἑτέρῳ τινὶ τῶν προειρημένων . . . γενῶν** *to another of the kinds we mentioned earlier.* It will turn out (at 62d–e) that the whole kind of knowing (previously mentioned at 31a), will be welcomed. In the end, they won't welcome the whole kind of anticipatory pleasures, even though they are pain free, because some such pleasures are false (as Socrates shows at 36e–40b).

32d5 **ὡς** *since.* This clause—going to the end of the sentence—gives the reason why pleasure and pain, like hot and cold, are only sometimes welcome: the pleasures and so on are not goods themselves, but they in some circumstances acquire goodness. Note the contrast between ἀγαθὰ ὄντα *being good* and δεχόμενα τὴν τῶν ἀγαθῶν φύσιν *accepting the nature of the good.*

32d6 **ἐνίοτε . . . ἔστιν ὅτε** *But sometimes . . . there are times when.* Badham (1878), followed by Bury (1897) and Hackforth (1945), found this an "intolerable tautology," in Bury's (1897) words.

32d9 **(ὡς)** Burnet (1901), following Badham (1878) wishes to excise. But such a ὡς can be causal, introducing a reason here (after a parenthetical εἴπερ clause) for the exhortation ἐννοήσωμεν *let's consider:* "Since (if the account being given is really so) there is pain when organisms are disintegrating and pleasure when they are being restored, let's consider about things that are undergoing neither disintegration nor restoration."

33a4 **ταύτην** It would be odd for an accusative to be the object of μεμνῆσθαι, for which we expect the genitive case, as at 33a3. As Bury (1897) says, "There are some instances of μεμνῆσθαι with accusative in poetry (e.g., Aeschylus, *Choephoroe* 492; Sophocles, *Oedipus Tyrannus* 1057), though this rare construction is certainly strange here." Instead of this rarity, one might take it as modifying κρίσιν *decision.* "One or more words may separate the demonstrative from its noun" (S §1317): πρὸς γὰρ τὴν τῆς ἡδονῆς κρίσιν οὐ σμικρὸν μεμνῆσθαι ταύτην ἔσθ' ἡμῖν ἢ μή *for toward this decision it is no small thing for us to bear in mind or not.* Such separation—here, of three words—often marks Socrates' style of speech in this dialogue. For ταύτην in an irregular word order, see note to 62a7–b2.

33b10–11 **ἄσχημον γοῦν αὐτῶν ἑκάτερον γιγνόμενόν ἐστιν** *each [thing,* i.e., the feeling of either pleasure or pain] *is, to say the least, unseemly of them.*

33b11 **τοῦτο** *this*—namely, the unseemliness of a divine life that is undergoing a feeling pleasure or pain. This pronoun is the direct object of ἐπισκεψόμεθα *we'll look at,* προσθεῖναι *to add* (c2), and προσθήσομεν *we'll add* (c3), and the unseemliness is the implicit subject of ᾖ *is* at c1.

33c5–6 **τό γε ἕτερον εἶδος τῶν ἡδονῶν . . . διὰ μνήμης πᾶν ἐστι γεγονός** *the other form of pleasures has all come to be through memory.* The periphrastic perfect ἐστι γεγονός = γέγονε. As at 32a9–b1, neither forms nor kinds come to be. Socrates is using the word εἶδος figuratively to refer to the members of the kind. Likewise, to speak of all as opposed to part of an εἶδος *form* is figuratively to refer to the items that share that form. See introduction: *Genos, Phusis,* and *Eidos.*

33c9 **ἀναληπτέον** *[we must] take up [a question]* plus accusative (Μνήμην . . . καὶ . . . αἴσθησιν). The verbal adjective can also mean *recall,* as at *Laws* 864b, and so there is wordplay here, as Stallbaum (1842) noted ("an elegant play of words" *facetus verborum lusus*).

33d2 **Θὲς** *posit that* plus accusative plus participle instead of the usual infinitive (LSJ B.II.5): τὰ μὲν . . . κατασβεννύμενα . . . ἐάσαντα . . . τὰ δὲ . . . ἰόντα . . . ἐντιθέντα *some are extinguished . . . , permitting . . . , while others, going . . . , set up . . .*

τῶν . . . παθημάτων *of the things undergone* [but not necessarily "experienced"] Genitive of divided whole with τὰ μὲν . . . τὰ δὲ (S §1317).

33d4 **τινα . . . ἴδιόν τε καὶ κοινὸν ἑκατέρῳ** *something specific to each and shared by both* (direct object of ἐντιθέντα). Perception involves two events like "shaking"—the specific sort of psychic movement a soul can undergo and the specific sort of somatic movement a body can undergo, yet the two events must share something in common in the act of perceiving.

33e2 **Τὸ λεληθέναι** *With respect to the [state of] having gone undetected* (S §1153f), or *with respect to the [expression] "having gone undetected"* (S §1153g). Gosling (1975) (following Hackforth 1945) treats the Τὸ not as making an articular infinitive but as making the word a name of itself: "When I say 'oblivious.'"

The Greek verb λανθάνω *to go undetected* and the noun λήθη *forgetting* are cognate. This is what Socrates is noticing and why he will at 33e10–34a1 introduce a different term to avoid confusion.

33e4 **δὴ** *now* a "temporal connective" (Denniston 1966, 238–39).

33e11 **ἣν** *which.* Grammatically, the feminine singular antecedent of ἣν ought to be τὴν ἀπαθῆ ψυχήν *the unaffected soul,* but sense requires us to understand the antecedent as τὴν τῆς ψυχῆς ἀπάθειαν *the soul's state of being unaffected.*

34a3 **Τὸ δ(έ) . . . τὴν ψυχὴν καὶ τὸ σῶμα . . . καὶ κινεῖσθαι** passive articular infinitive, accusative of respect *but with respect to soul and body being indeed moved.*

ἐν ἑνὶ πάθει . . . κοινῇ γιγνόμενον participle circumstantial to κινεῖσθαι *[the movement] occurring in common [to soul and body] in one effect.*

34a10 **Σωτηρίαν τοίνυν αἰσθήσεως τὴν μνήμην** *memory is a preservation of perception.* We learn at 34b11 that memory might also be the preservation of a μάθημα *thing learned.* In computer terms, a memory is not a storage location on a hard drive but an item, such as an image (i.e., perception) or song (i.e., thing learned) that is saved to that location. Once saved, that item might then be displayed on a screen or played on a speaker (i.e., become an object of awareness). The noun μνήμη occurs eleven times before this with a more ambiguous meaning. An instance of the meaning *an item in storage that can be brought to awareness* occurs at 19d2: things "lie side by side in" a μνήμη, as if two shapes in an image or two lines in a song. A different meaning occurs at 20b3, where a μνήμη is received from a god. I take it that in this context the μνήμη is still of course coming from the hard drive of the soul. The gift, in this context, cannot be the item stored, since that is *already* in Socrates' possession. Instead of the *item in storage*, the gift must be *the event of remembering*. Socrates disambiguates in this passage, calling the *item in storage* μνήμη and the event of remembering ἀνάμνησις *recollecting* (34b2–9). With this disambiguation, the noun μνήμη is changed (as Socrates predicted at 33e8) to a more precise meaning.

34b2 **λέγομεν** *[don't] we say that* plus accusative plus participle. In the rare cases when this verb of speaking governs a participle instead of an infinitive, the participle marks that the indirect statement is considered a matter of fact (Kühner 1904, 72, "Anmerk. 2").

34b11 **ὅταν . . . ἀναπολήσῃ . . . αὐτὴ** verb *whenever it [the soul] plows up [a memory] again*. "This rare word seems partly chosen for its likeness in sound to the preceding ἀπολέσασα: it is a metaphor from ploughing" (Bury 1897).

34c1 **ἀναμνήσεις (καὶ μνήμας)** *recollectings (and things recollected)*. The conjunction neatly distinguishes process from product. Recollection differs from memory in this account as subkind from kind. Any case of a recorded perception-motion is a generic memory (34a10–11). The cases of the soul either actively taking up that motion again within itself without the body, or, having lost that motion, plowing it up again, are specifically the kind of memory we call recollection. As Delcomminette (2006, 327) says, "This memory [which is a recollection] has the same nature as that which was originally preserved by the [faculty of] memory, but its origin is different: whereas the latter was the result of a perception, the former is the product of the soul working alone [*travail de l'âme seule*]." Alternative interpretations suppress καὶ μνήμας *and memories* (e.g., Burnet 1901) or revise the received text (e.g., Bury 1897; Diès 1949; Waterfield 1980, 57). For a defense of the received text, see Dixsaut (1999b, 254).

34c10 **πᾶσαν (τὴν) μορφὴν**. Burnet (1901) follows Badham (1878) in bracketing the article, "as the meaning should be *every* not *the whole*" *form* (Bury 1897). There is no need to bracket, if we accept that Socrates sometimes uses the word "form" figuratively to refer to a kind or the members of a kind. See introduction: *Genos, Phusis,* and *Eidos*. Accordingly, "to examine the whole form" might mean *to examine every subkind of that kind*.

34d5 **Ἀπολοῦμεν . . . καὶ ταῦτά γε** *we will lose [something] with respect to* these *issues at least*. Burnet (1901) brackets καὶ, but it has a place in the text as an intensifier of ταῦτά (see Denniston 1966, 320: "καί with substantives").

34e3–4 **Πρὸς τί ποτε ἄρα ταὐτὸν βλέψαντες . . . ἑνὶ προσαγορεύομεν ὀνόματι;** *After looking at what same thing do we refer to [these things, although differing so greatly] by one name?* This speech signals that Socrates is going to collect a kind. See introduction: *Genos, Phusis,* and *Eidos*.

34e7 **ἐκ τῶν αὐτῶν** *from the same things* [hunger, thirst, etc.] This prepositional phrase is "added by way of exegesis to 'Εκεῖθεν" (Bury 1897).

ἀναλάβωμεν *let us take up*. "Πάλιν [*again*] with ἀναλάβωμεν [*let us take up*] is not tautologous, since the preposition [ἐκ *from*] does not necessarily imply 'resumption'" (Bury 1897).

34e9 **Διψῇ . . . τι** *Something thirsts*. Indicative third person singular διψάω: note that this verb is irregular—διψῇ instead of διψᾷ. This appears to be direct discourse after the leading verb λέγομεν (for a similar example, see S §2590).

34a13–35a2 **Ἆρ' οὖν τὸ δίψος . . . μὲν πληρώσεως** *Now thirst is a desire?—Yes, for drink.—For drink, or for being filled with drink?—For being filled, I suppose*. Burnyeat (2004, 86) sees here a correction of *Republic* 437e4–5, where Socrates argues that thirst is a desire for nothing other than drink.

35a6 **ἔστιν [που] ὁπόθεν** *is there [anywhere] from which.* The antecedent of a relative adverb like που after ἔστιν is omitted (S §2515).

35a6–9 **ὁ τὸ πρῶτον κενούμενος . . . πώποτε ἔπαθεν** *[there is no source from where] one, beginning empty, [could be in contact with filling, neither through perception of this (emptiness) that one is at present undergoing, nor prior memory that] one ever underwent it.* My interpretation of this passage follows Delcomminette (2006, 333): rather than trying "to furnish an explanation of the empirical formation of the first desire," the premise is making a claim about "the possibility of desire in general." The role this premise plays in the argument is apparent if one notices that, logically, this proposition is equivalent to: "One who is empty could be in contact with filling in *only* two possible ways, either by sensation from his body or by memory." The linked premises are as displayed in the note to 32c–35d—*there is contact* (P10.1.2 = 35b6–8) and *the contact is not from the body* (P10.1.3 = 35b9)—from which the conclusion (P10.1) follows. The Greek verb ἐφάπτοιτ' ἂν *could be in contact* (at a7) is a potential optative and expresses a merely hypothetical condition. The premise does not take a stand whether or not organisms begin life empty.

The alternative interpretation (e.g., Tenkku 1956, 189; Hackforth 1945, 66n1; Waterfield 1982, 921; La Taille 1999, 69–70) takes this premise to make the claim that organisms do actually begin empty and without desire. Such an interpretation is not required by this premise, given the potential optative at a7. Such an interpretation contradicts other premises of this argument, such as 35a3–4, which claims that anyone who is empty desires filling. As Delcomminette (2006, 333) points out, such an interpretation also "is in contradiction with the conclusion that Socrates draws from his analysis of desire . . . that desire is ultimately the source [*en définitive le principe*] of all [animal] movement" at 35d2–3.

There is also a question as to whether the argument concerns *processes* of becoming full or empty, or *states* of being full or empty. The present tense verbal forms κενούμενος and πληροῦσθαι appear to indicate processes rather than states (see Rudebusch 2006). But it is odd to describe one who thirsts as in the process of emptying, rather than in an empty state, and it is difficult to give a reading of P10.1 (= 35b11–c1) in terms of *becoming* rather than *being* empty to begin with. Delcomminette gives a third alternative. After setting out the problems with both the processive and stative interpretations, he concludes that the word "filling" "is ambiguous" (*comporte une ambiguïté*), signifying sometimes the state of fullness and sometimes the process of filling, "an ambiguity that is fundamental to the structure of desire itself" (2006, 336). Delcomminette attributes to Plato an account according to which "the same desire" is both for *this particular drink* and for *the good* (2006, 340). As a fourth alternative, I propose to interpret "empty" and "filling" as relative terms, relative in the same way as *the more and less* and the *intensely and mildly* (24c1–3). I define those paradigms as *duos* of powers possessing antisymmetry, transitivity, and the unbounded, powers that inhabit different domains, such as the domains of food or drink in an organism. Taking that analysis as paradigmatic, I interpret emptying and filling here not as *mere* processes of food or drink coming to be present or absent, but as *ordered states*—in particular, processes ordered by antisymmetry, transitivity, and the unbounded. In this way, my interpretation might avoid the problems raised for the interpretations of "filling" as a reference to a *mere state*, a *mere process* or an *ambiguous term*.

35d2–3 **ψυχῆς σύμπασαν τήν τε ὁρμὴν καὶ ἐπιθυμίαν καὶ τὴν ἀρχὴν τοῦ ζῴου παντὸς** *Every impulse and desire and source of action of the whole animal belongs to the soul [by means of memory].*

In the note to 32c–35d I identify the argument for this premise (P10). Gosling (1975, 104–5) identifies a different argument for it as follows:

P10. "Desire is a psychic function."
Because:
1. "Something about the desirer apprehends replenishment."
   Because:
   1.1. "The first experience of deprivation is just that, with no apprehension of replenishment."
   1.2. "Desire is for replenishment not for the state of deprivation."
2. "A full description of the physical state has no bearing on statements about desire; for that we need reference to memory, knowledge, etc."

Because:

2.1. "The body has no apprehension" of replenishment.

2.2. The body, "far from having any contact with replenishment, is in a state of deprivation, the very same state experienced by the man who first feels thirst, where it has been agreed there is no desire."

Gosling (1975, 105) objects to premise 2.2 of his interpretation of the argument: "It is not clear . . . that sensation or thirst as the first experience of deprivation is hereby shown not to be mental." But his premise 2.2 is not in the text. His objection thus seems to be a reason to reject his alternative interpretation, not to condemn the argument of the text.

Delcomminette (2006, 334) interprets the main structure of this argument as I do, though he only mentions P10 = 35d2–3, P10.1 = 35b11–c1, P7 = 34a10–11, P8 = 34b2, P8.1.a = 34b6–8, and P8.1.b = 34b10–c1. But he embeds this whole argument in a proof by contradiction (*un raisonnement par l'absurde,* 2006, 333) with an unstated conclusion, which he supplies: "As a consequence, in order to explain the possibility of desire, we are obligated to suppose that to begin with, we are filled [*remplis*]: the state of repletion necessarily must precede all emptiness."

35b11 **Τὴν ψυχὴν ἄρα τῆς πληρώσεως ἐφάπτεσθαι** *[It remains that, in every case of impulse and desire] the soul [of an animal that is in any respect empty relative to something fuller] does contact the filling [relative to something emptier].* This conclusion P10.1 follows from its three supporting premises (P10.1.1–3; see note to 32c–35d). An alternative statement of this proposition (e.g., Hackforth 1945) is that, rather than "contact," the soul *apprehends* filling. The condition denoted by the Greek verb in question (ἐφάπτεσθαι) is one that body as well as soul is capable of (35b9). Since only souls apprehend, Hackforth's alternative faces an objection. I take it that the condition of *being in contact with* is the very same condition as that described just above, as a shared condition of body and soul, when either is disturbed, as it were, by a motion that might penetrate merely the body or both body and soul (P3 = 34a3–5), a motion that can be preserved in soul alone (P7 = 34a10–11). On my supplied qualifications to "empty" (relative to something fuller) and "filling" (relative to something emptier), see note to 35a6–9.

36b6 **ἐν τούτοις (τοῖς χρόνοις)** If we excise τοῖς χρόνοις *the times,* the text will read: *in these [respects].* If we leave the text intact: *at these times [he appears simultaneously to feel pain].*

36b13 **ἁπλῶς** adverb *simply.* Literally "without folds," a playful oxymoron with διπλοῦν *twofold.*

False pleasures

36C–E. SOCRATES AND PROTARCHUS DISAGREE WHETHER PLEASURES CAN BE FALSE.

In general, we call a thing false when its appearance and its reality disagree. Socrates establishes that pleasures are false in this general way by showing several distinct subkinds of such falsity: pleasures that are false representations; pleasures that are false in magnitude; merely apparent unreal pleasures; and the way in which the mixed condition of pleasure and pain can be false.

The discussion of false pleasure takes up a new question about pleasure. (An alternate interpretation is that false pleasures are a third kind of pleasure in addition to restorative and anticipatory.) At 31a7–10, Socrates summarized the main conclusions of the discussion to that point: Knowing is in the kind Cause, while Pleasure is in the kind Unbounded. He marked the transition to the next topic with the words: "After this it is necessary for us to consider, when [knowing and pleasure] come to be, both *in what things* and *from what circumstances* each comes to be. Pleasure first" (31b2–4). Having determined that the kind Pleasure as a whole comes to be *in* the kind Mix (31c2–11), while the two subkinds of pleasure—restorative and anticipatory—come to be *in,* respectively, animal organisms (31d4–6, restated 32a9–b2,) and souls (32c3–5), Socrates says, "Let us make use of this investigation of these circumstances [i.e., the circumstances of anticipatory pleasures and pains] for *this.*—For what?—For whether we will say that these pains and pleasures are (1) true, (2) false, or (3) some true and some false" (36c3–7). As I interpret it, this use of the investigation of the circumstances involved in anticipation (namely, in order to see whether such pleasures and pains are all true, all false, or some true and some false) is not a third subkind of pleasure alongside restorative and anticipatory, but a new question. Likewise,

Delcomminette (2006, 350) says, "the distinction between true and false pleasures is not a subdivision of . . . anticipatory pleasures, but is rather a new global division of pleasure." In order to make the point that the division of pleasures into true and false is a new global division of pleasures, it is not necessary to deny (as Delcomminette [2006, 350] implausibly does) that the antecedent of the demonstrative phrase "these pains and pleasures" (36c6) is the proximal demonstrative phrase "these circumstances" (36c3), which in turn must refer to "the doubly painful circumstance" at 36b12–13, as well as the circumstance of simultaneous pleasure and pain at 36b8–9. (Delcomminette 2003 presents a briefer, English version of his interpretation.)

Much of the secondary literature has focused only on the false anticipatory pleasures of *Philebus* 37–39. In contrast, Bravo (2003) tries to give a coherent reading to the whole discussion of false pleasure. The deep connection he proposes underlying Plato's use of "true" and "false" throughout the *Philebus* and *Republic* is the single theme of *truth as correspondence* in the spheres of epistemology, ontology, and morality (167–74). His account of the correspondence in *epistemology* is between representation and object; in *morality* between what is and what ought to be; and in *ontology* between a thing and itself. Mooradian (1996) criticizes the standard representational account endorsed by Bravo. Mooradian (1995) provides argument supporting Bravo's assertion (2003, 173) that "the ontological falsity of pleasure gives rise [*da lugar*] to epistemological falsity."

36d4 **λόγον . . . οὐ πάνυ σμικρὸν ἐπεγείρειν** *to stir up a not very small account.* The litotes οὐ πάνυ σμικρὸν *not very small* is translated, for example, as "very considerable" (Fowler 1925) or "weighty" (Frede 1993). Here Socrates marks the beginning of his discussion that pleasures can, like judgments, be both true and false.

36d6–7 **παῖ 'κείνου τἀνδρός** *son of that man,* "with no clear referent" (Nails 2002, 257). The possibilities are "'son of Philebus' because Protarchus was his student, or 'son of Gorgias' because Gorgias is a great figure discussed later in the dialogue, or 'son of [some man of mark]'" (Nails 2002, 257; following Fowler 1925). Socrates refers to Protarchus as ὦ παῖ Καλλίου *son of Callias* at 19b5. Burnyeat (2004) reviews yet other interpretations and defends that the reference here is to the intellectual father

Philebus. The only parallel use of the expression in Plato is at *Republic* 368a1–2, παῖδες ἐκείνου τοῦ ἀνδρός, which likewise arguably refers to an intellectual not biological father. Protarchus described himself as τοῦ λόγου διάδοχον *the successor of [Philebus'] argument* (19a6–7). At 18a1–2 Philebus asked about the relevance of Socrates' argument that every investigation should search for one and many; here Socrates would be referring to that Philebus to justify his asking about the relevance of the current change in topic to false pleasures. There are other allusions to the *Republic* in the *Philebus* (for the three Burnyeat lists, see notes to 20b6–7, 34e13–35a2, and 66a4).

36e1 **διὰ τέλους ἀεὶ** *permanently* (LSJ τέλος II.2.c) like διὰ παντὸς τοῦ βίου ἀεὶ at 39e5–6. For an account of Socrates' permanent wonder about falsity, see *Theaetetus* 187d–200c and the discussion in Rudebusch 1990.

36e7 **οὐδαμῶς** adverb *in no way.* Given the parallel with thinking developed below to establish this conclusion, Socrates seems here to endorse the conclusion that *if we think a false thought, we are in no way thinking.* This paradoxical result is a lengthy side issue. Although Socrates, perhaps by the principle of brevity just stated (36d9–10), does not defend such a paradox here, he establishes it in the *Theaetetus*. See note to 36e1.

37A–41A. FALSE REPRESENTATIONS THAT ARE PLEASURES.

Socrates begins by disambiguating the language of pleasure and thought, distinguishing in the case of the believer both the object (the thought) and the act (the thinking) and likewise distinguishing in the case of the enjoyer both the object (the pleasure) and the act (the enjoying, 37a1–b4). Then he elicits further parallels between thoughts and some pleasures (37b5–e9), but fails on the basis of these parallels to get Protarchus to see how there can be false pleasures. Even when pleasures arise in company with false thoughts, Protarchus calls only the thoughts false, not the pleasures (37e12–38a2). And so, Socrates develops a model of both the objects believed—namely, words written in the "book" of the soul—and of some objects that are enjoyed—namely, pictures painted there. With the model, he argues that there are false pleasures—namely, the pleasures that are false pictures in our souls. These false pictures are objects of the act of enjoying in the same way that false thoughts are objects of the act of thinking. I identify the argument in the note to 40b6–7.

37a2 **ἔστιν . . . τι δοξάζειν** The accent on ἔστιν marks it as existential not copulative; the infinitive is a verbal noun (S §1970). The indefinite pronominal adjective τι instead of the definite article τό changes the meaning: not *the opining exists* but *some opining exists.* Hackforth (1945) gives an idiomatic English translation: "there is such a thing as holding an opinion?"

37a2–b3 **ἔστιν γάρ πού τι δοξάζειν . . . τό γε ὄντως ἥδεσθαι δῆλον ὡς οὐδέποτ' ἀπολεῖ.** *There is such a thing as thinking . . . it is clear that the enjoying will never be nullified.* This passage as a whole argues for the conclusion that there are agreed parallels between pleasure and thought—namely:

a. There is such a thing as thinking (37a2–3).
a′. There is such a thing as enjoying (37a5).
b. [In cases of thinking] there is something that is thought (37a7).
b′. [In cases of enjoying] there is something that the one enjoying enjoys (37a9).
c. The thing that thinks, whether it thinks rightly or not, does not ever nullify the thinking (37a11–12).
c′. The thing that enjoys, whether it enjoys rightly or not, will never nullify the enjoying (37b2–3).

Penner (1970, 171–73) distinguishes between the *process* of believing or being pleased and the *product*—that is, *what* one believes or enjoys, and claims Plato is not fully aware of the ambiguity. But 37a2–9 (namely, statements a, a′, b, and b′) draws this very distinction and seems to show full awareness of the process/product distinction.

Delcomminette (2003, 216) rightly points out that the parallels drawn here are not themselves an argument that false pleasures exist, but instead merely a statement of analogous features of pleasure and thought. Nevertheless, the analogy here developed establishes the precise sense in which the argument for 40b6–7 proves that pleasures are false. Strictly speaking, the act of *enjoying* is no more false than the act of *thinking.* What is false is the object of the thinking—namely, the false thought, and the object enjoyed, that is, the false pleasure.

Plato states the analogy using forms of the Greek verbs δοξάζειν (to think, judge, consider, opine or believe) and ἥδεσθαι (to be pleased or to enjoy). An English translation of the analogy ought to reflect the following points. At 37a5 (= a′) and 37b2–3 (= c′), the act of enjoying is *complete.* An act is complete if to engage in the process of acting entails achievement of the product of the act. For example, at each moment where one enjoys, one already has enjoyed (see Aristotle, *Metaphysics* 9.6 and Rudebusch 2009b for a defense of Aristotle's distinction between complete and incomplete acts). The analogy requires, therefore, that the cognitive act mentioned at 37a2–3 = a and 37a11–12 = c also be complete. But the acts of judging and considering are incomplete: so long as I am judging, I have not yet judged; so long as I am considering, I have not yet considered. The analogy thus rules out the English verbs "judge" or "consider" as translations here of δοξάζειν.

Delcomminette proposes the verb "consider as" (*considérer comme,* 2006, 352n6), which expresses a complete action and is acceptable: as soon as I consider *X* as *Y*, I have considered *X* as *Y*. But the verb "consider as" is very awkward in translating 37a2–b3. Worse, *to consider X as Y* seems a subkind of δοξάζειν rather than equivalent to it. Verbs of thinking also express a complete action—as soon as I am thinking/believing/opining something, I have thought/believed/opined it. Thus, such verbs are a better translation of δοξάζειν.

In 37a7 = b and 37a9 = b′, the *thing believed* (expressed by a substantive formed from the present neuter passive participle of the verb, τὸ δοξαζόμενόν) and the *object of pleasure* (expressed by the object of the verb ἥδεται, which takes the dative case) are analogous. When Protarchus agrees to the analogy, the language used does not specify whether the thing believed and the object of pleasure are in the awareness (say, a thought and a sensation) or in the world (say, a man, or a meal). Accordingly, the translation should permit this ambiguity. "Tom is the man for the job? Is he your thought?"—"Yes." Delcomminette (2006, 354–56) argues that the passage refers unambiguously to internal thoughts and experiences rather than external objects, but his premises are all taken from passages *following* the present passage. It is not safe to assume that Protarchus in agreeing here already foresaw a future disambiguation.

37a7 **τὸ δοξαζόμενόν ἐστί τι** (the accent on ἐστί marks it as copulative not existential) *the thing being opined is something?*

37a9 **τό γε ᾧ τὸ ἡδόμενον ἥδεται [sc., ἐστί τι]**; *the thing by which the thing enjoying enjoys [is something].* Notice the parallel to a7: just as there is an object of my thought (any thought is "of" something), there is an object of my pleasure (any pleasure is "of" something).

37b2–3 **τὸ ἡδόμενον . . . οὐδέποτ' ἀπολεῖ** *The thing that enjoys, whether it enjoys rightly or not, will never nullify the enjoying.* At 40b6–7 Socrates' account of false pleasure will conform to this condition, that the enjoying really occurs even if the thing enjoyed is incorrect.

37b5–8 **Ὅτῳ ποτὲ οὖν δὴ τρόπῳ . . . <σκεπτέον>** *One question to investigate is how does thought manage to be true or false, while of pleasure there is only truth [as conventional wisdom claims], even though in both cases the thinking and the pleasing are equally real?* Mooradian (1995) rightly interprets Protarchus, like Protagoras in Plato's *Theaetetus* (156b), to hold that pleasures are inevitably true. Most likely, Protarchus assumes that a pleasure is *true* when the thing perceived as pleasant really is pleasant for the one enjoying it. For example, the pleasure I feel from possessing gold is *true* when the gold, which I perceive as pleasant, really is pleasant for me. Conventional wisdom cannot imagine how I could make a mistake about the pleasantness of gold for me. The anti-Protarchan argument for 40b6–7—that there are false anticipatory pleasures—is analogous to the anti-Protagorean argument that there are false perceptions of the future (*Theaetetus* 178b–179d).

An alternate interpretation is that Protarchus denies that pleasures are either true or false. Thus, for example, Migliori (1993, 211): "for [Protarchus], true and false apply only to items with cognitive content [*questioni con una valenza gnoseologica*], such as beliefs, and not to the other things," such as pleasure or pain. This alternative conflicts with the text at 36c6–9 and 37b7 and is no more charitable to the text than the Protagorean interpretation.

37b8 **<σκεπτέον>**. I propose that we let Protarchus' σκεπτέον at b9 finish the sentence that Socrates has begun, so as to avoid adding σκεπτέον, as Burnet (1901) does, at b8. This avoids emending the text.

37d2–4 **Ἂν δέ γε πονηρία . . . πονηρὰν δὲ καὶ ἡδονήν** *If some bad state should attach itself to either of them, then the thought becomes a bad one and the pleasure becomes bad, too.* For example, suppose I am thirsty in the desert and find water that is poisonous, yet I believe it safe to drink. Here the bad state of *being poison* belongs to the water, so that the thought (including *both* the proposition that it is safe *and* the act of thinking it) becomes *bad* for me, and the pleasure (including *both* the poisonous water *and* the enjoyment of it) becomes *bad* for me.

37d7 **ἂν ὀρθότητα ἴσχῃ** *if it [the judgment] possesses rightness.* Here is the familiar Platonic semantics: "Fx" is true if x possesses F-ness. Elsewhere the semantics is a premise in arguments that forms exist. (1) To say, "Simmias is taller than Socrates but shorter than Phaedo" is to say, "both *tallness* and *shortness* are in Simmias"; so "each of the forms exist" and "the other things [e.g., Simmias], by partaking of these, bear the name [e.g., 'the taller'] derived from these" (*Phaedo* 102b). (2) If one does not allow that "for each of the things that are there is an idea that is always the same . . . he will destroy the capacity for meaningful discourse"; so there are forms (*Parmenides* 135b–c). (3) "One soul is righteous and another unrighteous, and each becomes righteous by the presence [παρουσία] of righteousness, and opposite by the opposite, and the capacity for becoming present or becoming absent assuredly is something, so there is a form *righteousness*" (*Sophist* 247a–b).

37d8 **ταὐτὸν δὲ ἡδονήν** *and [is] pleasure the same thing* (that is, the same conditional holds true for pleasure). Bury (1897) takes ταὐτὸν as adverbial: *and pleasure equally.*

37e1–3 **Ἂν δέ γε ἁμαρτανόμενον . . . οὐδ' ὀρθῶς δοξάζουσαν** *If the thing believed is mistaken, then the thought that makes that mistake is not right and does not judge rightly.* Delcomminette (2006, 354) argues that the clause "the thing believed is mistaken" (ἁμαρτανόμενον τὸ δοξαζόμενον) suggests that "the thing believed" (τὸ δοξαζόμενον) refers to the content of the belief and not an external object of belief: "If τὸ δοξαζόμενον corresponded to the object of the belief, what could it mean to say that this object makes a mistake [*se trompe*]?" But the Greek participle ἁμαρτανόμενον *mistaken,* can have either a middle or passive grammatical voice. In the middle voice the participle τὸ δοξαζόμενον would naturally refer to the *subject* of the act of thinking: *the thing thinking.* But the passive voice would suggest that the thing believed was the *object* of the act of mistaking. In this voice τὸ δοξαζόμενον would naturally refer to *the thing believed*. The English past participle "mistaken" is ambiguous in precisely the same way. For example, a mistaken man might either be one who has made a mistake or a man about whom the mistake is made. So, Delcomminette's argument (that τὸ δοξαζόμενον cannot refer to an external object of belief) fails.

37e7 **τι τῶν καλῶν ὀνομάτων** in support of "fine names" v. "names of fine things" Bury (1897) cites *Cratylus* 411a2 and *Theages* 122d6. I add *Philebus* 43b1–2.

38a1 **τότε λέγομεν** *at that time we say [that the thought is false].* I follow Burnet (1901), who accepts Stallbaum's (1842) change from the manuscripts: τότ' ἐλέγομεν *at that time we were saying.*

38a8 **ἀνοίας** *want of understanding* or *folly* is in the manuscripts. Burnet (1901) and most others following Cornarius (1561) emend to **ἀγνοίας** *ignorance.*

38b9–10 **Ἕπεται μὴν ταύταις . . . ἀληθεῖ καὶ ψευδεῖ δόξῃ** *Pleasure and pain often come in the train of true and false thought.* As Delcomminette (2006, 355) remarks, this proposition takes for granted the existence of false thought, disregarding the theoretical problems with false thought raised at *Theaetetus* 188b–200c. See Rudebusch (1985) for discussion of the theoretical problems. If Socrates at a deeper level of analysis rejects the possibility of false thought, that rejection will not affect the parallel he develops here between thought and pleasure.

38b12–13 **ἐκ μνήμης τε καὶ αἰσθήσεως δόξα ἡμῖν καὶ τὸ διαδοξάζειν ἐγχειρεῖν γίγνεται ἑκάστοτε** *[i] Opining and [ii] the act of undertaking to maintain an opinion comes to be for us out of memory and perception.* In terms of the example that immediately follows, (1) δόξα *opining* is when in this case he says to himself ἔστιν ἄνθρωπος *it is a human being* (38d5–6) and (2) the act of undertaking to maintain the opinion includes his setting himself the question Τί ποτ' ἄρ' ἔστι τὸ παρὰ τὴν πέτραν τοῦθ' ἑστάναι φανταζόμενον ὑπό τινι δένδρῳ; *Whatever is this appearing to stand by the rock under a sort of tree?* (38c12–d1).

38b13 **διαδοξάζειν** *to maintain an opinion.* Bury (1897) infers that "διαδοξάζειν [is] silent (or πρὸς αὑτὸν) διαλέγεσθαι, just as δόξα is unspoken λόγος" from *Theaetetus* 190a: τὸ δοξάζειν λέγειν καλῶ . . . σιγῇ πρὸς αὑτόν *I call thinking silent speech to oneself.* The tendency of interpreters is to translate the present infinitive διαδοξάζειν as *to form an opinion* rather than, as I propose, *to maintain an opinion.* "Form a definite opinion" is the translation of LSJ, who follow Bury (1897) and are followed by many translators (e.g., Hackforth 1945, Gosling 1975, Waterfield 1982, and Frede 1993 and 1997). But the prefix δια is common, and commonly expresses that the action of the connected verb is performed *through* a space or time. For example, in the common verb διαλέγεσθαι the prefix entails *to maintain a speech* and because of its frequent use comes to be associated with an idiosyncratic meaning, speech *between* people. Likewise, in διανοεῖσθαι the prefix gives the meaning *to maintain in awareness* (at, e.g., *Theaetetus* 189e8, see note to 38e2 below). The compound διαδοξάζειν is extremely rare; hence the prefix should function without acquired idiosyncrasy and would here indicate that the holding of the thought is extended through time. In support of an idiosyncratic meaning for the prefix *to form* an opinion, LSJ refer to Iamblichus' *On the Mysteries* 4.6, lines 16–17, where Iamblichus writes that we must not make the gods the cause of any bad thing, περὶ οὗ πάντες Ἕλληνές τε καὶ βάρβαροι τἀναντία ἀληθῶς *διαδοξάζουσιν since such a view is opposite to the* opinion *that all Greeks and barbarians truly* maintain. In this occurrence, Iamblichus is using the verb to speak of *an opinion* that the Greeks and barbarians *maintain* (rather than a thought that they are *in the process of forming).* Thus, this occurrence does not support the idiosyncratic meaning LSJ wish to give the verb.

As another alternative, Bury (1897) explains the prefix as meaning here "to distinguish belief from belief." Diès (1949), followed by Migliori (1993, 217), translates δόξα ἡμῖν καὶ τὸ διαδοξάζειν ἐγχειρεῖν as "opinion in us, spontaneous or reflective" (*en nous l'opinion, spontanée ou réfléchie).* The spontaneous/reflective distinction is not what the Greek says; nor is it suggested in the illustration at 38c5–7 or the explanation at 39a2–3.

38b13 **γίγνεται** is the reading of manuscript T. Burnet (1901) follows manuscript Vat., γιγνεθ', a contraction for which *TLG* finds no other instance.

38c12 **ἄρ' ἔστι** *[what] then is [the thing appearing]?* Here ἐστί is written ἔστι because it follows ἄρα—a case not listed by S §187b.

38d10 **προσείποι** *he might say in addition* Bury (1897) finds the prefix "a strange use" and proposes that here it means *say instead.* LSJ lists only two meanings: either *say in addition* or *call X (accusative) Y (accusative).* Kyle Lucas suggested in a conversation that there is a sensible way to take the prefix in its ordinary use as *say in addition.* To understand the suggestion, imagine that the subject of the thought experiment, having said to himself that the object in view is a man, then asks himself, "But is it a man in the flesh or a man carved by shepherds?" The subject chanced to speak the truth (ἐπιτυχῶς) in calling the object a man, but in saying *in addition* that the man was a statue he went astray (παρενεχθείς). Interpreters have taken Socrates to speak of two alternative possibilities, one in which the man thinks the truth and the other in which he thinks falsely. But it fits the text better to take Socrates to be describing a single temporally extended possibility, in which the subject first thinks a truth and then, going off the rails, thinks something false.

38e2 **ἐντείνας εἰς φωνὴν** *after fitting [his thoughts] into vocal sound* (LSJ V.2). The word ἐντείνας *fitting* or *framing* suggests that the silent speech to oneself might have a different structure or grammar than the vocal speech. This would be a refinement on the equation of thought with silent speech to oneself that Socrates stated in the *Theaetetus* (τοῦτο γάρ μοι ἰνδάλλεται διανοουμένη οὐκ ἄλλο τι ἢ διαλέγεσθαι, αὐτὴ ἑαυτὴν ἐρωτῶσα καὶ ἀποκρινομένη, καὶ φάσκουσα καὶ οὐ φάσκουσα *[the soul], while it maintains this in thought, seems to me [to do] nothing other than converse, itself questioning and answering itself, and affirming and denying*, 189e7–190a2; and Οὐκοῦν εἰ τὸ λέγειν πρὸς ἑαυτὸν δοξάζειν ἐστίν *then if to think is to speak to oneself*, 190c5; and that the Eleatic Stranger stated in the *Sophist* (Οὐκοῦν διάνοια μὲν καὶ λόγος ταὐτόν· πλὴν ὁ μὲν ἐντὸς τῆς ψυχῆς πρὸς αὑτὴν διάλογος ἄνευ φωνῆς γιγνόμενος τοῦτ' αὐτὸ ἡμῖν ἐπωνομάσθη, διάνοια; *Then thought and speech are the same thing; except the train of speech that happens in the soul, to itself, without sound—to* this *we give the name "thought,"* 263e3–5).

39a1–3 **Ἡ μνήμη ταῖς αἰσθήσεσι συμπίπτουσα εἰς ταὐτὸν κἀκεῖνα ἃ περὶ ταῦτ' ἐστὶ τὰ παθήματα φαίνονταί . . . γράφειν.** *Memory, as it falls into line with perceptions [" falls into the same thing with perceptions"], and those effects concerned with [the lineup of memories and perceptions] seem to write.* The conscious experience of forming a thought is likened to putting pen to page and writing a sentence, which in turn is caused or "written" by both the matching of perception to memory and the associated effects in the soul of that matching. Here is an illustration in terms of 38b12–13. Suppose I have a memory of rustic statues made by herdsmen. When out in the country I perceive from a distance a man standing near a rock under a tree, I might falsely judge that the object I am perceiving is a statue. I may or may not formulate this judgment as an assertion. At the time of judgment, my soul is like a book. The writing, as it were, in the book happens as follows. The memory of a statue συμπίπτει εἰς ταὐτὸν (falls into line, 39a1) with the perceptions of that man under the tree. (Socrates uses a pair of metaphors for this mismatch of perception with memory at *Theaetetus* 193c5–6, where the memories are described as *imprints in the wax tablet* of the awareness, and the misapplication of perception to wax imprint is like *putting one's foot into the wrong shoe*. See Rudebusch 1985, 531 for discussion.) The memory, aligned—indeed, in this case *misaligned*—with perception, may give rise to effects (παθήματα, 39a2): perhaps pleasure that there is no one nearby, or a feeling of solitude. Socrates proposes that it is the aligned memory *and* the associated feelings (ἡ μνήμη . . . κἀκεῖνα ἃ περὶ ταῦτ' ἐστὶ τὰ παθήματα, 39a1–2) that together somehow write words and paint pictures in the book of the soul.

39a2 **παθήματα** *things undergone* [by the soul, such as the suffering of depletions or enjoyment of refillings]. This word, with its synonym πάθος, has a precise meaning in this dialogue, referring to the things that a body or soul undergoes—namely, *being moved* as opposed to moving something else. For translators, the problem is that English has only an obsolete verb with this meaning: *to suffer* as opposed to *acting*, an obsolete noun *affection* as opposed to *action*, the noun *effect*, which correlates better with *cause* than *act*, and *feeling*, which is appropriate only for the effects actually experienced or "felt" by the soul. As prior examples of παθήματα, Socrates has already mentioned (1) perceptions (34a3–5, 33d1–5), (2) depletings like thirst and hunger (35d5–6, e10, 32a1–3) and likewise replenishings, and so by definition (3) pleasures and pains (32b6–7), and finally (4) expectations, whether fearful or hopeful(36a1–5, see also 32c1–2). Thus, the παθήματα in this case might be fearful or hopeful expectations, other pleasures and pains, or still other perceptions circumstantial to the units formed from the perceptions falling in with memory. Gosling (1975) plausibly argues that fears and hopes cannot be included in the possible παθήματα on the grounds that in the present passage Socrates is explaining how expectations arise as a result of pictures and words, so that the expectations cannot belong to the creation of the words or pictures. In his own words, they are "based on the *logoi*" and "not the stimulus for them." In the context of Socrates' present analysis, then, these παθήματα that are nearby when perception fits into memory are most likely bodily pleasures and pains like drinking or thirst.

The περὶ ταῦτ' ἐστὶ *that are associated with these things* are the pleasures and pains in orbit, as it were, around the thoughts formed when sense perception conjoins with memories. If we take the neuter plural pronoun ταῦτ(α) to refer to the units formed when perceptions "fall in line with" memories, we produce a reasonable sense for these words. For more on this theory of thought formation, see *Theaetetus* 191c–d, where the faculty of memory is like a wax tablet, into which perceptions imprint memories (like "a signet ring pressing into wax") and the explanation of thought formation at 193c as matching a new sense perception to an old memory imprint (like "putting your foot into a shoe"). In the recent example, the perception of the thing under the tree forms a unit with memories of statues, the unit being a single *thought* or *statement:* "That thing under the tree is a statue."

39a4 **τοῦτο τὸ πάθημα** *this effect.* Apparently, this singular noun refers to the unit formed from both memory, falling in line with perception, and the circumstantial affections. The singular noun indicates these things are conceived as a single author, as it were.

39b3–7 **ἕτερον δημιουργὸν . . . ἐν τῇ ψυχῇ τούτων γράφει** *At such a time [to continue the comparison of soul to book], another artisan comes to be in our souls: a painter with the writer who draws images of his words in the soul.* Here is an illustration:

1. Suppose I am reading a handwritten letter with a passage that is not clearly legible. The illegible manuscript passage is parallel to the blurry percept of *something* near a rock under a tree (38c5–7).
2. I might well ask: "What are those letters, the ones that look like a backward letter *C* and a lowercase undotted I next to the legible series *A, T, O*?"—parallel to the question: "What could that be that appears to stand near that rock under a tree?" (38c9–d1).
3. Parallel to memory are the grammatical and orthographic comparisons I might bring to bear on the illegible passage.
4. Just as sometimes "memory falls into line with perceptions" (39a1), grammar and orthography might produce a match with the perception.

5. In imagination, the soul's "painter" supplies a mental image that enhances the perception. In that painted image, the painter has replaced the blurry perception of *something* near a rock under a tree with an enhanced image in which it is *a man* near a rock under a tree (39b3–7). Likewise, after grammar and orthography produce a match, I might "paint" or draw an enhanced version of the blurred manuscript. In the enhanced version, two blurry letters—*what looks like a backward letter C and a lowercase undotted letter I* next to the legible series "ato"—are now legible as the letters *P, l, a, t, o.*

The illustration is parallel to 38c5–e7, which concerns the present and past. The painting of the *man* near a rock under a tree is an enhancement of a blurry image of something near a rock under a tree, *presently visible or remembered from the past.* My parallel drawing of the word "Plato" is an enhancement of a blurry manuscript that itself is presently at hand or remembered from the past. Socrates extends his example to cases of the future at 39d7–e2. In future cases, there is no perception, present or remembered, to enhance. Yet it is possible for the soul's inner painting of a *bounty of gold* to be inspired solely by words ("If I win the lottery, I shall be rich!") Likewise, it is possible for the reader's soul to paint a *legible word, "Plato,"* without seeing the original illegible manuscript, solely on the basis of a verbal description (what looks like a backward letter *C* followed by an undotted lower-case letter I and then a legible string: "ato").

39c1–2 **ἢ τοῦτο οὐκ ἔστι γιγνόμενον παρ' ἡμῖν;** *or is this process not possible for us?* I take τοῦτο γιγνόμενον *this thing coming to be* as the subject of οὐκ ἔστι *is not possible.* Smyth's (1956, §2091) alternative translation is "or is not this something that takes place in us?"—taking the present participle γιγνόμενον as "a simple predicate adjective . . . with εἰμί." The accent of ἔστι permits either analysis (S §187b).

39c4–5 **αἱ μὲν τῶν ἀληθῶν δοξῶν καὶ λόγων εἰκόνες ἀληθεῖς, αἱ δὲ τῶν ψευδῶν ψευδεῖς** *the images of the true judgments and statements are true, and those of the false ones false.* Socrates' question and Protarchus' assent at 39c4–5 are conditional, expressing what happens *in general under certain conditions.* Socrates will proceed in his argument (identified in note to 40b6–7) to establish the actual, not the conditional, existence of false images and hence false pleasures.

Carpenter (2006, 14n20) gives the alternate interpretation that Protarchus at this point already agrees that there do exist false pictures. Her alternative faces two problems: it seems to ignore the conditional context of Protarchus' agreement, and it requires her to interpret the argument for false pleasure to be interrupted by an argument for an unrelated conclusion (that good human beings for the most part enjoy true pleasures, and that bad human beings enjoy false ones).

39d1 **αἵ . . . ἡδοναὶ καὶ λῦπαι ἐλέχθησαν** Rare use of passive voice of λέγω followed by ὡς plus indirect discourse (LSJ III.2): "the pleasure and pains . . . were mentioned, that they might precede . . ." That is, *we said . . . that the pleasures and pains . . . might precede . . .*

39d1–5 **Οὐκοῦν αἵ γε διὰ τῆς ψυχῆς αὐτῆς ἡδοναὶ καὶ λῦπαι ἐλέχθησαν ἐν τοῖς πρόσθεν ὡς πρὸ τῶν διὰ τοῦ σώματος ἡδονῶν καὶ λυπῶν προγίγνοιντ' ἄν, ὥσθ' ἡμῖν συμβαίνει τὸ προχαίρειν τε καὶ προλυπεῖσθαι περὶ τὸν μέλλοντα χρόνον εἶναι γιγνόμενον;** *As we said earlier* [at 32c3–5], *the pleasures and pains from the soul itself come to be beforehand* [that is, as expectations, 32c1–2] *before pleasures and pains from the body, with the result that enjoying and suffering happen to us beforehand, coming into existence with reference to the future.* Without this premise's recall of the earlier conclusion (at 32c3–5) that expectation is one form of pleasure, the argument for 40b6–7 would show only that some *expectations* in us are pictures that are false and would fall short of its conclusion that some *pleasures* in us are pictures that are false. This passage makes its point in terms of the distinction between αἱ ἡδοναί *objects that are enjoyed* as opposed to τὸ προχαίρειν *the enjoying [beforehand].* With the inner picture, Socrates presents a model. The inner picture is the pleasure enjoyed. The picture comes to be beforehand, before the predicted future that it represents. This premise affirms that there is an entailment relation between the existence of an inner *pleasure* beforehand and the existence of an *enjoying* of that pleasure, an enjoying that, like the picture, comes before the predicted future, which is why

Socrates calls it προχαίρειν *enjoying beforehand*. Without this entailment relation, the argument would show only that some *objects* within us are pleasures that are false, but would leave unsupported the conclusion at 40c1–2 that *we actually enjoy* those objects. La Taille (1999) consistently distinguishes act from enjoying in his translations.

The main alternative interpretations of this proposition do not clearly distinguish the object enjoyed from the enjoying: Diès (1949), Hackforth (1945), Gosling (1975), Waterfield (1982), Benardete (1993), Frede (1993, 1997), Migliori (1993), and Muniz (2014). This lack of fidelity to the text raises a further problem with this alternative: it cannot make sense of the entailment relation, which takes on the trivial form "p → p." Certainly the triviality is not reduced by taking the entailment relation to be from a-pleasure-*anticipating*-another-pleasure to a-pleasure-anticipating-a-pleasure-*in-future-time* (as suggested by the language in Diès 1949, Hackforth 1945, Gosling 1975, Waterfield 1982, Frede 1993 and 1997, and Muniz 2014). Hackforth (1945) states that this premise is intended to prove that it is possible to have judgments and images not based on sense experience, a statement without basis in the text. Gosling (1975) resorts to translating the result clause as an "in other words" clause, but such charity to the author comes at the price of infidelity to the text.

My translation takes the prefix προ- *pre-*, which is attached to the verbs γίγνοιντ' *come to be*, χαίρειν *enjoying*, and λυπεῖσθαι *suffering*, to be a temporal adverb, indicating that the action of the verb to which it is attached occurs *beforehand*. In the case of the verb γίγνοιντ' *come to be*, the prefix is cognate with a preposition πρό *before*, specifying before what the action occurs. In the case of the verbs χαίρειν *enjoying* and λυπεῖσθαι *suffering*, the prepositional phrase περὶ τὸν μέλλοντα χρόνον *with reference to the future* specifies the temporal reference for the prefix. Such a treatment of Greek prefixes, especially when they produce a rare word, as in these cases, is the most natural translation.

Delcomminette's alternative interpretation of the prefix προ- *pre-* is that, when attached to the verbs χαίρειν *enjoying* and λυπεῖσθαι *suffering*, "they show that the object enjoyed [*ce à quoi prend plaisir*] by the one who has a pleasure of anticipation is nothing else than the object that will be enjoyed in the future. In other words, the *content* of the pleasure of anticipation is identical to that of the future pleasure. The only thing that distinguishes them is the *time of their occurrence*" (Delcomminette 2006, 384, his italics). An earlier version of this alternative, unremarked by Delcomminette, is Harte (2004, 123–24), who argues that the same two prefixed verbs "show" (2004, n. 12) that "an anticipatory pleasure is understood to be an advance instalment of the pleasure anticipated," such that "this anticipatory pleasure is not a pleasure *in* the anticipated pleasure; it *is* (an advance instalment of) the anticipated pleasure" (italics and parenthetical remark are Harte's). These authors give no basis in Greek grammar for their contention that the prefix shows that the prior action is *identical in all but time* to the posterior action, and this alternative should be rejected as fanciful. I suppose that authors propose it because they believe the natural reading fails to yield a sound argument for false pleasures. My interpretation of the argument, which follows Frede (1985), has shown their belief to be false. I find the Harte/Delcomminette reading uncharitable in any case, because (1) Socrates' example at 40a9–12 makes clear that the object of the prior enjoying is a picture of gold and the object of the posterior enjoying is gold, and (2) it is uncharitable to suppose that Socrates mistakes a picture of gold for gold.

The analysis of the result clause (at 39d3–5, introduced by ὥσθ') is as follows. The noun phrase τὸ προχαίρειν τε καὶ προλυπεῖσθαι *the enjoying and suffering beforehand* is the subject of the verb συμβαίνει, which takes the personal dative ἡμῖν: *happen to us*. The prepositional phrase περὶ τὸν μέλλοντα χρόνον *with reference to the future* modifies the subject. The infinitive εἶναι *to be [pleasure or pain]* or *to exist* is most naturally read as complementing the participle γιγνόμενον *becoming*, and γιγνόμενον certainly modifies the subject. Thus, a precise translation is: "with the result that enjoying and suffering happen to us beforehand, coming into existence with reference to the future."

An alternative translation is Diès (1949): "Didn't we say earlier that the pleasures and pains that come from the soul alone [*venus par l'âme seule*] are able to precede the pleasures and pains that come from the body, so that it turns out that we have pleasures and pains beforehand about the future?" This translation takes the verb συμβαίνει to have an impersonal subject ("it turns out"), taking as its complement a subordinate clause where the subject is τὸ προχαίρειν τε καὶ προλυπεῖσθαι *the enjoying and suffering beforehand*, the verb is εἶναι *is* with a dative of possession ἡμῖν *for us*. The dative of possession is correctly translated into French or English by swapping subject and object and changing the verb from "is" to "have," so that the subordinate clause reads, "We have pleasures and pains." The problem with this translation is that it leaves the participle γιγνόμενον *becoming* untranslated. This same problem afflicts the translations of Hackforth (1945), Gosling (1975), Waterfield (1982), Frede (1993 and 1997), and La Taille (1999).

Benardete (1993), followed by Muniz (2012), also translates the verb συμβαίνει with an impersonal subject ("the result is"), this verb taking the ἡμῖν *for us* as an indirect object as well as governing a subordinate clause where the subject is τὸ προχαίρειν τε καὶ προλυπεῖσθαι *the enjoying and suffering beforehand*, the verb is εἶναι *is*, and the complement is the participle γιγνόμενον *becoming*. The resulting construction is reasonably translated into English with the verb rendered as an existential quantifier, "there is," and the participle as the noun "occurrence." Hence, Benardete's translation: "The result for us is that there is the occurrence of anticipatory enjoyment and anticipatory pain about future time." Although this translation is acceptable, it must strain to fit the word order of the text (according to Benardete's translation we might expect the γιγνόμενον to precede, not follow, the εἶναι, and both words to precede the τὸ προχαίρειν).

Some recent alternative translations.

Hackforth (1945): "We said previously, did we not, that pleasures and pains felt in the soul alone might precede those that come through the body? That must mean that we have anticipatory pleasures and anticipatory pains in regard to the future."

Gosling (1975): "Well, then, earlier we said of the forms of pleasure and distress that were purely mental that they preceded physical pleasure or distress. In other words we feel pleased or distressed in advance about the future."

Waterfield (1982): "In fact didn't we say earlier that the pleasures and pains of the soul by itself might occur before the pleasures and pains of the body? Doesn't it then follow that, where the future is concerned, we can feel pleasure and pain before the event?"

Benardete (1993): "Wasn't it stated in the previous account that the pleasures and pains through the soul itself, prior to the pleasures and pains through the body, would first come to be, and the result for us is that there is the occurrence of anticipatory enjoyment and anticipatory pain about future time?"

Frede (1993): "Now, did we not say before, about the pleasures and pains that belong to the soul alone, that they might precede those that go through the body? It would therefore be possible that we have anticipatory pleasures and pains about the future."

Migliori (1993), who gives a paraphrase rather than a translation: "Socrates recalls that it was already stated that pleasures and pains of the soul [*propri dell' anima*] are able to take place before bodily ones, as anticipations of the hoped-for or feared future"

Frede (1997): "Did we not say before, about the pleasures and pains of the soul itself, that they might precede those that go through the body, so that it happens that, concerning the future, we enjoy beforehand [*im voraus freuen*] or perhaps experience pain?"

La Taille (1999): "Wasn't it said earlier that the pleasures and the pains felt from the soul itself [*ressentis par l'âme seul*] were able to precede the pleasures and pains felt from the body, so that it turns out that we [*il nous arrive*] enjoy or suffer beforehand with regard to time to come?"

Muniz (2012): "Was it not said a little while ago that the pleasures and pains that come to us by means of the soul itself [*por intermédio da própria alma*] would be able to occur before the pleasures and pains that come to us by means of the body, so that it turns out, for us, that, in relation to future time, there is the occurrence of anticipatory pleasures and anticipatory pains?"

39d7–e2 **Πότερον οὖν τὰ γράμματά τε καὶ ζωγραφήματα, ἃ σμικρῷ πρότερον ἐτίθεμεν ἐν ἡμῖν γίγνεσθαι, περὶ μὲν τὸν γεγονότα καὶ τὸν παρόντα χρόνον ἐστίν, περὶ δὲ τὸν μέλλοντα οὐκ ἔστιν;—Σφόδρα γε.** *Then, are the texts and pictures, which a little before now we posited to come to be within us [*at 39a4–7 and 39b6–c2*], about the present and past, but not about the future?—Extremely much [about the future].* This passage, which provides premise P2 in the argument for 40b6–7 (see note to that passage), is made possible by P2.1 = 39c10–12 in the same argument: if the process can occur with reference to the future, then the product likewise might refer to the future. That the internal texts and pictures are *extremely much* about the future follows from 39e4–5 = P2.2 (such texts and pictures about the future are expectations) and P2.3 (we are full of expectations all our lives) in that argument.

39e10–40a1 *A righteous, reverent, and completely good man is loved by the gods, while an unrighteous and thoroughly bad man is completely hated by the gods* (premise P4.1 in argument for 40b6–7). Socrates does not state precisely how being loved/hated by the god entails enjoying true/false pleasures that are pictures of future states. The vulgar might assume that the process is a kind of magic (the gods supernaturally intervene in nature so that bad things do not happen to good people). By the dialogue's end, the philosophical will understand that a man's goodness is correlated not only with being loved by the god but also with the ability to predict and produce (thanks to the Divine Method) the successful mix of pleasures that gives one grounds for realistic hope.

40a6–7 **Λόγοι μήν εἰσιν ἐν ἑκάστοις ἡμῶν, ἃς ἐλπίδας ὀνομάζομεν** *there are statements in each of us that we call hopes.* The masculine noun Λόγοι is the antecedent of the feminine relative pronoun ἅς rather than the masculine relative οὕς. With a verb of naming (here ὀνομάζομεν) it is common for the relative to "agree in gender and number, not with the antecedent but with a following predicate noun" (here the feminine noun ἐλπίδας; see S §2502e).

40a6–9 *Our internal texts and pictures about the future are expectations* (premise P3 in argument for 40b6–7). This premise is a restatement of 39e4–5 = proposition P2.2. Often Plato's natural language restates premises that only play a single role in the structure of the argument. However, this premise is restated twice in the argument because it is used in two different inferences in the argument (supporting also the inference to proposition P2).

40a11 **ἐνεζωγραφημένον αὐτὸν ἐφ' αὐτῷ χαίροντα σφόδρα καθορᾷ** *he sees him[self] painted into the picture, rejoicing in himself exceedingly.* Some editors unnecessarily propose changing the αὐτὸν *him* to αὑτὸν *himself.* "The personal pronouns are sometimes used in a reflexive sense" (S §1222).

40b2 **τοῖς . . . ἀγαθοῖς . . . παρατίθεσθαι** *[things that have been painted] for good human beings to set before themselves.* The middle infinitive after the dative substantive here defines its datival meaning of purpose (S §2001, 2004).

40b2–4 **Τούτων οὖν πότερα φῶμεν τοῖς μὲν ἀγαθοῖς ὡς τὸ πολὺ τὰ γεγραμμένα παρατίθεσθαι ἀληθῆ διὰ τὸ θεοφιλεῖς εἶναι, τοῖς δὲ κακοῖς ὡς αὖ <τὸ> πολὺ τοὐναντίον, ἢ μὴ φῶμεν;—Καὶ μάλα φατέον.** *Shall we affirm or deny that, for the most part, true texts and pictures are set before good human beings, on account of their being loved by the gods, but for the most part (affirm or deny) oppositewise for bad human beings?—Very much indeed one must affirm.* With his affirmation, Protarchus provides premise P4 in the argument leading to the conclusion stated at 40b7: ψευδεῖς δὲ αὗταί *these [pleasures painted for bad human beings] are false.* An alternate interpretation of the argument (Guthrie 1978, 220; Carpenter 2006, 14n20) is that this affirmation is not necessary to the argument. But without premise P4, the other three premises—many internal pictures are about the future; some such pictures about the future are expectations; and some such expectations are pleasures—entail only that there exist pleasures that are pictures of the future and fall short of the conclusion, that some pleasures are *false.*

Socrates does not specify whether the images are false because (1) the bad man will not get the immense wealth, or because (2) the bad man, getting the wealth, will not after all enjoy it. It is a problem for Harte's interpretation (2004) that Socrates needs the more specific premise 2, yet neglects to say so. Harte argues that her interpretation is defensible, all things considered, on the grounds that the more faithful, less specific reading of this premise fails to escape Protarchus' objection that "the falsity in question applies only to some associated belief" (2004, 122), and on the grounds that the less specific reading of the argument will not "steer Plato clear of the various confusions" attributed to him by, for example, Gosling (1959). Harte (2004, 122) assumes that Protarchus' objection is not met by the most natural reading of Plato's argument. Although she refers to Frede (1997), she ignores Frede's point that Plato in fact does block this objection by distinguishing the process of thinking or enjoying—which is false in a derivative sense—from the thought or pleasant thing that is the object of the thinking or enjoying.

> Plato has blocked this objection [that a process is false only in a secondary sense] with his painstaking distinction (at 37a) between the enjoying itself and the *thing* enjoyed [*dem Sich-Freuen selbst und dem* Worüber *der Freude*]. The lengthy analysis of how beliefs come to be and the identification of hopes as beliefs establish the inference that the "object" of pleasure [*das "Worüber" der Lust*]—the intentional object be false in precisely the same way as the object of thinking. If someone's enjoyment consists in the assumption (and the corresponding picture) that he will get huge wealth, then not merely the picturing but also the enjoyed assumption—the picture—proves to be false (40a). The process of enjoying is admittedly false only in a secondary sense, but that [secondary falsity] is equally true also of thinking: the thinking—the process that takes place in our head—is "false" or misdirected because the belief is false, because the relevant facts do not obtain. In the same sense in which one speaks of "falsely thinking," one can also speak of "falsely enjoying." However, the "pleasure that . . ." rather than the mental process of enjoying is true or false in the prime sense. [*Primär wahr oder falsch ist dabei aber nicht der seelische Vorgang des Sich-Freuens, sondern die "Freude über . . ."*] Plato will not say more, and he does not need to assert more for his argument. (Frede 1997, 250; likewise, Frede 1993, xlv)

That Harte fails to recognize Frede's point is surprising, since Harte herself makes the process/product distinction about pleasure (2004, 112), endorses Socrates' parallel between belief and certain pleasures as "clearly right" (2004, 114), and happily speaks of the "false pleasures the wicked enjoy" (2004, 125)—false pleasures that are, in terms of Plato's analysis, precisely the pictures painted in their souls. Having established that these pictures are false, Plato has no need to infer that the mental event of *enjoying* these pictures is false in any but the derivative sense, exactly parallel to the primary falsity of beliefs and the merely derivative or secondary sense in which the event of *thinking* is false. Thus, there is no need for Harte to avoid the most natural reading of Plato's argument.

40b4 **πολὺ τοὐναντίον** *it is much the opposite.* The impersonal πολὺ τοὐναντίον with this meaning occurs at Isocrates, *Areopagiticus* 76.3 and Lysias, *In Agoratum* 51.8. Burnet (1901) follows Stallbaum (1842) in inserting <τὸ>, perhaps to get the meaning *for the most part it is the opposite*, but the addition seems needless.

40b6–7 **Οὐκοῦν καὶ τοῖς κακοῖς ἡδοναί γε οὐδὲν ἧττον πάρεισιν ἐζωγραφημέναι, ψευδεῖς δὲ αὗταί που.** *Painted pleasures are present to bad people no less [than to good people], but they tend to be false [while those present to good people tend to be true].* This statement is conclusion C in the analysis below. For a simpler presentation of the argument, I interpret conclusion C to be restated twice, at 40c4–6 *(There are false pleasures in human souls that are quite ridiculous imitations of true ones, and also such pains)* and 40c1–2 *(Worthless people for the most part enjoy false pleasures, while the good enjoy true).* As an alternative, one might interpret these three statements as two or three different premises with some sort of inferential relation between the following: "false pleasures *are present to* bad people"; "bad people *enjoy* false pleasures"; and "there are false pleasures *in human souls.*" I identify the argument for the single conclusion C as follows:

P1 As we said earlier (at 32c3–5), the pleasures and pains from the soul itself come to be *beforehand* (that is, as expectation [as said at 32c1–2]) before pleasures and pains from the body, with the result that enjoying and suffering happen to us beforehand, coming into existence with reference to the future (39d1–5).

P2 Our internal texts and pictures (postulated at 39a4–7, b6–c2) are emphatically about the future as well as present and past (39d7–e2). Because:

P2.1 We go through the painting process (described at 39b3–e3) about the future as well as present and past (39c10–12).

P2.2 All (texts and pictures about things future) are expectations about that time (39e4–5; restated at 40a6–9).

P2.3 We are throughout life full of expectations (39e5–6; restated at 40a3–4).

P2.3.a Example: Often a man sees (in an inner painting) a bounty of gold belonging to him, many consequent pleasures, and also himself, painted in, in intense joy about it (40a9–12).

P3 Our internal texts and pictures about the future *are* expectations (40a6–9; restatement of 39e4–5).

P4 The texts and pictures (that are expectations of many things in the future) inside good people are mostly true; inside bad people are mostly false (40b2–4).

P4.1 Because a righteous, reverent, and completely good man is loved by the gods, while an unrighteous and thoroughly bad man is completely hated by the gods (39e10–40a1).

I interpret conclusion C as validly following from its four premises. To make the validity of the inference to C easy to see, I provide the following order and simplification of the four premises:

1. Some pleasures are expectations. (P1)
2. Such expectations are texts and pictures about the future. (P3)
3. There are many such texts and pictures about the future (i.e., pleasures) in human souls. (P2)
4. Some of these texts and pictures (i.e., pleasures) are false. (P4)

Taking 39c7–8 ("If we have stated this [account] correctly, let us go on to consider the following [proposition based] on this account") to announce the beginning of the argument proper for C, I interpret

37a2–39c5 as background information for the argument to conclusion C rather than as premises. I take 40c4 ("according to our present statements") to indicate the inference to the final statement of the conclusion P. One alternative interpretation would be to incorporate some or all of these propositions into the argument for C as premises. I do not see a significant difference between such an alternative and my own. Another alternative interpretation is that there is *no* argument for conclusion C: "Plato offers . . . metaphors in lieu of arguments" (Russell 2005, 177). One might give the following argument in defense of the metaphor-not-argument interpretation. (1) The conclusion of my formal argument is a *restatement* not an inference from premise P4 ("Texts and pictures in the soul can be true or false," 40b2–4); and (2) premise P4 itself is only metaphorically true. Likewise, my argument for C has no more cash value than a metaphor. I reply that both premises of this argument are false.

Premise (2) of this argument is false. Protarchus admits that thoughts are true or false (36d1–2), that true and false thoughts are words in the soul that may be correct or incorrect representations of reality (38d5–e4) or texts in the soul that may be true or false (39a3–7). None of these admissions need be interpreted as more metaphorical than any propositional account of thought. And likewise, Protarchus' admission that images in the soul associated with true thoughts and statements would be true, while those of false thoughts and statements false (39c4–5) can be treated as being as literal as any discussion of imagination. And just as sentences can be literally false, images also can be. Accordingly, premise P4 ("Some people have inner texts and pictures that are true; others false") ought to be interpreted as literally true.

And premise (1) of the same argument is false. Premise P4 says nothing about pleasures and does not on its own establish proposition P. Other premises necessary to establish C are P1 ("Some pleasures are expectations" = 39d1–5), P2 ("There are inner texts and pictures about the future" = 39d7–e2), and P3 ("Expectations are inner texts and pictures about the future" = 40a6–9). Likewise, the conclusion C is more than a restatement of premise P4.

Following Frede (1985, 1993, and 1997), I interpret the "false" and "painted" pleasures in C (ψευδεῖς ἡδοναί, 40c1, c5) as *objects that are enjoyed* (as opposed to enjoyments of objects), such as Socrates' apt example of the false picture a man might enjoy, a picture of himself in the future surrounded by gold. Frede's interpretation enjoys numerous advantages over the alternatives.

1. Frede allows us charitably to evaluate the argument for conclusion C as sound.
2. Frede shows why Protarchus' earlier objection (at 37e12–38a2) fails. Protarchus had objected that merely to show that a pleasure *follows in the train of a false thought* will not entail that the pleasure, in addition to the thought, is false. Protarchus is right about the following sort of example (suggested by 37d1–e12, see note to 37d2–4). Suppose that I falsely believe, while thirsty in the desert, that this water is safe to drink and consequently find it a pleasure to drink. In this case, although the pleasure follows in the train of the false thought, the pleasure does not become false: neither the poison water nor the enjoyment of it is false, even though the pleasure might be bad and incorrect for me. Nonetheless, Protarchus must assent to conclusion C, since there Socrates identifies a different sort of example, according to which one falsely believes that one shall in the future enjoy immense wealth, and one enjoys an imaginary mental picture of that future. In this case, the picture enjoyed is indisputably false, and the enjoying of it is in a derivative sense false, precisely parallel to the falseness of a statement and in a derivative sense the believing of that statement.
3. Frede allows us faithfully to interpret the argument for conclusion C exactly as presented in the text, without needing to supply additional premises.
4. Frede conforms to Socrates' disambiguation of action and object at 37a2–b3.
5. Frede resolves the issue raised at 37b5–7, establishing a precise analogy between false thought and false pleasure.

6. Frede can easily give a sense to Socrates' claim in C that such pleasures are "ridiculous imitations" (40c5–6). A false picture of my future—say, of me happily surrounded by gold—is a ridiculous imitation of a true picture—say, of me in *poverty* or of me *miserable* while surrounded by gold. In contrast, there is no easy way to see how the enjoying of a false pleasure is a ridiculous imitation of the enjoying of a true pleasure.

The main alternative interpretation of the argument is that the false pleasures of conclusion C are *episodes* of enjoying pictures, as opposed to the *pictures* themselves. For example, Gosling (1975, 218): "The pleasure is most plausibly identified with the picturing." Gosling and Taylor (1982, 438) claim that this interpretation, which makes an "identification of pleasure with enjoyed activities," is "defensible" on the grounds that "it is in fact a possible sense of the plural *hēdonai,* as it is the most natural sense of the English 'pleasures.'" Despite its bare lexical possibility, this interpretation fails to enjoy any of the advantages listed above for Frede's interpretation, instead having the following disadvantages.

1. On this interpretation the argument for conclusion C is vulnerable to the objection raised alike by Gosling (1959, 1961), and 1975, 215–19) and Kenny (1960), for example. The objection is that the argument errs in moving from "bad people enjoy some false pictures" to "bad people falsely enjoy some pictures." As Gosling (1975, 218) puts this objection: "The pleasure is most plausibly identified with the picturing [i.e., the act of viewing the picture], but all that can strictly be said to be false is the picture."
2. The Gosling/Kenny objection stated as disadvantage 1 shows that, on this interpretation, the argument fails to meet Protarchus' objection, raised at 37e12–38a2. As Migliori (1993, 224n112) rightly objects to Gosling: if Plato conflated picture and picturing, "why did he not give more weight to [*non vale più*] Protarchus' objection? Why does a false thought become a false pleasure?"
3. On this interpretation, unless we attribute an equivocation to the text between *pictures* and *enjoying* pictures (as do, e.g., Gosling and

Taylor [1982, 438]), we must, like Kenny (1960), supply a suppressed premise (namely, that pleasure in false pictures is false pleasure). Dybikowski (1970), also assuming that the argument aims to show that enjoying (rather than pleasure) is false, attributes a different equivocation to the text, between picture and object depicted.

4. This interpretation, which identifies the pleasure with the picturing rather than the picture, does not fit with Socrates' disambiguation of *enjoying* and *object enjoyed* at 37a2–b3.
5. This interpretation does not produce a precise analogy between this type of false pleasure and false thought, an analogy affirmed at 37b5–7.
6. This interpretation does not easily give a sense to Socrates' claim in C that such pleasures are "ridiculous imitations" (40c5–6).

Another alternative interpretation of this argument is put forward by Hampton (1990, 58), who supplies a premise not found in the text: "The pleasures of wealth themselves are false in comparison to the true pleasures of which they are poor imitations." For this reason, according to Hampton, Plato condemns as also false the anticipatory pleasures of anticipating such pleasures. And there is no need to attribute such a premise to the argument. As my (Fredean) interpretation shows, the argument derives its conclusion without such a premise. Worse (as Delcomminette [2006, 388] notices), the supplied premise would have Socrates beg the question, since it assumes what it needs to prove.

40c6 **καὶ . . . δὲ** *and [pains] for that matter* (Rijksbaron 1997, 206).

40d5 **τὴν τούτων ἀντίστροφον ἕξιν ἐν ἐκείνοις** *the analogous condition of these in those.* Although there is no certainty about this line, I find it plausible, as Bury (1897) suggests, that τούτων refers to ταῦτά (d1, the "reality and groundlessness" of false judgments) and ἐκείνοις to the activity of judging and to the judgment. Socrates is asking Protarchus to discern that enjoying a false picture is like thinking a false thought. The taking pleasure, like the thinking, really exists. But the picture (i.e., the pleasure being enjoyed), like the thought, is false.

40d7–8 **ἦν μὲν χαίρειν ὄντως ἀεὶ τῷ . . . χαίροντι** *enjoying always really exists [as we now recognize]*, imperfect of truth just recognized (S §1902). The sentence construction is analogous to 40c8–10.

41B–42C. PLEASURES FALSE IN MAGNITUDE.

A second way for pleasures to be false is when they seem greater or less than they are, as happens when people mistake what will give them more pleasure.

41b3 **εἰσίν** *they exist.* Nonenclitic accent marks this verb as existential not copulative. This is an editorial change. The manuscripts have εἴπερ γέ εἰσιν *if indeed [pleasures] are [false in another way].*

41b5 **τοῦτο δὲ τὸ δόγμα ἕως ἂν κέηται παρ' ἡμῖν** *until we are familiar with this idea* [namely, the second way in which pleasure can be false—literally, "until this doctrine lies down beside us"]. Hackforth (1945) and Frede (1993) take the lying beside to entail that the idea is "established" or "accepted" rather than merely familiar. In its other six occurrences in Plato, the verb has that meaning in connection with law, where it occurs three times ([1]"laws are just [and (2), two lines below, 'good'] to the state that made them, so long as they 'lie,' i.e., are in force" [*Theaetetus* 177d1–5]; and [3] at *Laws* 841b6 something would "lie," i.e., be in force in the law). But in three other occurrences the verb has no such meaning: (1) at *Sophist* 257c2 the verb is used for the relation of denotation between word and object: "the utterances 'lie about' the things"; (2) *Parmenides* 148e7—if something "touches" itself, it must "lie" next to itself; and (3) *Republic* 477a7—a thing "would lie between being and not being." It is true that "to lie in the law" means "established," but it does not follow that if a thought "lies alongside us," it is established. Bury (1897) is not wrong to take κέηται here to mean merely "propounded as a thesis for discussion," not "established."

41c2–3 **δίχα . . . καὶ χωρὶς τῆς ψυχῆς . . . διείληπται** *has been taken apart from and separate from the soul in [what it undergoes].* The καὶ suggests both δίχα and χωρὶς are prepositions taking the same object. The verb's prefix δι(ά) with dative complement indicates the "place where"—that is, *the respect in which* body and soul are twofold and separated. As Bury (1897) notes, the relevant prior discussion was at 35a–c.

41c5–6 **τὸ μὲν ἐπιθυμοῦν ἦν ἡ ψυχὴ τῶν τοῦ σώματος ἐναντίων ἕξεων** *the thing desiring the opposite of the actual conditions of the body is the soul.* (The ἦν *is,* an imperfect with present meaning, is used to refer to a topic previously discussed: the "philosophical imperfect," S §1903.) There is a problem interpreting this proposition. It appears to entail that if the actual condition of the body is pleasant restoration, the soul then desires the opposite, which is pain! This cannot be correct; the object of desire is always pleasure. My interpretation is based on 35b11, which states that "in every case of impulse and desire the soul of an animal that is in any respect empty relative to something fuller does contact filling relative to something emptier." Accordingly, even when an animal's body is providing pleasure to the body—that is, when the body is refilling—the animal's desire will be for filling *relative to something emptier.* Hence, even at this time the soul is desiring the opposite of certain actual conditions of the body.

An alternative is Delcomminette (2006, 399), who sees here "an allusion to the fact that, insofar as every pleasure is insufficient for procuring happiness, the act of feeling a given pleasure in its incompleteness [*dans son incomplétude*] is no less able [than the act of feeling a pain] to stir up the desire for a pleasure more intense." Whereas the text at 35b11 establishes that every desire is for something fuller relative to something emptier, Socrates nowhere establishes the implausible claim that every desire is for the happiness that is not attained by the given pleasure. The text at 35b11 recognizes the fact that so long as I desire to drink, even while enjoying drinking, it is insofar as I remain thirsty to some degree. Delcomminette's interpretation, in contrast, is that everyone who enjoys drinking feels a *further* desire for the happiness that is unsatisfied with drinking pleasure.

Another alternative is Hackforth (1945, 78). When the body is providing pleasure, "what we desire then cannot be anything but the πλήρωσις [*filling*] of the awareness itself, namely the pleasure of acquiring knowledge, of which we shall hear later (52a)." This interpretation, like Delcomminette's, attributes an implausible claim to Socrates—that, when I enjoy the bodily pleasure of drinking, I must simultaneously desire a mental pleasure—on the basis of nothing to which Socrates can be referring in context.

41c6–7 **διὰ πάθος** *on account of what [the body] undergoes.* The word order—that διὰ πάθος qualifies both τὴν ἀλγηδόνα and τινα ἡδονὴν—in this passage is "somewhat peculiar," as Bury (1897) says.

41d1–2 **Γίγνεται τοίνυν . . . ἡδονάς, καὶ τούτων αἰσθήσεις.** *[In cases of desire,] pains and pleasures exist side by side, and there are simultaneous perceptions of these things that are opposite to each other.* This passage draws a subtle distinction between pleasure, a (perceived) restoration, and the perceiving itself, which is of the restoration. In terms of Socrates' prior example of the man suffering from poverty who enjoys a mental picture of himself rich in the future, the pains of poverty (say, the lack of proper food and drink) exist side by side with the pleasure, which is the picture at present in his soul (32b9–c1). The man simultaneously perceives his present bodily lacks and at the same time, in the picture, the things that are opposite to these lacks—namely, the pleasure of satisfying those wants (35b11).

41d2 **τούτων . . . ἐναντίων οὐσῶν** *[perceptions] of these [pleasures and pains lying side by side], which are opposites.*

41d9 **εἴτην** third person dual optative εἰμί *[the two] were.* The optative εἴτην is governed by the perfect εἴρηται at d5, repeated at d10. The perfect is a primary tense (S §1858). The rule for use of the optative: "No verb can be changed to the optative in indirect discourse except after a secondary tense" (S §2610). Despite this rule, in context the perfect εἴρηται refers to past time, permitting the optative, just as when present tense refers to past time (the historical present, S §1858a).

41e2–3 **τὸ βούλημα . . . βούλεται** *the intent intends to [figure out].* "The intent intends *X*" is an unusual expression in English, though Protarchus has no trouble understanding it in Greek. Just as a script can tell us what to say or a map can tell us where to go, an intent can tell us what to do—in this sense a script scripts, a map maps, and an intent intends. Just as previously for judging Socrates explicitly postulates an inner scribe who writes out a judgment, and for imagining an inner painter who paints an image for our soul to consult, enjoy, or fear, likewise also here, though implicitly, there seems to be an inner homunculus of intention that produces a written or painted intent that guides the soul. Gosling (1975) correctly identifies the agent of the intending as the *intent* in an idiomatic translation ("the aim of our judgment is . . . to decide").

41e4 **τίς μᾶλλον** *which [pleasure or pain is] more [pleasant or painful]* or *[happens] more [often]*. Protarchus repeats the adverb μᾶλλον, perhaps in the same sense, nine lines below. Frede (1993) translates them "more intensive . . . more so"; Gosling (1975) translates them "more . . . more in evidence"; and Hackforth (1945) translated the lines "degree . . . greater degree."

42a2–3 **ἐν λύπαις δ' ἄρα καὶ ἡδοναῖς οὐκ ἔστι ταὐτὸν τοῦτο γιγνόμενον** *Then, isn't it the same thing that happens in pains and pleasures?* The sameness has to do with eyesight: τὸ πόρρωθεν καὶ ἐγγύθεν . . . τὰ μεγέθη τὴν ἀλήθειαν ἀφανίζει καὶ ψευδῆ ποιεῖ δοξάζειν *the nearness and farness hide the truth about the magnitudes and cause false opinions* (41e9–42a1). The standard interpretation of the nearness and farness is that, "whereas in the case of eyesight the distance is distance in space, in the case of pleasures and pains the distance would be distance in time, as for instance when one compares a pleasure today with a pain or pleasure tomorrow" (Russell 2005, 183).

Delcomminette (2006, 401–2) objects that

> such an interpretation does not take account of the fact that this passage was introduced by recalling the mechanism of desire, when Socrates had strongly insisted on the *copresence* of the desired pleasure and the pain or pleasure of the body at the time of the desire, such that they were able to be placed side by side and compared. Therefore, it is not the temporal interval [*éloignement temporel*] that causes the exaggeration or under-estimation of the considered pleasure, but rather, as Socrates expressly says, the fact that they . . . accept the more and less.

The "copresence" premise of this objection is false. Just as there is a difference between gold and a picture of gold, so also there is a difference between a present anticipatory pleasure (which, in Socrates' example:

P2a = 40a9–12, is a picture of gold) and a future, desired pleasure (the gold itself). It is false that the *desired* pleasure (wealth) is copresent with the present pain (poverty), and it is uncharitable to interpret Socrates to make such a confused claim. What Socrates says in the passage referenced by Delcomminette (41d1–3) is that "whenever we desire" (ὁπόταν ᾖ ταῦτα, i.e., "whenever desires are in us," 41c1), two actions occur (the Greek uses the finite verb γίγνεται *there occur* with two complementary accusative-plus-infinitive constructions, παρακεῖσθαι λύπας τε καὶ ἡδονάς *pleasures and pains lie side by side*, and αἰσθήσεις γίγνεσθαι *perceptions arise*). The first event is that ἅμα παρακεῖσθαι λύπας τε καὶ ἡδονάς *pleasures and pains lie side by side at the same time*. As has just been shown, what lies in the soul at the same time beside a present pain (such as poverty) is an anticipatory pleasure (such as a picture of gold), not the desired pleasure (such as gold). The second event is that αἰσθήσεις ἅμα . . . γίγνεσθαι *simultaneous perceptions arise*. The perceptions are τούτων *of these things*—that is, of the pleasures and pains lying side by side. In the case of anticipatory pleasures, it goes without saying that a perception of the picture is also a perception of the thing pictured. Socrates specifies that the perception is οὐσῶν *of beings*, beings that are παρ' ἀλλήλας ἐναντίων *opposite to each other*. And it goes without saying that what is opposite to the pain of poverty is not the copresent anticipatory pleasure, a mere picture of gold, but the future, desired pleasure of the gold itself. Hence, we should not interpret the things that are the objects of the present perception, the things that are opposite to each other, to be copresent, but to be a present pain and a future pleasure, where the future pleasure is perceived in a picture that is present with the pain. Such an interpretation is at least as faithful to the text as the premise of Delcomminette's objection, and far more charitable.

The objection leads Delcomminette (2006, 402) to an alternative interpretation: "To examine a pleasure 'from afar' does not signify to consider a pleasure at some interval in the past or future, but to consider it in comparison to [*à partir de*] its opposite—that is, in comparison either to a pain or to a less intense pleasure." Mere "contrarity" (*contrariété*)—that is, "the opposition of the bigger and the smaller"—explains the error. He gives an example to illustrate how this occurs: "The color gray is able to appear white when it is compared to black." This alternative seems uncharitable. Certainly mere juxtaposition of two opposites can lead us to mistake the *absolute* value of one of the opposites, as the gray example shows. But the error that Socrates is concerned with is an error of *relative* value (41e2–6). The question would not be "How white is *that color*?" but "Which color is whiter *than the other* [πρὸς ἀλλήλας, 41e3–4]?" And a mere juxtaposition would never lead us to believe that black is whiter than gray.

Hampton (1990) rightly points out that no (false) exaggeration will occur without a comparison of pleasures and pains. She infers that a comparison of pleasures and pains requires a multipart soul, concluding that this second type of falsity must presuppose a multi-part soul in which rational and appetitive thoughts coexist. Her inference is invalid: a comparison of pleasures and pains requires only one part of the soul, a prudential part intent on minimizing pain or maximizing pleasure.

42a9 **ἀνεπίμπλασαν** *were filling up [the pleasures and pains with what they are undergoing].* If it were the case that only false judgments passed on their falsity (while true judgments did not pass on their truth), then the secondary "defiling" sense *infecting* (as in Gosling 1975, following Hackforth 1945) would be fitting; but since the condition passed on might be truth as well as falsity, better to translate with the primary meaning *fill up*, which is an apt metaphor.

42b2–4 **διὰ τὸ . . . θεωρεῖσθαι, καὶ ἅμα τιθέμεναι παρ' ἀλλήλας** *on account of their being viewed . . . while at the same time being placed side by side.* The mental comparison takes place at the same time as they are being viewed.

42C–44A. MERELY APPARENT PLEASURES THAT ARE NOT REAL AT ALL.

Socrates argues that a third type of false pleasure occurs when someone mistakes the neutral condition of being pain-free for pleasure. Socrates suggests that this third type of false pleasure is "even falser" than the above, both in "appearance and reality" (42c6–7). As Hackforth (1945, 81) rightly says:

> This third case differs in an important respect from the two others. In both of those there was a real pleasure or pain, containing an element of falsity; but now there is no . . . real pleasure or pain; this case is not covered by the formula of 37b ["the thing enjoying enjoys, whether rightly or wrongly; it is clear that he never destroys the act of really enjoying"]. On the contrary, we have what Protarchus "and everybody else" had asserted to be impossible, the case when a man [thinks he enjoys, but in no way enjoys] and [thinks he suffers pain, but does not suffer].

Likewise, Delcomminette (2006, 421): "This type of false pleasure shows the existence of [*nous met en présence de*] people who *believe* that they enjoy during the time when they do not enjoy at all." Unfortunately, Delcomminette contradicts this correct interpretation by affirming nonetheless that in such cases people "really and truly feel pleasure" (*prend bel et bien plaisir*, 2006, 420), that "the act of experiencing pleasure is not what is false in this case" (2006, 421), and that to have such a pleasure is "to take pleasure in something that is not a pleasure" (2006, 422).

Gosling (1975, 214) objects that if Plato considers such nonpleasures to be false, then he would be guilty of "straightforward equivocation." But the fact that Plato speaks of false pleasure in a number of ways is not sufficient reason to charge him with equivocation. The fallacy of equivocation only occurs if Plato asserts an argument that illicitly trades on different meanings of the same word. Gosling (1975) identifies no such argument. Frede (1993, 1997) is surely right that Plato here is cataloguing different manners of calling pleasures "false." But he is also engaged in the philosophical project (with, for example, Rorty 1970) that attacks the widely held thesis that human beings have incorrigible access to their own episodes of pleasure and pain.

42a5 **᾿Εναντίον δὴ τὸ νῦν τῷ σμικρὸν ἔμπροσθε γέγονεν** *the [falsity] now is opposite to the [falsity] a little earlier.* Gosling and Taylor (1982, 445) give the following illustrative example of the second type of falsity. "If I am dissatisfied with my job I may think that another job *will be* more satisfying than this one *is;* having made the change I discover to my chagrin that the new job *is* not more satisfying than the old one *was.*" Using this example, they raise the following objection. "Since we have no independent criterion either of how unpleasant my present job is in fact, or of how pleasant the alternative is in fact, we have no ground for the judgement that I exaggerate either the one or the other." Without an independent criterion, they argue, the most that "we can say is that a certain anticipation—that is, of how one *will* view the relative pleasantness of the two jobs—is falsified by the event, and hence that the pleasure in that anticipation was ill-founded. But that is precisely the first case of false pleasure of anticipation, where the falsity of an anticipation infects the pleasure in that anticipation with its falsity." The premise of their objection is true: we have no independent criterion either of how unpleasant my present job is in fact, or of how pleasant the alternative is in fact. But Socrates does not need such independent criteria to establish that the pain (the present job) and the pleasure (the future job) are false in a way that infects my thoughts. All he needs is that one of these pleasures might *be* more but *appear* less than the other. Socrates establishes the fact that there *is* a relationship between them of more or less at proposition 41d8–9. According to my interpretation, "pleasure accepts the more and less" entails that for all *x* and *y* pleasant things, there are relations (*less pleasant than, more pleasant than)* between *x* and *y*. Likewise, one pleasure is in fact more pleasant than another, whether or not we have criteria of the fact. (Frede [1997, 263–64] appeals both to "ordinary language" [*im Alltag häufig . . . zu sprechen*] and to Jeremy Bentham, rather than to 41d8–9, to defend Socrates' inference.) And the text at 42b2–6 establishes the fact that, while *being more,* one of these can *appear less,* since future pleasures are capable of being represented in pictures, and hence can be represented as more or less than they in fact are.

The first kind of false pleasure was a *mental picture* (of future gold or a job, say), illustrating and hence infected by the prior falsity of a thought about the future (a thought such as "I shall inherit" or "I won't have to speak to so-and-so at that job"). The second kind of false pleasure is not the mental picture but the *future gold* or *job.* There is a fact of the matter about whether this future object is more or less pleasant than some present pain (poverty or the present job), as the text at 41d8–9 establishes. And there are pictorial representations of this pleasure on account of which it appears falsely. The ability of the pleasure to appear falsely gives it the power to infect thoughts with its falsity, opposite to the first case (thoughts such as "wealth is more pleasant than poverty" or "working there is more pleasant than working here"). My interpretation follows Mooradian (1995).

42c2 **ἐπὶ τούτῳ . . . γιγνόμενον** *[the part] coming to be on this [appearance].* The manuscript has the accusative dual form τούτω, which has been corrected to τούτῳ. I follow the Badham (1878) reading, endorsed by Bury (1897): "That much then, by which either appears greater than it really is, that apparent and unreal quantity, you will cut off [from each], and you will neither say that the appearance itself is a right appearance, nor will you venture to call that part of the pleasure and pain which is founded upon it [τούτῳ, i.e., the apparent but unreal quantity], right and true." An alternative manuscript has ἐπὶ τοῦτο μέρος in 42c2, which Frede (1993) follows and translates: "you will neither admit that this appearance is right nor dare to say that anything connected with this portion of pleasure and pain is right and true."

42d3 **συμβαίνει γιγνόμενα** *come to be as a result.* The verb συμβαίνει and the participle γιγνόμενα have the same neuter plural subjunctive λῦπαί τε καὶ ἀλγηδόνες καὶ ὀδύναι καὶ πάνθ' ὁπόσα τοιαῦτ' ὀνόματα ἔχει, regarded as a collective (S §958).

42d5 **ὅταν καθιστῆται** with implied neuter plural subject *whenever [they] are becoming restored [into their proper nature].* This present indefinite temporal clause is part of the indirect discourse after ἀπεδεξάμεθα *we accepted*, depending on the accusative-plus-infinitive construction ταύτην . . . τὴν κατάστασιν ἡδονὴν *that this restoration [was] a pleasure.*

42e4 **οὐ κωλύει ἐμὲ** *it doesn't prevent* me. This is the text of B. Manuscript T has οὐ κωλύσεις με *you will not prevent me.* Burnet (1901) emends to κωλύεις *you do not prevent me.*

42e8 **ἐξ αὐτοῦ** *[consequence] of this.* Namely, as Protarchus will inquire (42e9) and Socrates confirm (42e10), *of the body not changing in either of the two ways.*

43a3 **ἀεὶ γὰρ ἅπαντα ἄνω τε καὶ κάτω ῥεῖ** *for all things are always in flux up and down,* a seeming quotation from memory of Heraclitus (Diels Kranz B 59; 60; A 1 [141, 24], citation from Frede 1997).

43a6–7 **ὑπεκστῆναι τὸν λόγον ἐπιφερόμενον τοῦτον βούλομαι** *I want to get out from under this speech that is bearing down on [us].* "The Heraclitean λόγος is likened to a charging foe—warrior or warship" (Bury 1897).

43b5–6 **ὀλίγου . . . τά . . . τοιαῦτα . . . πάνθ'** *all such things but a few,* ὀλίγου a genitive of quantity (S §1399).

43b8 **κάτω τε καὶ ἄνω γιγνόμεναι** circumstantial participle *going on "up and down."* See note to 43a3 for quotation.

43d4–5 **οὐκ ἂν εἴη τὸ μὴ λυπεῖσθαί ποτε ταὐτὸν τῷ χαίρειν** *To be free from pain is not ever the same thing as to feel pleasure.* This thesis is restated at 44a9–10. I interpret the argument for it is as follows:

P1 Because there are three [modes of] life: pleasant, painful, and what is neither (43c13–d2).

Because (inference indicated by Ἐκ δὴ τούτων τιθῶμεν *from these things let us posit,* 43c13):

P1.1 The middle (or neutral) manner of living could not be either pleasant or painful (42e11–12).

P1.1.1 Because (inference indicated by δὴ *then,* 42e11) in the middle, the body would be neither undergoing disintegration nor restoration (42e9–10).

P1.2 There is a [mode of] life that is free of pleasure and pain (43c8–12).

Because (inference indicated by Οὐκοῦν εἰ ταῦτα οὕτω *therefore, if these things are so)*:

P1.2.1 (Restatement of 31d4–6) Pain coincides with the disintegrating of an organism's nature (42c9–d3).

P1.2.2 (Restatement of 31d4–6) Pleasure is the same thing as the restoring of that nature (42d5–7).

P1.2.3 Only big (hence perceived) changes cause pleasures and pains, not moderate or small changes (43b7–9, 43c4–6).

P1.2.3.1 Because (inference indicated by τοίνυν *therefore,* 43b7) in almost all cases, we and other living creatures do not notice or perceive such processes as growth and other things we undergo (43b1–6).

Protarchus' assumption that "necessarily everything is changing in every way in us" (43a1–3) is not a premise of the argument. Socrates mentions the assumption in order to discount it, not infer from it.

43e1 **Τριῶν ὄντων οὖν ἡμῖν, ὧντινων βούλει** *if we have three [names]—whatever you wish.* Smyth (1956, §2527) cites this case (as "43d") as a rare instance of a pronoun before βούλει attracted to the case of its antecedent, but ὅστις is not subject to attraction (S: §2524). As an alternative, I understand the same tacit accusative noun ὀνόματα *names* as in the antecedent clause: *if we have three [names], [names] of whatever you wish.*

43e8 **λεγόμενος** *[the middle life] being said [to be pleasant or painful].* This assessment of proper speech replies to the man who speaks about these matters at 43d10 (Bury 1897; Delcomminette 2020).

44a6 **Φασὶ γοῦν** Protarchus only grants that they say this, not that they believe it—hence the next few questions by Socrates.

44a9–10 *There are people who falsely believe that they are pleased when they are merely free from pain.* Gosling and Taylor (1982, 450–51) object to this proposition as follows. First, they affirm that ill people and others whom Plato describes unmistakenly "do find a certain state enjoyable just because it is a state of freedom from distress. There is no misidentification involved here, any more than there is a mistake involved in finding a cool shady room pleasant just by contrast with the heat and glare outside." Second, taking themselves to have established the reality of such pleasures that are not processes of restorations, they conclude that such pleasures in states "provide further evidence of the inadequacy of [Plato's] general account" of pleasure as a process of restoration.

Gosling and Taylor's objection is unconvincing. They are right that the existence of such neutral states being pleasures is inconsistent with Plato's theory of pleasure as restoring. The force of their objection depends on their assertion that in illness the pleasure of recovery is true, and the only evidence they provide to regard such pleasures as true is the similarity they see between the pleasure of recovery and the pleasure taken "in a cool shady room . . . by contrast with the heat and glare outside." But the pleasures of the cool shady room are restoring processes, not neutral states. My overheated body takes pleasure as it restores itself by cooling down *just to the neutral point of body temperature*, after which further cooling is felt to be unpleasant. Likewise, the overstimulation of my eyes by the glare produces pleasure as my eyes find relief in the shadows *just to the point where I am relieved and become indifferent and, perhaps, bored with the lack of bright color and light.* I admit that *mere contrast as such* might be painful—for example, the contrast of light and dark caused by a strobe light. Such a pain is easy for Plato to explain: something like a headache is induced and magnified by the strobe. Likewise, I admit that some might find the same strobe effect to be pleasant, *merely as contrast*. But it is not difficult for Plato to explain such visual pleasure as relieving, with its stimulation, something felt as a kind of visual boredom, hence discomfort. In neither the case of the cool shady room nor the strobe light, therefore, do I find a convincing objection to Plato's argument.

44a10 **τοῦ μὴ λυπεῖσθαι καὶ τοῦ χαίρειν . . . ἑκατέρου** The sentence is awkward enough that some suggest emendations. Accepting the text, I analyze the articular infinitives to stand in apposition to ἑκατέρου: *[the nature] of each of the two, of feeling no pain and of feeling pleasure.*

44a11 **ἦν** *is*, an imperfect with present meaning, used to refer to a topic previously discussed: the "philosophical imperfect" (S §1903).

44B–51A. HOW THE MIXED CONDITION OF PLEASURE AND PAIN CAN BE FALSE.

Socrates argues that there are two ways that mixed pleasures are false, either by failing to be a net pleasure at all or by appearing greater than they are. Socrates does not refer to mixed pleasures as a fourth (or fourth and fifth) kind of falsity. Perhaps this is because the first kind of falsity in mixed pleasures—*a thing falsely seeming pleasant when not*—is the same kind of falsity as in type three, albeit that the neutral state is different from the mixed state, while the second kind of falsity in mixed pleasures—*a thing falsely seeming to be* just *pleasure when really a pleasure-and-pain*—is the same kind of illusion, produced by a contrasting background, as in type two. But there is a problem for such a reading. It is at odds with Socrates' criteria for classifying kinds of pleasure and knowledge at 31b2–3: "in what" (ἐν ᾧ) it is present and "through what *pathos*" (διὰ τί πάθος) it comes to be. His criteria do not include *by the way it seems* (e.g., seeming pleasant when it is not). According to Delcomminette (2006, 427), "the division between mixed and pure pleasures is a new, exhaustive, division [*nouvelle division exhaustive*] of pleasure according to a new criterion" (in note 2 on that page he reviews alternative interpretations).

44b1 **ἢ δύο μόνα** *or only two.* When the audience first hears this ellipsis, they will supply words from the first alternative: ἢ [sc., αἱρώμεθα παρ' ἡμῖν ταῦτ' εἶναι] δύο μόνα *or [shall we choose that the forms of life available to us are] only two.* By the time Socrates finishes the sentences, however, the words to supply come from the phrase standing in apposition: ἢ [αἱρώμεθα ταῦτα προσαγορεύεσθαι] δύο μόνα *or [shall we choose to call the forms of life by] only two [names].*

44b2 **αὐτὸ τοῦτο ἀγαθὸν ὄν** *this very thing [i.e., freedom from pains] being a good.* This circumstantial participle seems to be causal, giving the reason for calling a pain-free life pleasant: *since it's good, we call the pain-free life pleasant.* The missing premise in this enthymeme would be the hedonist thesis that *a good thing must be a pleasure.*

44b3 **προσαγορεύεσθαι** *for our purposes to call [pain something bad and release from pain good]* a middle infinitive depending on the deliberative subjunctive αἱρώμεθα *shall we choose*? To take προσαγορεύεσθαι as a middle infinitive is Gosling's (1975) reading: "or that there are only two, first distress, which we would say was a human evil, and secondly release from distress, which being itself good we should call pleasurable." An alternative is Hackforth (1945), who takes προσαγορεύεσθαι as a passive limiting the substantive ἀπαλλαγὴν "and release from pain being called pleasant" (S §2004). Frede (1993) follows Hackforth: "liberation from pain, also called pleasure." The advantage to Gosling's reading is that it explains the double accusative in the μέν clause, while the alternative must supply the participle of being, "pain being an evil."

44b6 **τοὺς πολεμίους** *the enemies [of Phileban hedonism].* The available historical data underdetermine who these enemies might be. Among many other alternatives (see Bury 1897), recent candidates have been Speusippus and his school (Schofield 1971; Dillon 1999) and Plato himself at an earlier time (Frede 1997, 268–71).

44c6 **δυσχερείᾳ φύσεως . . . λίαν μεμισηκότων . . . καὶ νενομικότων** *[divining not by expertise but by a sort of] disgust belonging to a not ignoble nature of human beings who intensely hate the power of pleasure and who consider it to be nothing healthy.* The noun φύσεως *nature* is a genitive of possession. As Badham (1878) analyzes, the genitives μεμισηκότων and νενομικότων depend on φύσεως. The pleasure haters are μάλα δεινοὺς λεγομένους τὰ περὶ φύσιν *said to be terribly clever at natural science,* οἳ τὸ παράπαν ἡδονὰς οὔ φασιν εἶναι *who deny that pleasures exist at all* (44b9–10), μαντευομένοις *divining* (44c5–6) their attitude toward pleasure οὐ τέχνῃ ἀλλά τινι δυσχερείᾳ *not by expertise but by a sort of disgust* (44c6), human beings φύσεως οὐκ ἀγεννοῦς *of a not ignoble nature* (44c6), μεμισηκότων τὴν τῆς ἡδονῆς δύναμιν καὶ νενομικότων οὐδὲν ὑγιές *who have developed a hatred of the power of pleasure and have come to the view that it is nothing healthy* (44c7–8).

As an alternative to "disgust," Pearson (2019, 258) refers to these natural scientists as "unspecified 'stroppy' characters (*duschereia*)." *Duschereia* (δυσχέρεια) is an abstract noun: it means "stroppiness," as Pearson's British-English translation has it, or "orneriness," a North American equivalent, or "cantankerousness," the more common or generic English word. The plural adjective is δυσχερεῖς, and indeed Socrates refers to them as οἱ δυσχερεῖς at 44e4.

The abstract noun δυσχέρεια names a possible part of human nature; the adjective δυσχερής describes the person who has such a nature; the process verb δυσχεραίνω refers to the activity that proceeds from such a nature, and the noun δυσχέρασμα is a cognate accusative of the verb, naming a product of that process. LSJ permits us to extend Pearson's sort of translation to all four words, listing the following meanings. For the abstract noun, *harshness* (δυσχέρεια **II.1**, citing 44c6), for the adjective, *ill-tempered, unfriendly* (δυσχερής **II.1**, citing Sophocles, *Electra*

929); for the verb, *cause annoyance* (δυσχεραίνω II.1, citing Sophocles, *Oedipus at Colonus* 1282), and for the cognate accusative of the verb, *harsh judgments* (δυσχέρασματα I.1, citing 44d2).

Despite LSJ's explicit recommendations for two members of this word family, translations like "harsh" or "stroppy" face a problem in interpreting 44c5–8, where Socrates would be saying that these *stroppy* people divine their attitude toward pleasure—an attitude that hates the power of pleasure and that views pleasure as nothing healthy—not by means of rational expertise but by means of *cantankerousness.* Now, my cantankerousness might help me divine without expertise that the world and everything in it deserves my hatred, and that nothing in the world is healthy. But such cantankerousness does not explain why I would single out pleasure for my ill temper.

As it happens, LSJ gives an alternative translation, which fits the context of the *Philebus* better. For the abstract noun, LSJ lists *loathing, nausea* (—and I add *disgust*—for δυσχέρεια **II.2,** LSJ citing Plato, *Protagoras* 334c), for the adjective, *fastidious* (that is, *disgusted,* δυσχερής **II.1,** citing Plato, *Republic* 475c); and for the verb, *be disgusted at* (δυσχεραίνω I.1, citing Plato, *Theaetetus* 195c). Although LSJ does not list such a meaning for the cognate accusative of the verb, δυσχέρασματα, the meaning *expressions of disgust* fits the context of 44d2 at least as well as LSJ's proposal there, *harsh judgments.*

A translation like "disgust" is superior to a translation like "stroppy" or "harsh" in giving us a satisfactory interpretation of 44c5–6. Socrates would be saying that these *fastidious* people divine their view of pleasure not by means of rational expertise but by means of *disgust.* Socrates would then be referring to a school of natural scientists who share feelings of disgust at pleasure. While they give a scientific explanation of all pleasures as mere releases from pain, they go further and deny that pleasure exists at all. On their account, αὐτὸ τοῦτο αὐτῆς τὸ ἐπαγωγὸν γοήτευμα *this very seductiveness of it* (i.e., of *release from pain*) *is bewitchment,* not pleasure (44c8). Their scientific explanation of pleasure as release from pain is insufficient to explain their overall view that pleasure is to be hated, that it is nothing healthy, that it is bewitchment and not pleasure at all.

It is their disgust, not their rational analysis, which explains their overall view, hating pleasure and divining that there is nothing healthy in it.

The means by which these fastidious scientists arrive at their overall view anticipates Nietzsche's means for arriving at his negative view of Plato, of Christianity, and of Arthur Schopenhauer—he "needs no refutation [*Widerlegung*]" because he "smells the decay [*riecht die Verwesung*]."[9] In other words, visceral disgust rather than cerebral analysis explains Nietzsche's overall view of these three philosophical systems. In contrast, Nietzsche's stroppiness by itself can give no explanation of his overall view. It is by means of his disgust, as opposed to his stroppiness, that Nietzsche divines his attitude and view of Plato and the others. In the same way, when Socrates says that a school of natural scientists makes divinations about pleasure by means of δυσχέρεια, we do better to interpret the means of divination to be *disgust* rather than *stroppiness.*

44c8 **αὐτὸ τοῦτο αὐτῆς τὸ ἐπαγωγὸν γοήτευμα** this very seductiveness of it [i.e., of *release from pain*]is bewitchment.

44d7 **Μεταδιώκωμεν** *let us pursue,* a metaphor from battle. In a battle, one might directly chase after a fleeing enemy, or one might chase after an ally who is chasing a fleeing enemy. Here the chase goes after the pleasure haters, who are themselves chasing after pleasure as they fight it.

44e7–8 **εἰ καὶ τὸ τῆς ἡδονῆς γένος ἰδεῖν ἥντινά ποτ' ἔχει φύσιν** *if [we were to wish] to see what sort of nature the kind Pleasure has.* A kind has a nature in virtue of having a form (as well as its members), and any form has a nature (as assumed at, e.g., 44e1). See introduction: *Genos, Phusis,* and *Eidos.*

45a1 **ἀκροτάτας καὶ σφοδροτάτας** [*If one wants to study pleasure, to see what kind of nature it has, one ought not to look at small-magnitude pleasures, but at those that are] most extreme and most intense.* A financial model of pleasure gives a charitable and faithful interpretation of

9. *Ecce Homo* "The Birth of Tragedy," §2. See Richardson (2004) for a defense of Nietzsche as a kind of natural scientist, a "neo-Darwinist," and the notes on p. 258 for more quotations documenting Nietzsche's preference for fastidiousness—whether we call it a sense of smell or an aesthetic judgment—over refutation as a means of reaching philosophical evaluations.

the distinctions Socrates draws. As pleasure is a process of restoring health in an organism, let *income* be a process able to restore financial well-being for a human being. Then call a process of income *extreme* or *large* if it involves the accumulation of an extreme or large amount of money. And call a process of income *intense* if the accumulation occurs in a very short period of time. By analogy to this model, a pleasure will be *extreme* or *large* if the perceived restoration is extreme or large, and *intense* if the restoration occurs very quickly.

45a4 **αἱ πρόχειροί γε** *the [pleasures] at hand [for purposes of the argument] at least.* The limitative γε implies that Socrates believes there are greater pleasures that are not at hand: there is a sense in which the pleasures of healthy people are "greater," as Socrates is about to mention. As an alternative, Frede (1993) reads πρόχειροί as "immediate" *to the person feeling pleasure,* which is perhaps a less obvious meaning for the word and does not improve the sense of the passage.

45a7–9 **μείζους εἰσὶ καὶ γίγνονται περὶ τοὺς κάμνοντας ἐν ταῖς νόσοις ἢ περὶ ὑγιαίνοντας** *[bodily] pleasures are larger when people suffer from an illness than when they are healthy.* Socrates takes care to distinguish this statement from the statement that healthy people feel more bodily pleasure, all things considered, than the extremely ill. The financial model of pleasure again (see note to 45a1) gives a charitable and faithful interpretation of Socrates' distinction between *larger* pleasures in an organism that enjoys *less.* A process of income might produce a large and intense *gross* income but a small, nonexistent, or even negative *net* income when the expenses associated with the income are taken into account. By analogy to this model, the very same process of restoration might be a large *gross* pleasure but a small, nonexistent, or negative *net* pleasure when destructive processes associated or "mixed" with the pleasure are taken into account (likewise at 45c1–5: τὰς μεγίστας ἡδονὰς *the greatest pleasures,* πλείω χαίρουσιν *enjoy more,* and μέγεθός . . . ἡδονῆς *magnitude of pleasure).*

45b9 **ἀποπληρουμένων** neuter passive, limiting ἡδονὰς: *[pleasures] of things being refilled.* If there is a sense in which pure pleasures are greater than pleasures mixed with pains, then the sick only have greater pleasures of refillings: the healthy might have greater pleasures when all pleasures are considered. As an alternative, Hackforth (1945) says "the genitive . . . could only be [a genitive of comparison] governed by μείζους" and thinks the genitive must be emended to the masculine nominative ἀποπληρούμενοι. As another alternative, Frede (1993 and 1997) without comment appears to take the genitive to be absolute, taking as subject the singular ἐνδείᾳ (returning as the plural ἐνδειῶν), so that it indicates a temporal condition, which gives a good sense: *the sick, when [their lacks] are being refilled, have greater pleasures [than the healthy]*—in her 1993 translation, "Do they not feel greater deprivations, and also greater pleasures at their replenishment?" Frede's analysis of the genitive as absolute appears to follow Gosling (1975), who perhaps translates better in leaving the subject of the replenishing undetermined in his translation: "being more closely acquainted with want, they surely get greater pleasure from replenishment." Gosling also translates the number of ἐνδείᾳ accurately as singular, "want," rather than using Frede's plural "deprivations."

45c1 **ὀρθῶς ἂν φαινοίμεθα λέγοντες ὡς.** It is most natural to take the participle λέγοντες to be complementary to φαινοίμεθα *might we evidently be speaking correctly, [saying] that* . . . As an alternative, some take λέγοντες as circumstantial: *might we appear correctly, saying that* . . . This seems to be Gosling's (1975) reading: "Should we seem justified in saying that . . ." (Likewise, Hackforth 1945 and Frede 1993, although their translations are freer.)

45c2–3 **οὐκ εἰς ὑγίειαν ἀλλ' εἰς νόσον ἰόντας δεῖ σκοπεῖν** *it is necessary to examine [those] going into sickness not health.* This translation takes ἰόντας as the direct object of σκοπεῖν with an implicit definite article for the participle (likewise with λεγομένους at 44b9, for example). For εἶμι plus εἰς: ἰόντες εἰς τὰς ὁμοίας *going into similar [wrestling grips, 13d7–8]*. For εἰς plus abstract noun: Thucydides, *History* 5.30.5.4, ἰέναι ἐς τὴν ξυμμαχίαν. Alternative translations tend to follow Bury (1897), who takes ἰόντας as circumstantial to an intransitive σκοπεῖν: *it is necessary* *to make an examination by going into sickness not health.* It might seem to tell against his reading that, as the subject of σκοπεῖν, we would expect a singular instead of plural participle, in agreement with the subject of the protasis at 45c1, τις *someone.* But he defends his alternative: "the plural after such an universalizing pronoun is common: cp. *Republic* 536a, *Prot.* 345e, etc."—and 45e9–10.

45c3 **μή με ἡγῇ διανοούμενον** One might expect here instead of a participle the infinitive διανοεῖσθαι: hence Badham (1878) proposes emending the text to μή με διανόου. But LSJ (ἡγέομαι III.2) recognizes "an attributive word" after ἡγῇ as well as an accusative-plus-infinitive construction: *that you do not regard me [as] intending (to ask you).*

45d2 **δείξεις** *you will be showing [the way].* The verbs ἕπομαι (*I follow [the way]*) and δείκνυμι (*I show [the way]*) likewise occur as antonyms at Plato, *Republic* 432c3–5, Sophocles, *Ajax* 813–14, and Xenophon, *Cyropaedia* 5.2.13.5, for example.

45d3 **ὕβρει** *wantonness* is an antonym to σωφροσύνη *soundness of mind* (occurring at 55b3).

45e3–4 **περιβοήτους ἀπεργάζεται** *[pleasure] produces [human beings] crying out* or *makes [human beings] notorious,* a pun.

45e9–10 **προελόμενον . . . ἐλέγομεν** Notice the switch from singular to plural: *it is necessary that some indefinite* one, *after choosing, examine in what way* we *say they are biggest.* Socrates restates this point at 46a2–3 ("Consider what there is about the pleasures of *such* diseases"), and refers to it at 46b3–4 ("the object of the present inquiry"). In this inquiry, Socrates elicits Protagoras' answer about one of these pleasures at 46a12 ("This is something mixed"), and he elicits Protarchus' answer about the whole class at 46b6–7 ("the [so-called 'pleasures'] that have a share [of pain] in their mixture").

46a5 **Τὰς (ἡδονάς) τῶν ἀσχημόνων** *the [pleasures] of the unseemly [ones].* The genitive νοσημάτων might be masculine, feminine, or neuter. Bury (1897) (followed by Gosling 1975) proposes we supply the feminine noun νοσημάτων: *unseemly illnesses.* This νοσημάτων readily comes to mind, because it likewise limited ἡδονάς just three lines earlier. But there are two problems making good sense of that reading. All illnesses are ἀσχήμων (*disfiguring*) in the sense that itches are, so ἀσχήμων νοσημάτων seems redundant on this reading. And surely the δυσχερεῖς hate above all not pleasures of disease but pleasures of wantonness. Likewise, Stallbaum's (1842) reading, that ἀσχήμων is masculine and refers to οἱ ἀσχήμονες (*unseemly people)* seems to give a good sense to the passage, since the "itches" that are cured by nothing more than "such actions as rubbing the skin" (τῷ τρίβειν καὶ ὅσα τοιαῦτα) will then refer to the δυσχερεῖς-hated pleasures. The verb τρίβειν can mean *masturbate* (Henderson 1991, 176). As an alternative, ἀσχήμων might give the same sense if we read it as neuter, *unseemly things.* Finally, we might read it as a feminine partitive genitive (τὰς τῶν ἀσχήμων ἡδονῶν) *pleasures taken from the unseemly pleasures.* This appears to be Frede's (1993) reading: "those pleasures of a rather repugnant type." On the identity of the δυσχερεῖς, see note to 44b6.

46a9 **οὐκ ἄλλης δεόμενα φαρμάξεως** *[whatever such things] not in need of another treatment.* While rubbing alone may be a φάρμαξις *treatment*, it is not an ἴασις *remedy* for scabies or dermatitis. Socrates' qualification seems to show that his topic—what the harsh-living pleasure-haters hate most of all—includes not the types of skin-rubbing that relieve the itching of skin disease (for which ancient medicine had other treatments, such as described in the note to 46e2) but the types of skin-rubbing that provide sexual pleasures to those itching for them. The Socrates of the *Gorgias* takes it to be a natural movement of thought to begin by asking about the one ψωρῶντα καὶ κνησιῶντα *itching and scratching* (494c6–7) and continue to ὁ τῶν κιναίδων βίος *the life of* kinaidoi *(*494e4), who were passive male partners in anal sexual intercourse.

46a12–13 **Σύμμεικτον τοῦτό . . . γίγνεσθαί τι κακόν** *this mix is something bad.* Hackforth (1945, 90) gives an alternative interpretation. Since Hackforth sees no reason why the pleasant factor should be regarded as bad, he proposes reading πάθος *a thing undergone* for κακόν *bad.* The resulting translation, in effect, is: "the relief from itching by rubbing, and all of that sort that needs no other remedy, is a mixed *experience* [of pleasure and pain]." But, as Migliori (1993) points out, Hackforth faces a problem (in addition to needing to emend the text): there is reason for Protarchus and us to regard this experience as something bad, since it is structurally the same as the experience of scratching an itch; moreover, even though we are capable of scratching itches, we all avoid getting such skin conditions. As the pleasure haters say, rightly, about this case: there is "nothing healthy" (44c8) about it. Hence, we rightly regard the overall experience as something bad.

46b1 **Οὐ μὲν δὴ Φιλήβου γε ἕνεκα** *not for the sake of Philebus.* Freer translations do not seem to improve the meaning: Gosling (1975), "to please Philebus"; Frede (1993) "with the intention of alluding to Philebus"; Hackforth (1945) "with any reference to Philebus." Gosling is closest to the text and, I think, gives the best sense. After Protarchus, with the decorum of an Athenian youth, refers to the sexual pleasures as "something bad," Socrates reminds him of Philebus, his character and practice. On Greek sexual morality see Dover (1974 and 1989).

παρεθέμην a causative middle (S §1725) *I did [not] cause [this argument] to be set out.* It is Socrates' characteristic method not to himself set out an argument but to cause his interlocutor to set it out.

46b2–3 **τῶν ταύταις ἑπομένων** With Bury (1897) I take **τῶν** to be feminine: *the [pleasures] that follow on these [rubbing pleasures].* Frede (1993), in opposition to Bury (1897), Hackforth (1945), and Gosling (1975), translates the participle as masculine *men* "who cultivate them," rather than as feminine, *pleasures following on them.* Frede's alternative faces a problem: Protarchus' reply indicates that Socrates is examining the συγγενεῖς *relatives,* not one particular form of pleasure together with the human devotees of that pleasure.

46b8–c4 *There are three kinds of mixtures of pleasures and pains—(1) bodily mixtures just in the body, (2) mixtures of pleasures and pains from both body and soul, and (3) soul mixtures just in the soul—and sometimes the [gross] pleasure and [gross] pain taken together amount to [net] pleasure; other times [net] pain.* The point of the three-part distinction is to show how widespread such kinds of falsity are. It is not surprising that Protarchus wonders, at the conclusion, if there are any true pleasures—that is, pleasures not contaminated with pain—at all (51b1–2).

46c6–7 **Ὁπόταν . . . τις . . . πάσχῃ** *whenever someone undergoes.* This first generalization illustrates αἱ μὲν κατὰ τὸ σῶμα ἐν αὐτοῖς τοῖς σώμασιν *mixtures of pleasure and pain within just the body* (46b8–c1). Illustrations of mixtures within just the soul, and then mixtures coming from both body and soul, will follow. According to Delcomminette (2006, 426), "the false pleasures of the first two species [namely, false pleasure of anticipation and of estimation] are found again explicitly subsumed under [*explicitement subsumés sous*] [this] species of mixed pleasures." It is true that in this passage, false pleasures of anticipation, which are false because they are false pictures of reality, are shown to be false in yet another way: as mixtures. Indeed, a pleasure can be true as a picture but will still be false because mixed with desire and pain.

46c9 **τὸ δὴ λεγόμενον πικρῷ γλυκὺ μεμειγμένον** *the so-called "sweet mixed with bitter."* Peponi (2002, 139–44) explains λεγόμενον, "so-called," as calling to mind in Plato's readers the epithet for *eros* in love poetry in for example Sappho (γλυκύπικρον *bittersweet*, *Fragment* 130) and Theognis (πικρὸς καὶ γλυκύς *bitter and sweet*, *Elegiae* 2.1353). As Peponi says, "*eros* in its physical aspect is essentially recalled but hardly ever mentioned in this part of the *Philebus*" (2002, 136).

46d1 **σύντασιν** *[makes a wild] straining.* This word occurs only one other time in Plato, when Diotima uses it in defining *eros* (ἡ σύντασις ἔρως ἂν καλοῖτο *the suntasis . . . may be called eros*, *Symposium* 206b2–3). LSJ lists the primary meaning as *tension, rigidity.* Although Henderson (1991) does not include it in his list of obscene words, it might have the meaning *tumescence* in both passages, as well as the transferred meaning *vehement effort, exertion* (the meaning that LSJ lists for these two passages). At this point Socrates is speaking in general of the bodily condition where there is firmness that is caused by swelling. As examples of this condition, he will include both pruritus caused by disease (when pain predominates over pleasure in relieving the itch) and male sexual arousal and orgasm (when pleasure predominates over pain in relieving the "itch"). Scientific understanding of the time connected itching with sexual pleasure. For example, Hippocrates explained the pleasure τριβομένου . . . τοῦ αἰδοίου *of the penis being rubbed* as ὥσπερ κνησμὸς *just like itching and scratching* (*De Semine* 1.7–8). See Peponi (2002, 153–56) for further discussion.

46d7–47a1 Editors and translators have proposed many emendations and alternatives for this passage. Before going into the details, I give in this note my edition of the passage followed by an account of how the different clauses fit together.

> Λέγε δὴ τὰς μέν, ὅταν πλείους λῦπαι τῶν ἡδονῶν γίγνωνται—τὰς τῆς ψώρας λεγομένας νυνδὴ ταύτας εἶναι καὶ τὰς τῶν γαργαλισμῶν—ὁπόταν ἐντὸς τὸ ζέον ᾖ καὶ τὸ φλεγμαῖνον, τῇ τρίψει δὲ καὶ τῇ κινήσει μὴ ἐφικνῆταί τις, τὰ δ' ἐπιπολῆς μόνον διαχέῃ, τοτὲ φέροντες εἰς πῦρ αὐτὰ καὶ εἰς τοὐναντίον ἀπορίαις μεταβάλλοντες, ἐνίοτε ἀμηχάνους ἡδονάς, τοτὲ δὲ τοὐναντίον, τοῖς ἐντὸς πρὸς τὰ τῶν ἔξω, λύπας ἡδοναῖς συγκερασθείσας, εἰς ὁπότερ' ἂν ῥέψῃ, παρέσχοντο τῷ τὰ συγκεκριμένα βίᾳ διαχεῖν ἢ τὰ διακεκριμένα συγχεῖν—καὶ ὁμοῦ λύπας ἡδοναῖς παρατιθέναι.

The main verb of the sentence is Λέγε δὴ *Do say* (i.e., *do remark* or *do note*), and it is followed by indirect discourse to the end of the sentence. The indirect discourse contains a temporal antecedent and its consequent. The sentence is complicated by two parenthetical remarks juxtaposed after the statement of the temporal antecedent. As Barbara Jane Hall has remarked, these juxtapositions in the text mirror the juxtapositions of pleasure and pain in the analysis. The temporal consequent begins and ends the indirect discourse, and is the main accusative-plus-infinitive construction after the verb of speaking, Λέγε.

> τὰς [sc., μείξεις] μέν . . . καὶ ὁμοῦ λύπας ἡδοναῖς παρατιθέναι, *some [mixtures] . . . put pains quite close beside pleasures.*

Taking the accusative τὰς [sc., μείξεις] μέν with the accusative παρατιθέναι to my knowledge was first proposed by Burnet (1901), who inserted hyphens to mark off the intervening eight lines of text. Gosling

(1975) seems in his translation to follow Burnet. Diès (1949), Frede (1993 and 1997), and Peponi (2002, 152) have no place for the accusative τὰς μέν in their translations, since they take the infinitive παρατιθέναι as articular, coordinate with τῷ . . . διαχεῖν and συγχεῖν. For example, Peponi (2002, 152) translates, "they provide themselves with . . . distress mixed with pleasure, . . . due to . . . the juxtaposing of pains along with pleasures." Bury (1897) raised a problem for such readings, in addition to leaving the accusative τὰς μέν untranslated: "This is saying that they do a thing by doing it"—which is meaningless. There is a meaning with Burnet's reading: when pains outweigh pleasures, such mixtures put *pains* close beside *pleasures:* in Socrates' example, the heat application places greater pain on the skin's surface close beside the lesser pleasure of internal relief. The predictable contrasting τὰς δε statement is left unstated: when pleasures outweigh pains, such mixtures put *pleasures* close beside *pains:* in Socrates' example of that mixture, the greater pleasure of sexual orgasm is placed close beside the lesser pain of teasing.

In my statement of the temporal consequent the three dots of elision stand for the remainder of the indirect discourse. That remainder begins by stating the temporal antecedent, a subordinate clause introduced by ὅταν.

> ὅταν πλείους λῦπαι τῶν ἡδονῶν γίγνωνται, *when pains come to be greater than pleasures.*

If this were all Socrates had said, the connection between the antecedent and consequent would not be clear. It would not be clear why, in certain mixtures, when pains outweigh the pleasures, the pains are put "quite close beside pleasures." The two parenthetical remarks make that connection clear. The first parenthetical remark is a short specification of the mixtures Socrates has in mind when pains are greater than pleasures. This remark is an accusative-plus-infinitive construction (ταύτας εἶναι) after Λέγε.

> τὰς τῆς ψώρας λεγομένας νυνδὴ ταύτας εἶναι καὶ τὰς τῶν γαργαλισμῶν *[do note that] these are [the mixtures] of the itch mentioned just now [i.e., the mixtures] of tickling irritations.*

The second parenthetical further describes the itch and a desperate response to it.

> ὁπόταν *(1a)* ἐντὸς τὸ ζέον ᾖ καὶ τὸ φλεγμαῖνον, *(1b)* τῇ τρίψει δὲ καὶ τῇ κνήσει μὴ ἐφικνῆταί τις, τὰ δ' ἐπιπολῆς μόνον διαχέῃ, τότε *(2a)* φέροντες εἰς πῦρ αὐτὰ καὶ εἰς τοὐναντίον ἀπορίαις μεταβάλλοντες, ἐνίοτε *(2b)* ἀμηχάνους ἡδονάς, τότε δὲ *(3)* τοὐναντίον τοῖς ἐντὸς πρὸς τὰ τῶν ἔξω, λύπας ἡδοναῖς συγκερασθείσας, εἰς ὁπότερ' ἂν ῥέψῃ, παρέσχοντο, ***when** (1a) the seething and inflammation are inside and (1b) by rubbing and movement someone is not able to reach [it], but (1c) they only disperse the things on the surface, **then,** (2a) carrying the [parts] to a hot fire and in their distresses changing about to the opposite [i.e., to cold water], **sometimes** (2b) by dispersing by force the compressed or compressing the dispersed they provide for themselves unsustainable pleasures, **and at that time,** (3) in whatever way they incline like a balance tilting, (3a they provide for themselves) the opposite for the inside things relative to the outside things, pains mixed with pleasures.*

Here there is a lengthy specification of the different stages (ὁπόταν . . . τότε . . . ἐνίοτε . . . τότε δὲ, *when . . . then . . . sometimes . . . and at that time*) of the time when, as a consequence, pains are put "quite close beside pleasures." Whereas the main verb of the first parenthetical was an infinitive (εἶναι), the main verb of the second parenthetical is finite (παρέσχοντο): unlike the first parenthetical, which is a subordinate clause depending on the verb of speaking Λέγε, the second parenthetical is an independent clause, composed of its own temporal antecedent (labeled 1a, 1b, and 1c), consequent (2a and 2b), and restatement of the consequent (3). It describes cases where the cause of the itch is inside the body and the patient cannot disperse it with the movements induced by rubbing. Since the rubbing does not produce relief at those times, as a desperate remedy the patient applies heat to the outside. The heat application eventually relieves the inside pain, and that relief according to Socrates' restorative account (first sketched at 31d–32b) is a pleasure. But at the same time the heat application causes pain on the outside of the body, and to relieve that pain the patient changes from the fire to the cooling water. Then the surface feels relief, but the pain returns on the inside. Both treatments, then, produce relief and pleasure but they do so at the price of causing pain. Hence, each treatment causes its own distinct "distress" (*aporia*, as stated in clause 2a): inside relief with outside pain that eventually is unendurable, or outside relief with inside pain that eventally is unendurable. The pleasures they provide for themselves in either case are therefore impossible to maintain—that is, "impracticable" or "unsustainable" (ἀμηχάνους, as clause 2b states). The verb of providing (παρέσχοντο) has the direct object "unsustainable pleasures" in clause 2b but has a second direct object in clause 3, "the opposite." As clause 3 states, they provide "the opposite for the inside things relative to the outside things." The accusative participle "pains mixed with pleasures" (λύπας ἡδοναῖς συγκερασθείσας) is appositive to and explanatory of the accusative "the opposite" (τοὐναντίον) in clause 3: the condition of unsustainable pleasure that they provide for themselves as they go back and forth from fiery heat to cooling water is a condition where "the opposite" is provided—namely, "pains mixed with pleasures." In other words, either act in the alternating treatment provides pleasure, but in each iteration it also provides the opposite, pain mixed with the pleasure. (The use of the same verb for two direct objects in different clauses puts them "quite close" side by side: the first direct object refers to pleasure, the second—as the appositive makes clear—refers to pain. Likewise, there is another beautiful mirroring in this passage between the sentence structure and the sentence analysis, the consequence of which is that in these cases pleasures and pains are put quite close together.) After Socrates states this second lengthy parenthetical, the connection between the temporal antecedent and its consequent becomes clear to Protarchus. To Socrates' imperative "Do say!" he replies, "[I say it] most truly" (Ἀληθέστατα, 47a2).

There are alternative interpretations of the passage, many of which I will mention in notes below. There is no certainty about the correct interpretation, but as a general rule any alternative that does not make good sense of some part of the passage, or advocates emendation or deletion, would seem to be inferior.

46d7 **τὰς μέν, ὅταν πλείους λῦπαι** *the [mixtures], on the one hand, when pains [come to be] greater.* The ὅταν is answered at 47a3, ὁπόταν αὖ, *whenever, again,* taking up the mixtures when pleasures are greater. This clause is subordinate to the statement that some mixtures of pleasures and pains place the pains quite close to the pleasures, and is the first condition for that consequence. Accordingly, it will be preferable to interpret the whole compound sentence as dealing only with mixtures where pains predominate. Socrates' example of predominating pains will be the itching of skin swollen from underlying inflammation, while the example in his next speech of predominating pleasure, though discretely left unnamed, is evidently the pleasure of rubbing an erect penis.

46d8–9 **—τὰς τῆς ψώρας λεγομένας νυνδὴ ταύτας εἶναι καὶ τὰς τῶν γαργαλισμῶν**—*these are the [mixtures] of pruritis and the [mixtures] of tickling irritations,* this accusative plus infinitive plus complement after Λέγε is an explanatory interjection in apposition to τὰς μέν. After both instances of τὰς I have supplied "mixtures." As an alternative, Hackforth (1945) supplies "pleasures," which would be an unexpected change of referent for τὰς from the previous line d7. Freely, for the sake of an idiomatic translation, Frede (1993) and others use the word "case," translating the feminine article τὰς as if it were neuter.

Following Burnet (1901), I put a hyphen after γαργαλισμῶν to mark the end of the interjection. An alternative proposed by Apelt (1922) (as defended by Arpe 1943 and followed by Frede 1993 and Delcomminette 2020) is to insert a full stop instead of hyphen.

46d9 **καὶ τὰς** epexegetic (only one case is described, and the class of tickling irritations includes penis-rubbing mixtures, too).

τῶν γαργαλισμῶν *of tickling irritations.* The noun has a narrow sense *tickle,* given as the only meaning in LSJ, but here it seems to have a broader meaning. LSJ gives to the verb γαργαλίζω the narrow sense *to tickle* but also the broader sense *to feel tickling or irritation.* I take it that the broader sense must be wide enough to refer to any irritation alleviated by rubbing or scratching. Such a sense must include both the feeling in a nose that induces a sneeze (*Symposium* 189a4) and the feeling of a tooth before it erupts (*Phaedrus* 253e6), as well, I suppose, as feelings of mosquito bites and scabies, but not of sunburn or a pebble in the shoe. As an alternative, Frede (1993) translates with the noun "scratching," which unfortunately has an active sense. Frede (1997) is more accurate in translating it as "*Juckreize*" (itching), followed by Delcomminette (2020): "*démangeaisons*," (itchings).

46d9–10 **ὁπόταν ἐντὸς τὸ ζέον ᾖ καὶ τὸ φλεγμαῖνον** *when the seething and swelling are inside*—that is, located inside the body. This is the second condition for the consequence that some mixtures of pleasures and pains place the pains quite close to the pleasures.

Burnet's 1901 addition <ἐν τοῖς> after ὁπόταν—boiling is "among the things [inside]" instead of "boiling is inside"—does not seem needed to most editors and translators. In either case the location prevents scratching and rubbing from providing relief, unlike when the cause of the itching is on the surface.

46d10 **τῇ τρίψει δὲ καὶ τῇ κινήσει** datives of means *by friction and movement.* As is often noticed (e.g., Frede 1992, 450), Socrates takes a medical and scientific tone in this passage.

Philip Willem van Heusde (cited in Burnet) removed the iota from κινήσει: τῇ τρίψει δὲ καὶ τῇ κνήσει *by means of rubbing and scratching.* Burnet (1901), Frede (1993), and many others accept this emendation without comment. I find no published justification of the emendation, but I suppose it is thought that there is some advantage in the replacement of the rare (or awkward or nearly nonsensical) coordination of the words τρῖψις and κίνησις by the much more common (or natural or sensible) coordination of the words τρῖψις and κνῆσις, an advantage accomplished merely by removing an iota. As it happens, such a thought is not supported by extant ancient Greek. A *TLG* proximity search produced no coordinations of τρῖψις and κνῆσις, while producing three of τρῖψις and κίνησις, all in scientific writings in the Aristotelian *Problemata:* coordinated by καί at 882a27 (αἱ δὲ κινήσεις καὶ αἱ τρίψεις τὴν μὲν κοιλίαν λεπτύνουσι, "movements and friction make the belly lean") and 927a14 (ἡ δὲ μῖξις τρίψει καὶ κινήσει, "the mixing [and consequent foaming of barley gruel or wheat flour with olive oil] is by friction and movement"), and by ἤ at 908b35 (ὅσα μὲν τῇ κινήσει ἢ τῇ τρίψει μεταβάλλοντα, "whichever [perfumes] undergo [chemical] change from motion or friction").

In addition to coordinations, the *TLG* search turns up other collocations of τρῖψις and κίνησις but no collocations of any kind of τρῖψις and κνῆσις. For example, Socrates in Plato's *Theaetetus* speaks of fire being born "from rapid motion and friction, and these two things are movements" (ἐκ φορᾶς καὶ τρίψεως· τούτω δὲ κινήσεις, 153a9–10). In scientific contexts, the movement of the internal parts of a body apparently was viewed as the effect of friction on its surface. For example, Aristotle thought that friction produces movement of semen out of the body (*Hist. An.* 581a29–31). Again, in theorizing why friction increases muscle mass (except for the curious case of the belly), the Aristotelian author remarks that the internal fluids of the body are always "in motion" (ἐν κινήσει), "which happens in friction" (ὃ ἐν τῇ τρίψει γίνεται, *Prob.* 965b38–966a2). Perhaps it is this assumed causal connection of friction (on the surface of the body) with movement (of internal parts) that explains Socrates' coordination of the words in the present passage. Or perhaps the coordination is between some external movement as the cause of the superficial friction, as at Aristotle, *De caelo* 289a19–21, *De mundo* 395b4–6, and *De respiratione* 475a9–10.

46e1 **τὸ δ' ἐπιπολῆς μόνον** *only the [seething/swelling] belonging to the surface.* Everyone accepts Schütz's (cited in Bury 1897) ἐπιπολῆς for ἐπὶ πολῆς of B and T (πολῆς is unattested). Note neuter accusative definite article with genitive noun, "the thing of the surface." Schütz emends τὸ to τὰ, which Gosling (1975) accepts "to have a plural antecedent for αὐτὰ at the end of the line." One can sensibly avoid this emendation by taking the antecedent of αὐτὰ to be τὸ ζέον καὶ τὸ φλεγμαῖνον (d9–10).

φέροντες . . . μεταβάλλοντες . . . παρέσχοντο *carrying . . . changing . . . they procure*, gnomic aorist. The plural number refers to the universalizing singular pronoun τις at e1 (S §1012). The present tense of the two participles perhaps indicates progressive aspect: continually carrying affected parts back and forth to heat and to cold and undergoing change.

Delcomminette proposes instead as the subject of παρέσχοντο and the participles φέροντες and μεταβάλλοντες "the triple infinitive construction that ends the passage"—namely, as he establishes the text, τῷ τὰ συγκεκριμένα βίᾳ διαχεῖν ἢ τὰ διακεκριμένα συγχεῖν, καὶ ὁμοῦ λύπας ἡδοναῖς παρατιθέναι (2006, 436n16). But neuter plural articular infinitives cannot be the subject of those masculine plural participles (S §958–959).

46e2 **ἀπορίαις** dative of cause *from the [events of] distresses.* Stallbaum (1842) considered emending the plural ἀπορίαις to the singular ἀπορίᾳ, presumably on the grounds that "it is in the singular that the term *aporia* can denote difficulty or even impossibility of finding a way out of a hard situation" (Peponi 2012, 149n32). Burnet (1901), presumably for the same reason, emended ἀπορίαις to πυρίαις, *steam baths (or any heat application),* a change perhaps anticipated in a scribe's note on W.[10] But there are many attested uses of the dative plural to refer either to more than one event of distress (e.g., Xenophon, *Cyropaedia* 1.6.24.8, συνεπικουρεῖν προθυμούμενον ταῖς ἀπορίαις αὐτῶν *eager to help them in moments of distress*) or to more than one kind of distress (e.g., Isocrates 12.140.8: ἐκ δὲ τῶν κοινῶν ταῖς ἰδίαις ἀπορίαις βοηθεῖν ζητούντων, *seeking to repair their own distresses from the public treasury*"; likewise, Isocrates 2.39.5, 3.44.7, 8.131.1, 15.281.5; Plato, *Statesman* 273d5, 274d5; and the Aristotelian *Problemata* 956b14). And the present passage plausibly refers to more than one kind of distress: first the inner pain that is not reached "by rubbing and scratching" (d10) and then the exterior pain from the application of fire's heat (e1). And the relative clause "*toward whichever of the two [the afflicted parts] are directed*" (e4) suggests a seesaw repeated back and forth, implying multiple events of these distresses. Likewise, the attested uses of the dative plural and the plausible meaning of the present pas-

10. "According to Diès' (1949) *apparatus*, the scribe seems not only to correct *supra lineam* the letter *ο* and change it into *υ* but also to think it necessary to repeat the letter *π* (replacing, that is, the existing ἀπο- with a new first syllable πυ-). Thus the scribe seems to be correcting the whole first syllable. If an examination of the manuscript verifies this understanding of Diès' *apparatus,* then the resulting reading after the whole correction should not be ἀπύριαις, as is Diès' (1949) understanding, but πύριαις. After all, the unattested word ἀπυρία can hardly make any sense. In Taylor (1956, 264n23) the editor thinks that even the reading ἀπύριαις "supports Burnet's conjecture πυρίαις" (Peponi 2012, 146n24).

sage do permit the plural dative ἀπορίαις in its meaning *distresses* or *events of distress*.

Peponi gives a second argument for Burnet's (1901) emendation: given the word ἀπορίαις, the passage at e1–2 speaks of those afflicted with pruritis "carrying them [the afflicted parts] to fire and, from their [repeated events of] distress, [continually] changing about to the opposite." Peponi's review of ancient medical texts makes a case that it is a mistake to assume that a commonly known medical prescription for pruritis was to alternate heat applications, "fire," with cold applications of fire's opposite, water (2012, 146–48). Hippocrates (*De humidorum usu* 6) even warns that suddenly alternating heat with cold as a treatment can irritate the skin. Granting the point about medical prescriptions, it might remain true that Socrates' audience was acquainted with a common practice of alternating hot and cold treatments. To give a contemporary parallel, although doctors today do not prescribe pain killers in combination with alcohol, in conversation one could sensibly allude to people, from their repeated distresses, combining pain killers with alcohol. The fact that experts advise against some medical practice, I suppose, is some evidence for the practice, and so the Hippocratic warning against combining alternate heat and cold treatment is possible evidence that the practice existed. Likewise, the evidence of ancient medical prescriptions does not give us evidence to emend ἀπορίαις, and might even lend support to keeping the word.

μεταβάλλοντες *and changing about to the opposite*. With, for example, Hackforth (1945) and Gosling (1975), I let καὶ coordinate φέροντες εἰς πῦρ *carrying to fire* with εἰς τοὐναντίον μεταβάλλοντες *changing to the opposite*. Frede (1993), as an alternative, lets καὶ coordinate only the two prepositional phrases εἰς πῦρ καὶ εἰς τοὐναντίον with both depending on φέροντες *carrying to fire and to the opposite*. On that reading there is no coordinating particle for the two participles, so that she must make one a parenthetical remark: "exposing them to fire or its opposite—they go from one extreme to the other"—a rare construction in Greek.

ἀμηχάνους ἡδονάς *enormous [*or *impracticable] pleasures.* The root passive meaning of ἀμηχάνους is *allowing of no means* (LSJ II) hence *impracticable* (LSJ II.1a and b), and Socrates speaks with this meaning at *Protagoras* 321d2 and *Republic* 548d3, for example. A more frequent meaning in Plato is *impracticable (to measure)* hence *immeasurable/enormous* (LSJ II.3). Translators unanimously have preferred *enormous* as the meaning here. But in this speech Socrates is considering cases where the pains are greater than the pleasures, so he oddly leaves unsaid that the pains are even bigger than *enormous.* Indeed, I know of no occurrence of ἀμήχανος in the sense of *immeasurably big/enormous* where nonetheless there is an explicit or implicit contrasting case of something even bigger. So, such a translation is problematic. To my mind, the meaning *impracticable* gives good sense to the passage. The patient tries to produce internal relief, but such a pleasure is impracticable because it requires a painfully hot external therapy. This impracticability explains the "distresses" (ἀπορίαις) of the patient: they cannot find a feasible relief—that is, a practicable pleasure—no matter how they change position.

46e3 **ἡδονάς . . . δὲ τοὐναντίον . . . , λύπας . . . , παρέσχοντο τῷ . . . διαχεῖν ἢ . . . συγχεῖν** *they provide pleasures to themselves and the opposite thing, pains, by means of dispersing or commingling.* I take the verb παρέσχοντο to have a plural subject (see second note to 46e1), three accusative objects—ἡδονάς, τοὐναντίον, and λύπας (*pleasures, the opposite thing,* and *pains)*—and two dative (of means) articular infinitives: διαχεῖν and συγχεῖν. The disjunction ἢ *or* coordinates two alternatives—dispersing things stuck together or commingling things pulled apart.

τότε δὲ τοὐναντίον τοῖς ἐντὸς πρὸς τὰς τῶν ἔξω *and at that time [they provide] to the things inside the opposite [experience] with respect to the [experience] of the things outside*—in other words, when they are feeling relief and pleasure on the inside, they are feeling heat pain on the outside, while when they give cooling relief and pleasure to the outside, the pain relief inside ends. I have made τοτε the paroxytone τότε *at that time* instead of the oxytone τοτέ *at other times.*

46e4 **εἰς ὁπότερ' ἂν ῥέψῃ** (third person singular aorist subjunctive) *toward whichever of the two they* (αὐτὰ, the seething and swelling parts) *are directed.* This is the meaning of ῥέπω plus the preposition εἴς (LSJ I.5), used by Gosling (1975). Hackforth (1945) and Frede (1993) translate ῥέπω as a metaphor of a balance scale (LSJ II), viewing the pleasures and pains as contending parties (LSJ I.3).

47a1 **καὶ** Burnet (1901) helpfully adds a hyphen, but proposes deleting the καὶ, which is not necessary if we take it to intensify the adverb ὁμοῦ *quite close.*

47a3 **κατὰ <τὰ> τοιαῦτα πάντα** *according to all such things [as follows].* This prepositional phrase seems to refer to the cases about to be described, where pleasure predominates. While the definite article τὰ typically precedes the phrase τοιαῦτα πάντα, it does not at 25a1; nor does it seem required by rule (S §1180). The text does not need emendation.

47a6 **συντείνει,** *braces up, makes intense.* As an opposite to χαλάω "droop down," it may refer to a male sexual erection.

47b8–9 **Πάντα . . . τὰ συμβαίνοντα πρὸς τῶν πολλῶν ἀνθρώπων εἰς δόξαν διεπέρανας** *you have thoroughly gone through all the things happening, in regard to opinion, for many people* (LSJ εἰς A.IV. 2: "in regard to," "in respect of"), taking the prepositional phrase εἰς δόξαν to modify συμβαίνοντα. The sense then is *you have covered what many people happen to opine.* An alternative is to take εἰς δόξαν to modify διεπέρανας, a conjecture of Bury (1897), followed by Robin (1950) and Delcomminette (2020): *you have gone through* to (our) expectation . . . , a reading that leaves unspecified the sorts of goings-on proceeding from most people.

47c3 **περὶ . . . ὧν** = περὶ ἐκείνων ἅ (S §2522) *concerning those [pleasures] with respect to which.* Both B and T read περὶ δὲ τῶν ἐν ψυχῇ, *concerning the things in the soul,* which is not sensible in context, instead of Burnet's (1901) περὶ δέ γ' ὧν ψυχὴ.

47c6 **ὁπόταν [αὖ] κενῶται** *whenever it is [again] empty.* As Delcomminette (2020) notes, if we do not excise αὖ *again*, then it meaningfully refers to the earlier discussion at 35a–b that no desire can arise the first time one is depleted, but when one is depleted *again,* desire and hope can arise.

47d1 **ψυχῆς . . . διαφερομένης** genitive absolute *when a soul differs [relative to a body],* which happens in cases where they bring opposites to experience.

47d2–3 **μεῖξις μία λύπης τε καὶ ἡδονῆς συμπίπτει γενομένη** *a mixture occurs, after becoming a unity* ["a one"] *of pain and pleasure.* On this reading, the participial phrase indicates the cause of there being a genuine mixture, not a mere jumble (distinguished at 64e1–3). Then the aorist tense of γενομένη makes sense as indicating a causal priority: the unity of the ingredients is the cause of the mixture occurring. This premise, that there is a single experience consisting of an opposed pleasure and pain, establishes again that any such mixture has a single net pleasure or pain, although consisting of both a gross pleasure and a gross pain.

As an alternative, translators tend to take μία to be an adjective modifying μεῖξις—for example Frede (1993), "a single mixture"; and Gosling (1975), "a single combination." And they treat συμπίπτω plus participle as an idiom equivalent to τυγχάνω plus participle (LSJ συμπίπτω II.3). But this makes the aorist participle γενομένη problematic: why does a single mixture occur *after* coming to be? Accordingly, Bury (1897) can see "no point in a departure from the regular present tense," and Burnet (1901) finds Badham's (1878) emendation of the aorist γενομένη to the present γιγνομένη worthy of mention in his critical apparatus.

47d7 **φῄς** *are you saying?* The present tense marks a peremptory question, instead of the more polite future tense.

47d9 **ἔφαμεν** *we said* (above at 46b).

47e6–9 The manuscripts have this: ἢ δεόμεθα ὑπομιμνῄσκεσθαι τὸ ὥστ' ἐφέηκεν τοῖς θυμοῖς καὶ ταῖς ὀργαῖς τὸ πολύφρονά περ χαλεπῆναι, ὥστε πολὺ γλυκίων μέλιτος καταλειβομένοιο. Burnet (1901), who is widely followed on this score, makes "considerable transposition and emendation" (Waterfield 1980, 61): ἢ δεόμεθα ὑπομιμνῄσκεσθαι [τὸ <ἐν> τοῖς θυμοῖς καὶ ταῖς ὀργαῖς,] τὸ "ὅς τ' ἐφέηκε πολύφρονά περ χαλεπῆναι ὅς τε πολὺ γλυκίων μέλιτος καταλειβομένοιο." Waterfield keeps the reading of the manuscripts, changing only ὥστ' to ὥς τ' and ὥστε to ὥς τε, placing a comma after ἐφέηκεν, and adding quotation marks to show that "ὥς τ' ἐφέηκεν" and "πολύφρονά περ χαλεπῆναι, ὥς τε πολὺ γλυκίων μέλιτος καταλειβομένοιο" are direct quotations. His translation: "Or do we need to be reminded 'that it incites' in passionate outbursts 'even the sage to wrath and that it is sweeter by far than trickling honey'" (1980, 61).

Waterfield (1980, 61–62) speaks to three problems that have been seen with the text of the manuscripts. (1) The manuscripts have repeated τό, but "τό regularly introduces quotations and here Plato has interrupted his quotation of *Iliad* 18.108–9 with a few words, so he repeats the τό when he resumes." (2) As usual, Socrates slightly misquotes Homer, and "as Benardete [1963] argued, when Plato misquotes Homer, . . . he does so on purpose. So here, given that Plato is omitting the noun (χόλος) which preceded Homer's ὅσ τε, clearly ὥς is preferable for [Plato]. Compare the omission of γάρ from *Odyssey* 1.351 at *Republic* 424b." (3) The manuscripts make Plato insert a few words of his own in the first line. But "any writer is at liberty to do this. Compare the interpolation of a few words into Hesiod, *Works and Days* 232–34, at *Republic* 363a–b, which serves exactly the same purpose, *viz.* that of filling in the context which is omitted in the quotation, as here Plato has omitted καὶ χόλος."

47e6–7 **τὸ <ἐν> τοῖς θυμοῖς καὶ ταῖς ὀργαῖς** article plus clause *the "in wrath and anger"*. Socrates quotes Homer (*Iliad* 18.108–9). The sense is made clear by the appositive lines e8–9. As an alternative, instead of reading this phrase as an article plus clause, one might accept Burnet's (1901) addition of ἐν to get an article plus preposition: *the thing in wraths and angers*. A more drastic alternative is to delete the entire phrase.

47e7 **τὸ** introducing quotation in next two lines in apposition to e6. The quotation is from Homer, *Iliad* 18.108–9. The lines are from Achilles' reply to his divine mother's prophecy that "right after Hector's" death, Achilles will die. Achilles is willing to die, since he grieves that he was not with Patroclus to "bear aid to [his] comrade at his slaying," lamenting that his wrath against Agamemnon made him a "profitless burden upon the earth," and hoping that with his death "strife perish from among gods and human beings," [καὶ χόλος,] ὅς τ' ἐφέηκε πολύφρονά περ χαλεπῆναι, / ὅς τε πολὺ γλυκίων μέλιτος καταλειβομένοιο, *[and anger], which incites to be harsh even one wise in much, and which is much sweeter than honey trickling down.*

47e8–9 **ὅς τ' . . . ὅς τε** Whereas B and T have repeated ὥστε, Burnet's (1901) emendation [ὅς τ' . . . ὅς τε] makes sense of the lines and follows the verse in Homer exactly.

48a8–9 *Also in the experience of comedies is there a mixture of pleasure and pain in our soul?* I interpret the argument for this thesis—raised as a question here and restated at 50b1–4—as follows:

P1 [In watching comedies, whether on stage or in life, we ridicule people not as enemies but as friends.] (This obvious premise goes without saying in the text.)

P2 When our friends are self-ignorant—with either would-be wisdom, would-be beauty, or would-be riches—in ways that are harmless to others, they are ridiculous (49d11–e2).

P2.1 Because of the definition of ridiculous: The ridiculous are those with the vice of self-ignorance (about their property, their body, or their soul) who are too weak to uphold their honor and take vengeance when ridiculed (49b6–8, 49c4–5).

Because:

P2.1.1 The ridiculous is a defective condition (of soul) (48c6, 49a4–5).

P2.1.2 It is the defect of self-ignorance, opposite to the Delphic virtue of self-knowledge (48c7–d2).

P2.1.3 The self-ignorance exists *about* three kinds of object (48d4).

P2.1.3.A Self-ignorance about *one's property*: when a man thinks he is richer than he is (48e1–2).

P2.1.3.B Self-ignorance about *one's body*: when a man thinks he is bigger, taller, more handsome, or better in any other bodily characteristic than he is (48e4–6).

P2.1.3.C The most widespread self-ignorance, about *one's soul*: when a man thinks he is better in virtue than he is, and in particular in the virtue of wisdom (48e8–49a2).

P2.1.4 Self-ignorance in those who have strength and power is not ridiculous (49b3).

P2.1.4.1 Because (definition) the *frightful and hateful* are those with the vice of self-ignorance (about their property, their body, or their soul) who are strong enough to uphold their honor and take vengeance when ridiculed (49b8–c1).

P2.1.4.1.1 (The self-ignorance of the strong is hateful and shameful) because it and any likeness of it is harmful to neighbors (49c2–4).

P2.1.5 Self-ignorance in those who are weak and powerless is ridiculous (49b4).

P3 When we ridicule things in our friends that are ridiculous, we are mixing pleasure in (an unrighteous) ill will, (a condition) where pleasure mingles with pain (50a5–7).

P3.1 Because ill will is an unrighteous mixture of pain and pleasure (49d1). Because:

P3.1.1 Ill will is a pain of the soul (48b8–9, restated at 50a7–8).

P3.1.2 The man of ill will takes pleasure in bad things occurring to his neighbors, such as ignorance and silly character (48b11–c2, restated at 50a8–9).

P3.1.2.1 Because ignorance is bad for us all (49d9).

P3.1.3 To be pleased (rather than pained) that bad things happen to friends is unrighteous (49d6–8).

48a10 **Οὐ πάνυ κατανοῶ** *I do not entirely understand.* Brianna Zgurich conjectures that Protarchus' confusion is that a comedy is typically perceived as *only* pleasurable and does not see how it involves a mixture. Socrates will attempt to prove that the experience of enjoying comedy must contain some aspect of pain.

48b8 **Τό . . . ὄνομα** accusative plus implicit infinitive εἶναι plus complement λύπην τινὰ after θήσεις *that the name [is a certain pain].* The metonymy—here, the use of a name to refer to the thing named—need not be viewed as "use/mention confusion."

48b8–9 *Ill will is a pain of the soul.* Socrates gives no support for this premise. Delcomminette (2006, 447) supports it with the following explanation:

"Insofar as the ridiculous man believes himself rich, handsome, or wise, he puts us in mind of goods that we do not possess and produces ill will [*suscite l'envie*]." Alternatively, Hampton (1990, 67) supports the premise that ill will is painful by making it arise after the pleasure of laughter, when we realize our similarity to the ridiculous man. Delcomminette (2006, 447) states the problem with this alternative: "It is difficult to see here the role of ill will," and according to this alternative, the pain is posterior to the pleasure, whereas "Socrates shows clearly that the pain is prior to the pleasure, insofar as the laughter presupposes ill will as a necessary condition [*sa condition de possibilité*]."

48c2 **Κακὸν . . . ἄνοια** *folly [is] something bad.* Burnet (1901), following Cornarius (1561), emends ἄνοια *folly* to ἄγνοια *ignorance.*

48c7–8 **ἐστὶ τοὐναντίον πάθος ἔχον** *[the ridiculous is] a condition that is [opposite],* taking τοὐναντίον as an adverb after ἔχον, and with Bury (1897) supplying τὸ γελοῖον as the subject of ἐστὶ and ἔχον. As an alternative, Ast (1821) inserts τὸ before τοὐναντίον. This definite article would change the indefinite πάθος *a condition* to the definite τὸ πάθος *the condition.*

48d1 **τὸ μηδαμῇ γιγνώσκειν αὑτὸν** articular infinitive *not knowing oneself at all.* Since shortly we see this "total" self-ignorance might be restricted in scope to money and so on, it is most charitable to interpret "not at all" as referring to one's degree of self-knowledge. To not know oneself *to any degree* (as we learn from *Apology* 23a5–b4; discussed by Rudebusch 2009a, 20) means *neither to know oneself nor to know one's ignorance.* It is essential to the comic effect of the self-ignorant that they not know their self-ignorance.

48d1–2 **τοὐναντίον μὴν ἐκείνῳ δῆλον ὅτι τὸ μηδαμῇ γιγνώσκειν αὑτὸν λεγόμενον ὑπὸ τοῦ γράμματος ἂν εἴη** *it is clear that "in-no-way-to-know-oneself"-being-stated-by-the-inscription would be opposite to [the-"know-oneself"-stated-by-the-inscription].* Christian Daniel Beck's alternative (cited by Badham 1878 and followed by others) is to delete λεγόμενον ὑπὸ τοῦ γράμματος as needless repetition. Evidently this deletion must suppose that a different opposition is meant (perhaps: "know oneself"/"in no way know oneself").

48e1–2 **Πρῶτον μὲν** [sc., **τὸ εἶδος**] **κατὰ χρήματα, δοξάζειν εἶναι πλουσιώτερον ἢ κατὰ τὴν αὐτῶν οὐσίαν** *[The form] according to wealth [is] first, [namely,] to think to be wealthier than according to their net worth.* This translation takes the subject of the sentence to be (τὸ εἶδος) κατὰ χρήματα, which coordinates with the second and the "the third form" (τὸ τρίτον εἶδος, 48e8). It takes the clause after the comma to be appositive to that subject, giving us the nature of the first form or condition. The prevailing alternative (e.g., Gosling 1975; Frede 1993; and Delcomminette 2020,) is to take the clause after the comma to be an accusative plus infinitive after an implied verb of speaking. According to this alternative, the accusative subject would appear to be the singular ἕκαστον from d9, becoming plural at the reflexive pronoun αὑτῶν at e2. Such a switch from singular to plural pronouns in an indefinite construction is possible in an indefinite construction, as in the English, "Someone is thinking of their wealth." The problem is that one would expect in that case the plural adjective πλουσιωτέρους instead of the singular πλουσιώτερον. On such an understanding, Badham (1878) called the manuscript reading "indefensible" and Stephanus (1578) (cited by Bury 1897) conjectured πλουσιωτέρους as an emendation.

48e8–9 **περὶ τὸ τρίτον εἶδος τούτων ἐν ταῖς ψυχαῖς διημαρτήκασιν** *they have gone quite wrong in their souls about the third form of these [three ways of being self-deceived: in property, body, and soul].* This translation takes τούτων with εἶδος, making the antecedent τρία at d8. Socrates is fulfilling his promise "to divide" (διελέσθαι, d6) "by three" forms (κατὰ τρία, d8): by the form *wealth* (κατὰ χρήματα, e1), by the form *body* (κατὰ τὸ σῶμα, e5), and now by the form *soul* (κατὰ τὴν ψυχήν). On this reading Socrates is saying people go wrong in their souls about the soul. The repetition of "soul" has a point: while it is more excusable for me to go wrong in my soul about *property* or *body*, it would seem less excusable for me to go wrong in my soul about *my soul*!

As an alternative, Burnet (1901) followed Badham (1878) in erasing this point from the text by emending τούτων to τὸ τῶν: *they go quite wrong about the third form, the [form] of the [things] in the soul,* leaving a puzzle: why such a laborious reference to the third form? Paley (1873) argued that such emendation was not needed since "the words in this dialogue are purposely so interlaced, that the author may have meant πολὺ πλεῖστοί τούτων [*by far the most of these (self-deceived persons)]*." And we can find the same antecedent with less interlacing of words by taking τούτων with ἐν ταῖς ψυχαῖς, *in the souls of these [self-deceived persons].*

49a4 **ἄν τις . . . ἂν εἴποι** *anyone might say that* [*every such condition is bad:* accusative (πᾶν τὸ τοιοῦτον πάθος) plus infinitive (sc., εἶναι) plus complement (κακὸν)]. Repeated ἄν foretells construction of sentence (S §1765a). This reading, following Hackforth (1945), Gosling (1975), and Frede (1993), permits the sentence to make a helpful transition to the next topic of division. There is an alternative: *Anyone, speaking rightly, might say that such a condition* (the condition of being ignorant about one's soul) *is all bad.*

49a7 **διαιρετέον** *we must make a division [in two of self-ignorance about one's soul].* Socrates has already divided the kind Self-Ignorance into three subkinds according to different objects of ignorance: the self's wealth, body, or soul. He now proposes to divide this last subkind "further" or "again" (ἔτι) into two, according to whether the self holds "strength and power" (ῥώμην καὶ δύναμιν, b3) or not. In this application of division, then, one and the same *genos* is given both a threefold and a twofold division. On division of kinds into subkinds, see Muniz and Rudebusch (2018 and n.d).

49a9 **πῶς οὖν τέμνομεν δίχα, λέγεις;** *in that case how are we cutting in two, do you say?* Burnet (1901) (whom I follow) follows T in giving this speech to Socrates, while B gives it to Protarchus.

49b1 **πάντες** left dangling without a predicate (a "nominative of suspense," S §941a, an *anacoluthon,* giving "to written language the vividness, naturalness, and unaffected freedom of the easy flow of conversation," S §3007), *all [who think . . .].* Perhaps the unstated predicate represents a pause in the conversation, as Socrates gives Protarchus time to think of a way to subdivide this kind.

49b6–7 **μετ' ἀσθενείας** *in company with weakness*—continuing the metaphor of following at b3.

49b9 **ἰσχυροὺς** *violent* (LSJ I.3). Paley (1873) translates the word in this "opprobrious sense" as "big bullies"). Schütz (cited by Burnet 1901) emends ἰσχυροὺς to αἰσχροὺς *causing shame/dishonoring.*

49c4 **ἡμῖν** *[while, on the other hand, the ignorance of a man who is weak] relative to us,* dative of relation limiting ἀσθενὴς. Alternatively, Gosling (1975) seems to take it as a dative of interest limiting εἴληχε or τὴν τάξιν τε καὶ φύσιν ("acquires for us the rank and character"). Another alternative is to leave ἡμῖν untranslated (e.g., Frede 1993 and Hackforth 1945).

49d1 **ἐστί** *[grudge] is.* Protarchus seems already to have recognized the mix of pleasure and pain in grudge, on the basis of Socrates' quotation from Homer at 47e8–9. In his reply here at d2 he recognizes the unrighteousness of grudge. The *OED* defines grudge as "ill-will or resentment due to some special cause, as a personal injury, the superiority of an opponent or rival, or the like." If φθόνος is such grudge, that is, the kind of ill will that is caused by a property of the begrudged object, then it may have subkinds, perhaps like the following:

Resentment: ill will caused by personal injury by the begrudged one.
Envy: ill will caused by superiority of the begrudged one.
Contempt: ill will caused by inferiority of the begrudged one.

Such an account of grudge gives us an interpretation of *Timaeus* 29e1–2: ἀγαθῷ δὲ οὐδεὶς περὶ οὐδενὸς οὐδέποτε ἐγγίγνεται φθόνος *into a good [person] no grudge ever is born about anything.* The "about anything" (περὶ οὐδενὸς) rules out that personal injury, superiority, inferiority or any other circumstance having to do with another will produce a grudge against that other. An alternative is that φθόνος is the kind of ill will that is not "specially caused" by some feature of the begrudged object, but is just a feature of the imperfect soul of the grudger: it bears ill will to all merely because it is malevolent. Such an interpretation might lead one to translate φθόνος as "malice," as does Frede (1993).

49d1–4 This passage is an aside, an argument for the conclusion that *to be pleased that bad things happen to enemies is not ill-willed* (φθονερόν, 49d3–4), from two premises:

P1 An ill will contains an unrighteous kind of pain and pleasure (49d1).
P2 To be pleased that bad things happen to your enemy is not unrighteous (ἄδικον).

Premise P2 seems contrary to the precept Socrates elicits from Polemarchus at *Republic* 335b–e—that it is unrighteous to bring troubles to anyone, friend or foe (and hence presumably also unrighteous to enjoy the arrival of such). I explain the discrepancy by referring to Socrates' dialectical method. He does not tell people his own thoughts but elicits what he needs for the project at hand, and he need not elicit that precept to make the point needed in this context. (On Socrates' dialectical method, see Rudebusch 2009c.)

49d3 **Οὐκοῦν . . . οὔτ[ε] . . . οὔτε . . . ἐστι . . . ;** *Now isn't it the case that [to take pleasure in the troubles of enemies] is neither [unrighteous] nor [grudging]?* The **Οὐκοῦν** expects a negative answer ("It is not the case . . .").

τοῖς τῶν ἐχθρῶν κακοῖς *the misfortunes of your enemies/bad things that happen to enemies.* The Greek is ambiguous: "the bad things of your enemies," which leaves open whether the enemy is the agent of or the recipient of the bad. But the previous mention of this phrase describes ὁ φθονῶν *the malicious man* as ἐπὶ κακοῖς τοῖς τῶν πέλας ἡδόμενος *taking pleasure at bad things of [his] neighbors* (48b11–12), which must mean bad things that happen to neighbors.

49e2 **ὅταν ἔχῃ τις [τῶν φίλων] τὴν ἀβλαβῆ** subjunctive in indefinite temp clause *whenever any [of our friends] has the [condition] harmless toward* plus dative. Aristotle gives a similar definition of comedy at *Poetics* 1449a31–37.

50b1–4 **Μηνύει δὴ νῦν ὁ λόγος ἡμῖν ἐν θρήνοις τε καὶ ἐν τραγῳδίαις, μὴ τοῖς δράμασι μόνον ἀλλὰ καὶ τῇ τοῦ βίου συμπάσῃ τραγῳδίᾳ καὶ κωμῳδίᾳ, λύπας ἡδοναῖς ἅμα κεράννυσθαι** *The argument now indeed reveals to us that pains are mixed together with pleasures in lamentations and in tragedies, not only for deeds on stage but also for the whole tragedy—and comedy—of life.* This speech expands on the conclusion drawn at 50a5–9, that *pleasure* is mixed with *pain* when we *laugh* at what is *ridiculous* in our friends. Socrates expands the conclusion by expecting Protarchus to see without further discussion the truth of the converse: that *pain* is mixed with *pleasure* when we *grieve* at *sorrow* for our friends. The many editors and translators who, with Burnet (1901), accept Hermann's (1855) addition of καὶ κωμῳδίαις after ἐν τραγῳδίαις at b2 do not give us this structure of drawing a converse conclusion. That addition changes the speech so that instead it makes a broader, but perhaps less elegantly stated, generalization.

50c11–d3 **ἆρ' οὐ πίστεως χάριν, ὅτι τήν γε ἐν τοῖς φόβοις καὶ ἔρωσι καὶ τοῖς ἄλλοις ῥᾴδιον κρᾶσιν ἐπιδεῖξαι, λαβόντα δὲ τοῦτο παρὰ σαυτῷ ἀφεῖναί με μηκέτι ἐπ' ἐκεῖνα ἰόντα δεῖν μηκύνειν τοὺς λόγους** answering Διὰ τί [*isn't it on account of being] for the sake of [two things]: (1) assurance that the mixture is easy to display in cases, at least, of fear and sexual desire and other things, and (2) that [you], after grasping this for yourself, allow that it is no longer necessary that I prolong the account by going at those things [i.e., the other cases of mixtures of pleasure and pain].* Interpreters have struggled with this passage. On my analysis, following Diès (1949), both the noun πίστεως ("assurance") and the accusative plus infinitive ([sc., σὲ] ἀφεῖναί) depend on χάριν. The prevailing alternative makes only πίστεως depend on χάριν, with two subalternatives. The first is to make both the ὅτι clause and the accusative plus infinitive (sc., σὲ) ἀφεῖναί depend on πίστεως: *isn't it on account of being for the sake of assurance that (1) the mixture is easy to display and that (2) [you] allow that it is no longer necessary that I prolong* (Stallbaum 1842; Delcomminette 2020). The problem with this subalternative is that clauses 1 and 2 do not seem to coordinate well: clause 1 speaks of an assurance to be provided to Protarchus; clause 2 of an assurance to be provided to Socrates. Hence the second subalternative, which makes only the ὅτι clause depend on πίστεως and proposes an implicit verb of speaking to govern the accusative plus infinitive (sc., σὲ) ἀφεῖναί: *isn't it on account of being for the sake of assurance that the mixture is easy to display; and [I hope that you] allow that it is no longer necessary that I prolong* (Hackforth 1945; Gosling 1975; Frede 1993). Others, seeing only πίστεως as depending on χάριν, have proposed various emendations noted by Bury (1897).

50d2 **ἐπιδεῖξαι** I have put a comma instead of Burnet's (1901) raised dot after ἐπιδεῖξαι, following Stallbaum (1842, not 1820). See previous note.

[χάριν σε] λαβόντα . . . ἀφεῖναί *[for the sake that you,] after grasping* [*this thing,* i.e., the mix of pleasure and pain in comedy], *allow that* plus impersonal infinitive μηκέτι δεῖν plus accusative με plus infinitive μηκύνειν plus accusative τοὺς λόγους. I take ἀφεῖναί to govern δεῖν in this reading. Bury (1897) takes δεῖν to govern ἀφεῖναί, presumably with this sense: *you ought to release me.* He notes that it is unusual to have an aorist rather than present infinitive (ἀφεῖναί) depend on χάριν.

51a2 **μεταβαλὼν** circumstantial participle to πειράσομαι *after making the change [from mixed to unmixed, I will try],* supplying the terms of the change from 50e5–6: μετὰ τὰς μειχθείσας . . . ἐπὶ τὰς ἀμείκτους.

51a5–9 *In the case of relief from pain, where pleasures are mixed with pains, (1) some pleasures are false in being apparent, but not in any way real, while (2) other pleasures are false in appearing to be both great and numerous, while being contaminated with pains and with cessations of the greatest pains and distresses of body and soul.* Socrates states that the entire discussion of the pleasure-haters serves to prove this proposition ("I use them as witnesses to prove," 51a4–5). Socrates uses them first to prove that, in the widespread case of pain relief, "some pleasures are apparent but not in any way real," (51a5–6) and then that "other pleasures appear to be both great and numerous, but are really contaminated with pains and with cessations of the greatest pains and distresses of body and soul" (51a6–9).

Socrates and Protarchus have already agreed (at 44a9), in the case of the neutral state seeming to be pleasant, that to be *merely apparent but not real* is to be false: this agreement explains why, in the case of mixed pleasures, the merely apparent pleasures will be false. Socrates and Protarchus have also agreed that a pleasure that *appears greater in magnitude than it is in reality* is false (at 42a2–3): this agreement explains why, to the extent that a passion has a misleading appearance of being a great pleasure, that passion will be false.

A successful interpretation of the argument for the conclusion stated at 51a5–9 must explain how mixtures can give rise to both types of falsity. I propose the following. Similarly to the way that accountants distinguish *gross* from *net* financial income, I take it that the argument distinguishes gross from net pleasure. In the argument, it is the difference between "bigger" (in gross) and "more" (in net): μείζους ἡδονάς—οὐ πλείους λέγω, 45d3 (see also 45a7–9, 45c1–8). The argument identifies some cases where the gross pleasure is great but there is no net pleasure. Just as there is an important sense in which we count only net income as true income, likewise Socrates counts only positive net pleasure as a truly pleasant event for the organism. Thus, when the net pleasure is nonexistent, any gross pleasure, even a huge gross pleasure, is false. This, then, is the case of mixed pleasure that Socrates describes as *merely apparent and not at all real*: where the gross pleasure does not exceed the gross pain (51a5–6; see also 44c5–d1).

The other case to consider is where the gross pleasure does exceed the gross pain. Socrates considers a case of titillating bodily pleasure where the pleasure greatly exceeds the pain (47a4–5). In this sort of case, although the pain is slight, its irritation is essential to the huge bodily pleasure, experienced as a release from that tension. Hence, Socrates seems justified in saying that such pleasures are mixed or contaminated with pain. It is in this case that the pleasure *appears greater in magnitude than it is in reality,* because the pleasure appears to be *merely* a large pleasure, but in reality it is mixed with pain.

The alternative, standard interpretation makes *all* mixed pleasures false simply because they are mixed with pain. For example, Gosling and Taylor (1982, 146: "they are not really pleasures . . . but pleasure/pains"). Likewise, (Frede 1993, i–li and 1997, 275: "these kinds of pleasure are false only in an extended sense [*in einem weiteren Sinne*] of the meaning of the word 'false'; these pleasures contain not only pleasure, as their name promises, but also pain"), and Irwin (1995, 329: "we confuse a state of pleasure with a mixed state of pleasure and pain"). This standard interpretation fails to explain why Socrates says at 51a5–9 that there are two kinds of falsity: some of these pleasures only *seem* to exist while others are real, but contaminated. This failure is a problem for the standard interpretation.

One might try to defend the standard interpretation by interpreting Socrates' reference to *pleasures that only seem to exist* as a reference to the seeming pleasures of 42c–44a. This defense has problems, too: Socrates first proposes to use the pleasure haters at 44c5; he does not need them before. Those—call them *proto-Epicureans*—from whom Protarchus hears that "pleasantest of all is to pass one's entire life painlessly" (43d7–8) are *not* the pleasure haters. Socrates uses the proto-Epicureans, *not* the pleasure haters, when he proves at 42c–44a that the proto-Epicurean experience (of the neutral state as the positive state of pleasure) is a case of having a false thought about whether one is feeling pleasure (44a9). Therefore, when Socrates says he "uses [pleasure-haters] as witnesses to the fact that (1) some pleasures are false in being apparent, but not in any way real while (2) other pleasures are false in appearing to be both great and numerous, while being contaminated . . ." (51a4–7), his reference to using the pleasure haters to prove case 1 is *not* a reference to 42c–44a.

51B–53C. TRUE PLEASURES.

51b–53c True pleasures are identified as perceived fillings of unperceived, hence painless, lacks. Socrates gives examples: abstract shape and color, pure sounds, fragrances, and pleasures of learning.

Socrates uses the noun phrase "true pleasures" *only* to refer to those defined at 51b1–7, the pleasures that are true because unmixed with pain. But there are three other ways in which pleasures might be true, in implicit contrast with the other ways of being false previously identified in the dialogue.

1. Some pleasures are representations that are true, mentioned at 39c4–5.
2. As a *difference* in distance can cause some sights and pleasures to appear falsely large or small (proposition 126.3–4 = 41e9–42a3), it seems safe to infer that being at the *same* distance might cause other pleasures to appear accurately and truly in comparison to one another.
3. As the middle, pain-free mode of life might falsely appear to be pleasant (128.2, 43e8–10), it is safe to infer that the pleasant mode of life might truly appear to be pleasant.

Some pleasures will simultaneously be instances of two different forms of true pleasure: true (in way 2) as truly appearing and true as unmixed with pain. Again, true pleasures of anticipation will typically be mixed with painful desire. In that case, there are true, mixed pleasures and hence in that case there are pleasures that are simultaneously true (in way 1) as representations and false as mixed. I suppose Socrates does not draw attention to these other ways for pleasures to be true because they are not relevant to the ranking of goods that is the goal of the dialogue.

51b1–7 *Those pleasures are true that arise when there are perceived and pleasant fillings of unperceived and painless lacks, as happens in the case of the so-called beautiful colors and shapes and in the case of most pleasures of fragrance and sound.* I follow Frede's interpretation (1997, 303): Plato defines the entire class here as the process (*Prozeß*, 303) of filling unfelt lacks. Since the lacks are unfelt, they are painless and thus the pleasure is "pure of pain."

There is a puzzle with Frede's interpretation: what painless lack do colors, shapes, sounds, and (in a less divine way) fragrances fill? Delcomminette (2006, 466) provides a solution: the *Timaeus* (47a1–e2) "presents vision and sound as divine gifts with the purpose of making human beings capable of attaining inner harmony [*harmonie intérieure*] by contemplating the exterior harmony presented by the beauty of the regular movements of the heavens or of music." People are not pained by this postulated inner disharmony as such—even though, of course, psychic disharmony is associated with numerous painful circumstances for human beings. People contemplate the regularities of audible harmony thanks to the instruments of music and the regularities of the motions of heavenly bodies thanks to the constructions of geometry (constructions comparable to those made by the tools of builders, 56b8–c2). Those regularities are pleasant precisely to the extent that they restore harmony to the movements of the soul.

An alternative to Frede's interpretation is Damascius' interpretation, according to which pleasures include both processes of filling and states of being full, an interpretation recently defended by Carone (2000), Bravo (2003), and Fletcher (2014). According to this alternative, there is no need to consider visions, smells and sounds to be fillings of unfelt lacks. The ὅσα clause (ὅσα τὰς ἐνδείας ἀναισθήτους ἔχοντα *as many things as have unfelt lacks* 51b5*)* about the filling of unfelt lacks is simply one more element in the list of pure pleasures.

Ogihara (2019, 110n14) explains why it is a strain to read the ὅσα clause as introducing a new item rather than generalizing from stated examples:

> Fletcher . . . cites *Philebus* 11b5, 21b1 as parallel passages where a ὅσα clause that follows καὶ introduces a new item. But καὶ plus ὅσα clause tends to have a *generalizing force* (26b1, 48e4–6; cf. 25c8–11, 54e4–5), and it does have it at 11b5, 21b1, where the reference of the ὅσα clause happens to exclude the preceding items because of σύμφωνα and ἀδελφά. She also cites *Sophist* 265c2 (she writes "c1"), where καὶ ὅσα certainly introduces a new item (see Fletcher 2014, n. 18). But here ἄψυχα that follows ὅσα makes it obvious that ὅσα ἄψυχα . . . refers to a new item besides animals, plants, etc. (c1–3). Nothing similar happens at *Philebus* 51b5–7.

Rudebusch 2006 (slightly revised) criticizes interpretations that add *states* of being full to *processes* of filling as follows:

> All sides agree on a processive interpretation of repletion: Plato means to count perceived *processes of filling* as pleasure. The issue is whether in addition there is a *stative* interpretation: that is, whether Plato also counts as pleasant *states of being full.* The motivation for Damascius and others is to enable them to assimilate Plato's account of pleasure with the sophisticated and plausible accounts of Aristotle and Epicurus (e.g., Bravo 2003, 59, 67–78), a reading that is charitable and therefore attractive. Despite its attractiveness, a number of reasons keep me from accepting this resurrection. There are four reasons of textual fidelity:
>
> 1. Movements are not states, and Plato classifies pleasure as a kind of movement throughout his middle and later dialogues, as Bravo himself carefully documents (Bravo 2003, 43–45).
> 2. Plato unambiguously dismisses the state of repletion following a process of repleting as neutral and neither pleasant nor painful at *Republic* 583c–585a and *Philebus* 42e.

3. Bravo defends the textual fidelity of the stative in addition to the processive interpretation: "According to the *Philebus*, the 'natural state' consists in harmony, and the attainment and the enjoyment of this harmony *is* pleasure" (*el logro y el disfrute de esta armonía es el placer*, Bravo 2003, 59). He bases this interpretation on his translation of 31c–d: "If in us organisms harmony is decomposed, then, at the time that the nature is decomposing [*se disuelve*] pains are born . . . But if the harmony is recovered [*recuperada*], and the proper nature reconstituted [*reconstituida*], the pleasure is generated." His word *recuperada* mistranslates the Greek *present* passive participle ἁρμοττομένης *getting tuned*, as if it were the *perfect* passive participle ἡρμοσμένης, *tuned*. (Likewise, his word *reconstituida* mistranslates a present as a perfect.) Plato follows standard Greek grammar in keeping the senses of present and perfect distinct, always using the present form unambiguously for the process of *becoming tuned*—for example, at *Republic* 349d and 591d—and always using the perfect form unambiguously for the state of *being tuned* (e.g., at *Republic* 410e, 443e, 554e, *Phaedo* 93d, and *Laches* 188d). Properly translated, *Philebus* 31d does not support the stative interpretation but counts against it. Likewise, Plato uses present not perfect forms at other passages cited by Bravo, such as the reiteration of this definition at *Philebus* 32e and 42d, as well as the complementary passages at *Timaeus* 64d (Bravo cites 64c) and *Republic* 585a. Likewise, Shorey (1930) systematically mistranslates present verbs as perfect.
4. Bravo also cites, without discussion, 32b. Socrates calls this definition a *reiteration* of the definition at 31d (ὅπερ ἔλεγον ἐν τῷ πρόσθεν, *the very thing I said before*), not as adding new meaning to that previous definition. The reiteration defines pleasure as τὴν δ' εἰς τὴν . . . οὐσίαν ὁδόν, ταύτην δὲ αὖ πάλιν τὴν ἀναχώρησιν, the way *to the [state of] being*, this return *back again*. The second clause is naturally read as restating the same meaning as the first clause. (LSJ lists αὖ πάλιν as an Attic pleonasm in the entry for αὖ.) Such a reading is confirmed by the immediately preceding

> use of "way" at 32a, not cited by Bravo, where Plato defines pleasure as "*the way back* to the same" (πάλιν δ' εἰς ταὐτὸν . . . ἡ . . . ὁδὸς): "the way back" must refer to the process of repleting, not the repleted state, which would be the *end* of the way.

In addition, there is a further problem of theoretical insufficiency. As I said above, Bravo, like Carone, wishes to assimilate Plato to Aristotle's attractive definition of pleasure as "unimpeded activation of the state that fits one's nature" (ἐνέργειαν τῆς κατὰ φύσιν ἕξεως . . . ἀνεμπόδιστον, *Nic. Eth.* 1153a14–15). There is no controversy that the *Philebus* defines pleasure as repletion. I have just argued that "repletion" refers unambiguously to the process not the state of repletion. If we, for the sake of argument, expand the definition to include the *state* as well as the *process* of repletion, then we can attribute to Plato, in addition to the repleting *processes* of, say, recovering one's health or of learning a skill, also the replete *states* of being healthy or of possessing skill. But such states are theoretically insufficient; they fall short of Aristotle's view. In order to be assimilated to Aristotle, Plato would need to admit as pleasure also the *activation* of one's states of, say, health or skill. Mere replete states are insufficient to count as activations, as Aristotle points out (*Nic. Eth.* 1095b31–1096a2, 1176a33–35). It is no wonder, then, that Aristotle did not take Plato's position to be assimilable to his own, as Bravo's discussion shows (Bravo 2003, 62–64). Likewise, in an early dialogue, Plato himself anticipates Aristotle's distinction between our merely *having* (κεκτῆσθαι) and *activating* (χρῆσθαι) a thing, and the Socrates of the *Euthydemus* affirms that mere having is insufficient for goodness (280c–d). Therefore, the stative interpretation falls short of the goal of attributing to Plato an attractive, Aristotelian theory of pleasure. The *Philebus* does admit that knowing can be *accompanied* by pleasure (ἡδονὰς . . . ἐπιστήμαις . . . ἑπομένας, 66c). But Socrates there appears to deny that the unimpeded activity of knowing itself *is* a pleasure. For he says that it is ἴσως οὐδὲν ἄτοπον *perhaps not unlikely* that the gods are aware and know—surely, without impediment—yet feel no pleasure; "at any rate" (γοῦν), for them to feel pleasure would be unseemly (33b3–11).

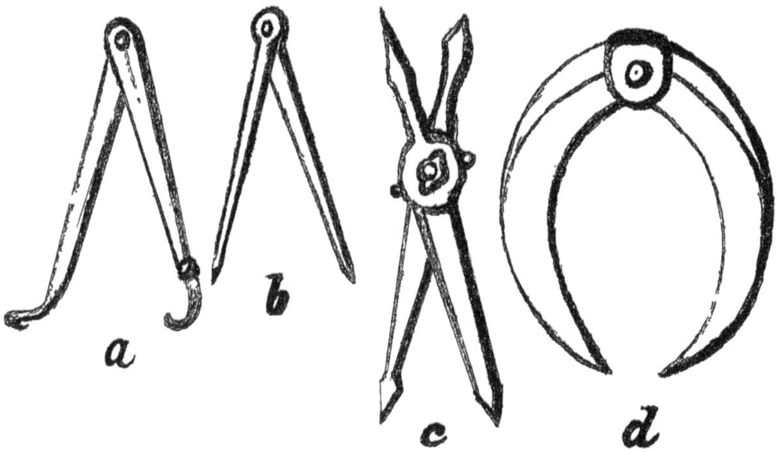

Figure 3. Four kinds of compass. Author's reconstruction from Blümner's drawing (1875, 232) of bronze implements found at Pompei. (*a*) Compass to measure interior spaces. (*b*) Compass for geometrical constructions and mechanical drawing. (*c*) Compass to change size of a two-dimensional image while keeping same proportions. (*d*) Compass to transfer measurements from a two-dimensional image to a three-dimensional construction.

51b5 **αἰσθητὰς καὶ ἡδείας [καθαρὰς λυπῶν]** *perceptible and pleasant [fillings], pure of pains.* Burnet (1901), in bracketing καθαρὰς λυπῶν, seems to accept Bury's (1897) assessment that the "clumsy tautology seems indefensible." Frede (1993), Gosling (1975), and Hackforth (1945) all leave the words out of their translations. But it is not a tautology to add to the description of the fillings in question as "pleasant" that they are also "pure of pain"—for not all pleasures are pure of pain. Nor is it tautology to infer step by step from the premise that *the lacks are imperceptible* (τὰς ἐνδείας ἀναισθήτους) to the intermediate conclusion that *the lacks are painless* (τὰς ἐνδείας ἀλύπους) to the conclusion that *the fillings are pure of pain* (τὰς πληρώσεις καθαρὰς λυπῶν).

51c4–5 **τόρνοις** *by means of compasses.* Blümner (1875, 232) shows four kinds in a figure drawn from bronze implements found at Pompei (see figure 3). Compton (1990) argues conclusively against an alternative translation, *lathe,* and defends *compass.* Yet, as a third alternative, he thinks that "pin-and-string" or "peg-and-cord" circle-construction devices are the compasses Socrates means (Compton 1990, 552). But

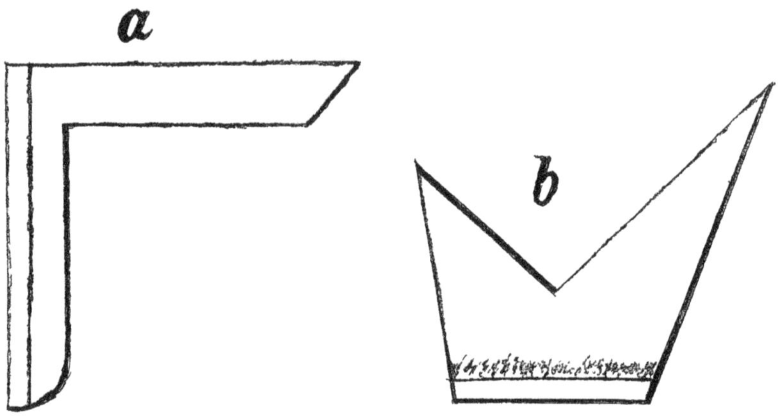

Figure 4. Two kinds of L-square. Author's reconstruction from Gruter's two drawings (1616, 644) of inscriptions of tools on Roman monuments to masons. (*a*) L-square to measure inside or outside of a right angle. (*b*) L-square to measure outside of a right angle.

idealized geometrical constructions, as we find in Euclid, seem to be what Socrates is referring to, and for those a geometrical compass (b) seems most appropriate, although I cannot rule out peg and cord and perhaps others in figure 3.

κανόσι *straight-edge rulers.* Carpenter rulers have regular intervals like inches marked on them, while a Euclidean straight edge is unmarked. Socrates seems to have in mind not the construction of a carpenter but of a Euclidean geometrician.

γωνίαις *L-squares,* Blümner (1875, 236) shows in a drawing on p. 237 two kinds, for measuring internal or external right angles. See figure 4. The drawings are after Gruter (1616, 644 [drawing 1 and drawing 2]), which he drew from Roman monuments to masons.

51d1 **οὐδὲν ταῖς τῶν κινήσεων προσφερεῖς** *similar in nothing to the [pleasures] of movements.* The movements are opposite to the immobility of the things ἀεὶ καλὰ καθ' αὑτὰ mentioned in the previous line. The prevailing alternative is to accept, with Burnet (1901), Heusde's emendation of κινήσεων to κνήσεων: *the [pleasures] of rubbing or scratching itches.* For a similar case, see note to 46d10.

51d2 **καὶ χρώματα δὴ τοῦτον τὸν τύπον ἔχοντα [καλὰ καὶ ἡδονάς]** *and colors that have this character [i.e., beautiful not relative to something but by themselves are] beautiful and [are] pleasures.* Stallbaum (1842), followed by Burnet (1901), would delete καλὰ καὶ ἡδονάς. Diès (1949) (citing Richards 1911 and followed by Delcomminette 2020) would move ἔχοντα after καλὰ καὶ ἡδονάς, apparently to avoid saying that colors *are* pleasures and to say instead the colors are "*sources* of pleasures" ("*sources de plaisirs,*" Diès) or that they "*have* pleasures" ("*comportent des plaisirs,*" Delcomminette).

51d6 **ἠχὰς** *sounds.* Following Burnet (1901), I accept Bury's (1897) proposal of ἠχὰς for τὰς in the manuscript, in order to make sense of the passage. Bury (1897) reasoned that the ἠ after δή might have been lost, and then the χ changed to τ.

51d7–8 *Such sounds are not beautiful in relation to anything else but are beautiful in and by themselves.* The musical tones that make up a single melody need not be pleasant as a relief from pain, but by virtue of their measure and symmetry, as Delcomminette (2006, 458) points out. Such measure and symmetry are pure pleasures because they restore an unperceived psychic lack of measure and symmetry (see note to 51b1–7).

An alternative interpretation (Frede 1997; Waterfield 1982) is that, instead of the tones being pleasant in themselves, each singular note by itself is pleasant. But as Delcomminette (2006, 458) points out, this alternative is unfaithful to the text, which takes up tones "producing melody," (τὰς . . . ἱείσας μέλος), not isolated tones by themselves.

51e1 **ἧττον . . . θεῖον** *less divine than.* Part of this proposition claims that pleasures of smell are less divine than visual and auditory pleasures, a claim not established by the premises. In support of Gosling (1975, 122), who points out that delight in "pure tunes" leads to "delight in numbers, whereas smells lead nowhere," I note that in giving "music" (τὸ μουσικὸν, 17b11) as an example to illustrate the Divine Method, Socrates remarks that the rhythm of a melody is "measured by numbers" (δι' ἀριθμῶν μετρηθέντα, 17d5). Delcomminette (2006, 457) suggests that we might establish the claim by supplying the premise that fragances activate more primitive cognitive processes than symmetrical forms and musical tones.

51e2 **τὸ δὲ μὴ συμμεμεῖχθαι ἐν αὐταῖς ἀναγκαίους λύπας** *but with respect to the fact that necessary pains are not mixed in together [with the kind Pleasures of Fragrances].* With this articular-infinitive accusative of respect Socrates posits the whole kind Pleasures of Fragrances as counterparts to the visible and audible kinds of pure pleasure *with respect to this fact.* Accordingly, Frede (1993) and Gosling (1975), for the sake of an intelligible translation, treat the accusative of respect as indicating a premise from which Socrates can draw a conclusion about how to posit the kind.

51e5 **ταῦτα εἴδη δύο λεγομένων ἡδονῶν** *these are two forms of [true] pleasures under discussion.* Burnet (1901) (citing Jackson) changes this text to: ταῦτα εἴδη δύο <ὧν> λέγομεν ἡδονῶν *these [are] two forms of [true] pleasures of which we speak.*

52a5 **μαθημάτων πληρωθεῖσιν . . . ἀποβολαὶ . . . γίγνωνται** *losses [of knowledge] occur to [people] after they are filled with knowledge.* The manuscripts have the genitive plural participle πληρωθεισῶν instead of Schütz's (cited in Burnet) widely accepted emendation to dative πληρωθεῖσιν. Without emendation the text gives us a genitive absolute with the meaning: *after lessons have been completed, losses occur.* For the passive sense *completed,* LSJ πληρόω III.3 cites Aristotle, *Mechanica* 854b29, which refers to a geometrical figure—and hence a lesson—being completed.

52b4 **Ἀληθῆ . . . λήθη** *truth . . . forgetting.* "Notice the wordplay both here and [at c1–d1] in μετρίως . . . ἀμετρίαν . . . ἐμμετρίαν" (Bury 1897).

52b6–8 *The [most divine pleasures, namely,] pleasures of learning—the ones enjoyed not by most people but by very few—are unmixed with pain.* Part of this proposition restricts the pleasures of learning to a very few, a restriction not established by the premises. We might infer this restriction from the premise: most people like to learn only because of the utility produced by the learning, not because of the pleasure of the learning itself (αὐτὰ τὰ τῆς φύσεως μόνον παθήματα χωρὶς τοῦ λογισμοῦ *the experience itself of its nature, apart from the reckoning,* b2–3).

52c3–4 *Let us by our reasoning attach lack of measure to the intense [i.e., mixed] pleasures, and measure to the opposite [mild, unmixed].*

An alternative interpretation is that pure pleasures cannot be bounded. Waterfield (1982, 123) edits and translates the text of 52c, a text that is corrupt, to produce such an alternative: "Whether [pure pleasures] occur commonly or rarely, whether they penetrate body and soul to a greater or lesser extent, we must say that they are members of our familiar indeterminate class, though some are moderate members." Delcomminette (2006, 481n55) raises a problem for Waterfield's alternative. Waterfield has edited and translated the text to avoid placing pleasure of any subkinds into the kind Bounded. But the text of 52c1–4 already entails that pure pleasures, since they are measured, are bounded. Hence, Waterfield must reedit an uncorrupt passage as well as the present passage in order to rid the text of the inconsistency he finds in it.

The problem Waterfield finds with allowing bounded pleasures to exist is that Socrates earlier (31a8–10) and later (65d8–9) puts pleasure in the kind Unbounded. How can he put the subkind Pure Pleasure, then, into the kind Bound? Hackforth (1945, 102–3), endorsed by Delcomminette (2006, 481n56), gives a workable solution (the following translations are from Hackforth 1945): pleasure and in general the "class" of the unbounded "does not and never will contain *within itself and derived from itself* (ἐν αὑτῷ ἀφ' ἑαυτοῦ) either beginning, or middle, or end" (31a10). Accordingly, "we must look for something other than the character of being unbounded to explain how an element of good [or truth, or purity] attaches to pleasures" (28a1–3). In general, the knowing attaches bound to unbounded to produce "bound unbounded"—that is, mix—and in the specific case of pleasure, the knowing attaches truth and purity to pleasure to produce "pure pleasure" in the kind Mix. In the same way, while high and low pitch and fast and slow tempo are unbounded in themselves and from themselves, the addition of harmony produces *musical* high and low pitch and *musical* fast and slow tempo (26a).

Hackforth (1945, 103) raises an objection to his own solution: "Although pleasure in the abstract belongs to the ἄπειρον γένος [*kind Unbounded*], any actual pleasure must be a μεικτόν [*mix*] of πέρας [*bound*] and ἄπειρον [unbounded]; it is the same as with Plato's own illustration of temperature: temperature in the abstract is an ἄπειρον [*unbounded thing*], a τὸ μᾶλλόν τε καὶ ἧττον δεχόμενον [*thing accepting more and less*] but any actual temperature is of a definite, determined degree. How then can Socrates say, as he does at 52c, that intense pleasures belong to the ἄπειρον γένος [*kind Unbounded*]?"

Hackforth finds no answer to this objection and accuses Plato of "a certain inconsistency." (Delcomminette [2006, 481] is silent about this problem.) Rudebusch (2021) provides a solution. It is not individual pleasures but the pleasure scale $\langle P, <_p \rangle$—that is, the domain of pleasant restorations P and the relations more and less *pleasant* $>_p$ and $<_p$ (relations that are antisymmetric, transitive, and without upper or lower bound)—that is in the kind Unbounded. And it is not individual pleasures that are bound or measured but a scale $\langle T, <_t \rangle$, constructed by expert knowledge, where T is the subset of P containing pleasant restorations that are not mixed with pain, where $>_t$ and $<_t$ are relations on T that possess an upper bound, and where $\langle T, <_t \rangle$ is *measured* or *Archimedean*—that is, there is an equality relation $=_t$, a binary operation $+_t$, and an identity element e on T with the same structure as Ra (the rational numbers), <, =, +, and 0. Rudebusch (2021) attributes only mathematical *intuition* of such scales to Plato, not *axiomatic theory*.

52c4–d1 *Let us propose for those pleasures—the ones that come to be big and intense—that they are of the kind of that unbounded less-and-more pleasant that pervades body and soul, and let us propose for the opposite pleasures that they are of the kind of the measured things.* The text I accept for my translation has grammar that is awkward and allusive, but feasible: καὶ τὸ μέγα καὶ τὸ σφοδρὸν αὖ καὶ πολλάκις καὶ ὀλιγάκις γιγνομένας τοιαύτας [sc., μεγάλας καὶ σφοδρὰς], τῆς [sc., ἡδονῆς] τοῦ ἀπείρου γε ἐκείνου καὶ ἧττον καὶ μᾶλλον διά τε σώματος καὶ ψυχῆς φερομένου προσθῶμεν αὐταῖς εἶναι γένους, ταῖς δὲ μὴ τῶν ἐμμέτρων. Alternative translations emend the text to produce a speculative but more grammatical text. With the exception of Waterfield (1982) (see previous note), there is little significant difference in the content of the translated proposition.

52c5 **<τὰς> . . . <δεχομένας>** *the [pleasures] that accept* plus accusative. This accusative (of respect) noun phrase is the antecedent of αὐτὰς at d1. With many others, I follow Stallbaum's (1842) changes to the text at c4–d1.

52d6 **Τί ποτε . . . πρὸς ἀλήθειαν εἶναι** *which is [directed* or *related] to truth? [The pure and unadulterated or the intense and the much and the large?]* As a less accurate alternative translation, Gosling's (1975) makes it a comparative question: "With regard to the truth," which is "better off?" Likewise, Frede (1993): "What is closer to it?"

52d8 **τὸ ἰταμόν** *reckless.* The manuscripts have ἱκανόν *sufficient,* which does not appear to make sense, given the connection of sufficiency to the good at 20d. Instead of Burnet's (1901) changing the word to **ἰταμόν,** Diès (1949), citing Jackson and followed by Frede (1993) and Delcomminette (2020), transposes ἱκανόν to the previous line, before ἤ.

53c–55b*: **Pleasure as process***

53c–55b Socrates argues that pleasure cannot be in the kind Good, because pleasure is a process of becoming, not a state of being, and becoming is inferior to being. A review of the overall aims of the *Philebus* makes clear the point of this argument. There are three theses under consideration in the dialogue:

1. *Socrates' interpretation of Philebus*: When we divide the kind Good we find pleasure as one subkind (among possible others, 11b4–6).
2. *Protarchus' interpretation of Philebus:* The good, without any division, is one and the same as pleasure (11d8).
3. *Socrates' thesis about pleasure:* Pleasure can take on goodness and badness as extrinsic characteristics: we can divide pleasure accordingly into good pleasure and bad pleasure (12c7–8).

Socrates refuted Philebus, as interpreted by Protarchus in thesis 2, at 20e–22c. The point of the argument at 53c–55b is to refute the Phileban thesis according to Socrates' interpretation (thesis 1), namely that "pleasure is something good" (54d7)—that is, generically good. Interpreters prior to Delcomminette (2006) did not understand this distinction and had difficulty seeing the point of 53c–55b (see, e.g., Hackforth 1945, 105;

Gosling 1975, 220). The two refutations together leave Socrates' thesis 3 the only remaining possibility.

53c4–5 **περὶ ἡδονῆς οὐκ ἀκηκόαμεν ὡς ἀεὶ γένεσίς ἐστιν, οὐσία δὲ οὐκ ἔστι τὸ παράπαν ἡδονῆς;** *Haven't we heard [in our conversation] that pleasure is always a process of becoming; that there is no being at all of pleasure.* The question expects a positive answer, "Yes, we have." It is reasonable to attribute these theses about pleasure (*is* a process of becoming; is *not* a being) to Socrates. Delcomminette (2006, 497) notices the alternative interpretation. "The fact that Socrates attributes this position to others, and that he never himself affirms it except conditionally (ἡδονή γε, εἴπερ γένεσίς ἐστιν, 54c6, d1), has made numerous commentators think that he is not taking it up as his own account, at least not for every subkind of pleasure, with the most widely cited exceptions being pure pleasures and pleasures of anticipation." Among others he cites Shorey (1933, 324), Taylor (1948, 427–29), Festugière (1950, 303), Crombie (1963, 263), Guthrie (1978, 229), Gosling and Taylor (1982, 153 and 236–37), Migliori (1993, 266), Carone (2000, 264–70), and Pradeau (2002, 64–65).

But the widely cited "exceptions" are not compelling reasons to abandon the plain sense of this passage. Pure and anticipatory pleasures might well be restorative. On pure pleasures, see note to 51b1–7. On anticipatory pleasures, see note to 32c3–5.

And there are problems with the alternative (that Socrates only conditionally affirms that pleasure is a process of becoming). Socrates affirms as his own account that pleasure is a member of the kind Unbounded (27e5–6) and that members of the kind Unbounded are always *becoming* more and less (24e7–25a2). Socrates is clever enough to recognize, as he does here, the obvious consequence: pleasure is always becoming.

Moreover, "it has been said repeatedly" by 42c1 that "the process of restoration is pleasure" (42d6), at 31d4–6 and 32a9–b2. The proposition that *restoration is pleasure* might mean that *restoration* constitutes *pleasure,* so that all pleasure is restoration, or it might mean that *restoration* is one form of *pleasure* among others. The context of 42d6 makes clear that restoration *constitutes* pleasure, so that all pleasure is restoration. For a life *without* (perceived) restorations will be pleasureless, "without charms, as we said" (43c11)—a reference to the pleasureless and hence charmless life of pure knowing (22b–22c and 21e1–2).

And yet the dialogue as a whole has a frame—namely, the question whether pleasure or knowing is or is closer to the good. Given the pleasure/knowing dichotomy, the argument proceeds to show that pleasure is a restoration. But in other frames, Socrates the dialectician need not accept the pleasure/knowing dichotomy. See note 22c5–6.

53e2 **Τὸ τρίτον ἔτ' ἐρῶ;** *shall I speak again for the third [time]?* All editors and translators follow Badham (1878), who made them the first words of Protarchus' speech instead of the last words of Socrates', after changing from τὸ τρίτον ἑτέρῳ *the third [thing] to another.*

55c6 **γενναίως** *nobly* modifies περικρούωμεν *let us strike all around.* It would show an ignoble love of victory rather than a noble love of truth if Socrates were to find impurity only in pleasure and not give a comparable critical examination of knowing.

55c8 **κρίσιν** *verdict.* "With this selection principle Socrates refers back to 52d–e, where he proposed, for simplicity [*zur Vereinfachung*] to seek out the pure forms. Diès [1949], who with Schleiermacher [1809] wants to read κρᾶσις here instead of κρίσις, seems to me to overlook this" (Frede 1997).

2. Likewise, we can classify and rank the forms of expert knowing.

55d–56e: ***Socrates classifies kinds of expert knowing relative to their clarity and precision in recognizing truth***

In interpreting this division, I have arranged the subkinds of the kind Expert Knowing (such as Applied versus Academic) from least to most perspicuous. I have not arranged the ultimate kinds of Expert Knowing, such as Shipbuilding versus House building, in any order.

1. **Expert knowing**
    - 1.1. Applied and Practical Expert knowing
        - 1.1.1. Less perspicuous: kinds of applied expert knowing that lack rule by mathematical knowledge
            - Playing the aulos
            - Healing

Piloting
Agriculture
Military strategy
[Sophistic and rhetorical persuasion, which are "most profitable" 58c2 and "superior in utility" 58c6]

1.1.2. More perspicuous: kinds of applied expert knowing that are ruled by mathematical knowledge
Building expertise
Shipbuilding
House building
Trading expertise (56e8)

1.1.3. Most perspicuous of the applied kinds of expert knowing: the mathematical kinds of expert knowing that give perspicuity to the other manually productive kinds of expert knowing (yet make computations—e.g., in counting armies or cattle—of units that in fact are unequal, 56d9–e1).
Applied arithmetic (56e7)
Measurement (56e7)

1.2. Academic Expert knowing

1.2.1. Philosophical counterparts to applied kinds of expert knowing (which only make computations when it is posited that no unit differs in the least from any other, 56e1–3).
Philosophical geometry (56e8)
Advanced computation (57a1)
[Music theory]

1.2.2. Dialectic

There are two main alternative interpretations of the division of the kind Expert Knowing. They differ in what they put in the kind Academic Expert Knowing. On the one hand, where I list only *philosophical* kinds of mathematics, Delcomminette (2006, 520) and Frede (1997, 322) list *both* applied and philosophical mathematics. On the other hand, Migliori (1993, 288) lists nothing at all under that heading.

To place the applied kinds of mathematics within the kind Academic Expert Knowing, as do Delcomminette and Frede, is unfaithful to the text.

Socrates and Protarchus agree that "arithmetic and whatever [other kinds of mathematics] are with these [i.e., the applied] arts" (Ἀριθμητικὴν . . . καὶ ὅσας μετὰ ταύτης τέχνας, 56c10–11) are the "most precise of these [i.e., the applied] arts" (Τούτων δὲ ταύτας ἀκριβεστάτας εἶναι τέχνας, 56c8). This text compels us to place the applied kinds of mathematics precisely where a charitable interpretation would seek to locate them, namely, in the kind Applied Expert Knowing. This text entails that the applied kinds of mathematics, as much as shipbuilding or playing the aulos, belong to the manual arts.

According to Migliori (1993, 288), Socrates' division places *nothing* in the kind Academic Expert Knowing. This alternative is faithful to the text of 56c, as shown above, in seeing some kinds of mathematics as a division of Applied Expert Knowing. Migliori differs from me in that he takes Socrates to *divide* these kinds of mathematics into applied and philosophical. Migliori rightly assumes that *if* the kinds of mathematics belong to the kind Applied Expert Knowing, then the result of any *division* of those kinds will also belong in the kind Applied Expert Knowing.

But the text does not compel us to interpret Socrates as *dividing* into two parts the kind of arithmetic that is part of the kind Applied Expert Knowing, with the nonsensical result that philosophical arithmetic is a kind of applied expert knowing. What Socrates elicits from Protarchus is that "one must speak of these [i.e., the kinds of mathematics that go with applied skills] as διττὰς *twofold* or *double*" (56d1–2).

Something might be διττὰς because it is *divided.* I take this be Migliori's reading, which entails, nonsensically, that philosophical arithmetic is a kind of Applied, not Academic Expert, Knowing. But something might also be διττὰς by *having a counterpart.* And so, when Socrates says that these kinds of mathematics are διττὰς, we can read him as saying that the kinds of applied mathematics have counterparts. Leaving aside this contested passage, the Greek word διττὰς, "twofold," is used nowhere in the *Philebus* to indicate a division. According to my proposed counterpart reading, Socrates is not dividing the kinds but rather identifying a corresponding set of kinds, a corresponding set that need not fall anywhere under the kind Applied Expert Knowing. Such a reading permits philosophical arithmetic to be a kind of Academic Expert Knowing, which makes good sense. Given a choice between two faithful readings of the text, charity requires us to interpret Socrates and Protarchus to make as sensible an agreement as possible.

As shown above, the text of 56c8–11 compels us to list the applied kinds of mathematics, but not the philosophical kinds of mathematics, as applied expert knowing. The text divides the kinds of applied expert knowing into three: the less precise (such as playing the aulos), the more precise (such as the building arts), and the most precise (the mathematics associated with the more precise arts).

There is an intuitive distinction between *measurable* and *immeasurable* differences of superiority. One way to make precise the distinction is to define measurable differences as those found on a *ratio* scale. On such a scale, as defined by Archimedes, for any positive number x, no matter how small, and for any number y, no matter how large, there exists an integer n, such that $nx \geq y$. In contrast, what are often called *lexical* superiority relations are not measurable on a scale fulfilling the Archimedean property. As dictionary users are aware, any entry under the heading A, no matter how long, will be prior to any entry under the heading B, no matter how short. (On such "trumping" and other forms of lexical orders of priority, see Griffin 1986, 83–86.)

I take it that Socrates observes the measurable/immeasurable distinction in the text with his contrast between *more* (πολὺ, 57c9) and *immeasurably* more (ἀμήχανον, 57d1). This passage tells us that, *within* the kind Applied Expert Knowing, the difference in the degree of accuracy attained by the applied kinds of mathematics is a measurable (in some sense) "more" versus less. In contrast to this measurable difference *within* a kind, Socrates says that the superiority of the *academic* to the *applied* kinds of mathematics is "immeasurable." I interpret this immeasurable difference to confirm my interpretation, that academic kinds of mathematics are outside while applied kinds of mathematics are inside the kind Applied Expert Knowing.

55d1 **τῆς περὶ τὰ μαθήματα ἐπιστήμης** *[the one part] of knowledge concerning what can be learned*. Badham (1878) reasonably complains that "knowledge concerning what has been learned" is redundant. Bury

(1897) replies that perhaps τὰ μαθήματα is to recall the "learning" discussed at 52a–b. I propose that Socrates adds the prepositional phrase περὶ τὰ μαθήματα with the ἡμῖν to make clear that he is talking about the knowledge that we humans have attained as opposed to whatever knowledge remains undiscovered.

δημιουργικόν *craftworking.* It will make the most sense of Socrates' division of expert knowing to notice the root sense of this word, *deme-working*—that is, *working in service to the deme*—what we might call "applied" expert knowing.

55d2 **παιδείαν καὶ τροφήν** *education and nurture.* In opposition to applied expert knowing, educational nourishment seems to be expert knowing that completes the soul—what we might call "academic" expert knowing—rather than deriving its value by application to external ends.

55d5 **Ἐν δὴ ταῖς χειροτεχνικαῖς** *among the practical skills.* I take the prefix χειρο-, *manual* or *hands on,* in the sense of *practical.* These skills are the members of the *deme-working* part of expert knowing mentioned in the note to 55d1.

55d6 **τὸ μὲν ἐπιστήμης αὐτῶν μᾶλλον ἐχόμενον, τὸ δ' ἧττον ἔνι** *with respect to the one part of these [practical skills] holding itself more closely to expert knowing while the other part [of these having] less [expert knowing] in (itself).* Plato sometimes places ἔνι = ἔνεστι *is in,* after its dative complement noun (*Theaetetus* 180a1) or with its noun unstated (*Theaetetus* 194e7; *Republic* 431a5).

55d11 **χωρίς** adverb *[one must take the ruling parts of each of these arts] separately,* taking ἑκάστων αὐτῶν as a partitive genitive. An alternative is to take χωρίς as preposition plus the genitive object ἑκάστων αὐτῶν *[one must take the ruling parts] without [each of these arts].*

55e2 **ὡς ἔπος εἰπεῖν** *almost, practically,* qualifying as too absolute the expression that, stripped of arithmetic and measurement, there will be nothing fine left of any practical skill.

55e7 **προσχρωμένους** *using in addition [the powers].* "The subject of προσχρ. is the possessors of senses" (Badham 1878).

56a3–7 **Οὐκοῦν μεστὴ μέν που μουσικὴ πρῶτον, τὸ σύμφωνον ἁρμόττουσα οὐ μέτρῳ ἀλλὰ μελέτης στοχασμῷ, καὶ σύμπασα αὐτῆς αὐλητική, τὸ μέτρον ἑκάστης χορδῆς τῷ στοχάζεσθαι φερομένης θηρεύουσα, ὥστε πολὺ μεμειγμένον ἔχειν τὸ μὴ σαφές, σμικρὸν δὲ τὸ βέβαιον.** *Accordingly, music I suppose is full [of guesswork] in attuning to what agrees in sound not by measurement but by a guesswork born of practice, indeed aulos-expertise as a whole [is full of] it* [i.e., guesswork], *in hunting by guesswork for the measure of each plucked note as it is being carried [through the air], so that it has much unclarity mixed up in it and but little certainty.* There are no difficulties in the manuscripts. Nevertheless, many emendations have been proposed (most recently, three were deemed necessary by Borthwick 2003) to make sense of the text.

56a3 **μεστὴ [sc., στοχαστικῆς] . . . μουσικὴ** *music [is] full [of guesswork, supplied from 55e7].* Bury (1897) remarks that "the ellipse with μεστή is most awkward," but it is in keeping with the elliptical style of the *Philebus.* Barker (1987, 105) rightly worries that the translation "guesswork" is "potentially misleading," since "certainly the musician does not *guess* at the correct intonation, whether he is tuning the instrument or playing it." Barker is right that the meaning of the verb "guess" is misleading, if we take the meaning to be the *OED*'s fifth entry, to act "at random or from indications admittedly uncertain." But the first entry of the *OED* is more accurate: to act on the basis of "an approximate judgement . . . without actual measurement." Musicians by practice improve their skill at hitting the right note by approximating without measurement—*by feel*, as it were—so that the approximation can reliably be within a small enough range to serve the purposes of the scale.

μέν μουσικὴ *while music [is full of guesswork]* is answered at b4 by Τεκτονικὴν δέ *with respect to building skill . . .* The μέν marks the most inaccurate kinds of expert knowing, while the δέ introduces kinds that are one degree more accurate.

πρῶτον *[music,] first.* The first member of the list is music; the list is continued at b1–2, as indicated by the conjunctions Καὶ μὴν . . . τε καὶ . . .

καὶ . . . which coordinate different instances of the expertises with the lowest degree of accuracy.

56a4 **καὶ** (after στοχασμῷ) coordinates (1) a general thesis (μεστὴ [sc., αὐτῆς] μέν που μουσικὴ *music is full of guesswork*) plus the circumstantial participle (τὸ σύμφωνον ἁρμόττουσα οὐ μέτρῳ ἀλλὰ μελέτης στοχασμῷ *in attuning to what agrees in sound not by measurement but by a guesswork born of practice*) with (2) an illustrative instance of the general thesis (σύμπασα [sc., μεστὴ] αὐτῆς αὐλητική *aulos-expertise as a whole is full of* guesswork*)* plus an illustrative instance of the circumstantial participle (τὸ μέτρον ἑκάστης χορδῆς τῷ στοχάζεσθαι φερομένης θηρεύουσα *in hunting by guesswork for the measure of each plucked note as it is being carried through the air*).

56a5 **σύμπασα αὐτῆς αὐλητική** *aulos-expertise as a whole [is full of] it [*i.e., guesswork]. This is Paley's (1873) reading, defended by Barker (1987, 104) against many alternatives:

> There is a purpose in delaying αὐτῆς (from a3, where it might have appeared next to μεστὴ. [The delay] signals the fact that μεστή . . . αὐτῆς attaches not only to μουσική in a3 but also to σύμπασα . . . αὐλητική in a5. The sense is "Music is full of this . . . and so is the whole of αὐλητική." This construal has the advantage of giving a simple and coherent syntax to the whole sentence [without emendation], which is hard to find in [the alternative readings].

αὐλητική, τὸ μέτρον ἑκάστης χορδῆς τῷ στοχάζεσθαι φερομένης θηρεύουσα *aulos-expertise as a whole [is full of] it* [i.e., guesswork], *in hunting by guesswork for the measure of each plucked note as it is being carried [through the air].* The root meaning of χορδή is *gut,* hence *string of gut,* but LSJ lists just for this one passage the meaning *musical note,* driven to give an ad hoc meaning because there are no gut strings on an aulos. As an alternative to giving χορδή an ad hoc meaning, the second hand of manuscript Ven. 189 adds καὶ κιθαριστική (*cithara-skill*) after αὐλητική, an addition to the text followed by many, again because there are no gut strings on an aulos. Still other emendments have been proposed. There is a way to avoid both LSJ's ad hoc meaning for χορδή, the second hand's addition of words to the text, and other emendments. The solution is to let φερομένης refer, as Paley (1873) suggests, "to the notes of the [cithara] passing, as it were, to the ear of the player who accompanies it on the [aulos]." Thus Barker (1987, 107): "The *aulete* was notoriously compelled to adjust the pitch of every note in the act of playing it. The pitch that such an instrument emits is not fully determined by the fingering, but depends crucially on such variables as the pressure of the player's breath and the position and tension of his lips on the reed." (Barker, however, follows LSJ to translate χορδή here as *musical note*).

56b9–c1 **κανόνι** *straight-edge ruler.* While at 51c4–5 Socrates seemed to mean the Euclidean straight edge, here in the context of building he seems to mean the carpenter's rule, which has intervals like inches marked on it.

τόρνῳ *compass.* See note to 51c4–5.

διαβήτῃ *A-frame level,* a plumbline and weight hanging from the apex of an A-shaped frame. This level stands bestride a surface to determine if it is level. The word comes from a form of the verb διαβαίνω (*to step or stand with legs apart*) with an agentive suffix: *bestrider.* This has led some (e.g., LSJ, followed by Compton 1990, 550) to identify it with a straight-leg compass. But an A-frame level is equally well called a "bestrider" and was identified as the διαβήτης (Latin *libella)* without controversy by nineteenth-century German scholars such as Blümner (1875, 235–36), who gives two drawings of the διαβήτης (see figure 5, where [b] in the figure represents an A-frame level that could double as a triangle square). The sources of those drawings are inscriptions of tools on the tombs of Roman masons (for such a drawing, see Gruter 1616, 644).

στάθμῃ *plumbline* (as identified by Blümner 1875, 234–55)—that is, "a string with a lead [*Bleistück*] at one end, which serves to measure whether a surface is made exactly vertical or not" (Blümner 1875, 234). An alternative translation is *carpenter's line*—that is, a chalked string that is stretched and snapped to leave a straight line on a surface (LSJ gives both meanings but cites this passage as an instance of *carpenter's line,* followed by Compton 1990, 550).

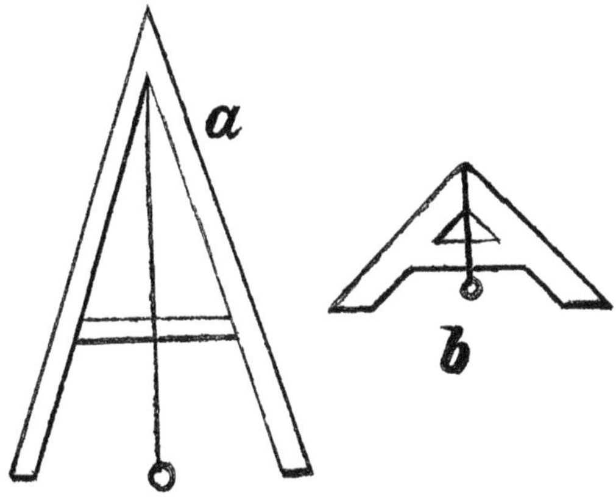

Figure 5. Two kinds of A-frame level. Author's reconstruction from Gruter's drawing (1616, 644) of an inscription of tools on a Roman monument to a mason. Drawing (*b*) shows an A-frame level that also measures interior right angles.

τινι προσαγωγίῳ κεκομψευμένῳ *a sort of device held against the object being measured that is ingenious.* Waterfield (1982) argues that the kind of *prosagōgion* referred to here must be a "try-square" (that is, an L-square: see figure 4 in note to 51c4–5) perhaps called "ingenious" because recently invented. It is "clearly" a try-square, he claims, in a second-century BCE Boeotian inscription (εὐγωνίους πρὸς τὸ προσαγωγεῖον *well-angled against the prosagōgeion*). Compton (1990) agrees and gives the same text. Since Socrates describes it as "ingenious," I propose it is a triangle square (which would equally well fit the Boeotian inscription). Figure 6 shows one with a tail as an added feature (from Blümner 1875, 237: "after an iron original in the Zürich collection [*Züricher Sammlung*]"). Even without the tail—which allows one to measure exterior ninety-degree angles as well as interior 135-degree angles—a triangle square has uses that are not obvious. Like an L-square (identified as a γωνία in a note to 51c4–5), a triangle square permits one accurately to measure a line perpendicular to the edge of a board (hence the "square" in the name). A triangle square has another obvious use: measuring forty-five degrees (or, with a triangle of another shape, sixty- and thirty-degree angles). But it has other truly ingenious uses. Notice the pivot point on the tool at the bottom right corner

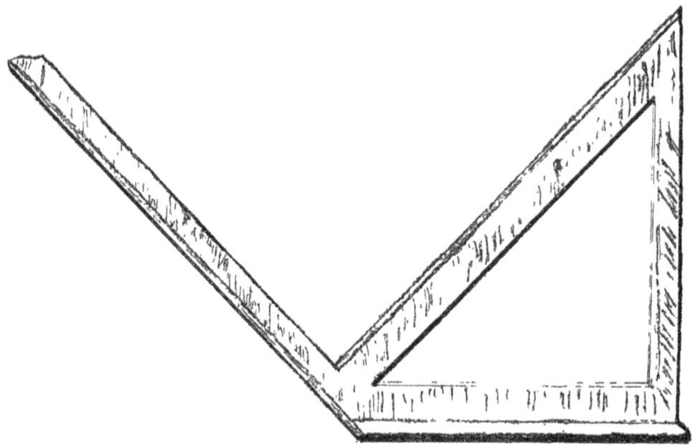

Figure 6. One kind of triangle square. Author's reconstruction from Blümner's drawing (1875, 237) of an iron original "in the Zürich collection." The kind shown is remarkable for its added tail, giving the builder greater versatility.

of figure 6. This, together with the equivalent of a pencil (a dirty fingernail will do the job), permits one accurately to copy and reproduce angles, for example, in cutting rafters to pitch a roof. A similar triangle square with a pivot point, enhanced with additional features by Albert Swanson in 1925 and known as the "speed square," is still in use by carpenters.

56c1 **ὀρθῶς λέγεις** *you are speaking rightly.* Socrates is speaking rightly and is speaking of right angles.

56c4 **τὰς λεγομένας τέχνας** *the mentioned arts* = the arts that are productive for the deme, the χειροτεχνικαί of 55d5.

56d1 **διττὰς** *twofold, double, two.* Notice the difference between *having a double* and *being divided in two* (διχῇ, 56c4). This matters for how we understand the division tree of expert knowing. See my assessment of Migliori's interpretation in note to 55d–56e.

56d5 **φιλοσοφούντων** *who is the philosopher.* As, it seems, this is the character with knowledge of how to rule that appears in the *Republic*, not the ignoramus searching for that knowledge who is praised by Socrates in the *Apology*.

56e–59d: ***Relative to their precision, Socrates ranks kinds of expert knowing from dialectic, philosophical mathematics, applied mathematics, the sciences that rely on mathematical expert knowing, and at last the non-mathematical kinds of expert knowing.***

56e1–3 *Of the mathematical disciplines, there are those of philosophers* (56d5–6), *which only compute when it is posited that none of those unboundedly many units differ in the least from any of the others.* Following Grote (1875, 66), interpreters rightly refer to Mill (1872, 170–71):

> In all propositions concerning numbers, a condition is implied, without which none of them would be true; and that condition is an assumption which may be false. The condition is, that 1=1; that all the numbers are numbers of the same or of equal units. Let this be doubtful, and not one of the propositions of arithmetic will hold true. How can we know that one pound and one pound make two pounds, if one of the pounds may be troy, and the other avoirdupois? They may not make two pounds of either, or of any weight . . . All units must be assumed to be equal in that other respect; and this is never accurately true, for one actual pound weight is not exactly equal to another, nor one measured mile's length to another; a nicer balance, or more accurate measuring instruments, would always detect some difference. What is commonly called mathematical certainty, therefore, which comprises the twofold conception of unconditional truth and perfect accuracy, is not an attribute of all mathematical truths, but of those only which relate to pure Number, as distinguished from Quantity in the more enlarged sense.

Mill knew the *Philebus* and may well have had 56d5–e1 in mind as he wrote this passage.

56e3 **θήσει** [*unless*] *one will put* or *one will posit.* This future indicative protasis with its optative apodosis indicates a "mild future," that is, neither emotional/minatory nor potential optative (S §2356a). "The others would have nothing to do with them except on the postulate that none of the myriad units under discussion is in any way different from any of the others" (Gosling 1975).

56e4 **τευταζόντων** Bury (1897) notes a scholiast who gives the meaning: *being employed upon, engaged in, concerned with a thing* plus περὶ plus accusative.

56e5 **δύ' αὐτὰς εἶναι** *that these [arithmetical expertises] are two [stands to reason].* This infinitive clause is the subject of λόγον ἔχειν *stands to reason.*

56e7 **λογιστικὴ καὶ μετρητικὴ** *a logistic skill and a measuring skill [in building and business].* The <ή> is not in manuscripts B or T but is added in manuscript Ven. 189 from a desire to make the noun phrase definite: "*the* logistic," and so on. There is no verb conjugating with this nominative. "A sentence may begin with the nominative as the subject of thought in place of an oblique case" (S §941). Bury (1897) notes this "less common" sort of nominative plus verbal adjective construction occurs also at *Republic* 460b (δοτέον . . . ἀφθονεστέρα ἡ ἐξουσία *more frequent permission . . . one must give*) and *Sophist* 223b (ἡ . . . θήρα προσρητέον . . . σοφιστική *sophistry . . . one must call the hunting [of human beings]*).

57a11 **προβεβληκέναι** *to have thrown X forward* or *to have propounded X.* But what is its direct object *X*? The adverb ἐνταῦθα (*here, there)* rarely might mean *the things here* hence, as Gosling (1975) and others take it, *these considerations,* allowing us to preserve the manuscripts. Gosling notes:

> Others follow Schleiermacher [1809] in reading προβεβηκέναι *to have reached,* in which case the sense is: "It seems to me that in its search for an analogue to the pleasures the discussion has reached this point of enquiring whether . . ." The change, however, seems unnecessary. If it is felt that "these considerations" harks too far back, there are still two possibilities: (1) one could with Stallbaum [1842] cite *Hippias Major* 293d1–4, and claim it as an example of προβάλλειν without an object. (2) One could cite the same passage, claiming that προβάλλειν as well as ἐλεήσας *pitying* takes "inexperience and lack of education" as an object, and say that in the present passage it, as well as ζητῶν *seeking* takes ἀντίστροφον *analogue* as its object. For (1) the translation would be: "It seems to me that the argument, in its search for an analogue to the pleasures, puts one forward by enquiring . . ." I have

preferred to go back to "these considerations" as the object because I think the word in 57a5, προηνεγκάμεθα *we have brought forward* is probably being picked up by προβεβληκέναι—Socrates brings before the meeting what the argument throws before the meeting.

57b6 **ἀνηυρήκειν** *[the argument has attempted—to what?] To have discovered [that one expertise is more clear and another more unclear than another]*. There is no finite verb in this sentence, leading Schütz (cited in Bury 1897) to emend this infinitive to the perfect ἀνηυρήκει and Bury (1897) to the present tense ἀνεύρισκε. These changes are needless, if we suppose that Socrates has interrupted (with Τί οὖν; *To what?*) and completed (with ἀνηυρήκειν *to have discovered*) Protarchus' verb ἐπικεχείρηκεν *[the argument] has attempted.*

57b9 **τινα τέχνην ὡς ὁμώνυμον φθεγξάμενος** *after [the argument] called a particular expertise by a name with two referents ["called it using a homonym"]*.

57b10 **εἰς δόξαν καταστήσας** ὡς μιᾶς *after putting (the name "arithmetic"] into our opining as [a name] of a single [expertise]*. Gosling (1975) puts this into idiomatic English: "giving the impression that it was the name of a single skill."

57c1 **[πάλιν ὡς] δυοῖν** *again [after putting the name "arithmetic" into our thought] as [a name of] two [expertises]*. Gosling (1975) is idiomatic: "and then, suggesting it is the name of two."

57d4 **ὁλκήν** literally: *drawing, dragging*—for example, of hair. Metaphorically: *[skilled in] drawing [words to a false meaning]*.

58a1 **Δῆλον ὁτιὴ πᾶς ἂν τήν γε νῦν λεγομένην γνοίη** *it is clear that anyone might recognize the [power] now under discussion.*

58b3 **ἐναντία τίθεσθαι** *to take an opposite position* (in discussion or in war: ἀντία τὰ ὅπλα ἔθετο *he placed the troops opposite,* Xenophon, *Anabasis* 4.3.26.3; ἐναντία μὲν ἔθετο τὰ ὅπλα *he placed the troops opposite,* Xenophon, *Hellenica* 7.3.9.2–3) Socrates will play on this ambiguity in his reply.

58b4 **αἰσχυνθείς** *feeling ashamed.* Shame would keep Protarchus from saying "weapons," perhaps because, as Frede (1993) notices, "rhetoric persuades and does not use force."

58c1 **διαφέρει τῷ μεγίστη καὶ ἀρίστη**—what to do with the τῷ? One manuscript (Burnet's Ven. 189) = Bury 1897 Ven. Σ) adds εἶναι after ἀρίστη. Paley (1873) takes that infinitive to be understood: *differs in [being] greatest and best.* I propose instead that we treat it as an article-plus-clause construction (S §1153g): *excels in the [title] "greatest and best."*

58c5 **ὅρα – . . . – τὸ καθαρὸν** Burnet (1901) adds the hyphens to indicate that Socrates breaks off his command *to see* for some ten lines until he resumes the thought below at d6. Accordingly, the main sentence (ὅρα . . . τὸ καθαρὸν νοῦ τε καὶ φρονήσεως εἰ ταύτην μάλιστα ἐκ τῶν εἰκότων ἐκτῆσθαι φαῖμεν ἂν ἤ τινα ἑτέραν ταύτης κυριωτέραν ἡμῖν ζητητέον *consider if we might affirm that this [expert knowing] most of all possesses the pure part of awareness and knowing, as seems likely, or we must seek some other [expert knowing] more authoritative than this*) is interrupted by a lengthy parenthetical remark. Frede (1997, 77) suggests that Plato intends Socrates' negligence for the clarity and intelligibility of this "nearly impenetrable [*schwer durchdringbaren*] . . . mammoth, twelve-line sentence" to indicate at the dramatic level his concentration on the nature of the clearest, most intelligible science.

58c6 **τῇ τέχνῃ ὑπάρχειν διδούς** *conceding that it falls to the skill [of that man to be superior in respect of need].* The participle διδούς (*giving* hence *conceding)* here takes an accusative-plus-infinitive complement (LSJ III.2), and the infinitive ὑπάρχειν has an unstated impersonal accusative subject and a dative complement. LSJ (III.1) translates this clause "assigning as a property of [the] art."

58c7 **ᾗ δ' εἶπον ἐγὼ νῦν** = τῇ δὲ πραγματείᾳ ἣν εἶπον ἐγὼ νῦν *but to that discipline that* I *was talking about now.* This phrase correlates with τῇ μὲν . . . τέχνῃ (58c5–6) as the second dative complement of ὑπάρχειν. The dative relative pronoun ᾗ has been attracted into the case of the antecedent τῇ (πραγματείᾳ), which in turn has been omitted, as often happens (S §2522).

59a11 **Τούτων . . . ὧν** = Τούτων ἅ *of these things, which.* It is rare for a nominative relative pronoun to be attracted to the case of the antecedent (S §2523).

59b1 **ἔσχε . . . κατὰ ταὐτὰ** "held according to the same things," *were in the same condition.* I take this to be the familiar Platonic point about the compresence of opposites in perceptible objects, in other words: for a given property P, perceptibles are and are not P. Intelligible objects, in contrast, do "hold in the same way"—that is, for any P, they "unchangingly" are P.

59b4 **ἡντινοῦν** In every case of the twenty-three other occurrences in Plato of this feminine singular accusative pronoun, there is an obvious feminine antecedent. Here there is no obvious antecedent. Now, when the feminine singular dative pronoun ᾗ has no antecedent, it may be an adverb of place, *where* (LSJ I.1). This is why Frede (1993) and Gosling (1975) conjecture that the pronoun ἡντινοῦν refers in the same way to place—namely, the subject area where the labor takes place. But τέχνη has been in the consciousness of the speakers since 58e5 and it might be the implicit antecedent: *with respect to any skill whatsoever.*

59b7 **ἔχουσα** agrees only with ἐπιστήμη not νοῦς. Possibly its sense applies to both, as Gosling (1975) translates ("there is no understanding or branch of knowledge relating to them that has the complete truth"). But more likely its sense applies exactly as the grammar has it: *there is neither awareness about them nor any expert knowing that possesses the most truth.*

59c3 **εἰλικρινές** *unmixed-pure* in contrast to καθαρόν = *cleansed-pure.* "Pure" seems a better English word than "unmixed" to translate εἰλικρινές. The word is coordinated with ἀμείκτοις *unmixed* at 32c7 and with καθαρόν *clean* at 52d7. It refers to the features of being μόνον καὶ ἔρημον *alone and isolated* at 63b8. It is opposed to φαῦλον *base* at 29b7 and is associated with καλῶν *noble* at 30b6.

τὰ ἀεὶ κατὰ τὰ αὐτὰ *the things always according to the same things* or *always in the same way.* On this feature—and the opposite feature of *accepting change*, see, for example, *Phaedo* 78c–d.

59c4 **[δεύτερος]** There is a Greek proverbial expression: δεύτερος πλοῦς "a second sailing," meaning *the next best way* (LSJ δεύτερος A.I) famously used at *Phaedo* 99d and, perhaps echoing that use, above at 19c. Accordingly Schleiermacher (1809), followed by Stallbaum (1842), proposed that δεύτερος is elliptical for δεύτερος πλοῦς. Bury (1897) called this proposal "hardly conceivable," and most translators seem to have followed him in supposing the word δεύτερος must be cut from the text. In defense of Schleiermacher, the literary style of the *Philebus* features many puzzling ellipses (see introduction: Stylistic Ambiguity).

59d4–5 **Ταῦτ' ἄρα ἐν ταῖς περὶ τὸ ὂν ὄντως ἐννοίαις ἐστὶν ἀπηκριβωμένα ὀρθῶς κείμενα καλεῖσθαι.** This sentence has been a tough nut to crack. There are two main problems: what is the complement of the main verb ἐστὶν, and what is the function of the infinitive καλεῖσθαι? Not seeing any solution, Badham (1878), Jackson, and Bury (1897) all proposed emending the text, as in effect do translators who ignore the infinitive καλεῖσθαι (such as Fowler 1925, Gosling 1975, and Frede 1993). Here is my proposal for solving the two problems:

1. Ταῦτ' . . . ἐστὶν ἀπηκριβωμένα *these [names] are exactly fitted.* The perfect participle is often used as a predicate adjective with ἐστὶν (S §2091).
2. ἀπηκριβωμένα . . . καλεῖσθαι *exactly fitted to be given.* When the subject of the passive verb καλεῖσθαι is a person, the verb means *to be called,* but when the subject is a name, the same verb means *to be given* (LSJ II.1, citing Euripides, *Hecuba* 1271: τύμβῳ δ' ὄνομα σῷ κεκλήσεται *a name shall be given to thy tomb*). One might worry that there is no parallel case of the infinitive καλεῖσθαι as complement to the verb ἀπακριβόομαι. But at *Timaeus* 33b7–c1 the verb seems to govern an accusative plus infinitive: λεῖον δὲ δὴ κύκλῳ πᾶν ἔξωθεν αὐτὸ ἀπηκριβοῦτο *outside, he fitted it all [to be] in a circle and smooth.*)

Finally, I take the prepositional phrase to modify κείμενα as follows: ἐν ταῖς περὶ τὸ ὂν ὄντως ἐννοίαις . . . κείμενα *when [these names are] applied or invoked in our reflections about what is really real.* (On κεῖμαι used of names, see LSJ IV.5; on "invoked," see I.3). This produces the following sensible, accurate, and grammatical translation: *These [names: "awareness" and "knowing") are exactly fitted to be given, when used in our reflections about what is really real.*

59d10–e3 Paley (1873) remarks that this sentence provides yet another example of Socrates' "purposely involved style" in this dialogue. As Barbara Jane Hall has pointed out, the speaker's interweavings in the present context are an image of how we make a combined life.

59e2 **ἐξ ὧν ἢ ἐν οἷς δεῖ δημιουργεῖν τι** *out of which* or *in which it is necessary to craft something.* Commentators mainly take the antecedent of both relative pronouns to be ἀλλήλων *pleasure plus knowing*, giving this sense: *out of which, like ingredients, or in which, like an artist's medium, the craft is worked.* As an alternative, one might take the plural antecedent to be the most proximate fitting word, ἡμῖν. Protarchus and Socrates (and the audience and we readers as well) are to craft the product—the best life as a proper mix of the matter—either *out of ourselves* or *in ourselves.*

PART IV. RANKING THE ELEMENTS IN THE MIXED LIFE

1. The answer to the Happiness Question: Knowing ranks after three Forms—Measure, Beauty, and Truth—that capture what is good in the mixed life, ahead of Pleasure.

60a–64b: ***Socrates restates the main structure of the argument of the dialogue. Socrates argues that, for a body possessed by a soul, all forms of knowing but only some forms of pleasure (true and pure pleasures and those of health, temperance, and virtue) may be included in the mix that is the good for such a creature.***

60c2 **Ὧι παρείη τοῦτ' . . . , προσδεῖσθαι . . . δὲ ἔχειν** *[it might be agreed by us that] what this might be present in . . . needs in addition . . . and possesses . . .* The verbs προσδεῖσθαι and ἔχειν are infinitive because they are part of indirect discourse after ἂν συνομολογοῖτο *it might be agreed* at b7–8. The relative clause ᾧ παρείη τοῦτ' *what this might be* *present in* uses an optative because its sense expresses the protasis of a future remote (S §2344): εἴ τινι παρείη τοῦτο *if this were to be present in something.* Although τοῦτ' *this* is the subject of the protasis, the dative relative pronoun Ὧι *in what* gives the implied subject of the protasis. Since there is no particle ἄν in the apodosis προσδεῖσθαι . . . δὲ ἔχειν, this apodosis does not correspond to an optative-plus-ἄν apodosis in direct discourse (S §2611) but regularly corresponds to a present indicative, producing a mixed conditional (S §2355) with the effect of a present general conditional sentence (S §2360a).

60d5 **τῆς αὐτῆς ἰδέας τιθέμενος** *positing that (A, B, C, and D) are of the same character.* This "genitive of classification," as Bury (1897) calls it, is a type of partitive genitive (LSJ τίθημι B.II.4).

61a1–2 **Οὐκοῦν τό γε τέλεον καὶ πᾶσιν αἱρετὸν καὶ τὸ παντάπασιν ἀγαθὸν οὐδέτερον ἂν τούτων εἴη;** *Therefore, the perfect and choiceworthy thing for all, i.e., the wholly good, could be neither of these.* In another context, the neuter singular noun phrase τὸ παντάπασιν ἀγαθὸν *the wholly good* might refer to the form *good itself.* But here that noun phrase is coordinate with οὐδέτερον τούτων *neither of these*—namely, neither to have pleasure without any knowing nor "to have knowing without any pleasure" (ἄνευ πάσης ἡδονῆς φρόνησιν ἔχειν, 60e2). Likewise, in this context τὸ παντάπασιν ἀγαθὸν is *to have the wholly good for a human being*—namely, to have a mix of both pleasure and knowing. Such a mixed life might be appropriate for a human being but might not for a god. It would therefore seem to be too specific to identify with the good itself.

61a4–5 **Τὸ τοίνυν ἀγαθὸν ἤτοι σαφῶς ἢ καί τινα τύπον αὐτοῦ ληπτέον** *then one must either grasp clearly the good or [grasp] some impression of it.* As at a1–2, the context suggests that τὸ ἀγαθόν here is not the form *good itself* but the (wholly) good possession that makes human life go as well as possible. One would have to be godlike to understand *that* possession clearly, as Socrates argues in the *Apology.* Nevertheless, in order to settle the dialogue's question, taken up at 22c8, whether pleasure or knowing wins second prize in the competition, it will be enough to get "a sort of impression" (τινα τύπον) of that possession, as happens at 61b4–64b4: that possession will be a mix of knowing, pleasure, and truth.

61a7 **ὁδὸν μέν τινα ἐπὶ τἀγαθὸν** *a sort of path heading to the good.* The metaphor will recur, the path eventually taking them to the "dwelling" (οἴκησις, 61a9, 64c2) of the good possession.

61a9–b1 **εἴ τίς τινα ἄνθρωπον ζητῶν τὴν οἴκησιν . . . πύθοιτο αὐτοῦ** *if someone, seeking a human being, were to learn his dwelling.* The meaning of the metaphor given in this protasis seems to be: *if the argument, seeking the condition that makes human life truly happy, were to learn the dwelling of that condition* [then it would have a big clue to finding that condition]. This "dwelling," it seems, would be the framework, the "impression" or "outline" (τύπος), referred to at 61a4. The recipe metaphor is one way to see the difference between learning the good possession and learning an outline of it: to learn the good would be to learn the precise recipe, while to learn the outline of the recipe might be to learn only that it contains, say, barley, hops, malt, and water in proper measures, without learning those measures. It will turn out that finding, not entering, the dwelling—that is, learning the outline, not the precise recipe—will be sufficient to settle whether pleasure or knowing wins second prize.

61c1 **εἴτε Διόνυσος εἴτε Ἥφαιστος εἴθ' ὅστις θεῶν** *whether Dionysus or Hephaestus or whoever of gods.* As Diès (1949) observes, Hephaestus acts as cup-bearer to the gods on Olympus (*Iliad* 1.596–600).

61e7–8 **τὸν ἀγαπητότατον βίον ἀπεργασάμενα παρέχειν ἡμῖν** *[sufficient] to completely produce the most beloved life and provide it to us. TLG* finds these two verbs collocated and sharing a direct object in Plato in three other passages (*Euthydemus* 291b6–7; *Timaeus* 89a1; and *Laws* 667d10–e1). In all three cases the deponent ἀπεργασάμενα has its usual active meaning. As an alternative, Delcomminette (2020) translates ἀπεργασάμενα here with a passive meaning ("the ingredients would be sufficiently completed [*accomplies*] to provide us") although not attesting other such instances. Socrates' concern, as shown from the following thought experiment of a person knowing some things but not others, is that the mix be sufficient to produce the best life, not that the ingredients be sufficiently mixed together.

61c5 **μέλιτος [sc., κρήνῃ]** *[to a fountain] of what is sweet as honey.* The verb ἀπεικάζοι regularly takes a dative complement, while the case of μέλιτος is genitive; following Bury (1897), I supply κρηνῃ. According to LSJ (μέλι I.2) the noun μέλιτος can refer in a comparison to "anything sweet." Socrates' simile in the previous line likens Protarchus and himself to οἰνοχόοις τισὶ *wine-pourers,* which requires that the word μέλιτος refers to οἶνος μελιηδὴς *honey-sweet wine*—as opposed to οἶνος αὐστηρός *dry wine.* The standard translation "honey" might suggest that Socrates is speaking here of a wineless mixture: as if in Socrates' image honey is literally flowing from one fountain (despite the problem that honey would dribble, not flow) and water from another. Such an alternative makes pointless Socrates' contrasting adjectives for the fountain of water: νηφαντικὴν καὶ ἄοινον *sobering and wine-free,* since both honey and water are wine-free. There were wineless offerings of such mixes, but they were to chthonic goddesses, and I am unable to find any explanation about how such offerings could fit the context. Moreover, such offerings were not of water and honey but of water and milk sweetened with honey, and the word for that mixture was μελίκρατα *honey-mix* not μελί *honey* (see Jebb 1907, 28). Likewise, there is no way to take the word μέλιτος *of honey* literally in this passage. Either it is a metonym for a wineless *honey-mix* or a simile for *wine sweet as honey.*

61d1 **πρότερον** *before [mixing]:* Socrates is assembling the ingredients before mixing them.

62a7–b2 **κύκλου μὲν καὶ σφαίρας αὐτῆς τῆς θείας τὸν λόγον ἔχων, τὴν δὲ ἀνθρωπίνην ταύτην σφαῖραν καὶ τοὺς κύκλους τούτους ἀγνοῶν, καὶ χρώμενος ἐν οἰκοδομίᾳ καὶ τοῖς ἄλλοις ὁμοίως κανόσι καὶ τοῖς κύκλοις** *and having an account of the [divine] circle [itself] and the divine sphere itself, but being ignorant of this human sphere and these circles, and using in the* same *way in [this human] housebuilding the* other *[divine] straight-edges and circles [despite the fact that, of course, the procedures used in formal geometry and material housebuilding are* not *properly used* *in the same way].* The attributive position of the demonstrative ταύτην is irregular (S §1176). This reading of the somewhat indeterminate Greek has become standard since Hackforth (1939).

62b1 **χρώμενος . . . ὁμοίως κανόσι καὶ τοῖς κύκλοις** While the grammar is straightforward, commentators are unsure how to understand the meaning. One possibility: *using . . . straight edges and circles in the same way* (that is, trying to use perceptible straight edges and circular objects using only knowledge of the intelligible form *straightedge itself* and *circle itself*). Also possible: *using straight edges and circles in the same way* (that is, confusing when to use a circle and when to use a yardstick).

62d4 **Ὁμήρου** *of Homer.* The genitive indicates that Socrates is quoting Homer (*Iliad* 4.453) with the word μισγαγκείας *meeting of waters.*

62d9 **πρῶτον** Socrates proposed this procedure—to mix only pure with pure—at 61e6–7. At 52e and 55c he wants the pure parts of each for a different reason, to judge second prize.

63d5–6 **τὰς ψυχὰς ἐν αἷς οἰκοῦμεν ταράττουσι διὰ μανικὰς ἡδονάς** *[the biggest and most intense pleasures] disorder the souls in which we [kinds of knowing] dwell, on account of [being] manic pleasures.* Editors, including Burnet (1901), emend the text in various ways. Rather than emend, I read διὰ μανικὰς ἡδονάς as an ellipsis for διὰ μανικὰς ἡδονάς [ὄντας]. Likewise, *Statesman* 270a7–8: διὰ δὴ τὸ μέγιστον ὂν *on account of being the biggest.*

63e3 **ἄλλας τε ἡδονὰς ἀληθεῖς καὶ καθαρὰς ἃς εἶπες** *and other pleasures, true and clean, which you spoke of.* Burnet (1901) emends the text: ἀλλ' ἅς τε ἡδονὰς ἀληθεῖς καὶ καθαρὰς [ἃς] εἶπες *but [those] that you called true and clean pleasures.*

63e9–64a3 **ὅτι καλλίστην ἰδόντα καὶ ἀστασιαστοτάτην μεῖξιν καὶ κρᾶσιν, ἐν ταύτῃ μαθεῖν πειρᾶσθαι τί ποτε ἔν τ' ἀνθρώπῳ καὶ τῷ παντὶ πέφυκεν ἀγαθὸν καὶ τίνα ἰδέαν αὐτὴν εἶναί ποτε μαντευτέον** *after (1) seeing whatever [is] a mix and blend most beautiful and freest from factions, (2) to try to learn in this [mix] what is by nature good in a human being and in the universe and (3?) what form one must divine it [namely, the form of this good in the mix] to be.* This speech by the kinds of knowing is a signpost for the reader. It sets out the two (or perhaps three) steps of the ὁδός *path* (61a7) that Socrates and Protarchus are on.

Clearly, they begin to see the mix—the first step—when they begin the mixing with a prayer at 61b11, and they complete this step after they have added all the ingredients into the mix (that is, all the kinds of knowledge, some but not all pleasures, and truth) and are unable to think of additional ingredients (64b5–6). Socrates marks the step as completed when he says that "the argument now appears to be completed" (ὁ νῦν λόγος ἀπειργάσθαι φαίνεται, 64b7–8) and that they stand before the front doors of the good (64c1).

Equally clearly, they begin the second step—trying "to learn in this mix what is by nature good in a human being and in the universe"—when Socrates asks, "What in the mixture is most valued (τιμιώτατον, 64c5)?" And Socrates marks that they have completed the second step with his words σὺν τρισὶ λαβόντες *after grasping the good with three [forms]* at 65a2.

The statement of the third step is ambiguous. Perhaps we make the most sense of the text by taking the καὶ before τίνα ἰδέαν as epexegetic, so that there are only two steps, the second step being stated twice. On this reading, *to try to learn in this mix what is by nature good* is nothing other than *to try to learn what form one must divine it [namely, the form of the good in the mix] to be.* The language of divination (μαντευτέον, 63a3) refers to the result that, in trying to learn what is good in this mix, they were unable to identify or "hunt it down" with a single form and only grasped the target with three forms (65a1–2). Even so, rather than say that there are three goods in the mix, Socrates says we most rightly refer to the target οἷον ἓν *such as one* not such as three. Given such a result—catching the target with three forms but holding it to be such as a one—if we were asked τίνα ἰδέαν αὐτὴν εἶναί *what form it is* (64a2), it seems we cannot give an account of that form but instead only divine it, in some mysterious way speaking of three forms as if one.

The alternative interpretation is that the third step is different from the second. Such a third step cannot be found in the dialogue. One might try to explain the absence of the third step with the last line of the dialogue, when Protarchus says that σμικρὸν ἔτι τὸ λοιπόν *what remains is a small matter* (67b11). The problem with this alternative is that, if *divining what form the good in the mix* is were a small matter, it has already been done: capture that target with three forms and then divine that the three are such as one. If the divination is something more than that—and surely it would be unsatisfactory to expect a rational account of divination—then it does not make sense for Protarchus to call it σμικρὸν *a small matter.* For another possible bit of unfinished business, see note to 11c2.

What is good in the mix for the human being will turn out to be measure, beauty, and truth, not knowing or pleasure. Thus, Socrates can truly say that the good, understood as these three, will be in the mix for the human being and the universe.

64a2 **τίνα ἰδέαν αὐτὴν εἶναί** *what form [one must divine] it to be,* an accusative (αὐτὴν) plus infinitive (εἶναί) plus complement (τίνα ἰδέαν) after μαντευτέον. There is a similar construction at 25b5–6: τὸ δὲ τρίτον . . . τίνα ἰδέαν . . . ἔχειν *what form will we say the third [kind] to have?* An alternative analysis is to take αὐτὴν as intensive: *[one must divine] what a form itself is* or perhaps *what form itself is*—but neither of these translations makes sense in the context. Frede (1993, "to get some vision of the nature of the Good itself"), Migliori (1993), and Gerson (2010, 274, "what the idea of the good itself should be divined to be") translate inaccurately, as if there were a definite article modifying ἰδέαν: αὐτὴν τὴν ἰδέαν τίνα εἶναί, as at *Euthyphro* 6e3–4: Ταύτην τοίνυν με αὐτὴν δίδαξον τὴν ἰδέαν τίς ποτέ ἐστιν *teach me then what this form itself is.*

The antecedent of the pronoun αὐτὴν must be feminine. The nouns μεῖξιν *mix* and κρᾶσιν *blend* are explicit possible antecedents, but an obvious implicit antecedent fits the context better: τὴν ἰδέαν τὴν τοῦ ἔν τ' ἀνθρώπῳ καὶ τῷ παντὶ ἀγαθοῦ *the form of the good in the human being and in the universe.* Socrates in the *Phaedo* is careful to distinguish the forms themselves from the forms in us, speaking, for example, of "not only the *tall itself* . . . but also the *tall in us*" (οὐ μόνον αὐτὸ τὸ μέγεθος . . . ἀλλὰ καὶ τὸ ἐν ἡμῖν μέγεθος, 102d6–7). The *tall itself* eternally is unchanging, while the *tall in us* does change, coming to be and ceasing to be. He appears to observe the same distinction in the *Philebus.*

64a3 **μαντευτέον** *one must divine.* Socrates, in speaking of diviners at 44c5–6, explained that some do not divine by expert knowing, implying that some divination is expert knowing. Socrates refers to his own μαντεία *power of divination* at 66b5 and refers to τῶν ἐν μούσῃ φιλοσόφῳ μεμαντευμένων . . . λόγων *arguments that divine by means of philosophical music* at 67b6, evidently including the arguments of this dialogue. This is how Protarchus and company seem to understand Socrates at 67b8–9: "we all affirm that (they, namely Socrates' arguments) ἀληθέστατα . . . εἰρῆσθαί *have been spoken most truly.*

64b2 **Ὧι μὴ μείξομεν ἀλήθειαν** *what we will not mix truth with.* The future indicative μείξομεν takes μὴ in a relative conditional clause (S §2560). Likewise, Frede (1993) translates as a relative clause ("Wherever we do not mix in truth") while Gosling (1975) translates as a conditional ("If we will not mix truth in with whatever we have in hand").

Although Socrates explains why truth must be added to the mix (64a7–b3), the reasoning is not obvious, and scholars have proposed alternative explanations. No doubt it will strike many readers as strange that Plato makes truth an *ingredient* in the mix. But it is an ingredient in the sense established at 27b1–2—namely, *an object of a craftworking skill.* It is not clear to me if Delcomminette (2006, 557; cf. Boussoulas [1952, 149n1]) agrees when he says that "the 'adding' of truth must without doubt be understood as the emphasis [*la mise en évidence*] of an essential aspect of the mix that we have obtained."

Horn (1893), quoted in Bury (1897, 208), raises an objection to Plato: there is no further need to add truth to the mix, because we have already added truth in adding "true knowledge and true pleasure" (*wahre Erkenntniss und wahre Lust*). Bury (1897, 208) rightly replies that "it is one thing to have [truth in] the constituent *elements* . . . and quite another to have truth in the mixture itself as a *process.*" Friedländer (1969, 347) and (Dixsaut 2003, 256) follow Bury (1897).

Rodier (1900, 296) and Hackforth (1945, 132–33) give an alternative translation of ἀλήθεια as "reality" (*la réalité*). Such a translation leads Rodier to this interpretation: without reality, the mix "would lack [*manquerait*] an essential condition of being good"—"a sort of ontological argument." Hackforth is similar: "It is Plato's way of expressing his hope and faith that the kind of life indicated is no impossible ideal, and his recognition that unless it is so all his labour in the dialogue has been vain" (1945, 133).

Migliori (1993, 305–6) rightly rejects this alternative translation on the grounds that the dialogue has used the word ἀλήθεια to refer not to *reality* but to *an accurate correspondence between representation and reality* at 39a and to refer not to reality but to *the accuracy of knowing* at 59a–b, so that it would be "a misleading simplification" (*una lettura elementare e fuorviante*) to translate ἀλήθεια as "reality" here. Migliori's explanation about why truth is added is that Plato must "emphasize that [the being of the good] is a principle provided with epistemological value," in addition to the ontological and axiological values it already carries (1993, 306). There is a seeming problem with Migliori's explanation. The mix being produced is a good life, neither a mental representation like a painting nor a kind of knowing. Hence, it cannot be true in the standard epistemological sense of correspondence of representation to reality. Nonetheless, when craftworking skill produces a mix that comes to be, that mix will possess a more or less accurate correspondence of *product* to whatever *paradigm* the maker used. Thus Hackforth (1945, 139, followed by, e.g., Davidson 1990, 231) interprets truth here as "truth to type." As Hackforth sees it, this is Bury's (1897, 204) interpretation. Likewise, Frede (1997, 356): "Truth functions as one of the most important criteria in judging pleasure and knowing. If it is mentioned again specifically as a requirement for the mixtures themselves, this is presumably not only because its elements must fulfill the condition of truth, but also because only a successful [*geglückte*] mixture is a genuine [i.e., true] mixture." Moreover, in defense of Migliori's seemingly problematic claim of an *epistemological* value, I point out that for Plato the relation of product to paradigm *is* epistemological: the product represents the paradigm, and the product provides us with a kind of knowing, albeit an imperfect one, of the paradigm, as Plato says at *Republic* 505e–506a. Shadow (or painted) images share with physical objects the "comparative clearness and obscurity" (509d9) that characterize representations, and thus both possess "truth" (510a9), albeit in different degrees, in how clearly they give us knowing of what they represent. Having defended the Davidson/Frede true-to-type interpretation and having made the true-to-type relation out to be epistemological, I would also point out how this interpretation connects to the actual reasons (at 64a7–b3) that Plato uses to establish that truth must be added to the mix. Here I follow Damascius (1959, §236.1–3, 12–13): "Truth [i.e., truth to type] makes each thing *only* and *wholly* what it is, so that it is not a mere appearance [εἴδωλον] and not intermixed with something else [τινὶ ἑτέρῳ συμμεμιγμένον]," and hence "preserves the fullness [πλήρωσιν] of each thing."

64b6–7 **καθαπερεὶ κόσμος τις ἀσώματος ἄρξων καλῶς ἐμψύχου σώματος** *just as if a certain bodiless order, that is going to beautifully rule an ensouled body.* The noun phrase ἐμψύχου σώματος refers to τ' ἀνθρώπῳ καὶ τῷ παντὶ *both a human being and the universe* (64a1–2: at 29b–30d Socrates argued that the universe is an ensouled body). The nominative case of the noun phrase κόσμος τις ἀσώματος *a certain bodiless order* indicates that the likeness indicated by the adverb καθαπερεὶ is to ὁ νῦν λόγος *the present argument.* This gives us three elements of an analogy: as a bodiless order rules an ensouled body, so the present argument rules some fourth item, which I interpret to be ὁ νοῦς *the awareness* that apprehends this argument. Such an analogy produces an elegant hierarchy. In the first place, the formal argument rules over an awareness of that argument just as the good order of a soul rules over the body of that soul. In addition, the awareness will rule over the good order of the soul possessing that awareness.

As an alternative, Bury (1897) completes the analogy by interpreting the argument to rule over the σύγκρασις *mixture* mentioned at b5. Frede (1993) freely translates: "our discussion has arrived at the design of what might be called an incorporeal order that rules harmoniously over a body possessed by a soul." This translation identifies the argument's "design"—namely, the outline of the mixture—with the ruling order, which is unsatisfactory. It would not be the outline of the mixture but the precise mixture itself that would rule an organism. Moreover, the mixture is a possession of the organism, like its life. Such a possession, containing pleasures, is the wrong sort of thing to be the ruling element.

64b7–8 **ὁ νῦν λόγος ἀπειργάσθαι φαίνεται** *the present argument appears to have been completed.* The νῦν λόγος *present account* must refer to the account of the mixed life that is superior to unmixed pleasure or unmixed knowing as a life. As instances of the sorts of knowing described at 63e9, Socrates and company now have seen the καλλίστην καὶ ἀστασιαστοτάτην μεῖξιν καὶ κρᾶσιν *mixture and blend most beautiful and freest from factions.* There will be further argument in the remainder of the dialogue in order to determine if knowing or pleasure is closer to first prize in their competition—that is, to answer the Happiness Question raised at the beginning of the dialogue.

64b9 **δεδόχθαι** impersonal perfect infinitive passive δοκέω *[it] to have seemed* (LSJ II.4.b). There is a parallel use of this impersonal in an (implied accusative) plus infinitive construction at Xenophon, *Hellenica* 5.3.23.4.

64c1–3 **Ἆρ' οὖν ἐπὶ μὲν τοῖς τοῦ ἀγαθοῦ νῦν ἤδη προθύροις [καὶ] τῆς οἰκήσεως ἐφεστάναι [τῆς τοῦ τοιούτου] λέγοντες ἴσως ὀρθῶς ἄν τινα τρόπον φαῖμεν;** *Then perhaps we would be speaking in some way rightly in saying that we stand now on the portico of the good and of the dwelling [of the thing that is such as the good].* The etymological meaning of προθύροις is *before doors,* and the word refers to the front entrance of a dwelling grand enough to possess double doors: a covered front porch or "portico." The portico-of-a-dwelling metaphor brings to completion the first step of the path-to-a-dwelling metaphor begun at 61a7–b1 and signposted at 63e9–64a3. Since it is the same metaphor, τοῦ ἀγαθοῦ *the good* here, as earlier, is the good in a human life—that is, the possession that makes human life truly happy (see notes to 61a1–2, 61a4–5, and 61a7). It is this clarification that Socrates seems to make with the epexegetic καὶ, coordinating τοῦ ἀγαθοῦ *the good* with τῆς οἰκήσεως τῆς τοῦ τοιούτου *the dwelling of the thing that is such [as the good].* The τοιούτου *thing that is such as the good*, then, is the possession that makes human life truly happy, and from the portico they can see the *dwelling*—that is, framework (see note to 61a9–b1)—of that good in a human life, but they are not in view of it.

As an alternative to my translation—*of the good and of the dwelling of the thing that is such [as the good]*—Frede (1993) translates: "of the good and of the house of every member of its family." This translation is less accurate, but it allows Frede to interpret the dwelling to be the kind containing good objects rather than an outline of the precise recipe for the good in a human life. Such an interpretation of the dwelling as the kind leaves unclear how one can see the kind without seeing the members of that kind.

Burnet's (1901) alternative is to cut the bracketed words from the text. If we follow Burnet, we get *of the dwelling of the good,* which is Gosling's (1975) reading, "of where the good is to be found."

64c1 **μὲν** with no answering δέ clause, called μέν *solitarium,* is used in contrast with something that the speaker does not "intend to express in words" (Denniston 1966, 380). Located within the prepositional phrase ἐπὶ τοῖς προθύροις *on the portico,* the unstated δέ clause might be *on the portico but not inside the dwelling in view of the good in a human life.* As other instances of μέν *solitarium* in Plato, Denniston cites *Charmides* 154a3, *Theaetetus* 148d3, and *Republic* 453c7 and 557c7.

64c–67a: ***Socrates answers the Happiness Question in the terms developed in the course of the discussion. Neither pleasure nor knowing but a mixed life is the good for human beings. What makes that mixed life good is its possession of measure, beauty, and truth. The kind Knowing is more akin to this good than Pleasure in being far more measured, beautiful, and true.***

At 66a6–8, b1–3, b5–6, b8–c2, and c4–6 Socrates argues for the following numerical ranking: *In the mixture that is a human life, the first rank goes to the effect of measure (namely, being measured and timely), second rank to the effect of measure and beauty (namely, being complete and sufficient), third to the effect of measure, beauty, and truth (namely, the power of knowing and awareness), fourth to the effects of knowing in the soul (namely, the sciences and kinds of expertise), and fifth to the effects of activities of science and expertise (namely, pleasures that are free of pain).* Pleasures of health and temperance are necessary for a good life (62e8–10) and therefore extrinsically good. They are excluded from this five-part ranking because, unlike pure pleasures, they are not intrinsically good.

I interpret the argument for this proposition as follows (square brackets enclose unstated premises):

P1 The good is a trinity of three forms—[in rank order:] *measure, beauty,* and *truth*—explaining why mixtures are [measured, beautiful, and true] and therefore good (65a1–5).

Because:

P1.1 Measure is the most valuable thing in any mixture and the ultimate cause why the occurrence of any such condition is loved by human beings (64c5–7).

P1.1.1 Because without measure, that is, the nature of symmetry, every mixture will necessarily destroy its ingredients and first of all itself (64d9–11).

P1.1.1.1 Because there would be no blending in such cases but in truth an unblended jumble that will be a real disaster for anything caught up in it (64d11–e3).

P1.2 [Beauty is second in causal or explanatory order after measure.]

Because:

P1.2.1 Measuredness—that is, symmetry—everywhere turns out to be beauty and excellence (64e6–7).

[P1.2.2 To constitute something is to be prior in causal or explanatory order.][11]

P1.3 Truth is mixed into the blend with them (measure and beauty) (64e9–10).

Because:

[P1.3.1 Nothing other than measure and beauty could cause truth to be in the mixture.]

P2 Knowing is more akin to the highest good and of more intrinsic value than pleasure (65a7–b2).

P2.1 Because knowing is more akin to truth, measure, and beauty than pleasure (65b5–9).

11. I supply this premise to make explicit that "constitutes" (or whatever verb one uses to translate συμβαίνει γίγνεσθαι, 64e7) entails causal or explanatory priority. With P1.2.1, this premise establishes P1.2. The premise is most plausible when we interpret beauty as "the complete and sufficient" (τὸ τέλεον καὶ ἱκανὸν, 66b2) in the mixture, as I do below, since it is by being measured that a mix is complete and sufficient both in its elements and for its purpose.

Because:

P2.1.1 Knowing is more akin to truth than pleasure (65c2–3).

Because:

P2.1.1.1 Pleasure is the greatest impostor of all, by general account, and in connection with the pleasures of love, which seem to be the greatest of all, even perjury is pardoned by the gods, as if pleasures were like children, as mindless as possible (65c5–d2).

P2.1.1.2 Knowing either is the same as truth or of all things it is most like it and most true (65d2–3).

P2.1.2 Knowing is more akin than pleasure to measure (65d4–6).

Because:

P2.1.2.1 Nothing is more outside all measure than pleasure and excessive joy (65d8–9).

P2.1.2.2 Nothing is more measured than being aware and expert knowing (65d9–10).

P2.1.3 Being aware is more akin than pleasure to beauty (65e1–3).

Because:

P2.1.3.1 No one, awake or dreaming, past, present or future, could ever see awareness and knowing to be ugly (65e4–7).

P2.1.3.2 When we see anyone actively engaged in pleasures, especially those that are most intense, we notice that their effect is quite ridiculous, if not outright obscene; we become quite ashamed ourselves and hide them as much as possible from sight, and we confine such activities to the night, as if daylight must not witness such things (65e9–66a3).

There are a number of questions about this ranking.

1. Why does Plato provide a numerical ranking?
2. Is Plato consistent in his first three ranks? (a) In particular, is symmetry of the first or second rank? (b) And does the third rank belong to truth or to knowing and mental awareness?
3. Why does Plato list the good as a trinity of ingredients?
4. Why does he list the ingredients in the order he does?

5. What is the relation between the first three ranks—the trinity of the good—and the fourth and fifth ranks?

I propose answers to these questions and consider a few alternative interpretations in this note.

1. Why does Plato provide a numerical ranking?

I endorse the answer given by Delcomminette (2006, 620):

> If the conflict between pleasure and knowing had been resolved in the terms in which it had been introduced [11d–12a] . . . nothing [would be] good in itself; a particular thing or action [*telle ou telle chose ou action*] could only be said to be more or less good than some other such particular. This is why it is essential to replace that contrariety of more and less by determinate relations that allow us to locate the terms in relation to each other without in so doing to throw them back into indeterminacy. It is only on that condition that these terms may be joined together to form a harmonious whole . . . This is the goal of the final scale of goods [proposition 151 = 66a6–8], which, thanks to the notion of *number* . . . will determine the rank that each of the goods must occupy within the good life so that it might be a harmonious whole.

2a. Is Plato consistent in his first three ranks? In particular, is symmetry of the first *or* second *rank?*

The dialogue gives four different statements pertaining to the first three ranks. Socrates first states the trinity at 65a2: "We grasp the good with three forms, *beauty* and *symmetry* and *truth* [κάλλει καὶ συμμετρίᾳ καὶ ἀληθείᾳ]." Second, Protarchus tentatively restates this trinity at 65b8 as "beauty, truth, and measuredness [κάλλους καὶ ἀληθείας καὶ μετριότητος]"—a restatement that Socrates endorses as correct (65b10). Third, they use the trinity as criteria for a comparison of pleasure and knowing: truth (ἀληθείας, 65b10), measuredness (μετριότητα, 65d4), and beauty (κάλλους, 65e3). Fourth, they explicitly rank the three: "First about measure [πρῶτον μέν πῃ περὶ μέτρον, 66a6] . . . second about symmetry and beauty [δεύτερον μὴν περὶ τὸ σύμμετρον καὶ καλὸν, 66b1], and if you put knowing and awareness third you would not stray very far from the truth [or from truth] [τὸ τοίνυν τρίτον, ὡς ἡ ἐμὴ μαντεία, νοῦν καὶ φρόνησιν τιθεὶς οὐκ ἂν μέγα τι τῆς ἀληθείας παρεξέλθοις, 66b5–6]." The four statements seem to be inconsistent. For the first statement (65a2) to be consistent with the restatement (65b8) and the criterial statement (65b–e), symmetry and measuredness must denote the *numerically same* element of the trinity: call it "measure." But measure and symmetry appear to be *numerically distinct,* ranked first and second, in the explicit ranking (66a–b).

To resolve this inconsistency, I propose the following interpretation. The key is the distinction between cause and effect implied by the mixing metaphor. In cooking, for example, there is a difference between the *ingredient* used by the chef, say *sugar,* and the effect of that ingredient in the cooked product, *sugared*. The ingredient sugar is not the sugared product but the cause of it. Just so, Socrates marks this distinction between the *cause* (αἰτίαν) of value, measure, and the *mixtures* that come to be valuable (64d3–4). In Socrates' terms, mixtures that come to be "have a share of" (μετείληφε) the ingredients that cause them, just as awareness "got a share of beauty (κάλλους μετείληφε) so as to be beautiful" (65e1–3). Socrates also marks the distinction by referring to the causally prior ingredients—say measure, beauty, and truth—as three "forms" (ἰδέαι, see also 65a2), while referring to their effects—say measured, beautiful, and true—as "properties" (see also κτῆμα, 66a5) of the mixed product. The same sort of distinction between forms as causes and their effects in the things that come to be is also in the *Phaedo,* drawn for example between "the opposite thing that comes to be" and "the opposite itself" (103b3–4).

I use this distinction between ingredient cause and effected property to provide an accurate translation of the explicit ranking at 66a–b, a translation that avoids attributing inconsistency to Plato's ranking. In the explicit ranking, the statement of the first rank is parallel to the statement of what is *not* of the first rank: "Pleasure is not a property first [in rank]" (ἡδονὴ κτῆμα οὐκ ἔστι πρῶτον, 66a5–6). Rather (supplying the unstated parallels): "The measured and timely [are properties] first [in rank] [πρῶτον μέν . . . καὶ τὸ μέτριον καὶ καίριον], and whatever we must suppose to be such [καὶ πάντα ὁπόσα χρὴ τοιαῦτα νομίζειν, 66a6–8].” The grammatical subject of this statement is “the measured and timely and whatever we must suppose to be such.” The grammatical subject is modified by a prepositional phrase: “somehow about measure” (πῃ περὶ μέτρον). The adverb “somehow” (πῃ) and the preposition “about” (περὶ) with its object, as here, in the accusative case imply as their basic meaning *motion that takes place round about, in some way,* the object. In context the motion is the coming to be of certain properties of the mixed life. I propose that “somehow round about” means in this context *as the effect of* the object. These properties that have come into being as the effect of measure are *the measured* and *the timely* and suchlike—just as *the sugared* comes to be in cooking as an effect of the causal ingredient sugar. Thus, there is a distinction in this statement of the first rank between the causally prior ingredient *measure*, marked as the object of the preposition περὶ, and its effect in the mixture that comes to be, *the measured and timely and suchlike.*

Socrates marks the same distinction with the same preposition in the statement of the second rank, again in parallel. “As the effect of [both] symmetry and beauty, the complete and sufficient [are properties] second [in rank], and whatever is of this family” (δεύτερον μὴν περὶ τὸ σύμμετρον καὶ καλὸν καὶ τὸ τέλεον καὶ ἱκανὸν καὶ πάνθ’ ὁπόσα τῆς γενεᾶς αὖ ταύτης ἐστίν, 66b1–3). By observing this distinction with an accurate translation, I avoid attributing inconsistency to Plato. It is undeniable that for the first statement 65a2 to be consistent with the restatement 65b8 and the criterial statement 65b–e, symmetry and measuredness must denote the *numerically same* element of the trinity: call it *measure.* However, I avoid the contradiction because symmetry is *not* ranked second at 66b1–3. The *complete* and the *sufficient* and suchlike—in a word, the *beautiful*—are ranked second. The beautiful is second because it is the effect of *both* symmetry (i.e., measure) *and* beauty. The beautiful in the mixed life is the effect of beauty in precisely the same way that the measured in that life is the effect of measure. The beautiful is *also* the effect of measure because beauty itself is causally posterior in some way to measure, as stated above at P1.2. Nothing in this statement of the second rank entails the inconsistency that symmetry (i.e., measure) is *numerically distinct* from measure in the ranking.

It is a consequence of my interpretation that the ranking is not a ranking of the ingredient causes measure, beauty, and the rest but of what comes to be as their effect in the mixed life: first the measured, second the beautiful, and so on. This consequence will also provide an answer to questions about the ranks further below.

The standard alternative translation and interpretation has its modern origin in Maguire (1874, 442). This alternative ignores the distinction within the first two ranks between *ingredient cause* and *effect that comes to be in the mix,* translating both alike as objects of the preposition περὶ. Likewise, Maguire 1874 translates πρῶτον μέν πῃ περὶ μέτρον καὶ τὸ μέτριον καὶ καίριον καὶ πάντα ὁπόσα χρὴ τοιαῦτα νομίζειν (66a6–8) as "the first (possession) in a manner has to do with Regulation and with that which is submitted to Regulation and has (thereby) become suitable to something and (has to do with) all things of such a kind," a translation quoted and followed by Bury (1897, 171), followed in turn by Hackforth (1945, 139–40), Diès (1949, 90–91), Gosling (1975, 70), Waterfield (1982, 147), Hampton (1990, 85), and Benardete (1993, 83). Frede (1993, 81) is ambiguous in her translation of the first rank: "First comes what is somehow connected with measure, the measured and the timely." This translation leaves open, just as the Greek leaves open, whether the noun phrase "the measured and timely" is in apposition to the noun "measure" or to the noun phrase "what is somehow connected with measure." Unfortunately she does not extend the ambiguity to her translation of the second rank: "The second rank goes to the well-proportioned and beautiful, the perfect, the self-sufficient." This sort of translation leads her (1997, 362) to make measure (*Maß*) and symmetry (*Maßhaftes*) numerically distinct—as Gadamer does (1991, 211). Likewise, neither Frede's nor Gadamer's interpretations avoid inconsistency. Migliori (1993, 315) correctly makes the causal distinction at the first rank but fails to do so at the second rank. "The first is in the vicinity of measure, whereby [*di ciò che*] it is measured and appropriate . . . The second rank lies in that which is in the vicinity of the proportionate [*proporzionato*], beautiful, complete, sufficient." This translation leads him, too, to affirm that measure and symmetry are numerically distinct ("*occupano due posti separati*," 316). Most recently, Delcomminette (2006, 622) likewise misses the distinction in describing "at the first rank, measure in [*sous*] its different forms: μέτρον, μέτριον, καίριον." The standard alternative appears to go back to the ancient commentators. For example, Syrianus puts measure in the first rank and symmetry in the second rank (Damascius 1959, note to §§253–54). I reject this standard alternative on the grounds that it must attribute inconsistency to Plato's ranking. (There are other alternative interpretations to other aspects of this passage. See Bury [1897, 169–78] and Gosling [1975, 137–38] for discussion.)

2b. *Is Plato consistent in his first three ranks? In particular, does the third rank belong to truth or to knowing and awareness?*

As I pointed out above, the dialogue gives four different statements pertaining to the first three ranks. In the first statement (65a2), the restatement (65b8), and the criterial statement (65b–e), the third element is truth. But in the explicit ranking (66a–b) knowing and awareness are mentioned as "not far from the truth [or from truth]." Does Plato assign the third rank to truth or not? The distinction between *ingredient cause* and *effect that comes to be in the mix* provides an answer to this question as well. *Truth* is the ingredient cause and its effect is that the mix is *true to type* (see note to 64b2). The mix here is the human life, which is a type of life characterized by the leading powers of the human rational soul, namely knowing and awareness. I take it that premise P2.1.1.2 = 65d2–3 is Protarchus' attempt to describe the causal relation between truth and knowing. As above, the ranking is not a ranking of the ingredient causes measure, beauty, truth, and the rest but of what comes to be as their effect in the mixed life: first the measured, second the beautiful, and third truth, which causes knowing and awareness.

3. *Why does Plato describe the good as a trinity of these ingredients: measure, beauty, and truth?*

   I endorse Delcomminette's answer to this question: "The good appeared in the division of pleasure via the dialectical difference between good (pure) and bad (impure) pleasures. This difference was precisely identified with the characteristics of measure [52c3–4] and beauty and truth [53b10–c2]" (Delcomminette 2006, 588). Likewise, in the discussion of knowing, measure's effects—arithmetic, measurement, and weighing—appeared as the ruling element of any expertise (55e1–3), while beauty and truth's effects—coming to be beautiful and true—appear at 58a3–6 and 59c8–d6.

4. *Why does Plato list the three in this order?*

   Although each of the three—measure, beauty, and truth—mutually require the others and hence are each complete, there is a causal or explanatory priority among them. Measure is the ultimate cause (P1.1 = 64c5–7). To be measured turns out to be what beauty is (P1.2.1 = 64e6–7). Beauty and measure are explanatorily prior to truth in the mixture (64e9–10).

5. *What is the relation between the first three ranks—the trinity of the good—and the fourth and fifth ranks?*

   The relationship of cause and effect continues into the fourth and fifth ranks. As shown above, the third rank belongs to the effect of truth on the mix, that effect being the leading powers of the human rational soul, knowing and awareness. The effects of these powers in the human soul are the activities of science, expertise, and true thought. In Socrates' words, "Fourth, those [activities] we assigned to the soul itself, called sciences, expertises, and true thoughts" (66b8–9). Likewise, the pain-free pleasures are effects in the soul of cognitive activities, including perception: "Fifth, what we defined as pain-free pleasures of the soul itself . . . consequences of scientific activities and perceptions" (66c4–6).

64c5–9 **τί δῆτα ἐν τῇ συμμείξει τιμιώτατον ἅμα καὶ μάλιστ᾽ αἴτιον εἶναι δόξειεν ἂν ἡμῖν τοῦ πᾶσιν γεγονέναι προσφιλῆ τὴν τοιαύτην διάθεσιν; τοῦτο γὰρ ἰδόντες μετὰ τοῦτ᾽ ἐπισκεψόμεθα εἴθ᾽ ἡδονῇ εἴτε τῷ νῷ προσφυέστερον καὶ οἰκειότερον ἐν τῷ παντὶ συνέστηκεν** (1) *What, then, in the mix might seem to us to be the most precious and at the same time most of all cause why such an ordered condition is beloved by all? After seeing this,* (2) *we will then consider whether it is more closely attached and more akin to pleasure or to awareness in the universe.* This question and announcement are signposts.

The double question—"What is most precious and the cause of this mix's being beloved?"—announces the next step of the inquiry, a step foretold in the speech by the kinds of knowing: after seeing the most beautiful mix, ἐν ταύτῃ μαθεῖν πειρᾶσθαι τί ποτε ἔν τ᾽ ἀνθρώπῳ καὶ τῷ παντὶ πέφυκεν ἀγαθὸν *to try to learn from it what is by nature good in a human being and in the universe* (see note to 63e9–64a3). Socrates will state the answer to this question at 65a1–5. Note that the discussion continues to be about the good in a human being and in the universe. Accordingly, references in this discussion to *measure, beauty,* and *truth* are to those forms in us and in the universe, not to these forms in themselves.

The announcement tells what step the argument will take (at 65a7–66a3) after the attempt to learn this good.

64d9–11 **Ὅτι μέτρου καὶ τῆς συμμέτρου φύσεως μὴ τυχοῦσα ἡτισοῦν καὶ ὁπωσοῦν σύγκρασις πᾶσα ἐξ ἀνάγκης ἀπόλλυσι τά τε κεραννύμενα καὶ πρώτην αὑτήν** *Because without measure, that is, the nature of symmetry, every mixture of any sort will necessarily destroy its ingredients and first of all itself.* In order to get a consistent ranking (see note to 64c–67a), I translate the καὶ in μέτρου καὶ τῆς συμμέτρου φύσεως as epexegetic—"measure, *that is,* the nature of symmetry"—rather than as a conjunction of two numerically distinct ingredients.

μὴ is here used with a participle since it can be resolved into a conditional clause (LSJ B.6).

64e2 **τοῖς κεκτημένοις** *for the possessors.* Frede (1993) freely interprets these owners to be the components of the mixture: "whatever happens to be contained in it." Gosling (1975) is ambiguous: "whatever is afflicted by it." Frede (1997) is accurate: "Besitzern" *owners,* as is Delcomminette (2020): "ceux qui la possèdent" *those who possess it.*

64e5 **ἡμῖν** *for us* is a dative of interest ("of advantage or disadvantage") with a verb of fleeing (S §1483). The attempt to hunt down and capture the good by means of measure alone has failed. See note to 65a1, where the hunting metaphor continues.

64e6–7 **μετριότης γὰρ καὶ συμμετρία κάλλος δήπου καὶ ἀρετὴ πανταχοῦ συμβαίνει γίγνεσθαι** *measuredness—that is, symmetry—everywhere turns out to be beauty and excellence.* In order to get a consistent ranking (see note to 64c–67a), I translate the καὶ in μετριότης καὶ συμμετρία as epexegetic ("measuredness—*that is,* symmetry") rather than as a conjunction of two numerically distinct ingredients. On δήπου, see note to 12c7–8.

64e9–10 **ἀλήθειάν . . . αὐτοῖς ἐν τῇ κράσει μεμεῖχθαι** *Truth is mixed into the blend with them [namely, measure and beauty].*

65a1–5 **εἰ μὴ μιᾷ δυνάμεθα ἰδέᾳ τὸ ἀγαθὸν θηρεῦσαι, σὺν τρισὶ λαβόντες, κάλλει καὶ συμμετρίᾳ καὶ ἀληθείᾳ, λέγωμεν ὡς τοῦτο οἷον ἓν ὀρθότατ' ἂν αἰτιασαίμεθ' ἂν τῶν ἐν τῇ συμμείξει, καὶ διὰ τοῦτο ὡς ἀγαθὸν ὂν τοιαύτην αὐτὴν γεγονέναι.** *If we are not able to hunt down the good [in the mix] with one form, then, while grasping [it] with three [forms]—*measure, beauty, *and* truth*—let us say that of the things in the mix we would most correctly hold this [good], as it were a one, as the cause, and [say] that on account of this, since it is good, [the mixture] has come to be such [as the good in it].* The sentence hypothetically exhorts us to say something. The hypothesis is our inability to say what the good in the mix is in terms of one form, while we are in the circumstance of having grasped what it is in terms of three forms. The exhortation is to make a statement of cause and effect. That statement is reported twice in indirect discourse after λέγωμεν, first as a ὡς clause and then as an accusative-plus-infinitive construction. The main verb of the ὡς clause, a verb of holding responsible or imputing cause (ἂν αἰτιασαίμεθα), is optative in mood. The optative verb is limited by the superlative adverb ὀρθότατα *most correctly.* The optative with adverb (*we would most correctly hold . . .*

as cause) has the force of a conditional: *if we were to impute cause most correctly, we would hold this good as cause* (S §1825). Following Fowler (1925), I take the partitive genitive τῶν ἐν τῇ συμμείξει *of the things in the mix* limits τοῦτο *this*. This ὡς clause answers the question asked at 64c5–7: τί δῆτα ἐν τῇ συμμείξει τιμιώτατον ἅμα καὶ μάλιστ᾽ αἴτιον εἶναι δόξειεν ἂν ἡμῖν τοῦ πᾶσιν γεγονέναι προσφιλῆ τὴν τοιαύτην διάθεσιν *what, then, in the mix might seem to us to be the most precious and at the same time most of all cause why such an ordered condition is beloved by all?* The καὶ introducing the accusative-plus-infinitive construction is epexegetic, since that construction answers the same question in other words: διὰ τοῦτο ὡς ἀγαθὸν ὂν τοιαύτην αὐτὴν γεγονέναι *on account of this [namely, the good in the mix], since it is good, it [namely, the mix] has become such [as the good in it].* While there may be other reasons we might correctly identify as to why the mixed life is good, the sentence exhorts us to say that we will *most correctly* identify the cause of this effect to be the good in the mix. The exhortation is qualified by the condition that we were not able to say what that good is by means of a single form, while we did grasp it with the help of three forms—*measure, beauty,* and *truth.* Accepting the conditional grasping, we might suppose that the cause is three things. But the sentence tells us that we ought not to refer to the cause as three things but "as it were a one" (οἷον ἕν).

65a1 **εἰ μὴ μιᾷ δυνάμεθα ἰδέᾳ τὸ ἀγαθὸν θηρεῦσαι** *if we are not able to hunt down the good with one form.* As Bury (1897) notices, to try to capture the object of inquiry μιᾷ ἰδέᾳ *with one form* recalls the description of the divine method at 16d1–2: ἀεὶ μίαν ἰδέαν περὶ παντὸς ἑκάστοτε θεμένους ζητεῖν—εὑρήσειν γὰρ ἐνοῦσαν *having posited in each case one form always for everything, to search for it—for [it is needful] that we shall find [it] present in [them].*

The metaphors of hunting down (θηρεῦσαι) and catching (λαβόντες) τὸ ἀγαθὸν *the good* continue the metaphor of ἡ τοῦ ἀγαθοῦ δύναμις *the power of the good* fleeing for refuge (καταπέφευγεν, see note to 64e5). 64e5 tells us that we cannot capture the good with the single form *measure*; we likewise cannot capture the good either with the single form *beauty* or the single form *truth.* Of course, the first wave of single-formed candidates—pleasure and knowing—also failed to capture the good, as shown at 20b–21c. If it is the same hunt now as earlier, then it must be the same target, and that target has never been the good itself but always the good in a human being and in the universe. This is a problem for Delcomminette's alternative interpretation, that this clause is evidence that "the investigation of the *Philebus* has succeeded in providing what the *Republic* denied us: the *logos* of the good" (Delcomminette 2006, 586), since that good in the *Republic* is the good itself. Another interpretation of 65a1–7 denies that "form" here refers to a Platonic Form (for example, Festugière [1950, 311n9], who leaves the reasons for this thesis unstated).

65a2 **σὺν τρισὶ λαβόντες, κάλλει καὶ συμμετρίᾳ καὶ ἀληθείᾳ** *after grasping [the good] with three [forms]—measure, beauty,* and *truth.* The verb of grasping is modified by a prepositional phrase σὺν τρισὶ *with three.* The preposition σύν *in company with,* here has a "collateral notion of help or aid," as in the expression σὺν θεῷ *with God's help* (LSJ σύν A.2) and is equivalent to a dative of means (LSJ σύν A.7), coordinate with the dative of means μιᾷ ἰδέᾳ at a1. Gosling (1975) inaccurately makes the "trio" the thing *grasped* rather than the things *with which* the good is grasped. Frede (1993) does better to translate σὺν τρισὶ as an adverbial prepositional phrase. But her translation, "in a conjunction of three," suggests that σύν with a plural object τρισὶ means that the three are *thought of as singular* (OED, "in" I.3), likewise Frede (1997): "in a threefold form" (*in dreifacher Gestalt*—an unattested meaning for σύν with a plural). The addition of the singular noun—"conjunction" or "*Gestalt*"—is not required in this passage and seems inadvisable in a dialogue that pays careful attention to the metaphysical differences between one and many (although sometimes Socrates does appear indifferent to singular versus plural expressions, as, for example, when he uses a plural noun phrase τὰ παθήματα *the feelings* at 39a2 as the antecedent of the singular pronominal phrase τοῦτο τὸ πάθημα *this feeling* at 39a4). The direct object of the verb of grasping is τὸ ἀγαθὸν *the good [in the mix],* and this neuter singular noun is the antecedent of the neuter singular pronoun τοῦτο *this* at a3.

65a3 **λέγωμεν** *let us say.* On my reading, this verb of speech governs first a ὡς-plus-finite-verb clause and then an accusative-plus-infinitive clause, coordinated by an epexegetic καὶ. Thus Gosling (1975): "let's . . . say that this [i.e., the good] is the element in the mixture that we should most correctly hold responsible, that it is because of this [i.e., the good] as something good that such a mixture becomes good." Likewise, Diès (1949), Frede (1997), and Delcomminette (2020).

As an alternative, Frede (1993) (followed by Muniz 2012) finds but a single ὡς clause after λέγωμεν: "let us affirm that these should . . . be held responsible for what is in the mixture, for its goodness is what makes the mixture a good one." This translation inaccurately reads the coordinating conjunction καὶ at a4 as if it were an inference indicator γάρ *for.*

τοῦτο οἷον ἓν *this [i.e., the good in the mix] as a one.* The antecedent of the neuter singular τοῦτο is the neuter singular τὸ ἀγαθὸν *the good [in the mix]*—that is, the object that the argument was unable to hunt down with one form, while grasping it with three forms. Although it required three forms to grasp it, nonetheless it is *as a one,* not as three, that it is the cause of the mix itself being good. Diès (1949), Gosling (1975), Frede (1993), and Muniz (2012) take the antecedent of τοῦτο to be the three things—measure, beauty, and truth—which antecedent is grammatically irregular and unnecessary for good philosophical sense.

οἷον ἓν *just as a one* or *as it were a one.* The adverb οἷον *as* occurs ten other times in the *Philebus,* all in speeches by Socrates, who uses it in only two ways. In six cases it means *as for instance* and introduces examples (LSJ οἷον V.2.b). In four cases it means *just as* or *as it were* and introduces a simile: οἷον βέλη *as it were missiles* (23b8); οἷον γράφειν *as it were to write* (39a3); τερπόμενος οἷον ἀποθνῄσκει *from the pleasure he as it were is dying* (47b3–4); and οἷον φειδόμενοι *as it were showing mercy* (55c5, LSJ οἷον V.2.a or d). Here at 65a3 οἷον does not introduce an example but is easily understood as introducing a simile: the target good (captured with three forms) is *just as* a one, that is, like a one.

As an alternative, Harte (1999, 385–401) interprets οἷον ἓν to mean that beauty, proportion, and truth are represented as identical in this passage, evidently giving the word οἷον a different meaning from its other two uses in the *Philebus.* LSJ (οἷος root meaning and II.7) permits οἷον ἓν to mean *such as a one* or *a sort of a one.* But even with either of those meanings the passage does not seem to license us to say they are literally one and the same. For Frede (1997, 359), beauty and truth are "*causae cognoscendi*" of the goodness of a mix—the cause of the mix's being known to be good—while only measure is the "*causa essendi*"—the cause of the mix's being good. If this had been Socrates' view, it seems he would have said that he had been able to capture the cause of the mix's being good with a single form: measure. Therefore, Socrates' denial at 65a1 that he had been so able raises a problem for her interpretation. Gerson (2010, 273) translates οἷον ἕν "in a way one," which is less definite than the Greek, which tells us the way in which the captured good is one: it is *a likeness to* one. His interpretation makes the three forms *effects* of the good itself ("they differently express or represent . . . the presence of this one idea") and he permits all three to be *causae cognoscendi* (they "serve as a kind of litmus test for the presence of this one idea"), but he does not clearly permit the three forms to be *causae essendi* of the goodness of the mix, seeming to give that power only to the good itself and not its image in the mix—namely, the captured good. Yet another alternative is to read οἷον *as it were* as οἷον *alone*, as suggested by Sayre (1983, 171n 81).

65a3–4 **τῶν ἐν τῇ συμμείξει** Bury's (1897) much-followed alternative analysis makes this genitive of effect: *[cause] of the things in the mix*. To say that the good in the mix is the cause of the things in the mix is an answer to this question: "Why are these things (namely, all the kinds of knowing, only the true pleasures, and the trio of ingredients truth, measure and beauty) in the mixed life that is best for human beings?" One problem is that this is a question that is never asked in the dialogue. Another problem is that its answer, in part, is that truth, measure, and beauty (taken as the good) are the reason why truth, measure, and beauty are in the mixed life—which is hard to make sensible. These two problems make it seem that one should read τῶν ἐν τῇ συμμείξει as a partitive genitive with Fowler (1925) rather than as a genitive of effect with Bury.

65b6 **<ὡς> μᾶλλον συγγενὲς** *as more akin*. Burnet (1901) accepts Badham's (1878) addition of ὡς to make sense of the text.

65c4 **οἶμαι** plus accusative (πολὺ διαφέρετον) plus infinitive (supply εἶναι). Following the ancient commentator Damascius (1959, §248, p. 117), some object that Protarchus errs by only considering gross pleasures in his comparison and ignores in particular the pure and true pleasures. Rodier (1900, 296–97), Hackforth (1945, 134), and Delcomminette (2006, 616) propose a solution to the problem. It is necessary to evaluate pleasure before it is mixed with truth and limited by measure, so as to determine its value as it is in itself "by nature" (πεφθκός, 65d9). In the same way, the ranking of the kinds of knowing shows that dialectic is what knowing is by its nature or in itself.

65c7 **τὸ ἐπιορκεῖν συγγνώμην εἴληφε παρὰ θεῶν** *to make a holy vow falsely has received lenient judgment from the gods [in the case of pleasures of sexual desire].* Likewise, says Pausanias at *Symposium* 183b–c, as Delcomminette (2020) points out.

66a1 **αἴσχιστον** *ugliest.* Socrates makes the same judgment at *Hippias Major* 299a, as Delcomminette (2020) points out.

66a4 **Πάντῃ . . . ὑπό . . . ἀγγέλων πέμπων** *everywhere . . . by sending messengers* perhaps echoing Pindar *Olympian* 9.36 παντᾷ ἀγγελίαν πέμψω *I will send a message everywhere.* Burnyeat (2004, 85) notes the parallel between this announcement of the first of five prizes and *Republic* 580b8, where Socrates urges that heralds be sent to declare which is the best of five lives.

66a7 **πάντα ὁπόσα τοιαῦτα** *whatever [is] such*—the contrast is between the forms and the things that are like the forms. We becomers are able in some sense to possess causes—that is, forms like the measured (which are beings)—and also to possess their effects—that is, things that are such as the measured, for example, a healthy meal or appropriate clothing.

66a7–8 **[χρὴ νομίζειν τὴν ἀίδιον ᾑρῆσθαι φύσιν]** It is impossible to reconstruct this passage with any confidence. The square brackets follow Gosling's (1975) conjecture that this is a scribe's comment on the text—*we ought to think that the eternal nature has been captured*—which is not part of the original text.

66c1–2 **τοῦ ἀγαθοῦ γέ ἐστι μᾶλλον [ἢ] τῆς ἡδονῆς συγγενῆ** *[these things] are more of the kind of the good than of the kind of pleasure.* If, with Burnet (1901), and following Stallbaum (1842), we bracket ἢ, we get *[these things] are more of the kind of the good than pleasure [is].*

66c8 **Ὀρφεύς** Delcomminette (2020) notes that according to West (1983, 118), "these six generations would be: (1) Night; (2) Heaven and Earth; (3) Ocean and Thetys; (4) Phorcys, Kronos, Rhea and the other Titans; (5) Zeus, Hera and the other Olympians; (6) 'all others.'"

66d1–2 **ὥσπερ κεφαλὴν ἀποδοῦναι τοῖς εἰρημένοις** continues the metaphor of an Orphic ritual: *as it were to assign the crown to what has been said.*

66d4 **τὸ τρίτον τῷ σωτῆρι** *the third [libation] to the savior.* Bury 1897 compares Aeschylus, *Eumenides* 759, *Supplices* 27, Plato, *Charmides* 167a, *Republic* 583b, Pindar, *Isthmian* 6 (5).11, and a scholiast on *Charmides* 167b.

66d7–8 **τἀγαθὸν . . . ἡμῖν ἡδονὴν εἶναι πᾶσαν καὶ παντελῆ** *that every pleasure was the good for us, and was perfectly/completely the good [for us] in every way.* Plato uses the adjective παντελῆ six times, and in every other case—*Republic* 414b2; *Timaeus* 31b1; *Laws* 698a10, 796c1, and 796d8—in modifying some *X* it means *perfectly/completely X in every way.* Gosling, Frede, and Delcomminette give it meanings not found in the lexicon. Gosling (1975): "our good in life consisted of pleasure." Frede (1993): "every pleasure of every kind is the good (likewise Frede 1997). Delcomminette (2020): the good is "complete and total pleasure" (*le plaisir complet et total*).

66d10 **τὸν ἐξ ἀρχῆς ἐπαναλαβεῖν δεῖν λόγον** *that we must take up the argument again from the beginning.* This subordinate clause after the verb of speaking ἔλεγες appears to stand in apposition to Τὸ τρίτον.

2. Epilogue: Some small part is missing from the discussion.

67b*: Protarchus recalls some details that remain to be discussed.*

See notes to 11c2, 22c7–d1, and 63e9–64a3 for some missing "small points."

67b6 **τῶν . . . μεμαντευμένων . . . λόγων** deponent participle μαντεύομαι *[than] arguments that divine [in philosophic music].* An alternative is to take the participle to be passive: *arguments that have been divined.*

WORKS CITED

Adam, James. 1900. "Emendation of Plato, *Philebus* 17e." *Classical Review* 14:264.

Ahbel-Rappe, Sara, and Rachana Kamtekar. 2006. *A Companion to Socrates*. Oxford: Blackwell.

Annas, Julia, and Christopher J. Rowe. 2003. *New Perspectives on Plato, Modern and Ancient*. Center for Hellenic Studies Colloquia 6. Cambridge, MA: Harvard University Press.

Apelt, Otto. 1922. *Platon, Philebos*. 2nd ed. Leipzig: Meiner. Reprinted, Hamburg: Meiner, 1955.

Arpe, Curt. 1943. "Platon, *Philebos* 46d–47a." *Philologus* 95:161–65.

Ast, Friedrich. 1821. *Platonis Quae Exstant Opera*. Vol. 4. Leipzig: Weidmann.

Badham, Charles. 1855. *The Philebus of Plato*. 1st ed. London: J. W. Parker.

Badham, Charles. 1878. *The Philebus of Plato*. 2nd ed. London: Williams & Norgate.

Bailly, Jacques. 2003. *Plato's* Euthyphro *and* Clitophon. Newburyport: Focus.

Barker, Andrew. 1996. "Plato's *Philebus:* The Numbering of a Unity." *Apeiron* 29:143–64.

Barker, Andrew. 1987. "Text and Sense at *Philebus* 56a." *Classical Quarterly* 37:103–9.

Barnes, Jonathan, ed. 1984. *The Complete Works of Aristotle*. Vol. 1. Princeton: Princeton University Press.

Bast, Friedrich Jacob. 1809. *Epistola critica ad J. F. Boissonadum super Antonio Liberali, Parthenio et Aristaeneto*. Leipzig: Weidmann.

Baxter, Donald. 1988. "Many-One Identity." *Philosophical Papers* 17:193–216.

Beck, Christian Daniel. 1816. *Platonis Opera*. Vol. 3. Leipzig: Karl Tauchnitz.

Bekker, Immanuel. 1817. *Platonis Dialogi Graece et Latine*. Berlin: Reimer.

Benardete, Seth. 1963. "Some Misquotations of Homer in Plato." *Phronesis* 8:173–78.

Benardete, Seth. 1993. *The Tragedy and Comedy of Life: Plato's* Philebus. Chicago: University of Chicago Press.

Benitez, E. E. 1989. *Forms in Plato's* Philebus. Assen, Netherlands: Van Gorcum.

Blümner, Hugo. 1875. *Technologie und Terminologie der Gewerbe und Künste bei Greichen und Römern*. Vol. 2. Leipzig: Teubner.

Borthwick, E. Kerr. 2003. "Text and Interpretation of Plato *Philebus* 56a." *Classical Philology* 98:274–80.

Boussoulas, Nicolas-Isidore. 1952. *L'Etre et la Composition des Mixtes dans le "Philèbe" de Platon*. Paris: Presses Universitaires de France.

Bravo, Francisco. 2003. *Las Ambigüedades del Placer: Ensayo Sobre el Placer en la Filosofía de Platón*. Sankt Augustin, Germany: Academia Verlag.

Burnet, John. 1901. *Platonis Opera*. Vol. 2, *Tetralogiae* 3–4. Oxford: Oxford University Press.

Burnyeat, Myles F. 1997. "First Words." *Proceedings of the Cambridge Philological Society* 43:1–20.

Burnyeat, Myles F. 2004. "Fathers and Sons in Plato's *Republic* and *Philebus*." *Classical Quarterly* 54:80–87.

Bury, Robert G. 1897. *The Philebus of Plato*. Cambridge: Cambridge University Press.

Carone, Gabriela Roxana. 2000. "Hedonism and the Pleasureless Life in Plato's *Philebus*." *Phronesis* 45:257–83.

Carpenter, Amber. 2003. "Phileban Gods." *Ancient Philosophy* 23:93–112.

Carpenter, Amber. 2006. "Hedonistic Persons: The Good Man Argument in Plato's *Philebus*." *British Journal for the History of Philosophy* 14:5–26

Chalmers, David, David Manley, and Ryan Wasserman. 2009. *Metametaphysics*. Oxford: Oxford University Press.

Compton, Todd. 1990. "What are the TOPNOI in *Philebus* 51C?" *Classical Quarterly* 40:549–52.

Cordero, Nestor-Luis. 1993. *Platon: Le Sophiste*. Paris: Flammarion.

Cornarius, Janus. 1561. *Platonis atheniensis philosophi summi ac penitus divini opera quae ad nos extant omnia*. Basel: Froben.

Cooper, John M., ed. 1997. *Plato Collected Works*. Indianapolis: Hackett.

Crombie, I. M. 1963. *An Examination of Plato's Doctrines 2: Plato on Knowledge and Reality*. London: Routledge.

Damascius. 1959. *Damascius: Lectures on the* Philebus *Wrongly Attributed to Olympiodorus*. Text, translation, notes, and indices by L. G. Westerink. Amsterdam: North Holland.

Dancy, Russell. 1984. "The One, the Many, and the Forms: *Philebus* 15b1–8." *Ancient Philosophy* 4:160–193.

Dancy, Russell. 2005. "The Limits of Being in the *Philebus*." Paper presented at 79th Annual Meeting of the American Philosophical Association, Pacific Division, San Francisco. (Appearing under the same title in 2007 in *Apeiron* 40:353–70.)

Davidson, Donald. 1990. *Plato's* Philebus. New York: Garland.

De Almeida, Custódio L. S. 2002. "O Princípio Incondicionado da Dialética no *Filebo* de Platão." *Veritas* 47:209–21.

Delcomminette, Sylvain. 2002. "The One-and-Many Problems at *Philebus* 15b." *Oxford Studies in Ancient Philosophy* 22:21–42.

Delcomminette, Sylvain. 2003. "False Pleasures, Appearance, and Imagination in the *Philebus*." *Phronesis* 48:215–37.

Delcomminette, Sylvain. 2005. "The Fourth Genus and the Other Three: A Note on *Philebus* 27a8–9." *Classical Quarterly* 55:614–16.

Delcomminette, Sylvain. 2006. *Le* Philèbe *de Platon: Introduction à l'Agathologie Platonicienne*. Leiden: Brill.

Delcomminette, Sylvain. 2014. "Odysseus and the Home of the Stranger from Elea." *Classical Quarterly* 64:533–41.

Delcomminette, Sylvain. 2020. *Philèbe*: Introduction, traduction et commentaire. Paris: Vrin.

Denniston, John D. 1966. *The Greek Particles.* Oxford: Oxford University Press. 2nd edition revised by Kenneth J. Dover. Reprinted 1996, Indianapolis: Hackett.

Desjardins, Rosemary. 2004. *Plato and the Good: Illuminating the Darkling Vision.* Leiden: Brill.

Diès, Auguste. 1949. *Platon: Oeuvres Complètes.* Vol. 9, part 2. Paris: Société d'Edition "Les Belles Lettres."

Dimas, Panos, Russell E. Jones, and Gabriel R. Lear. 2019. *Plato's* Philebus: *A Philosophical Discussion.* Oxford: Oxford University Press.

Dillon, John 1999. "Speusippe et le plaisir." In Dixsaut 1999b, 83–98.

Dillon, John, and Luc Brisson, eds. 2010. *Plato's* Philebus: *Selected Papers from the Eighth Symposium Platonicum.* Sankt Augustin: Academia Verlag.

Dixsaut, Monique. 2003. *Platon : le désir de comprendre.* Paris: Vrin.

Dixsaut, Monique, ed. 1999a. *La Fêlure du Plaisir: Études sur le* Philebe *de Platon.* Vol. 1, *Commentaires.* Paris: Vrin.

Dixsaut, Monique, ed. 1999b. *La Fêlure du Plaisir: Études sur le* Philebe *de Platon.* Vol. 2, *Contextes.* Paris: Vrin.

Dover, Kenneth J. 1974. *Greek Popular Morality in the Time of Plato and Aristotle.* Oxford: Blackwell.

Dover, Kenneth. 1989. *Greek Homosexuality.* Cambridge, MA: Harvard University Press.

Drozdek, Adam. 2000. "The Four Kinds of Reality in the *Timaeus* and *Philebus.*" *Diálogos* 76:125–41.

Dybikowski, James C. 1970. "False Pleasure and the *Philebus.*" *Phronesis* 15:147–65.

Ferber, J. 1912. "Platos Polemik gegen die Lustlehre." *Zeitschrift für Philosophie und philosophische Kritik*: 129–81.

Festugière A.-J. 1950. *Contemplation et vie contemplative chez Platon.* 2nd ed. Paris: Vrin.

Ficino, M. (1496) 2000. *The* Philebus *Commentary.* Critical edition and translation by M. J. B. Allen. Tempe: Arizona Center for Medieval & Renaissance Studies.

Fine, Gail, ed. 2019. *The Oxford Handbook of Plato.* Oxford: Oxford University Press.

Fletcher, Emily. 2014. "Plato on Pure Pleasure and the Best Life." *Phronesis* 59:113–42.

Fowler, H. N. 1925. *Plato: Statesman, Philebus, Ion.* Loeb Classical Library 164. Cambridge, MA: Harvard University Press.

Frede, Dorothea. 1985. "Rumpelstiltskin's Pleasures: True and False Pleasures in Plato's *Philebus.*" *Phronesis* 30:151–80.

Frede, Dorothea. 1992. "Disintegration and Restoration: Pleasure and Pain in Plato's *Philebus.*" In Kraut 1992, 425–63.

Frede, Dorothea. 1993. *Philebus.* Indianapolis: Hackett.

Frede, Dorothea. 1997. *Platon: Werke, Übersetzung und Kommentar.* Vol. 3, part 2, *Philebos.* Göttingen: Vandenhoeck & Ruprecht.

Friedländer, Paul. 1969. *Plato.* Vol. 3, *The Dialogues, Second and Third Periods.* Translated by H. Meyerhoff. Princeton, NJ: Princeton University Press.

Gadamer, Hans-Georg. 1991. *Plato's Dialectical Ethics.* Translated by Robert M. Wallace. New Haven, CT: Yale University Press.

Geis, Michael. 1973. "*If* and *Unless.*" In *Issues in Linguistics: Papers in Honor of Henry and Renée Kahane,* edited by Braj B. Kachru, Robert B. Lees, Yakov Malkiel, Angelina Petrangeli, and Sol Saporta, 231–53. Urbana: University of Illinois Press.

Gerson, Lloyd. 2010. "Beauty, Commensurability, and Truth in Plato's *Philebus.*" In Dillon and Brisson 2010, 272–78.

Goodwin, William W. 1890. *Syntax of the Moods and Tenses of the Greek Verb.* Enlarged ed. Boston: Ginn and Heath.

Gosling, J. C. B. 1959. "False Pleasures: *Philebus* 35c–41b." *Phronesis* 4:44–54.

Gosling, J. C. B. 1975. *Philebus.* Oxford: Clarendon Press.

Gosling, J. C. B. 1961. "Father Kenny on False Pleasures." *Phronesis* 6:41–45.

Gosling, J. C. B. 1999. "Y a-t-il une Forme de l'indéterminé?" In Dixsaut 1999a, 43–59.

Gosling, J. C. B., and C. C. W. Taylor. 1982. *The Greeks on Pleasure*. Oxford: Clarendon Press.

Graham, Daniel W., and Justin Barney. 2016. "On the Date of Chaerephon's Visit to Delphi." *Phoenix* 70:274–89.

Griffin, James. 1986. *Well-Being: Its Meaning, Measurement and Moral Importance*. Oxford: Clarendon Press.

Grote, George. 1875. *Plato and the Other Companions of Socrates*. Vol. 2. London: Murray.

Grube, G. M. A. 1935. *Plato's Thought*. London: Methuen.

Gruter, Janus. 1616. *Inscriptionum romanarum corpus absolutissimum*. Heidelberg: Commelinianus.

Guthrie, W. K. C. 1978. *A History of Greek Philosophy*. Vol. 5, *The Later Plato and the Academy*. Cambridge: Cambridge University Press.

Hackforth, Reginald. 1939. "On Some Passages of Plato's *Philebus*." *Classical Quarterly* 33:27–28.

Hackforth, Reginald. 1945. *Plato's Examination of Pleasure*. Cambridge: Cambridge University Press. (I follow the pagination in *Plato's Philebus*, Cambridge: Cambridge University Press, 1972.)

Hampton, Cynthia. 1990. *Pleasure, Knowledge, and Being: an Analysis of Plato's Philebus*. Albany: State University of New York Press.

Harte, Verity. 1999. "Quel prix pour la vérité?" In Dixsaut 1999a, 385–401.

Harte, Verity. 2002. *Plato on Parts and Wholes: The Metaphysics of Structure*. Oxford: Oxford University Press.

Henderson, Jeffrey. 1991. *The Maculate Muse: Obscene Language in Attic Comedy*. 2nd ed. Oxford: Oxford University Press.

Hermann, Karl Friedrich, ed. 1855. *Platonis Opera*. Leipzig: Teubner.

Horn, Ferdinand. 1893. *Platonstudien*. Vienna: Tempsky.

Huffman, Carl. 1999. "Limite et illimité chez les premiers philosophes grecs." In Dixsaut 1999b, 11–31.

Hume, David. (1779) 1998. *Dialogues Concerning Natural Religion*. Indianapolis: Hackett.

Irwin, Terence. 1995. *Plato's Ethics*. Oxford: Oxford University Press.

Irwin, Terence. 2019. "The Platonic Corpus." In Fine 2019, 69–92.

Jackson, Henry. 1882. "The *Philebus* and Aristotle's *Metaphysics* I 6." *Journal of Philology* 10:253–98.

Jebb, Richard C. 1907. *Sophocles: The Plays and Fragments*. Part 2, *The* Oedipus Coloneus. Cambridge: Cambridge University Press.

Johnson, B. 2000. "Metaphor, Metonymy, and Voice in *Their Eyes Were Watching God*." In *Zora Neal Hurston's Their Eyes Were Watching God: A Casebook,* edited by C. A. Wall, 41–58. Oxford: Oxford University Press.

Jowett, Benjamin. 1892. *The Dialogues of Plato*. Oxford: Oxford University Press.

Kenny, Anthony. 1960. "False Pleasures in the *Philebus:* A Reply to Mr. Gosling." *Phronesis* 5:45–52.

Kraut, Richard. 1992. *The Cambridge Companion to Plato*. Cambridge: Cambridge University Press.

Kühner, Raphael. 1904. *Ausführliche Grammatik der Griechischen Sprache*. Part 2, *Satzlehre*. Hannover: Hahnsche

La Taille, Antoine. 1999. *Philèbe* 31b–44a. Paris: Ellipses.

Ledger, Gerard. 1989. *Re-counting Plato: A Computer Analysis of Plato's Style*. Oxford: Clarendon Press.

Lewis, David. 1991. *Parts of Classes*. Oxford: Blackwell.

Liddell, H. J., R. Scott, H. S. Jones, and R. McKenzie. 1940. *A Greek-English Lexicon*. Oxford: Clarendon Press.

Liebesman, David. 2011. "Simple Generics." *Noûs* 45:409–42.

Löhr, Gerhard. 1990. *Das Problem des Einen und Vielen in Platons* Philebos. Göttingen: Vandenhoeck & Ruprecht.

Lorenz, Hendrik. 2019. "Intelligence as Cause: *Philebus* 27c–31b." In Dimas, Jones, and Lear 2019, 90–105.

Maguire, Thomas. 1874. "The *Philebus* of Plato and Recent English Critics." *Hermathena* 1:441–67.

Mason, Andrew J. 2014. "On the Status of *Nous* in the *Philebus*." *Phronesis* 59:143–69.

Matthiae, August. 1827. *Ausführliche griechische Grammatik*. Vol. 2. Leipzig: Vogel.

Meinwald, Constance. 2019. "The *Philebus.*" In Fine 2019, 337–58.

Menn, Stephen. 1995. *Plato on God as* Nous. *Journal of the History of Philosophy* Monograph Series. Carbondale: Southern Illinois University Press.

Menn, Stephen. 1998. "Collecting the Letters." *Phronesis* 43: 291–305.

Migliori, Maurizio. 1993. *L'uomo fra piacere, intelligenza e bene: Commentario storico-filosofical al "Filebo" di Platone.* Milan: Vita e Pensiero.

Mill, John Stuart. 1906. *A System of Logic*. 8th ed. London: Longmans, Green.

Mooradian, Norman. 1995. "What To Do About False Pleasures of Overestimation? *Philebus* 41a5–42c5." *Apeiron* 28:91–112.

Mooradian, Norman. 1996. "Converting Protarchus: Relativism and False Pleasures of Anticipation in Plato's *Philebus* [36a3–41a5]." *Ancient Philosophy* 16:93–112.

Moravcsik, J. M. 1979. *"Form, Nature, and the Good in the* Philebus." *Phronesis* 24:81–104.

Moutsopoulos, Evangelos. 1959. *La musique dans l'œuvre de Platon.* References are to the 2nd edition (1989), Paris: Presses Universitaires de France.

Muniz, Fernando. 2012. *O* Filebo *de Platão.* Rio de Janeiro: PUC-Rio: Loyola.

Muniz, Fernando. 2014. "Propositional Pleasures in Plato's *Philebus.*" *Journal of Ancient Philosophy* 8:49–75.

Muniz, Fernando, and George Rudebusch. 2004. *"Philebus* 15b: A Problem Solved." *Classical Quarterly* 54:394–405.

Muniz, Fernando, and George Rudebusch. 2018. "Dividing Plato's Kinds." *Phronesis* 63: 392–407.

Muniz, Fernando, and George Rudebusch. n.d. "*Genos* and *Eidos* in Plato." Forthcoming in *Ancient Philosophy.*

Nails, Debra. 1995. *Agora, Academy, and the Conduct of Philosophy.* Dordrecht: Kluwer.

Nails, Debra. 2002. *The People of Plato.* Indianapolis: Hackett.

Nicomachus. 1895. *Harmonicum enchiridion, in Musici scriptores Graeci.* Edited by K. Jan. Leipzig: Teubner.

Ogihara, Satoshi. 2019. "The Independence of the Soul from the Body: Philebus 31b–36c." in Dimas, Jones, and Lear 2019: 106–23.

Ogle, William. 1987. *Translation of Aristotle's* On the Parts of Animals. In Barnes 1984: 994–1085.

Paley, F. A. 1873. *Translation of Plato's* Philebus. London: Bell.

Pearson, Giles. 2019. "Putting the 'Stroppies' to Work: *Philebus* 42c–47d." In Dimas, Jones, and Lear 2019, 141–62.

Penner, Terry. 1970. "False Anticipatory Pleasures: *Philebus* 36a3–41a6." *Phronesis* 15:166–78.

Peponi, Anastasia-Erasmia. 2002. "Mixed Pleasures, Blended Discourses: Poetry, Medicine, and the Body in Plato's *Philebus* 46–47c." *Classical Antiquity* 21:135–60.

Poste, Edward. 1860. *The* Philebus *of Plato*. Oxford: Oxford University Press.

Pradeau, J.-F. 2002. *Platon: Philèbe*. Paris: Vrin.

Ratzsch, Del. 2005. "Teleological Arguments for God's Existence." In *Stanford Encyclopedia of Philosophy*. Stanford University, 1997–. http://plato.stanford.edu/entries/teleological-arguments.

Rheins, Jason. 2016. "World-soul, Intellect and Cause in Socrates' Cosmological Argument in the *Philebus*." Paper presented at the Ninth Annual West Coast Plato Workshop: Plato's *Philebus*. Northern Arizona University, Flagstaff, AZ, May 2016.

Richards, Herbert. 1911. *Platonica*. London: Grant Richards.

Richardson, John. 2004. *Nietzsche's New Darwinism*. Oxford: Oxford University Press.

Rickless, Samuel. 2007. *Plato's Forms in Transition: A Reading of the Parmenides*. Cambridge: Cambridge University Press.

Rijksbaron, A. 1997. *New Approaches to Greek Particles*. Amsterdam: Gieben.

Ritter, C. 1923. *Platon, sein Leben, seine Schriften, seine Lehre*. Vol. 2. Munich: Beck.

Robin, Léon. 1950. *Platon: Œuvres complètes*. Paris: Gallimard (La Pléiade).

Rodier, Georges. 1900. "Remarques sur le Philèbe." *Revue des Études Anciennes* 2–4:281–303.

Romspert, George. 1881. *The Western Echo: A Description of the Western States and Territories of the United States*. Dayton, OH: United Brethren.

Rorty, Richard. 1970. "Incorrigibility as the Mark of the Mental." *Journal of Philosophy* 67:399–424.

Ross, William David. 1951. *Plato's Theory of Ideas*. Oxford: Clarendon Press.

Rudebusch, George. 1985. "Plato on Sense and Reference." *Mind* 94:526–37.

Rudebusch, George. 1990. "Does Plato Think False Speech is Speech?" *Noûs* 24:599–609.

Rudebusch, George. 1991. "*Sophist* 237–239." *Southern Journal of Philosophy* 29:521–31.

Rudebusch, George. 1999. *Socrates, Pleasure and Value.* Oxford: Oxford University Press.

Rudebusch, George. 2006. Review of *Las Ambigüedades del Placer: Ensayo Sobre el Placer en la Filosofía de Platón*, by Francisco Bravo. *Ancient Philosophy* 26:192–96.

Rudebusch, George. 2009a. "Pleasure." In *A Companion to Aristotle*, edited by Georgios Anagnostopoulos, 404–18. Oxford: Wiley-Blackwell.

Rudebusch, George. 2009b. Review of *Plato and the Art of Philosophical Writing*, by Christopher Rowe. *Philosophical Books* 50: 79–86.

Rudebusch, George. 2009c. *Socrates.* Oxford: Wiley-Blackwell.

Rudebusch, George. 2016. *Argument Analysis of Plato's* Philebus. Archelogos.com. http://www.archelogos.com/xml/toc/toc-phil.htm. Full text available at https://www.academia.edu/8710106/Philebus_Argument_Analysis_and_Commentary_with_Appendices_and_Bibliography.

Rudebusch, George. 2018. Review of *Clitophon's Challenge: Dialectic in Plato's* Meno, Phaedo, *and* Republic by Hugh Benson. *Philosophical Review* 127:229–32.

Rudebusch, George. 2020. "*Philebus* 11b: Good or The Good." *Apeiron* 53:161–85. https://doi.org/10.1515/apeiron-2019-0004.

Rudebusch, George. 2021. "*Philebus* 23c–26d: *Peras*, *Apeiron*, and *Meikton* as Measure Theory." *Plato Journal* 22:53–67.

Rudebusch, George, Hayden Niehus, and Brianna Zgurich. 2020. *Philebus: Greek Text and Basic Grammar*. Seattle: Kindle Direct Publishing. https://www.academia.edu/39309001/Philebus_Greek_Text_and_Basic_Grammar.

Rudebusch, George, and Christopher Turner. 2014. "A Philosophical Solution to the Problem of Socrates." *Journal of Ancient Philosophy* 40:1–39.

Russell, Daniel C. 2005. *Plato on Pleasure and the Good Life*. Oxford: Clarendon Press.

Ryan, Paul. 2012. *Plato's* Phaedrus*: A Commentary for Greek Readers*. Norman: University of Oklahoma Press.

Sayre, Kenneth M. 1983. *Plato's Late Ontology*. Princeton, NJ: Princeton University Press. Reprinted Las Vegas: Parmenides 2005.

Schleiermacher, Friedrich. 1809. *Platons Werke*. Vol. 3, part 2, *Phaidon, Philebos, Theages, Die Nebenbuhler, Der erste Alkibiades, Menexenos, Hippias, Kleitophon*. Berlin: Realschulbuch.

Schofield, Malcolm. 1971. "Who were οἱ δυσχερεῖς in Plato, *Philebus* 44 a ff.?" *Museum Helveticum* 28:2–20, 181.

Schumann, Walter L., ed. 1961. "Index of Passages Cited in Herbert Weir Smyth: Greek Grammar." Greek, Roman, and Byzantine Studies Scholarly Aids 1. Watertown, MA: Eaton.

Shorey, Paul. 1930. *Plato: The Republic*. Vols. 1 and 2. Loeb Classical Library 237 and 276. Cambridge, MA: Harvard University Press.

Shorey, Paul. 1933. *What Plato Said*. Chicago: University of Chicago Press.

Smyth, H. W. 1956. *Greek Grammar*. Revised by G. M. Messing. Cambridge, MA: Harvard University Press.

Soames, Scott. 2009. "Ontology, Analyticity, and Meaning: The Quine—Carnap Dispute." In Chalmers, Manley, and Wasserman 2009, 424–43.

Stallbaum, G. 1820. *Platonis* Philebus. Leipzig: Teubner.

Stallbaum, G. 1842. *Platonis* Philebus. London: Gothae.

Stephanus, Henri Estienne. 1578. *Platonis Opera Quae Extant Omnia*. Geneva: Henri Estienne. https://www.plato-dialogues.org/stephanus.htm

Striker, G. 1970. *Peras und Apeiron: Das Problem der Formen in Platons* Philebos. Göttingen: Vandenhoeck & Ruprecht.

Taylor, A. E. 1948. *Plato: The Man and his Work*. London: Routledge.

Taylor, A. E. 1956. *Plato: Philebus and Epinomis*. Edited by R. Klibansky. London: Thomas Nelson and Sons.

Tenkku, Jussi. 1956. *The Evaluation of Pleasure in Plato's Ethics*. Helsinki: Acta Philosophica Fennica, 11.

Thesaurus Linguae Graecae Digital Library. n.d. http://stephanus.tlg.uci.edu/abridged.php.

Thomas, C. 2006. "Plato's Prometheanism." *Oxford Studies in Ancient Philosophy* 31:203–31.

Vogt, Katja Maria. 2019. "Rethinking the Contest Between Pleasure and Wisdom: *Philebus* 11a–14b." In Dimas, Jones, and Lear 2019, 17–33.

Von Fintel, K. 1992. "Exceptive Conditionals: The Meaning of *Unless*." *Proceedings of the North East Linguistics Society* 22:135–51.

Waterfield, R. 1980. "On the Text of Some Passages of Plato's *Philebus*." *Liverpool Classical Monthly* 5:57–64.

Waterfield, R. 1982. *Plato: Philebus*. London: Penguin.

West, M. L. 1983. *The Orphic Poems*. Oxford: Clarendon Press.

West, M. L. 1992. *Ancient Greek Music*. Oxford: Clarendon Press.

Wheeler v. Kassabaum. 76 Cal. 90, 11,299. Supreme Court of California. *Pacific Reporter* 18 (1888):119–20.

GENERAL INDEX

INDEX OF PASSAGES

www.ingramcontent.com/pod-product-compliance
Ingram Content Group UK Ltd.
Pitfield, Milton Keynes, MK11 3LW, UK
UKHW011007210826
474623UK00001B/41